Underground Structures
of the Cold War

To Rebecca

Underground Structures of the Cold War

The World Below

Paul Ozorak

Pen & Sword
MILITARY

First published in Great Britain in 2012
and reprinted in this format in 2022 by
Pen & Sword Military
an imprint of
Pen & Sword Books Ltd
47 Church Street
Barnsley
South Yorkshire
S70 2AS

ISBN 9-781-39907-450-6

A CIP catalogue record for this book is
available from the British Library.

Typeset in Ehrhardt by Phoenix Typesetting, Auldgirth, Dumfriesshire

Printed and bound by CPI Group (UK) Ltd, Croydon CR0 4YY

Pen & Sword Books Ltd incorporates the Imprints of Pen & Sword Aviation,
Pen & Sword Maritime, Pen & Sword Military, Wharncliffe Local History,
Pen and Sword Select, Pen and Sword Military Classics, Leo Cooper,
Remember When, Seaforth Publishing and Frontline Publishing.

For a complete list of Pen & Sword titles please contact
PEN & SWORD BOOKS LIMITED
47 Church Street, Barnsley, South Yorkshire, S70 2AS, England
E-mail: enquiries@pen-and-sword.co.uk
Website: www.pen-and-sword.co.uk

Contents

Preface

The Cold War was one of the costliest times in mankind's history. During those forty-five years, billions were spent on weapons and manpower in dozens of countries to keep everyone safe from each other. Funding was also spent on the supporting infrastructure – that is the military bases – that kept those troops employed and that housed those weapons. The bases were prime symbols of that great geopolitical-conflict-that-never-was, and while the public often knew or suspected what went on there, there were times when they did not because those bases were designed to be secret. And secret they remained until the final curtain of the Cold War drama was lowered.

Those bases that were secret often had an underground component. They were so designed because governments wanted to protect their occupants from one of man's most destructive inventions, the A-bomb. The structures were erected to shield government leaders, weapons and military troops, and in some countries they were even built to store material necessary for a nation's survival. The facilities came in all forms such as earth-covered bunkers, tunnels, re-inforced basements, silos and even windowless surface concrete blockhouses. In a fairly large majority of cases, the public did not truly know what lay behind a barbed wired fence, but as the sands of time have passed and as these places were closed, you and I can learn about them.

This book builds on my earlier work on the subject, *Bunkers Bunkers Everywhere*. Since that volume was published in 1998, I have been greatly helped by many new good books. In the United Kingdom, I have found Nick McCamley's book *Cold War Secret Nuclear Bunkers* particularly useful. In fact, I have kept the British chapter of my own book purposefully short since I did not want to repeat, in any great detail, his work. On the other hand, I have filled some gaps from his book with such items as the Ground-Launched Cruise Missile shelters at Greenham Common and Molesworth, and have said more on High Wycombe than he did. Then there was Cocroft and Thomas's book *Cold War. Building for Nuclear Confrontation*, which I thought was priceless. I also note other commendable works such as David Stumpf's book on the Titan II ICBM, Pavel Podvig's epic *Russian Strategic Nuclear Forces* (banned in Russia, smuggled out of Russia, and published in the United States), and Valery Yarenich's work on the Russian command and control system. For the Canadian chapter, I have been immeasurably helped by government files now declassified at Library and Archives Canada. In France, books such as *Les Sentinelles de la Paix*, which gives an excellent overview of that country's IRBM programme, was a great source of reference. Also highly recommended is Stefan Best's very detailed work on East German bunkers, *Geheime Bunkeranlagen der DDR*. In Latvia, one acquaintance suggested that I pick up a copy of the *Latvija autoceļu atlants* (Latvian Road Atlas) since it showed all the former Soviet military properties in that country as red stars. This too was of great help. When it comes to American continuity of government, Daniel Ford's *The Button* was of prime importance, not just to me but also apparently to the Soviet government when it was published in 1985. I look forward to the day when similar such books are published on the Soviet continuity programme.

To write a book such as this required me to consult a large number of other references. Much of what I have learned also comes from magazines, newsletters and newspapers, not to mention academic journals and the odd television documentary. I also relied heavily on the Internet, without which I probably would not have learned so much about the Minuteman ICBM. The Internet has also been useful in that it has allowed me to confirm the location of several installations through satellite imaging sites. Here, however, I must repeat a warning sounded by others that not all online material is factual. Just because something is mentioned on a website does not make it true. At the same time, I noticed long ago that military organizations change often. A regiment that was said to be at some base five years ago might no longer exist, and a particular action in a missile launch procedure might no longer be performed. NATO, for one, drastically changed its organizational structure a few years ago by getting rid of its regional commands, and the United States major attack plan, the Single Integrated Operational Plan, has gone through endless revisions. I, therefore, cannot guarantee that everything in this book is totally accurate or up-to-date.

One thing that has struck me through my readings and by talking to various people is the arrogance of the Russian government. I have come across several examples of this over the years, from the forced annexation of the three Baltic states, Lithuania, Latvia and Estonia, by the Soviets in 1940, to the willingness of the Soviets to sacrifice the entire Czechoslovakian army during a nuclear war (as stated by Johnson et al. in *Eastern European Military Establishments*), to the mistrust of fellow Warsaw Pact officers at the Falkenhagen, Germany, bunker, not to mention of course the Soviet-led invasions of Hungary in 1956 and Czechoslovakia in 1968 and the downing of Korean Air Lines flight 007 off the Pacific coast by an air defence jet fighter in 1983. There are also stories of the Soviet army accidentally killing civilians in southwestern Poland with artillery fire. As well, when the Russians left the various Eastern European countries in the 1990s, they took whatever they could with them, even electrical cabling and toilets, and left behind numerous environmental disasters such as the contaminated nuclear reactor at the Paldiski, Estonia, naval training centre. Their attitude has caused many, many former Soviet bunkers throughout the Eastern bloc to be stripped of anything useful to historians. It is as if the Russians were telling their former socialist brothers-in-arms to go do sexually unnatural things to themselves.

By digging into old government files, one can learn much that is interesting. An old Canadian Department of Foreign Affairs file describes the mistrust Western governments had for the International Civil Defence Organization, an outfit that was ostensibly created to share information on public protection, rescue and relief, radiological defence etc. and that was based in Geneva. The president of the ICDO, Dr Milan Bodi, had asked Canada to participate in such events as the 1964 International Symposium on Civil Defence in Monaco, but Ottawa declined to answer his request. NATO had agreed years earlier not to send any representatives to these symposia, and Canada, as a member of the Alliance, was no doubt pressured into following the lead. Both R.B. Bryce, director of the Canadian Emergency Measures Organization, and the Canadian Under-Secretary of State for External Affairs would not even reply to Bodi, the Under-Secretary baldly stating that 'we see no reason to re-open the matter of Canadian relations with ICDO'. While NATO had been afraid the ICDO would have been used as an instrument of communist propaganda against nuclear testing, the real reason for the mistrust of the Organization was that its regular meetings were attended by Eastern bloc representatives. Even today, neither Australia, Canada, Germany, Italy, Japan, Norway, Sweden, the United Kingdom nor the United States belong to it.

This book is by no means meant to be the definitive book on Cold War bunkers. It is only designed to give an idea of the kinds of places that existed in various countries. I have found through my research and travels that nations such as Sweden, Germany and Switzerland had huge numbers of underground installations. If someone like Stefan Best can write a 240-page book on East German bunkers alone, imagine what a comprehensive book that covered the entire world would look like. My life is too short for that.

Underground Structures of the Cold War is not entirely for the uninitiated. When I wrote it, I made some assumptions of you, the reader. I have assumed you know what an ICBM, IRBM and SAM is, what is continuity of government (in its basic form) and how radar works. I also assumed you know what NATO, NORAD and the STASI are, and that you are familiar with the basic roles of the British Home Office. Should you lack some particular knowledge, I suggest a trip to Wikipedia.

This book is more than just about bunkers. Knowing why they were built can be just as important as where they were. One could talk about the characteristics of a missile silo, but I think it would be equally interesting to talk about the weapons themselves. I have thus touched on several other subjects in this volume, in addition to the obvious topics such as civil defence and continuity of government, such as strategic targeting, stockpiling, command and control systems, communications methods, civil engineering, radiation detection and emergency legislation.

My subject can thus be considered oxymoronic. By this, I mean that bunkers were such a small aspect of the Cold War, yet when you consider their different uses, it becomes a truly vast topic. I can, therefore, only scratch the surface (pun intended) of the subject. By doing so, however, I think we will succeed at looking at the world below.

Paul Ozorak
Ottawa, Canada
December 2011

Acknowledgments

In addition to the various media I have mentioned in my introduction, some of what I have learned has come from individuals whom I've met on my many trips. Some of those persons have imparted knowledge to me that was not available from the Internet, and to them I tip my hat. Others have been nice enough to drive me to places not accessible by public transport, or have made my trips less costly by sheltering me. Among these individuals, I thank David and Andrea in London, Mike G. in Manchester, along with Rupert Allason, Dan McKenzie, James Fox and Paul Stokes of the United Kingdom. I also thank John Bex of Alconbury Developments. In Poland, I am grateful to Marta and Pawel of Wroclaw, Joanna Lamparska, Professor Janusz Miniewicz and Tomas. In Estonia, Mati Õun, Jiri and Francoise were of great help. I also thank the Estonian Police for allowing a visit of the former KGB bunker by Lake Paunküla. In Germany, there was Werner Bochert of Zossen, Claus Röhling of Urft, Burkhard Baumgartner of Kerkel, Tomas of Eichental and Frank Tausche and Diethelm Markowski of the Finow air museum. In Switzerland, it was Jean-Christophe Moret and Rudolf Steinmann, the former who takes care of Battery A46 at Martigny, and the latter who gave me a tour of the Bloodhound missile site near Zug. Liz Laan of Ottawa was kind enough to proof-read the Canadian chapter, and John Clearwater, also of Ottawa, provided valuable assistance, as did Dave Peters and Bob Borden of the Diefenbunker museum. Architect David Warne of Toronto also helped, as did the Newmarket Historical Society and Orianna of Aurora. I am also grateful to Warrant Officer Doug Powell of the Canadian Forces for allowing a tour of the only remaining Cold War bunker in operation in Canada. In Sweden, I must thank Lars Hansson of Nyköping for driving me around his area, and volunteers at the Säve air museum for giving me a peek inside the former air control centre there. I also thank Sven Scheiderbauer in Norway, along with acquaintances from Russia, China, Spain and Sweden. In France, I thank Stéphane Bréard of the Defence Historical Service in the splendid Chateau de Vincennes in Paris.

In the United States, I thank Mark Morgan, Charlie Simpson of the Association of Air Force Missileers, Gary Powers Jr, Pavel Podvig and Bob Norris of the Natural Resources Defense Council. (In fact, anyone interested in learning more about nuclear weapons and targeting is encouraged to read the NRDC's *The US Nuclear War Plan. A Time for Change*, which he co-wrote with McKinzie, Cochran and Arkin.) I am also grateful to Joe Kaufman from Texas for opening a door hitherto closed to me. Muchas gracias JK.

Where governments are concerned, very few provided any kind of help, but I must thank at least SAC Historian Jerry Martin, Kay Goss and Catherine Light of FEMA for help provided years ago, and Karin Hirsbrunner of the Swiss Office of Civil Protection. I am also grateful to the Library of Congress for allowing the reproduction of missile site-related photos.

The lack of co-operation from the various governments (along with NATO) that I have just mentioned came from all sides. STRATCOM would not confirm to me whether the Major Attack Options that I describe in the American chapter are still called as such. FEMA still will not say anything about Mount Weather, even though everyone and their grandmothers know what's there, although it has provided information to me on the underground Federal Regional Centers. And the British government will not release a harmless photo of a blast door at RAF Neatishead, nor will it say anything about its long-closed nuclear weapons depots in Germany. I expected this kind of secrecy from the Russians and the Chinese, not from the British and Americans. Always in the name of 'national security', they say.

Another problem I have had to deal with is censorship. For years, one had a bird's eye view of the NATO bunker outside Lisbon on the Internet, until someone covered it. Similarly, one could also see the location of the Polish bunker in the Pyry forest in Warsaw on the net relatively clearly until recently, but now that particular part of Pyry is blurred out. Also, the French government has blurred out satellite images of its active air bases. I also remember that, years ago, photos of the SAC bunker at Barksdale Air Force Base in Louisiana were available on ebay, but the photos soon mysteriously disappeared. I doubt very, very much if any of this would have really hurt 'national security'.

Glossary

AAA	Anti-Aircraft Artillery
AAOR	Anti-Aircraft Operations Room
ABC	American Broadcasting Corporation
ABM	Anti-Ballistic Missile
AC&W Sqn	Aircraft Control and Warning Squadron
ADM	Air Defence Missile
ADOC	Air Defense Operations Center
AEC	Atomic Energy Commission
AFB	Air Force Base
AFNWC	Air Force Nuclear Weapons Center
AFOC	Air Force Operations Centre
AFS	Air Force Station
AGT	Alberta Government Telephones
ALCM	Air Launched Cruise Missile
ANMCC	Alternate National Military Command Center
APS	Auxiliary Power Supply
ARADCOM	Army Air Defense Command
ARP	Air Raid Precautions
AT&T	American Telephone and Telegraph
Autodin	Automatic Digital Network
Autovon	Automatic Voice Network
AWACS	Airborne Warning and Control System
AWDREY	Atomic Weapons Detection Recognition and Estimation of Yield
BBC	British Broadcasting Corporation
BIRDIE	Battery Integrated Radar Display Equipment
BMAT	Ballistic Missile Analyst Technician
BMEWS	Ballistic Missile Early Warning System
BND	Bundesnachrichtendienst (German Intelligence Service)
CAOC	Combined Air Operations Center
CBC	Canadian Broadcasting Corporation
CCR	Canadian Censorship Regulations
CDBS	Command Data Buffer System
CENTAG	Central Army Group
CEP	Circular Error Probable
CFB	Canadian Forces Base

CFS	Canadian Forces Station
CGS	Chief of the General Staff
CGWHQ	Central Government War Headquarters
CIA	Central Intelligence Agency
CMC	Central Military Commission
COFAS	Centre d'opérations des forces aériennes stratégiques
CRC	Control and Reporting Centre
CSS	Coded Switch System
DHS	Department of Homeland Security
DIADEM	Directional Indication of Atomic Detonations by Electromagnetic Means
DIPEF	Defense Industrial Plant Equipment Facility
DMCCC	Deputy Missile Combat Crew Commander
DND	Department of National Defence
DoD	Department of Defense
DOSAAF	Volunteer Society for the Cooperation with the Air Force, Army and Navy
DOT	Department of Transport
DPRK	Democratic People's Republic of Korea
DPW	Department of Public Works
DSO&P	Directorate of Survival Operations and Plans
DUCC	Deep Underground Command Center
EAM	Emergency Action Message
EASE	Experimental Army Signals Establishment
EHF	Extremely High Frequency
EKV	Exo-atmospheric Kill Vehicle
EMO	Emergency Measures Organization
EMP	Electromagnetic Pulse
EOC	Emergency Operations Centre
ERCS	Emergency Rocket Communications System
ERR	Emergency Radio Relay
EWO	Emergency War Order
FBI	Federal Bureau of Investigation
FCC	Federal Communications Commission
FEMA	Federal Emergency Management Agency
FLQ	Front de Libération du Québec
FOST	Force Océanique Stratégique
FRG	Federal Republic of Germany
FSB	Federal Security Service
GAMA	GLCM Alert and Maintenance Area
GBI	Ground-Based Interceptor
GLCM	Ground-Launched Cruise Missile
GPO	General Post Office
GRU	Soviet/Russian military intelligence

GSFG	Group of Soviet Forces in Germany
GWEN	Ground Wave Emergency Network
HEW	Health, Education and Welfare
HF	High Frequency
HIPAR	High Power Acquisition Radar
HMCS	Her Majesty's Canadian Ship
HMS	Her Majesty's Ship
HMSO	Her Majesty's Stationery Office
IAEA	International Atomic Energy Agency
ICBM	Inter-Continental Ballistic Missile
IFF	Identification Friend-or-Foe
IG	Inspector General
IRBM	Intermediate Range Ballistic Missile
KGB	Committee for State Security
LCC	Launch Control Center
LCO	Launch Control Officer
LLC	Line Load Control
LOPAR	Low Power Acquisition Radar
MAF	Missile Alert Facility
MCC	Military Control Center
MCCC	Missile Combat Crew Commander
MDA	Missile Defense Agency
MFT	Missile Facilities Technician
MIMS	Missile Inspection and Maintenance Shop
MIRV	Multiple Independently-targetted Re-entry Vehicle
MoD	Ministry of Defence
MPVO	Local Anti-Aircraft Defence Organisation
MS	Mobile Support, Missile Squadron
MTR	Missile Tracking Radar
MWC	Missile Warning Center
MWEAC	Mount Weather Emergency Assistance Center
NAC	NORAD Air Center
NARA	US National Archives and Records Administration
NATO	North Atlantic Treaty Organization
NBC	Nuclear, Biological, Chemical
NCS	National Communications System
NDFRS	Nuclear Detonation and Fallout Reporting System
NMD	National Missile Defense
NORAD	North American Air Defense
NRP	Nudet Reporting Post
NSA	National Security Agency
NSI	Nuclear Surety Inspection
Nudet	Nuclear detonation
NVA	Nationale Volksarmee (East German National People's

	Army)
OCD	Office of Civil Defense
OCIPEP	Office of Critical Infrastructure Protection and Emergency Preparedness
OEP	Office of Emergency Preparedness
ORI	Operational Readiness Inspection
OSAX	Ottawa Semi-Automatic Exchange
PAL	Permissive Action Link
PHS	Public Health Service
PJHQ	Permanent Joint Headquarters
PRC	People's Republic of China
PVO	Protivovozdushnaya Oborona (Soviet air defence)
PWC	Provincial Warning Centre
QRA	Quick Reaction Alert
RADIL	ROCC-AWACS Digital Interface Link
RAF	Royal Air Force
RCA	Royal Canadian Artillery
RCAF	Royal Canadian Air Force
RCMP	Royal Canadian Mounted Police
RCN	Royal Canadian Navy
REACT	Rapid Execution and Combat Targeting
RGHQ	Regional Government Headquarters
RN	Royal Navy
RNAF	Royal Norwegian Air Force
ROCC	Region Operations Control Centre
RSG	Regional Scat of Government
RWR	Regional War Room
SAC	Strategic Air Command, Second Artillery Corps
SACDIN	Strategic Air Command Digital Network
SAM	Surface-to-Air Missile
SAOC	Sector Air Operations Centre
SCC	Space Control Center
SHAPE	Supreme Headquarters Allied Powers of Europe
SIOP	Single Integrated Operational Plan
SLBM	Sea Launched Ballistic Missile
SLCM	Sea Launched Cruise Missile
SMES	Strategic Missile Evaluation Squadron
SMS	Strategic Missile Squadron
SOC	Sector Operations Centre
SRC	Sub-Regional Control
SRF	Strategic Rocket Forces
SRHQ	Sub-Regional Headquarters
START	Strategic Arms Reduction Treaty
STRATCOM	Strategic Command

TAHQ	Target Area Headquarters
TEL	Transporter Erector Launcher
TTR	Target Tracking Radar
UDMH	Unsymmetrical dimethyl hydrazine
UHF	Ultra High Frequency
UKWMO	UK Warning and Monitoring Organisation
VHF	Very High Frequency
VLF	Very Low Frequency
WSAC	Welfare Service Accommodation Centre

❑ AFGHANISTAN

As a people that have been invaded several times by foreign forces, Afghanis have learned to make use of local geographical features to protect themselves. Afghanistan is mostly rough country, with about two-thirds consisting of the Central Highlands. This topography makes it difficult to travel through, or from a military perspective to fight in, as the countless ridges, hills and mountainsides provide an ideal environment for a defender. The Afghan people must have learned Sun Tzu's dictum of 'he who is prudent and lies in wait for an enemy who is not, will be victorious'.[1]

As all attacking forces have discovered, whether they were British, Soviet or American, the Central Highlands are full of caves and tunnels. These have been used by Afghan defenders for various purposes, such as storage depots, observation posts, barracks and command centres. In his book *Afghanistan Cave Complexes, 1979–2004*, Mir Bahmanyar describes one of the larger complexes that was built in the eastern part of the country near the Pakistani border. The Zhawar Kili base was an al-Qaeda stronghold that included a training centre, supply depot and public-relations office. Outside, one only saw houses for the terrorists' families, along with a reinforced tunnel entrance. Inside, though, underground tunnels led to two complexes that consisted of a veritable warren of branch tunnels and rooms used for equipment repair and storage, along with a hotel and mosque. Many rooms had their own ventilation shafts that led above. The two complexes could also be reached by tunnels hidden in the outside buildings, and also possessed several emergency exits. The base had been bombed by Allied aircraft in 1998 in response to terrorist attacks in Kenya and Tanzania, but in 2002, US Navy Seals and US Marines visited the complexes for intelligence purposes. The base was then destroyed.

Another large cave complex existed north of Zhawar Kili at Tora Bora. Again, it was located very close to the Pakistani border.[2] This huge complex occupied an area 5 miles long by 7 miles wide and was set in hills that were very difficult to reach, so much so that only mule convoys and foot soldiers could travel there. The base included entrances that were so inclined that it was difficult for attackers to enter and for guided munitions to inflict serious damage inside. According to one website, tanks were kept in some of the tunnels, and if this is true, they would have had to have been taken apart below, dragged up piece by piece, and re-assembled inside. The complex also consists of various stores, living and eating areas and, as above, ventilation shafts and emergency exits. Of course, it also had its own power source.[3]

Another underground facility in Afghanistan lies beside the presidential palace in Kabul. The bunker was built to give President Karzai protection from his many enemies. The magazine *Time* reported that it had been built with the help of the US Army's 769th Engineer Battalion.

❑ ALBANIA

The small country of Albania can be described, first and foremost, as a bunker-phile's delight. The tiny Balkan nation is said to have the highest concentration of bunkers in the world with the figure of 700,000 often quoted. The passion, or obsession, with underground places came from Prime Minister Enver Hoxha who, like Switzerland, was determined to protect his country from foreign aggressors. Hoxha had never been overly fond of Moscow's rule, and this dislike became serious enough for him to leave the Soviet camp in 1960. When the Soviet army invaded Czechoslovakia in 1968, he decided it would be better to adopt a more 'concrete' protectionist policy.

The structures were placed everywhere. These could be seen in farmers' fields, beaches, along a roadside or in someone's back garden. The bunkers varied in size from small infantry posts to larger urban public shelters. One journalist estimated that there was one structure for every four residents. Some were even placed in cemeteries, perhaps as a way of protecting the dead. Today, the bunkers have either adopted new roles as storage facilities or discos, or have been simply left to withstand the whims of Mother Nature. Some say that perhaps Hoxha built the bunkers as a way for his people to remember him.

Underground facilities known to exist in Albania include the following:

- For the air force, as aircraft hangars, at the Gjader, Rinas and Kucovë air bases. The Gjader air base was opened in 1974 and saw a number of fighters deployed there, such as Chinese F-7As of the 5646th Regiment, until 2001. The Rinas air base, which is part of Tirane's international airport, was home to the 7594th Regiment and is still active today, as is the Kucovë aerodrome, 40 miles south of Tirane;
- For the navy, on a spit of land north of Durrës near Porto Romana and Rinie, and at Porto Palermo, west of Qeparo; and
- For the national government under Mount Dajti, east of Tirane.

Finally, there is no doubt the communist-era civil-defence organization the Zshnum trained civilians in radiation monitoring, rescue and shelter usage. Zshnum was an Albanian acronym for the Society for Aid to the Army and for Defence.

❑ AUSTRIA

The Austrian government's alternate seat of government was located under a house and tennis court near the town of Grafenhof, south of Salzburg. The five-storey bunker doubled as an air-defence operations centre. It opened in 1982 and employed 250, and is apparently no longer in operation.

The Austrian Army also had a number of field fortifications along the Czech border. One of the bunkers, about 6 miles southwest of Villach in the Wurzenpass, was built in 1963 and used until 2002. It is now a museum.

❑ BELARUS

Very little has ever been disclosed about Cold War bunkers in Belarus, but it is known that public shelters were built in public parks in the capital, Minsk. In addition, the Soviet Strategic Rocket Forces had ICBM silos at several places that belonged to the 50th Missile Army. SRF units in Belarus can be found in Appendix M.

❑ BELGIUM

Perhaps one of the most important bunkers in Western Europe lies next to NATO headquarters at Casteau southwest of Brussels. The facility is designed to be the primary war-conducting centre for the Supreme Headquarters Allied Powers Europe. Here, staff are trained to conduct land, sea and air operations using the best technology and the latest intelligence gathered from points throughout Europe. The bunker is connected to regional underground facilities in several countries (e.g. Brunssum in the Netherlands and Linnich-Glimbach in Germany) as a way to keep track of activities in their area of responsibility. The staff in the operations centre in the underground complex use a War Headquarters Information Dissemination and Display System to visualize current operations and to keep track of unusual naval and air activity. Many of the staff here hold 'Cosmic Top Secret Atomal' security clearances.

The SHAPE bunker at Casteau relies heavily on communications for its work. Every method of communications is used to ensure it stays in contact with all NATO sub-units, with certain foreign Ministries of Defence and with the Pentagon and Strategic Command in Omaha. SHAPE relies on the civilian telephone system to link it with its microwave relay towers, and has its own satellite communications network called the NATO Integrated Communications System.[1] For years, and perhaps even now, it could rely on a small number of EC-135 aircraft codenamed 'Silk Purse' to disseminate attack orders, and it can make use of a convoy of trucks as a mobile command post.[2] SHAPE also has high-frequency radio links with all its subordinate commands and in addition can utilize American systems, such as the Digital European Backbone, to issue orders.

Other underground facilities in Belgium are:

- At Florennes air base for US Ground-Launched Cruise Missiles. The USAF's 485th Tactical Missile Wing was to receive 48 GLCMs in 1987, but the INF Treaty of that year cancelled the deployment. The three bunkers south of the air base were never used for their intended roles;

- Under Mount Kemel outside the town of Heuvelland. This was built as an air-defence operations centre for the Belgian air force in the 1950s using a design similar to British ROTOR stations. As of 1963, the bunker became the national war headquarters for the armed forces, although it was rarely used as such. The facility, accessed from a farm house, consists of offices, the operations centre, communications rooms, eating and sleeping areas and power and air filtration rooms. In total, the two-storey facility contains approximately fifty rooms. Local residents always suspected something secret lay there, but never knew exactly what. Today, the facility is a tourist attraction;
- Under a car park in Ghent;
- At Kanne, for NATO's 2nd Allied Tactical Air Force. The bunker was in an old quarry right on the Dutch–Belgian border. Here, it was possible to enter on the Belgian side and to exit on the Dutch side. NATO ceased using the facility in the early 1990s;
- At Kleine Brogel air base. Each of the eleven hardened aircraft hangars had a WS3 vault below that could hold two B61 nuclear gravity bombs. The weapons were in the custody of the USAF's 52nd Munitions Support Squadron, but would have been used by Belgian F-16s of the 23rd and 31st Squadrons on the base; and
- In addition to the Mount Kemmel bunker, the Belgian air force operated two radar stations in bunkers. These were at Glons and Semmerkaze.

❏ BOSNIA

Underground facilities in Bosnia include:

- A bunker at Han Pijesak, a small town on Highway 19 east of Sarajevo. This was built during the communist era and was used in the 1990s by Ratko Mladic of the Bosnian-Serb Army. Its entrance lies near Villa Javor;
- A bunker on top of Pljesevica Mountain. This was built in 1947 as a Yugoslavian air force radar and communications station. It was used by NATO during the Balkan War;
- Mountain hangars at Zeljava air base outside the city of Bihac. The facility was known as Object 505 and was built between 1957 and 1965. It was used by such units as the air force's 117th Fighter Aviation Regiment. Part of the base lies in Croatia;
- A facility near a chalet on Mount Gola. From this bunker, tunnels ran down to the Zeljava air base;
- A shelter for former President Tito near Bugojno; and
- A nuclear shelter for the government at Konjic.

❏ BULGARIA

During the Cold War, public shelters were built under the hills of central Plovdiv. One source claimed there were at least fifty such structures, with three of them turned into restaurants. Similar bunkers were likely constructed in the capital, Sofia.

Also, two bunkers can be seen at what seems to be an old anti-aircraft site east of Tsaratovo, which is north of Plovdiv.

❏ BURMA

The website channelnewsasia.com reported several years ago that the Burmese air force was building a large bunker for its MiG-29s at Taungdwingyi.

❏ CANADA

The Diefenbunkers and Emergency Government
To say that the Cold War had an impact upon Canada would probably be an understatement. Nestled between two superpowers, Canadian politicians knew that if a third world war was to ever break out, the country, long aligned with the United States, would feel the wrath of the Soviet Union's strategic menace. This fear caused an eagerness within political and military leaders in Ottawa to develop an extensive air defence network, to bolster its anti-submarine warfare capability, and to emulate, up to a point, the American defence mindset. That mindset included an elaborate continuity of government programme.

The whole purpose of the government's continuity plan in Canada, as in other countries, was the survival of the political leadership and the machinery of government. Politicians and senior military officers had every intention of resisting the Russians and helping Canadian cities cope with devastation. Working in co-operation with provincial governments (which in Canada are akin to American state governments), plans were set up by the national government to allocate resources, rescue those in need and maintain communications as well as law and order if war had ever broken out. Every government ministry was expected to participate in the continuity planning process, and many staffers at both the federal and provincial levels were chosen to man 'special facilities' during times of crises. The federal government in Ottawa had the largest of these facilities.

The quiet rural town of Carp is 28km west of Parliament Hill in the nation's capital. In 1959, construction crews moved into the area to construct a new military base quite unlike anything that had been built before in Canada. The previous year, Prime Minister John Diefenbaker ordered the construction of a bunker large enough to accommodate himself, his Cabinet, government staff and senior military and police personnel of sufficient numbers to maintain this continuity in government. Within this facility, this group would have had the onerous

The Carp bunker was located on Canadian Forces Station Carp west of Ottawa. This photo was taken in 1994 when the bunker was closed. (Photo: Author)

task of managing an entire nation. It would be Canada's chief centre for policy-making in wartime.

Although first known as the National Emergency Headquarters, the facility would later officially be known as the Central Emergency Government Headquarters. Government planners first envisaged that this complex would consist of three separate but interconnected underground buildings, but this was later changed to two, then one. The contract to build it was awarded by a crown corporation that specializes in military projects, Defence Construction Limited. The final 100,000sq ft bunker cost $25 million (land, building and equipment included) and involved over 1,000 contractors and miles of concrete-reinforcing steel rods. Project director Lieutenant-Colonel Edward Churchill of the Royal Canadian Engineers was given the task of building the structure and, using a new engineering management tool known as Critical Path Networking, completed the project on time and on budget in 1961.[1] For thirty-three years, the 'Diefenbunker', as it came to be known, was kept in stand-by mode ready to accept a large crew of key public and private sector personnel who would have been needed when the Bomb had dropped.

Typically of nuclear shelters, the Diefenbunker at Carp was designed for self-sufficiency. This meant an independent power supply and underground water reservoirs, kitchen, messes, dorms, offices, washrooms and a decontamination suite. A small Canadian Broadcasting Corporation (CBC) radio studio was maintained complete with a 78rpm turntable and audio tape player along with prerecorded messages for public announcements. Since NATO's Military Committee predicted that a nuclear war would consist of a brief attack of a few weeks duration followed by a long period of reorganization, provision levels were set at thirty days to cover the first phase only. After this, radiation levels were expected to be such that surface life could resume as before, although this is an argument that has oft been questioned. The bunker was built to protect its residents from both radioactive fallout and blast pressures up to 100lb per sq in, and

One of the
entrances to the
Carp bunker.
(Photo: Author)

its sloped exterior was designed to deflect the pressure wave from a nearby detonation. In total, it was expected to house 550 persons.

Physically, the bunker is a large blockhouse supported by huge inverted cement cones. These are called capitals and are so shaped to spread shock waves. The bunker's ceiling consists of 5ft of reinforced concrete and the walls themselves are 3ft thick. It is estimated the structure can withstand a 5 megaton blast 1.1 mile away. Its particular design was chosen after research was done by the National Research Council and the Defence Research Board using data compiled by the US Army and US Navy. The data showed what design would work to provide shock resistance and optimal living conditions. Indeed, the capitals were painted with vertical black and white stripes to give residents the illusion of higher ceilings.

The Carp facility is four storeys high, or rather deep. It is accessed from a linear walkway with entrances at both ends, with two blast doors half-way down, one for freight and the other for personnel. The doors are located at right angles from the tunnel to avoid the effects of a channelled blast wave. The top-most floor contained primarily medical and administrative sections such as decontamination cubicles, medical inspection room, offices and, for those heavily affected by radiation, two medical lockups.[2] One also found a Message Centre with classified communications and cryptographic equipment, an RCMP vault for records, the switchboard and two emergency exits leading to top-side hatches.

The next floor down housed the Ottawa Semi-Automatic Exchange (OSAX), which would have been the government's main telephone exchange in case of war. There was also an Information Co-ordination Centre that would track such things as nuclear detonations and fallout and that would estimate casualty levels. This floor also had ladies' sleeping quarters, the CBC studio and conference centre, an officers' lounge, as well as the Prime Minister's minuscule office, bedroom and lavatory. Finally, a conference room was established for use by the War Cabinet. For ease of communications, the various staff rooms were interconnected by closed-circuit television.

The Ottawa Semi-Automatic Exchange, what would have been the government's main switching centre during a war. It was operated by the Canadian Army's corps of signals. The room was shielded against radio frequency interference. (Photo: LAC, DND Collection, RE72-1305)

This same floor also had a Military Information Centre. The MIC monitored foreign and friendly troops, and maintained communications with NATO and NORAD. The MIC included a large screen called an Iconorama upon which could be displayed an image of North America and another projection, this one overlaid, that could show an air battle in progress, more or less as it was represented in the film *Failsafe*. This device, which was manufactured by Canadian Aviation Electronics of Montreal at a cost of over $372,000, was only used until 1969.

On the third floor (or Level 2) were the men's quarters. The dining facilities nearby served food classed as excellent and could accommodate 180. During crises, the staff would have been fed regular food for seven days, and after that army rations for twenty-three days. The bottom floor contained the heavy diesel generators with a thirty-day supply of oil, filter intake and exhaust plena, offices, stores and battery rooms. The plena also doubled as emergency exits. Much of the heavy machinery was spring-mounted for shock absorption and, indeed, the entire building was buffered by crushed gravel for the same reason. The air filters installed in the intake plena were reputed to provide 99.5 per cent pure air. The morgue was also located on this floor and although never used as such, it made a good food freezer.

Attached to the bottom floor by a high-ceilinged hallway was a vault designed to keep the Bank of Canada's gold reserves. The structure consisted of a double outer wall that had a narrow airspace in between for security in case of tunnelling attempts. The vault's 10-ton door was built by Mosler Safe of Ohio, the same company that manufactured the Greenbrier bunker doors and the vault doors at Fort Knox. An air duct and fan with its own safe-type door were built in the wall beside it to allow air in as it is not possible to open a door to a hermetically sealed room. The vault never served its intended purpose and by 1970, the Bank of Canada decided it would not have used it in times of war. It would only have stored archival records and selected national treasures. On a day-to-day basis, the vault acted as a supply depot and its access hallway doubled as a gym.

Carp was built over an eighteen-month period between 1959 and 1961 by the Foundation Company of Canada. In its first year of operations, the bunker employed 203 military personnel and 50 civilians. The property included not only the bunker proper but also above-ground engineering workshops, a junior ranks' mess hall, sewage lagoons, a helicopter landing pad and a guard house complete with its own mini-bunker. Just a few feet away was another bunker built to house a bulldozer that would have been used to clear debris, and that also contained mobile CBC equipment.

The Carp facility was in peacetime the responsibility of the Department of National Defence (DND) and the Canadian Army. Its major user, however, was the federal government's Emergency Measures Organization (EMO). While the Army's Directorate of Survival Operations and Plans (DSO&P) prepared guidelines for casualty rescue, re-entry into a bombed area, attack warning and emergency communications, EMO was the agency tasked with overall government survival planning and relocation. It maintained the *Government Emergency Book* (Volume I for natural disasters and Volume II for war) and ran the

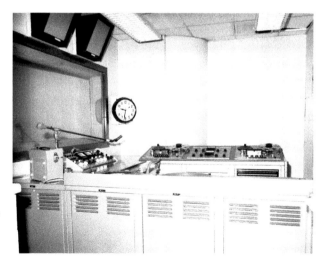

The CBC studio at Carp. (Photo: LAC, DND collection, REC93-2251, October 1993)

This separate bunker at Carp stored a bulldozer that would have been used to clear debris, along with mobile CBC equipment. (Photo: Author)

occasional exercise. The Army, on the other hand, was the bunker's caretaker. Costs of running the facility were shared between DND and EMO, but it was only in 1968 that the formula was finalized. The $447,700 annual price tag was split fifty-fifty between the two organizations.[3] DND, through the Canadian Army, was also responsible for maintaining the food supply.

Civil defence was not new to Canada as it was applied during the Second World War. After the war ended, the concept disappeared from the minds of the politicians but when the Cold War gained momentum, there was a resurgence of interest in the matter and the requirement for new plans. A civil defence controller was formally created in 1948, but from then on, the thorny question of whom to assign overall responsibility was never answered with permanence. Policy-makers could seemingly never make up their minds which department to put it under. Civil defence was first made a Department of National Defence matter but in February 1951, it was transferred to the Department of National Health and Welfare. In 1959, it was given to the Privy Council Office, and subsequently to the Department of Defence Production (which later became the Department of Industry). In 1968, it was returned to DND but later was listed as an independent organization, albeit still partially controlled by DND. In September 1992, to reduce administrative overheads, civil defence again became a direct DND responsibility. Unlike in the United States, where the director of the Federal Emergency Management Agency is a civilian who reports to the President, the director of Emergency Preparedness Canada, as it was then called, now reported to a military officer, the Deputy Chief of the Defence Staff. As of the time of writing, it was included in the ministry called Public Safety Canada. The Canadian emergency measures outfit suffered the same identity crisis as FEMA since it was renamed several times, viz:

Civil Defence Co-ordinator
Federal Civil Defence Co-ordinator

Emergency Measures Organization
Canada Emergency Measures Organization
National Emergency Planning Establishment
Emergency Planning Canada
Emergency Preparedness Canada
Office of Critical Infrastructure Protection and Emergency Preparedness
Public Safety and Emergency Preparedness Canada
Public Safety Canada, Emergency Management and National Security
    Branch

Many provinces also had their own EMOs, and some of them were afflicted by the same titular schizophrenia. Alberta's emergency management outfit was first known as Alberta Civil Defence, then Emergency Measures Organization, Disaster Services and then Public Safety Services Agency. It later became a division of the provincial ministry Alberta Transportation and Utilities, but is now an independent organization known as Alberta Emergency Management Agency.

Because of the huge job of running a nation after an attack, many men and women were selected for occupancy at Carp. As mentioned before, the Prime Minister had a reserved suite waiting for him. There was also an outer office for his secretary. As his wife was deemed non-essential, there were no quarters for her. Another suite awaited the Governor-General – a nominal head of state whose functions include granting Royal Assent to new legislation, while small single bedrooms were allotted to the RCMP Commissioner and the President of the CBC. Other residents were to include select Privy Councillors (advisers to the Prime Minister), and twelve Cabinet ministers, six of whom would have formed the War Cabinet. Space was also reserved for senior members of the RCMP and the Department of National Defence, medical personnel, communications operators and technicians, maintenance engineers and guards. In the 1960s, the following ministries would have been represented at Carp:

Agriculture
Defence Production
External Affairs
Fisheries
Justice
Labour
Finance
National Defence
Transport
Public Works
Postmaster
National Health and Welfare

With the Canada Mortgage and Housing Corporation responsible for emergency housing construction, it too gained a spot. The Canadian Security Intelligence Service was also represented after it was formed in 1984 when it was given counter-espionage functions from the RCMP. From the private sector, personnel were selected for their expertise in running the electric grid, the telephone system and the oil supply.

Except for the Prime Minister, the Governor-General and others mentioned above, all were bunked several to a room. Because of the insufficient number of beds, people would have had to sleep in shifts. In a personal memo from the Canadian Army's Chief of the General Staff to R.B. Bryce of the Privy Council Office, the bunker's ultimate superintendent, it had been recommended that women not be employed at Carp, 'thus avoiding the need for any separate facilities', and that staff be strictly male. Since ladies' dorms and washrooms appear on a 1961 floor plan, one can conclude this recommendation was never accepted.

To maintain contact with the outside world, the bunker at Carp was linked to several remote facilities. Chief of these was a separate transmitter station a few miles east of Perth, Ontario, off Lanark County Road No. 10, called the Richardson Detachment. Richardson was connected by underground landline to Carp and was located far enough away from Carp for survivability and to reduce interference with its equipment. At first, the station was given Marconi HS51 transmitters but due to their many periods of unserviceability, these were replaced by the more dependable Harris FRT-510s.

To ensure the twenty-or-so required communications personnel at Richardson would survive the holocaust, a two-storey 18,000sq ft bunker was built on the property. It had been originally planned for a site near Cedar Hill west of Pakenham but when civil engineers realized the geology was inadequate for a bunker, excavation was stopped and a new site near Perth was found. The Richardson bunker came complete with mess hall, sleeping quarters, first-aid

The entrance to the Richardson bunker. Richardson had radio connections to several other emergency facilities along with buried landlines to Carp and the federal building in Smiths Falls, which, along with Carp, was also a relocation site. (Photo: Author)

Blast doors at
Richardson. (Photo:
Author)

post, offices and power room and, as with Carp, decontamination cubicles. It cost $134,739 to build and was completed in 1962.

When construction began at Carp, the government attempted to hide the project's true purpose. Work crews may have understood what was going on but as far as the public was concerned this was an experimental radio station with the cover name of Project EASE – Experimental Army Signals Establishment. Trying to keep a lid on the subject proved impossible as both leaks and the Prime Minister's statement in the House of Commons on 31 May 1960 announcing the construction of emergency facilities fuelled media speculation and rumours. Major-General A.E. Wrinch, director of the Army's survival operations branch and chief bunker planner, felt that keeping up Carp's pretence as a strictly signals establishment was pointless since the press had already pierced through the veil of secrecy. In fact, the Canadian Broadcasting Corporation had requested permission in November 1959 to film the bunker under construction, one month before building work began, but was politely refused this permission by the Army. George Brimmell of the *Toronto Telegram* had also heard the government was building something secret at Carp, and when during a helicopter overflight his photographer, Ted Grant, saw the unusually large number of toilets waiting to be installed, Brimmell knew the facility was no ordinary radio station. (He would be the first journalist to use the word 'Diefenbunker', a play on the then-Prime Minister's name.) In the article he wrote for his newspaper, he showed everything. So incensed was Diefenbaker at his revelation that he demanded that the *Telegram* fire him. General Wrinch thought the Canadian Army was now being 'held up to ridicule fairly frequently' by the media and recommended leading publishers and editors be given a classified briefing in the hope that the speculation would end. A previous memo to the Minister of National Defence to this effect was rejected, but this did not deter Wrinch from pressing on. To maintain the illusion of some secrecy, EMO recommended military survey parties wear civilian clothes.

Despite Wrinch's desire for secrecy, a surprising amount of information on survival planning and continuity of government was made public through unclassified publications such as the *EMO National Digest* and the *Canadian Army Journal*. Personnel working in these bunkers were still sworn to secrecy, however, and needed at least a security clearance level of Secret. If this personnel required access to atomic information, they needed a clearance level of Top Secret to ZED standards. This level was necessary if they were required to take the Atomic, Biological and Chemical Warfare Course at the Joint Atomic, Biological and Chemical Warfare School at Camp Borden, or if they were to be given access to British or American nuclear-related documents. The Department of National Defence formed the Joint Special Weapons Committee in the 1950s to grant these ZED clearances and assigned the responsibility for doing so to specific Navy, Air Force and Army Control Officers. In 1960, the Army ZED Control Officer was Lieutenant-Colonel James C. Bond.

Despite the security around EASE, if anyone wanted to find out what was truly going on, all they had to do was ask the local Monk Rural Telephone Company operator. For two months in 1959, the operator served as the contractor's unofficial gossip and kept everyone informed of progress. Upon learning of her indiscretions, the project's security director had a discussion of the problem with the telephone company manager. The gossiping soon stopped.

Perhaps more worrisome than the talkative telephone operator were the foreign sightseers bearing diplomatic licence plates. Since it represented a valid military target, the Russians took an interest in Carp early on. On 25 September 1959, the Russian military and assistant military attachés, Colonel Nikolai Evsikov and Captain Aleksandr Pavlov respectively, were noticed driving around the project's perimeter to survey the site.[4] Two months later, two more diplomatic vehicles, Czech and Russian, were spotted looking around. The Russians this time were Aferiev and Third Secretary Evgeny Lopatin, known to be electronics experts. Since all were within the travel limit imposed upon diplomats by the Department of External Affairs, no action could be taken against them.

The designation of Carp as an Experimental Army Signals Establishment followed a long tradition of using research or some other bland excuse as a cover for any kind of special activity, a tradition adopted not only in Canada but also by many other countries and one that continues to this day. For instance, during the Second World War, British Security Co-ordination ran a commando school, Special Training School 103, at Oshawa, Ontario. More commonly known as Camp X, it was in fact called 'Project J' by the Department of National Defence. Also, the Canadian Army's secret radio station at the same location was known as 'Military Research Centre No. 2' from 1944 to 1947. The Army's secret wartime monitoring station at the National Research Council's Montreal Road campus in east Ottawa was known as the Royal Canadian Signals Experimental Station. Furthermore, the Department of National Defence's wartime signals analysis organization, the No. 1 Discrimination Unit, became the Communications Research Centre in 1946. In fact, current Canadian military signals intelligence personnel are known as Communications Research

Operators. Several other examples of cover organizations in other countries are found in Appendix L.

During peacetime, Carp acted as a government communications network centre manned by the Army with technical operations looked after by the Royal Canadian Corps of Signals' 1 Army Signal Squadron, specifically by the Squadron's EASE Signal Centre Troop. During the armed forces reorganization in the mid-1960s, the base was renamed Canadian Forces Station Carp and put under the aegis of the Canadian Forces Communications System and the Signal Centre Troop, redesignated 701 Communications Squadron.[5] Perhaps fittingly, CFS Carp's heraldic crest featured Cerberus, a three-headed dog which acts as the guardian to the gates of hell.

With the station acting as a military radio/telephone/teletype network centre, all defence-related calls from Ottawa to other points in Canada passed through it. One radio link was also established with RAF Boddington, England, at Barrow in Gloucestershire to communicate with the British government. Carp served the Canadian Switched Network and the Automated Defence Data Network, two systems used for message processing. Signals intelligence obtained from Canadian Forces Supplementary Radio System stations across Canada was routed here through the Canadian Supplementary Military Network. At least one of those stations, Canadian Forces Station Alert in the far north, had a direct radio connection to Carp.

Project EASE was divided into two basic functional subsets: the primary and secondary areas. The primary areas included technical sections in the bunker such as the Facility Control Centre (the communications circuits monitoring and testing centre), Message Centre, the OSAX node, On-Line Crypto section and remote receiver and transmitter sites. Warning centres capable of relaying attack information to local authorities were located in every province and linked to Carp through the OSAX. Secondary areas seem to cover more the information input/output functions such as the Military Information Centre, CBC studio and the Emergency Radio Relay.

The Cornwall federal building was one of the government's relocation sites. Staff would have used the basement as an operations centre. The building is now the city's public library. (Photo: Author)

The ERR was one of Carp's links to the outside world. It was connected to six remote locations, which acted as additional government relocation sites. These six points were at Pembroke, Arnprior, Smiths Falls, Cornwall, Carleton Place and Kemptville, all in Ontario, most of which were upwind from a nuclear cloud over Ottawa. In the first four towns, they were located in the basement of the local post office, and at Kemptville and Carleton Place, they were in the basement of specially built facilities that looked like military barracks.

In the government's emergency plan, in addition to Carp, some civil servants would have relocated to the above six buildings while others would have gone elsewhere. At one point, the Post Office Department would have moved to the post office in Pembroke. The CBC and members of the media, who would have formed the National Emergency News Pool, might have found themselves at the post office in Smiths Falls, and members of foreign diplomatic missions would have been quartered at the Ontario Agricultural College in Kemptville. The Civil Defence College in Arnprior and Camp Petawawa were also designated relocation points, the former to be used by the Department of National Health and the RCMP and the latter by the Army Alternate Emergency Headquarters and, as one of the attack warning control points, the Alternate Federal Warning Centre. Indeed, the Arnprior college had been the government's first main relocation site prior to Carp's construction and Camp Petawawa the second. As for Air Force Headquarters and Naval Service Headquarters, they would have moved to RCAF Station Trenton and to a naval armoury, HMCS *Cataraqui*, in Kingston, Ontario, respectively.

The basements of these six secondary relocation sites were hardened to protect offices, dining facilities, a generator, a radio room and a medical station. Since they were below ground, they had ample blast protection. The dormitories normally had a total capacity for over 100. Throughout the continuity of government programme's lifetime, military personnel kept freeze-dried rations stored there and replenished the stock every two years. The communications equipment was installed by the Army's Corps of Signals and maintained on a regular basis.

In the early 1960s, it was planned that government support staff would move to the Kemptville, Carleton Place, Arnprior and Smiths Falls relocation sites by special Colonial Coach buses following procedures listed under the federal dispersal plan, called 'Rustic'. In the early days of the COG programme, these four sites, sometimes called Central Relocation Units and sometimes Federal Departmental Relocation Sites, would have housed the following:

Kemptville	Carleton Place
Cabinet Group	War Supplies Agency
External Affairs	Agriculture
National Health and Welfare	Finance/Bank of Canada
Transport	Fisheries
	Public Works

Smiths Falls
Labour
Justice
CBC

Arnprior
RCMP
National Health and Welfare

The two other relocation sites, at Pembroke and Cornwall, were only developed later on. Another site had been examined in Renfrew, again in the basement of the post office, but it was rejected as too costly to modify.

The Smiths Falls Central Relocation Unit was a bit different to the other five CRUs. The Cabinet Committee on Emergency Plans later decided there should be a back-up to the War Cabinet at Carp in case the CEGHQ was ever attacked. This was needed to prevent an interruption of Parliament. Thus, an alternate War Cabinet consisting of six other federal ministers was slated for residency at Smiths Falls.

The facilities at Carleton Place and Kemptville were special in that they were the only CRUs built specifically as relocation sites. They were first known as Welfare Service Accommodation Centres (WSACs), a name that suggests they may have been initially reserved strictly for the federal Department of National Health and Welfare's Emergency Welfare Service. In wartime, the EWS would have served as an advisory and assistance body to the provinces in all matters of public welfare, such as emergency clothing and feeding, and would have continued processing family allowance and old-age payments. The WSACs' role as emergency facilities was not kept secret since they were listed in the Department of Public Works 1962 public annual report as used for 'Emergency Military Operations'.

Both WSACs, later renamed Readiness Units, were two-storey huts with offices and small roomettes on the top floor and a kitchen, dining room, separate male and female washrooms, more roomettes and other offices on the bottom floor. Some windows were painted and screened for security. Normally, however, these facilities were used by government staff for training purposes; the

The Kemptville relocation facility. The emergency exit can be seen in the centre. This building no longer exists. (Photo: Author)

RCMP and the Canadian Security Intelligence Service have occupied the Carleton Place building during security exercises.

The WSAC basements were themselves self-contained units in that they had their own eating and living facilities. The government kept sufficient food stocks for fourteen days in the kitchenette along with menu lists for each day. The male and female dorms were long rooms with bunk beds along each longitudinal wall with each dorm having its own sanitary station and sand-filled emergency exit leading above ground. Another section housed an operations centre and at the opposite end, a Message Centre contained radio and telephone equipment with lines connected to several other emergency facilities. The building's power plant was also on this floor. The basement walls were 12in thick and the entrance door was of heavy steel. At the Carleton Place WSAC, the white and olive drab wall colour scheme in the operations centre left something to be desired so red, orange and yellow cloth panels were installed. Government staff totalling 256 would have occupied both floors along with the basement during times of tension.

Military facilities in North America and Europe were connected with Carp through the Richardson radio transmitter site and through receiver sites at Almonte and Woodlawn, Ontario. Some of the telephone lines to and from the bunker passed through a secret network centre at an armoury in Renfrew. Also, as of the early 1970s, overseas communications were processed through a satellite ground station located in a separate building just west of the bunker. This satcom terminal operated as a component of NATO's Integrated Communications System and allowed messages to be sent to and received from foreign terminals: in the 1980s, NATO's primary communications satellite was simply numbered '4A'. As well, communications with the United States were so critical the Prime Minister had direct access to the Pentagon through an American-owned KY-3 secure voice circuit in his office. The circuit's designation was CANHOUSWASH/VOICE. Weather reports, crucial for radioactivity plotting, were sent by a then-new invention, a fax machine.

The Canadian Army's Directorate of Survival Operations and Plans (DSO&P) considered everything when building Carp. Some nuclear drills were held to test the movement of emergency personnel and the quality of life under brief locked-down conditions. Even before it was fully manned, Army personnel were brought to Carp for a simulated lock-down to see how well they would react. This research showed that the accommodations were such that extended stays in the bunker were both possible and practical.

In its planning, DSO&P took advantage of the fact a railway line ran conveniently close to the bunker. Some public servants were to be brought in by a special Canadian National Railways train when the threat of attack loomed. The four-coach 'Special Train' was kept parked at Ottawa Union Station and switched over to a loading platform within twenty minutes of an alert, and had to load and depart within another ten. On the way to Carp, stops were made at various points within the city of Ottawa, such as at Hurdman's Bridge, Pleasant Park Drive and Merivale Road, to pick up further passengers. The railroad plan was maintained after Union Station moved to its current Tremblay Road location in 1966. Arrangements for the Prime Minister were somewhat different in that a special helicopter was to be brought in from the Trenton air base during alert phases and kept on stand-by at the Rockcliffe airfield in east Ottawa. If and when the attack was announced, the helicopter was to pick the Prime Minister and a few others up in front of the Parliament buildings for a quick trip to the bunker.

The Carp facility, its associated transmitter site at Richardson, and the six government relocation sites around Ottawa were only part of the Canadian continuity of government programme. At the same time Project EASE was being built, Ottawa politicians decided that for the programme to be truly effective, the provinces would have to be brought on board. The Canadian Constitution gave certain responsibilities to the federal government and others to the provinces, and politicians thought that this public-service duality would be maintained, even during a nuclear war. Provincial Premiers guard their powers jealously, and under no circumstances (or almost) would they have abdicated these.[6] The federal Cabinet realized this and decided at the outset that members of provincial governments would also be housed in protected facilities. The plan was therefore made to build subterranean Regional Emergency Government Headquarters in all ten provinces.

Where staffing was concerned, these REGHQs were to have representatives from every crucial provincial government department. During wartime, these civil servants would have been needed to look after road and bridge repairs, sources of energy and food, public communications, the maintenance of law and order and public health. In these bunkers, spaces were earmarked for the Premier, support staff, departmental advisers and co-ordinators, and a small regiment of clerks and typists. Total staff varied from 150 men and women for the Prince Edward Island facility to 387 for the Ontario bunker. These public servants would not have been alone since some space was also set aside for federal workers (who looked after federal responsibilities) and for Army personnel. At the Ontario bunker, which was located at Camp Borden north of Toronto, staff from the following ministries were planned in the early 1960s:

Federal	Provincial
RCMP	Health
National Health & Welfare	Welfare
Post Office	Agriculture
Agriculture	Transport
Transport	Labour
Labour	Provincial EMO
Bank of Canada	Public Works
CBC	Premier
War Supplies Agency	Attorney-General
Judiciary	Energy-Resources

Co-ordinator	Lands and Forests
Regional Commissioner	Treasurer
EMO	Highways
Finance	Ontario Provincial Police
Public Works	Ontario Fire Marshal
Canadian Army	

Each provincial bunker had its codename consisting of the word 'Bridge' followed by a number. Ontario's bunker was Bridge 5.

All the provincial bunkers had roughly the same two-storey design that consisted of power units on the ground floor and offices, living quarters, decontamination centre and entrances on the upper floor. The structures varied slightly in size; the Ontario bunker at Camp Borden measured 71,000sq ft and the one at Penhold, Alberta, 66,000sq ft.[7] All had 15in reinforced concrete walls and emergency exits on the roof. They were built for fallout protection except for the one at Camp Valcartier – it had blast protection in the form of heavier doors and blast valves in the air intakes and outlets – since its proximity to the target community of Quebec City made this imperative.

The main functions of these provincial bunkers, in addition to the relocation of public servants, would have been the co-ordination of emergency work and the issuance of warnings to the public. All REGHQs had within them a Provincial Warning Centre (PWC) with personnel responsible for analyzing attack data and

The Regional Emergency Government Headquarters at Canadian Forces Base Borden. This would have been used by the armed forces and the provincial Premier along with his staff. Other provincial government employees would have relocated to other locations. This bunker no longer exists. (Photo: Author)

activating air-raid warning sirens. During peacetime, two emergency wardens, an Army Captain and a Sergeant, were kept busy testing the air-raid sirens, monitoring the weather, receiving air defence surveillance data from NORAD, testing communications with the nearest CBC studio and carrying out nuclear drills. The latter involved running imaginary attack scenarios on their computers and predicting which cities would be blasted or contaminated by fallout. In wartime, the number of staff assigned to the PWCs would have increased to eight or nine.

In addition to the above, plans were made in most provinces to evacuate federal and provincial support personnel to nearby auxiliary sites, much like the federal dispersal plan for Ottawa. These sites were called

Blast doors at the CFB Shilo bunker in Manitoba. When the bunker was being built, someone suggested installing a periscope as a way to assess nearby battle damage. The periscope was never put in. (Photo: RCA Museum)

Regional Relocation Units, and again they were often sited in the basement of post offices. In Ontario, some civil servants would have moved to RRUs at Orillia and Barrie, and in British Columbia, those not going to the REGHQ would have been sheltered at the RRUs in the provincial courthouse or at the Pacific Biological Station in Nanaimo. Here, staff would have continued their normal functions; for instance, agricultural personnel would have given advice to farmers on crop protection, and the provincial departments of justice would have continued providing support to the courts. Probably for reasons of cost, some

The British Columbia REGHQ was at Camp Nanaimo on Vancouver Island. It cost approximately $2 million to build. Today, it is sealed up and a new highway runs almost over it. (Photo: R.V. Stevenson)

The Ontario Ministry of Natural Resources training centre at Dorset was one of the provincial government's relocation facilities. It had no bunker, but was far enough away from major urban centres to provide good protection. When photographed by the author in 2009, it lay abandoned. (Photo: Author)

RRUs, such as at Truro, Nova Scotia, and Hinton, Alberta, were never activated.

When Parliament in Ottawa decided to plan for continuity of government, many of the provinces followed suit. Provincial emergency measures staff began planning government dispersal programmes for personnel not going to REGHQs or RRUs. Relocation facilities were chosen outside provincial capitals – usually in existing accommodations – in buildings that would house all the equipment needed to continue operating. Ontario's Ministry of Municipal Affairs and the Department of Lands and Forests (later renamed the Ministry of Natural Resources), for example, would have relocated to the post office in Bracebridge and to the Leslie M. Frost Natural Resources Centre in Dorset respectively. In British Columbia, the provincial Forest Research Station at Lake Cowichan was similarly considered. The Province of Alberta, on the other hand, would go one step further and construct two purpose-built bunkers for the relocation of its staff in the Edmonton suburb of Jasper Place.

If the Central Emergency Government Headquarters was the main wartime centre for policy-making, and the Regional Emergency Government Headquarters were the primary seats of operational governments, it remained for yet other centres to act as front-line units. When Prime Minister Diefenbaker secretly announced in 1958 that he wanted a national COG network, he decided upon a decentralized system, much like the current federal-provincial-municipal structure. What was thus needed were more local headquarters, offices with staff that could look after emergencies within their small jurisdictions. If a city had been devastated by an atomic weapon, personnel would have been required to co-ordinate traffic, look after the wounded, control looting, help rebuild damaged areas, and ensure the public had enough to eat. Such personnel would have been found in Zone Emergency Government Headquarters (ZEGHQs).

There were to be thirty-four ZEGHQs across Canada. These were sited in the basement of existing federal buildings, much like the Central and Regional Relocation Units, with a few exceptions such as at Guelph, Ontario, where space was made for it in the basement of Johnston Hall at the University of Guelph. They would have sections for manpower, supplies, transport, postal services, engineering, finance, emergency communications, along with police, fire, health, welfare and public information, and would be led by provincial Cabinet ministers. They would have no military functions. Their main duties were to implement directives from the REGHQs, to provide direction to municipalities in their areas, and to co-ordinate rescue and relief operations. They were also expected to take over from REGHQs if these were ever destroyed. Each ZEGHQ would have been staffed by about fifty men and women and hold sufficient food rations for fourteen days.

Toronto's emergency operations centre was located under an old house in Aurora. The house was bought by the city in 1962 and converted into a command post the following year. Besides the EOC proper, there were three radio rooms, a generator, and a supply of food and cots. Municipal politicians would not have relocated here, but rather at St Andrew's College. The bunker ceased to be maintained in the 1980s, after which it was used by Toronto police for tactical training. Today, it sits unused. (Photo: Anonymous)

Yet other emergency government facilities were established in Canada during the Cold War. Even with the thirty-four zone headquarters created to handle local emergencies, municipalities were still encouraged to set up a secure location from which they could continue operating, in a sense what were considered alternate city halls. The federal government thus decided to rent out space in local federal buildings to the cities for a small fee for this purpose. These Municipal Emergency Government Headquarters were equipped with suitable furniture, radios, telephones and maps and had the same responsibilities as ZEGHQs, namely rescue, health, food supply, transport, law enforcement and public information. Each municipality was expected to appoint a civil servant as emergency measures officer, and it was this person's responsibility to ensure that the emergency government would run smoothly. At least one Canadian MEGHQ would be located in a bunker: Toronto's command centre was placed several miles north of the city under the lawn of an old house in Aurora.

The duality of federal-provincial governments that is so firmly entrenched in Canadian society exists for at least one reason: some services can be delivered more effectively if a more local government handles them. Some portfolios, such as natural resources, can be better developed if they have a more local character. This implies that what works for Alberta may not work for Nova Scotia. This two-track approach to public service would, however, cause a serious problem in the REGHQs: that is, who would be in charge? If there was to be any co-ordination of relief or efforts at reconstruction, who would, in the event of a disagreement, make the final decision? It was decided that each bunker would be run by a Regional Commissioner, someone who would give executive direction, as required, to federal agencies of government, who would 'coordinate joint operations of the federal and provincial agencies of government', and who would 'arbitrate serious matters of conflict between federal and provincial agencies of government'. But in drafting these Terms of Reference, the federal government in Ottawa would create a major problem.

While the federal Cabinet had already decided that the Regional Commissioners would be federal officers, some provinces were extremely reluctant to yield any control to these individuals. Such displeasure was made clear at a federal-provincial civil defence conference held in November 1961. Every time some individual was considered for the role, there was an objection from either the federal or provincial side. It was suggested that Lieutenant-Governors, persons who are in effect the Queen's representatives to the provinces, be given the role. As he is the individual who gives provincial laws Royal Assent, having him relocate to an REGHQ would have ensured his survival. On the other hand, some people could not accept having a Queen's representative double as a senior civil servant. This would have blurred the line heavily between the executive and legislative functions of a democratic society. Provincial Premiers were also suggested as Regional Commissioners, but some federal politicians shot that idea down as they feared their efforts would have been too greatly slanted towards the provinces and not towards the nation as a whole. It was further suggested that federal Cabinet ministers be appointed to the role, but some feared they would not have been able to reach their respective bunkers on time. No matter who was suggested, there were always objections.

When C.W. Bunting, the director of policy at the Emergency Measures Organization, wrote his recommendations to the federal Cabinet, he concluded that provincial Premiers be chosen as Regional Commissioners, hoping they could set aside their provincial biases and concentrate on the well-being of the entire nation. The Premiers present at a 1965 federal-provincial conference concurred with the idea but, although draft acceptance letters were prepared for the Prime Minister to sign, they were never, at least as recently as the 1970s, signed by him. The question of who to put in charge thus seemed to never have been settled.

The choice of Regional Commissioners was not the only problem facing Ottawa. Inevitably, there would be some disagreements over the siting of the bunkers. EMO's Quebec regional officer wanted the Quebec bunker built near Montreal closer to his and other federal offices. Provincial staffers and the Canadian Army, on the other hand, preferred the proximity of Camp Valcartier outside Quebec City. The EMO regional officer complained to Ottawa that the Army and province were being selfish. Upon being advised of this objection, Lieutenant-General Simon F. Clark, Chief of the General Staff, thought the EMO officer felt 'more important than he should and that he will have full powers of the Prime Minister and his Cabinet as soon as there is an emergency'. Clark suggested the EMO director settle the matter, and in the end the bunker was placed at Camp Valcartier.

As previously mentioned, continuity of government in Canada originally meant that each of the ten provincial governments would have its own bunker on

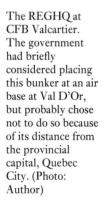

The REGHQ at CFB Valcartier. The government had briefly considered placing this bunker at an air base at Val D'Or, but probably chose not to do so because of its distance from the provincial capital, Quebec City. (Photo: Author)

a nearby military property. As it transpired, only six provinces got theirs: British Columbia, Alberta, Manitoba, Ontario, Quebec and Nova Scotia. According to a 1960 letter to the Chief of the General Staff from the Privy Council, Prime Minister Diefenbaker was quoted as saying he felt 'we had too many of these centres (planned)' so construction was delayed on the others and by 1963, deferred indefinitely. One memo stated Canada's foreign exchange crisis that year contributed to the freeze. With Saskatchewan – Diefenbaker's home province – as a non-recipient, the CGS thought this could lead to embarrassment, although some say the real reason this province never got its bunker was because the leftist New Democratic government there wanted nothing to do with COG. Canada's smallest province, Prince Edward Island, was given such a low priority its continuity plans were delayed, and when funding for new emergency government facilities was cut back by Cabinet order in January 1968, it was permanently dropped from the eligibility list. It would live out its existence as an Interim Regional Emergency Government Headquarters in the basement of the federal building in Charlottetown. The lower number of bunkers meant some would have housed Premiers and civil servants from more than one province.

Newfoundland had its REGHQ and PWC for a few years in a leased Superior Rubber Company factory in Holyrood on an interim basis. In 1964, the lease was not renewed and the federal government allocated one of the buildings at a recently closed US Army base in St John's, Fort Pepperell, for emergency

The Edenvale, Ontario, remote communications bunker. It had radio links to CFBs Valcartier, Shilo and Petawawa along with Chicago, the latter possibly to the US Army. After its closure in 1994, it was sold to a private individual. Today, it lies abandoned with some of its power panels slowly rusting away. (Photo: Author)

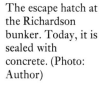

The escape hatch at the Richardson bunker. Today, it is sealed with concrete. (Photo: Author)

government. Curiously, this one was manned during normal business hours only, as if the Soviet strategic forces worked nine to five weekdays only.

As late as 1988–89, the federal government considered building a bunker for the New Brunswick government outside Fredericton at a new forestry complex, this to replace an interim facility in the basement of a downtown public building. The province's then-Premier, Frank McKenna, was delighted at the federal government's munificence, but nevertheless torpedoed the idea as being unnecessary in an age of fiscal restraint. As with some American congressmen and the Greenbier bunker, McKenna also did not like the idea of leaving his loved ones behind during a war, an idea that was shared by his predecessor, Richard Hatfield.

Following the pattern set for Carp, the REGHQs had their own transmitter facilities built underground at remote locations. These one-storey structures were smaller than the provincial shelters and, as with Richardson, were designed to be used by communications personnel only. They had the standard assortment of eating and living quarters, stores, power and air filtration rooms, a decontamination chamber and an emergency exit. The transmitter halls usually contained twenty transmitters and the total surface area of these bunkers measured approximately 15,000sq ft. These were opened in 1964.

Among the three military services, the Canadian Army was the key player when it came to national survival. Not only did it maintain the network of Diefenbunkers, it was given several other tasks. In 1952, a decision was made by Ottawa to acquire and store medical supplies that would have been used in damaged areas. The government's Emergency Stockpile Program was designed to supply medical facilities with drugs and equipment of all types, such as Mobile Feeding Units and transportable Advanced Treatment Centres, to local health-care personnel in times of danger. Although funded and co-ordinated by the Department of National Health and Welfare's Emergency Health Services Division, storage was at the Army's large depot on Gladstone Avenue in Ottawa and at several Regional Medical Equipment Depots (RMEDs) located on military bases across the nation (e.g. at Camps Chilliwack, British Columbia, Petawawa, Ontario and Debert, Nova Scotia.) Some equipment, such as mobile field hospitals, was stored at some REGHQs. Military facilities were chosen since they provided protection to the stocks, especially of narcotics, and because many were far enough away from major urban centres to survive destruction. The RMEDs were useful in another way in that when disaster struck in foreign lands, they were the ones from which supplies were sent; when a gas plant exploded in Mexico in 1985, medical supplies were shipped from the depot in Calgary, Alberta.

In the bunkers themselves, the Canadian Army had several other roles. There, it would have managed national survival operations (a term it preferred over civil defence), which meant allocating troops where necessary, maintaining lines of communications, liaising with other armed services or police forces, looking after the warning sirens, and caring for the bunkers. Army signal troops maintained the communications equipment, such as the VHF radios, the KL-7 and RACE cryptographic machines and the Secure Conference Network telephones. They also programmed monthly crypto codes into the portable Secure Telephone Units that were used by senior government and military officers. The signallers also regularly tested emergency government circuits between the REGHQs and other facilities during exercises to ensure their constant working order.[8] Some of the REGHQs had radio links with US Army units that would have been used to warn the latter of threats from the north. Communications personnel (along with Military Policemen) were also responsible for protecting the bunkers from outsiders during wartime.

Another role assigned to the Canadian Army was the co-ordination of re-entry operations in cities subjected to bombardment. With the help of volunteers, the Army reserve was to rescue the trapped and injured as soon as practical and ship the unfortunates to the nearest medical facility or welfare reception post. It was also ready to help fix water supplies and clear roads. For such things as evacuation or traffic control in Ontario, the Army could count upon the assistance of a new police organization created in 1954, the Civil Defence Auxiliary Police. On occasion, the Army reserve would practise these re-entry operations. Initially, sixteen cities were classed as potential enemy targets by the federal government, and in consequence each was given a Target Area Headquarters 25 to 50 miles away for rescue planning and co-ordination. The TAHQs were officially created as military entities in August 1961. Many of them were located on military properties, but these locations changed as requirements dictated. The sixteen target cities and their TAHQs were:

Calgary	Olds armoury
Edmonton	Wetaskiwin armoury
Halifax	Windsor armoury
Hamilton	Camp Hagersville

London	RCAF Station Centralia (later Station London)
Montreal	St Jerome
Niagara Falls	Welland armoury
Ottawa	Almonte armoury
Quebec City	Camp Valcartier
St John's	Holyrood
Saint John	Camp Gagetown
Toronto	Newmarket, Old York Manor
Vancouver	Camp Chilliwack
Victoria	Duncan armoury
Windsor	Chatham armoury
Winnipeg	RCAF Station Portage la Prairie

TAHQs were categorized by target city size and staffed accordingly. In peacetime, they employed fifteen to twenty individuals who spent their time collecting information necessary for the implementation of their plans such as population densities, fire hazards and availability of routes. The knowledge of usable roads was particularly important for evacuation purposes, and indeed the Army even published special maps called Military Town Plans to help its planning and rescue teams. In wartime, the number of personnel assigned to TAHQs would have greatly increased. These men received their training at the Joint Atomic, Biological and Chemical Warfare School at Camp Borden, using such manuals of training as *Nuclear Warheads Basic Characteristics and Employment*.

One of the key functions of TAHQ personnel during a nuclear war would have been the unenviable task of quantifying the radiation of an affected city. This meant sending out reconnaissance detachments in protective gear and radiation meters to take readings at selected locations for charting. The Canadian Army had learned that a 5 megaton bomb would:

- Destroy everything within 2 to 3 miles;
- Damage beyond repair all buildings within 5 or 6 miles;
- Cause major damage to most buildings within 8 or 9 miles; and
- Create a cigar-shaped radioactive cloud about 200 miles long and 25 miles wide.

The duties of these reconnaissance troops were therefore to take measurements at various locations where a blast had occurred, and mark on maps green zones that indicated where re-entry was possible, and red zones where re-entry was to be avoided. They would then enter the city from an upwind direction. If the city was only affected by fallout, TAHQ staff would again take radiation readings and mark the levels on maps. Re-entry troops were naturally expected to avoid areas with high levels.

The Army also set up several Mobile Support (MS) Groups throughout the country to assist civil powers if needed. These units were columns of regular and specialist Army personnel who were taught those trades necessary for emergency work such as communications, reconnaissance, engineering and first aid. The Royal Canadian Engineers would have looked after route clearing and water supply, the Royal Canadian Army Service Corps would have provided cooked rations and transport and Royal Canadian Ordnance Corps staff would have handled decontamination. If any riot control was necessary, the soldiers would have been given tear gas, billy clubs and, for psychological effect only, firearms. As examples of staffing, in eastern Ontario, 307 MS Group were members of the 1st Light Anti-Aircraft Regiment of Picton and 308 MS Group consisted of staff assigned to two military schools at Kingston. If Canadian Army personnel were not sufficient for this task, Army Headquarters had the authority to call upon troops from the RCAF and RCN for assistance. The RCAF, for example, had light transport aircraft squadrons in major Canadian cities ready to help with evacuation, along with reserve Medical Units of personnel trained to act as emergency medical response teams. There had even been the suggestion of using selected penitentiary inmates for relief work, but it is not known by the author if formal plans for this were ever prepared.

Offers of assistance could come from the most unexpected quarters. In 1950, the national civil defence co-ordinator, General F.F. Worthington, received a letter from the Chief Executive Commissioner of the Boy Scouts Association. In his letter, the Commissioner offered the service of Boy Scouts across Canada to do such things as messenger work, light rescue and damage surveys. The Commissioner was confident the young scouts could be successfully trained in these matters. Worthington must have accepted the offer as Boy Scouts were indeed used during a 1954 large-scale exercise at the Civil Defence College as runners.

Yet another role for the Army was the management of a national network of sites that would have recorded atomic blasts and that would have tracked the resulting radioactive fallout, a network called the Nuclear Detection and Fallout Reporting System (NDFRS). The first component of this system was the Nudet (nuclear detonation) Reporting Post. At any of the forty-five NRPs established, personnel could tell from Bhangmeters a weapon's yield, and from Indicator Position of Nuclear Bursts the position and height of an atomic detonation; it remained only for the information to be transmitted to higher authorities by radio. The posts were also equipped with personal dosimeters, compasses and radiacmeters. The NRPs were small bunkers built under or above ground or on the roofs of government buildings, at Army camps, on Customs or RCMP posts and at RCAF stations. Out of necessity, some of the sites in Ontario were built on civilian properties such as at the Seaway Building in Cornwall, the Ontario Agricultural College in Kemptville and the H.J. Heinz ketchup plant in Leamington.

One of the Victoria, British Columbia, NRPs was planned for Saturna Island. This post would have been of the surface type and would have measured approximately 30ft by 15ft. It would have contained the instruments previously mentioned along with radio equipment for communication with the nearest Provincial Warning Centre. The structure would have contained living ameni-ties such as bunk beds, a kitchenette, generator, air filtration system and chemical toilet. The walls would have been doubled concrete blocks with sand in between and the roofs were to be 10in thick covered with sand. Government records show this mini-bunker would have been built next to the lighthouse, but it is not clear if construction ever went ahead.

Another major component of the NDFRS was the fallout reporting network. Approximately 2,000 Fallout Reporting Posts (FRPs) were installed across Canada to trace the spread of radioactivity once a blast had occurred. These were equipped with 1M108 atmospheric Radiac radiation meters and CDV 700 meters to detect radioactivity on food, water or personnel. The posts were also complete living units with everything needed for independent survival such as food, blan-kets, fire extinguishers and first-aid kits. FRPs were built in existing basements, in surface blockhouses, on bridges or in bunkers either on government, railroad or private property. The odd one was put in country general stores, such as at Notre Dame de la Salette, Quebec. FRPs and NRPs would have been manned by government, military, railroad or police staff during alerts only.

As an example of a typical Fallout Reporting Post, site EO-46 at Peterborough, Ontario, at 452 Charlotte Street, consisted of a room in the basement of what was then the local Ontario Provincial Police detachment. The five-year lease was negotiated with the building's owners, Scott and Mary Medd, at $1 per year effective May 1962. The Army then installed its equipment and instructed the OPP on how to use it if the Soviets ever attacked.

Once information was collected by fallout or nuclear detonation posts, it would have been sent to Filter Centres for correlation, and from there to a Nuclear Analysis and Prediction Centre at a Provincial Warning Centre for action.[9] At the PWCs, the locations of atomic blasts and the spread of radioactivity would have been plotted on large maps, and rescue planning would have commenced. The CBC would then have sent warning messages to the public from their studios. All non-military messages, such as detonation, fallout and weather reports, would have been sent through a new communications network called the National Survival Attack Warning System. It was also through this system that the network of air-raid sirens

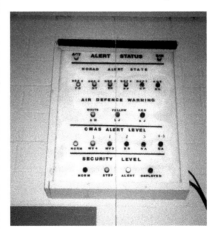

The alarm panel at an REGHQ at Debert, Nova Scotia. This now sits at the nearby Debert Military Museum. (Photo: Author)

would have been activated. NSAWS code words were adopted to signify various stages of alert with TROT indicating that PWC warning personnel be placed on stand-by, and CANTER designating a full alert.

In addition to control, communications and rescue, the Army also conducted research on the effects of atomic blasts. In 1960, the Canadian Army Operational Research Establishment secretly prepared a series of estimates of attack casualty levels for major Canadian cities. These figures were in turn used for rescue and evacuation planning. The estimates were based on yield of weapon used, mode of detonation (airburst or groundburst) and whether a warning was issued and rescue attempts initiated. Casualty figures were listed by deaths, serious injuries and light injuries. The tables showed airbursts were normally less lethal than groundbursts and that warnings reduce casualty rates, a logical corollary to the usefulness of evacuation and sheltering.

It was clearly enunciated in the government's action plan that military troops called out to aid civil powers were there to assist and not replace them. The one exception was for times where damage was so severe and widespread local civil defence authorities would have been overwhelmed. Under those circumstances, the plan stated the Army could 'assume completely the functions [of the local civil defence organization] because the alleviation of suffering and the restoration of civilian activity is of immediate importance to the war effort'. The plan's absolutist wording worried George F. Davidson, Deputy Minister of National Health, that it would provide an excuse for non-co-operation by some provinces and municipalities, namely Ottawa, Montreal and the province of Quebec. This implies there was resistance to civil defence initiatives by Quebec, a suggestion that contrasts with Premier Duplessis' perfect attendance record at civil defence meetings. With respect to the city of Ottawa, when the 1955 edition of the federal plan was prepared, the city had no emergency script to speak of even though smaller cities such as London, St Catharines and Brockville did. Municipal emergency measures officers such as in the small city of Kingston had even gone as far as examining various buildings to see how many persons they could hold.[10] Davidson recommended to General Worthington, the current federal civil defence co-ordinator, that he 'soft-pedal' the plan's offending section.

EMO personnel proper at the REGHQs had several tasks, one of which was the compilation of facilities that would require special protection in wartime. This Vital Points Program database consisted of such places as docks, petroleum pumping stations, natural gas facilities, key bridges, nuclear power plants and telephone exchanges that could be subject to sabotage or attack. During alert conditions, all would have been guarded by either members of the RCMP, Canadian Army or local law enforcement.

The idea of maintaining a Vital Points register or database was not a new one. According to declassified government documents, such a list was first established in Canada in 1938. During the Second World War, the list would have been needed by the Canadian Army to plan the deployment of guarding forces. At some time during the postwar period, the Vital Points register was somehow dropped, but when certain Quebec individuals began terrorist action in the autumn of 1970, the list was reborn. Today, the Vital Points database is managed by the RCMP, and local Army reserve units will sometimes carry out VP protection exercises.

To support its war plans from a legal perspective, the government had in place emergency legislation such as the *War Measures Act* and certain Orders-in-Council.[11] The government has the prerogative to decide what constitutes an emergency and has instructions to implement certain services, such as the internment of enemy aliens, the movement control of individuals and the establishment of temporary organizations, as soon as an attack is declared. But the legislation and lack of judicial oversight could in effect have turned the nation into a dictatorship. Walter S. Tarnopolsky writing in 1972 as a legal academic but who later became an Ontario Court of Appeal judge understood that emergency government action was then not subject to judicial review and that courts did not want to 'argue with the doctrine of parliamentary sovereignty'. This is no longer the case.

Tarnopolsky's statements were made before the implementation of the *Canadian Charter of Rights and Freedoms* and some judges now say that the government's actions, specifically its violation of civil liberties, could be contested for reasonableness. Section 1 of the *Charter* states government actions are acceptable only when they 'can be demonstrably justified in a free and democratic society' clearly suggesting the possibility of judicial review. Had the *Charter* and its racial equality provision and a strong Supreme Court existed during the Second World War, the mass internment of Japanese-Canadians that took place in 1942 would not have occurred. The *International Covenant on Civil and Political Rights*, to which Canada agreed to in 1976, also prevents the curtailment of civil rights such as the imposition of slavery, the arbitrary deprivation of life or the subjection to cruel and unusual punishment, even in an emergency. While the application of emergency legislation has never been examined by the Supreme Court of Canada, this same court has decided in one review that international instruments such as the *Covenant* are applicable to Canadian jurisprudence.

One of the primary criticisms of the *War Measures Act* was its all-or-nothing approach. Jacques Janson of Emergency Preparedness Canada stated it was unable to 'deal with peacetime disasters and emergencies with the moderation that is desirable'. Many civil libertarians had objected to its usage by Prime Minister Pierre Trudeau during the 1970 terrorist scare, usage that included the rounding up of hundreds of innocent persons by police. Desperate times requires desperate measures, was the current thinking. During the 1984 federal election, however, a promise was made by the leader of the Official Opposition, Brian Mulroney, to repeal the *War Measures Act* and replace it with a more reasonable law.

After his accession to power, Mulroney remained true to his word and passed the *Emergencies Act* in July 1988. In the House of Commons, all three major political parties, the Conservatives, the Liberals and the New Democrats, took pride in the new law. Perrin Beatty, Conservative Minister of National Defence, vowed that 'never again . . . will there be the ability to use the *War Measures Act* to knock on the door in the dark of night, to sweep up our citizens, to hold them without charge and without the right to *habeus corpus*'. Speaking for the Opposition, Liberal Member of Parliament Bob Kaplan said he was quite pleased with the new law, although Derek Blackburn of the New Democratic Party, who was also pleased, took the time to point out that the Liberals, who were the ones who had used the law in 1970, made no serious effort to change it afterwards and rarely showed up when the new legislation was being debated in parliamentary committee meetings. Such is Parliament.

What the three political parties took pride in was the fact that the *Emergencies Act* gave greater guidance to the government during a crisis by, for example, incorporating certain limitations on its actions; the *Act*'s forty-two pages provides greater clarity of the government's rights and duties than the *War Measures Act*'s four pages. For instance, the new law breaks emergencies down into four categories – public welfare for natural disasters, public order for domestic situations, international emergencies and war emergencies – with each category given its own rules. While the war emergency subsection allows for the search and seizure of persons or things, the public welfare subsection does not. The act also contains a provision for the review of its application by a parliamentary review committee – something else the *War Measures Act* lacked – and also provides for compensation for those who suffered unfairly as a result of its usage. It is interesting to note that the new legislation's preamble directs the government to respect both the *Charter* and the *Covenant*.

Since law enforcement in Canada is primarily a provincial matter, it is educational to look at what provincial emergency legislation can allow. The *Alberta Public Safety Services Act* gives the government a wide range of powers abrogating civil rights during an emergency. Section 16 of the *Act* states any qualified person can be ordered to render assistance where those qualifications allow and that the government may restrict or prohibit travel in any part of Alberta. In the first instance, medical personnel can be ordered to assist the injured and in the latter, persons can be prevented from getting too close to a damaged area, an especially useful section to prevent looting. This same section authorizes the government forcibly to evacuate persons or livestock – reminding one of the plight of Japanese-Canadians during the war – except that the subsection contains the caveat 'from any area that may be affected by the disaster'. Arbitrary forcible relocations would therefore not be allowed. On the other hand, a further subsection states the government may enter any premises without warrant and in yet another, it can conscript any person 'needed to meet an emergency'. The latter implies forced labour and appears to contravene the *Covenant*.

While the above is one example of provincial legislation, it is assumed other provinces have similar enactments. In 1984, the Nova Scotia Parliament's Select

Committee on Emergency Measures recommended the passage of laws that would 'require any person to remedy or alleviate any hazard to persons or property by a condition, use, operation or process that is going on' and that would have given the government the right to confiscate any personal property or to enter any building without a warrant. The legislation also included protection for the government from liability. It is not known by the author if this law was ever adopted.

Having emergency legislation such as Acts of Parliament and Orders-in-Council was one thing, having the necessary infrastructure for continuity of government was another. While the federal Emergency Measures Organization was the main planner for COG, every government ministry was expected to prepare itself for the worse. According to declassified government documents, this is in fact what happened. The federal Department of Transport (DOT), for instance, had prepared orders for the subjugation of all domestic rail, maritime, broadcasting and aeronautical facilities as well as the seizure of certain foreign vessels during a war. If an alert had been sounded, each mode of transport would have been subject to a separate government unit supervised by DOT. Railroads would have been put under the management of an Emergency Rail Transport Control Organization, and airlines similarly controlled with the smaller ones and the flying clubs co-opted for reconnaissance and the transport of emergency personnel. The same was true for shipping.

Since broadcasting facilities were then a Transport responsibility, radio and telecommunication services would have been controlled by DOT's Emergency National Telecommunications Organization, working in conjunction with the Canadian Broadcasting Corporation. Once a YELLOW warning was issued by DOT, all civilian broadcast stations were to remain on the air for only fifteen minutes to warn the public after which they were to shut down. The shutdown was thought necessary to prevent Soviet bombers from using the stations as navigation aids. Some stations, mainly of the CBC network, would have been allowed to reopen later on to provide advice to the public and to keep it informed of events. The CBC even maintained its own national emergency communications centre in Watrous, Saskatchewan, for several years.

Standard Emergency Broadcast messages stocked by the CBC in the various emergency government facilities were prepared for each level of crisis. As an example, for an evening attack on central Sudbury, Ontario, and a warning of fallout, EB 6 would have aired as follows:

> A nuclear weapon exploded in the Sudbury area at 9 p.m. Everyone within 20 miles of downtown Sudbury take shelter against fallout which will start to come down within 20 minutes. A much larger area will eventually be affected as the upper winds will cause fallout to drift east from Sudbury toward North Bay at about ten miles per hour. The estimated times at which fallout will affect the localities east of Sudbury will be broadcast in a few minutes. The situation will be easier to follow if you have a road map.

Some of the legislation authorizing the take over of radio stations was found in the *Radio Act* of 1938. Section 3, for instance, allowed the government to censor stations during an emergency and section 11 allowed it to take over any station at any time, in peace or war. These two sections can still be found in the current *Radiocommunication Act*.

For those times when the media would not have been completely shut down, the government still had the option of control. Broadcasts could accidentally contain information of use to the enemy, as could any form of print media. Moreover, there is always the possibility of unpatriotic individuals using the media to Canada's detriment, much as Lord Haw-Haw did against Britain during the Second World War, although from another country. The federal government realized this early on and prepared a set of control guidelines, known as Canadian Censorship Regulations (CCRs), to be implemented in wartime by a temporary agency of the Justice Department known as the Office of Censorship.

The Office of Censorhip was broken down into divisions with each responsible for a different mode of communication. The Director of Censorship had below him Assistant Directors as well as the following:

Chief Postal Censor
Chief Telecommunications Censor
Chief Information and Records Censor
Chief Censor of Publications (English)
Chief Censor of Publications (French)
Chief Radio Broadcasting Censor for Canada

As an example of duties, the Chief Postal Censor worked with the Postmaster General to censor and control international and, under some circumstances, domestic mail. The Chief Censor of Publications controlled all written media and required all printers to keep complete records of all printing orders. He also had the authority to search any incoming vessel for prohibited documents. Details of these regulations are still classified today.

Unquestionably, the Department of National Defence was a key player in the nation's preparedness for war. Besides providing guidance and support to the armed services, one of its lesser known tasks was the compilation of lists of individuals that could act against the state if hostilities neared. These security-intelligence target lists were drawn up with a view to keeping senior government officials informed of possible attempts at sabotage, terrorism and subversion. They would have been disseminated to any province or municipality requesting military assistance under the Aid of the Civil Power programme, presumably to allow police to make quick arrests. The federal government makes no secret of maintaining these lists today.

Other government departments had elaborate continuity plans in keeping with their general mandate. These plans were listed in departmental War Books. The Department of Agriculture was prepared to establish an Animal Health

Emergency Organization ready to deal with sabotage or biological attacks on crops or livestock. It was also ready to assist in the prevention of large-scale epidemics. Upon activation by Order-in-Council, a temporary crown corporation, the War Supplies Agency, would have looked after the rationing of food and fuel, controlled any kind of printing (to avoid a shortage of ink), purchased goods required by the federal government and controlled industrial production. One of the Department of Finance's roles was to advise Cabinet on the imposition of emergency taxes. In addition to censorship, the Department of Justice was responsible for creating emergency orders and ensuring these would not conflict with provincial responsibilities. Basically, all these programmes ensured the government could continue running with minimal disruption to itself while managing with utmost efficiency.

As previously stated, the Department of National Health and Welfare stockpiled medical equipment and drugs at Army bases across Canada. It also stored emergency equipment at non-military depots in such cities as Guelph and Brockville, Ontario, Nanaimo, British Columbia, Shawinigan, Quebec and for a while at an old air base at MacDonald, Manitoba. The Brockville facility consisted of a warehouse leased from Industrial Avenue Realties Limited with a floor space of 34,042sq ft, rented at $1 per square foot per year. Located on the south side of Parkedale Avenue east of North Augusta Road, it kept alcohol, towels, pumps, blankets, generators and oxygen cylinders, and included a walk-in vault for classified publications. Security came in the form of electric eyes.

The RCMP was another organization that would have been very busy if war had been declared. Each of its major divisions had its own relocation plan. While headquarters staff would have moved to Carp, divisional personnel in the provinces would have dispersed to REGI IQs and other centres. In Ontario, home of the force's 'O' Division, its staff would have gone to the bunker at Camp Borden while others would have relocated to Owen Sound, a small city 100 miles northwest of Toronto, probably to its local offices. One of the roles of the RCMP would have been the rounding up and processing of enemy aliens at temporary detention centres, such as at Camp Borden or in Gatineau Park outside Ottawa, prior to their shipment to federal penitentiaries. In 1969, the federal police had a list of 800 such persons. The RCMP would also have been responsible for the security of certain installations, port and travel security control, and the co-ordination of all police forces.

Not only did the government of Canada make plans to relocate its staff, provide advice and warnings to the public and create medical stockpiles, it also provided training to rescue personnel that would have been needed in damaged areas. In the early 1950s, the federal government created a national training centre where public servants at all levels of government and selected civilians could learn what to do during emergencies. Parliament was firmly committed to the survival of the public if a nuclear holocaust was to occur (keeping budgetary constraints in mind), and so it wanted to train as many rescue workers as possible. Therefore, the Canadian Civil Defence College was established.

Buildings at the
Canadian
Emergency
Measures College
in Arnprior. These
are gone now.
(Photo: Author)

The CCDC offered a wide variety of programmes to cover every aspect of civil defence, from both a theoretical and practical perspective. Courses were offered in national survival planning and operations, casualty simulation and emergency feeding. Students could also learn the mechanics of an emergency clothing supply system and how to provide for public welfare. In addition to training federal and provincial staff, the college also offered its courses to members of the public such as nurses, doctors and pharmacists. On occasion, it also hosted conferences for mayors, members of the clergy, and the media. It even ran shelter studies in its own underground experimental bunker. For most of its life, the College was located on the site of a former Second World War airfield at Arnprior near Ottawa. Eventually, it was renamed the Canada Emergency Measures College.

Despite the thousands of dollars spent on emergency government facilities across Canada, they were not without problems. As mentioned previously, many of them were located in the basement of federal buildings. EMO admitted these were not necessarily the best places to have offices since they were not meant to be used regularly by humans. As an example, the two provincial civil servants employed at the ZEGHQ in Sudbury, Ontario, had often complained about headaches and nosebleeds in the early 1970s because of the poor air quality of their below-ground facility at the post office. An investigation by EMO confirmed the complaint and recommended the office be relocated.

Another problem arose at the Orillia, Ontario, Regional Relocation Unit. The federal government had contracted to modify the basement of the federal building to a Toronto contractor, Ayube Ally, in 1967 for its use as an RRU to support the REGHQ at Borden. By the following year, Ally had still not been paid, so he contacted the local newspaper and his Member of Parliament and invited them for a visit. Ally called the expenditure of funds a waste of taxpayer money, partly because the facility was not even fallout-proof since there was a gap between the entrance door and the floor. The government replied that it had not paid Ally because of a disagreement over the type of water tanks installed.

Government records consulted by the author do not show how the disagreement was settled.

There were also differences of opinion between the federal and municipal governments over the MEGHQs. As with RRUs and ZEGHQs, these head-quarters were normally located in the basement of federal buildings. In Ontario, municipalities were charged $0.65 per square foot in rent for these headquarters. When Ottawa tried to increase the rent to $1.00 per square foot, the cities and the provincial emergency measures branch objected. This, they said, threatened municipal participation. The threat worsened when the federal government reduced its annual grants to the provinces, which had been a source of funds to pay for these rents. Again, historical records consulted by the author do not show how the situation was resolved.

Over the years, several stories have emerged about the Carp and Richardson facilities. For instance, there have been rumours that Richardson was connected to Carp by long underground tunnels complete with high-speed vehicles. Similar stories have arisen with respect to the White House in Washington, DC. These rumours have no basis in fact. There have also been people who swear that Carp was connected to the Parliament in downtown Ottawa by a secret tunnel. This is also hogwash. On the other hand, as described in the Russian section, such secret tunnels do exist under Moscow, as does a huge underground complex at Ramenki next to Moscow State University that could hold an estimated 10,000 persons with supplies for up to 30 days. According to some sources, including ex-KGB officers, dignitaries and public servants would have travelled there in times of war by special underground trains. Ramenki is still a government secret because the Russian Ministry of Defence denies knowledge of its existence.

With some of the Canadian bunkers set low in the ground, there was always the risk of them becoming swimming pools. On a few occasions at Richardson, when personnel opened one of the blast doors, several gallons of water rushed in. The water, the result of melted snow, had trickled down the inclined walk-way and had built up in front of the entrance, the drains being incapable of diversion. The remedy came in the form of an automatic sump-pump and the laying of a mound of asphalt at the upper entrance.

Other rumours have it that there exists a bottle of whiskey and an electric cement packer in the concrete walls at Richardson. These were dropped by construction crews in the mix most likely by accident. There were also occasions when lightning hit the power lines and caused them and the bus bar to melt causing the input sections to the low-frequency transmitters to blow.

Some people actually enjoyed living in these citadels for extended periods. One particular serviceman enjoyed living in the Carp bunker so much that he refused to set foot outside for weeks. Apparently, some co-workers began worrying about his pale complexion and eventually, word got to the brass. This may have been the reason that, from the 1980s on, no one was allowed to live in the bunker and everyone had to find accommodations either in town or on the nearest military base, Canadian Forces Base Ottawa.

Carp was also a favorite posting for officers but for reasons entirely different than for bunkerphiles. As a military station, it was always commanded by a Major. One of the advantages of a posting there was that it almost always led to a promotion for the Commanding Officer. The basis for this advantage was not clear but one theory has it that if anyone could run a unique installation such as Carp effectively, that person would have the ability to command larger installations just as effectively. And since these larger bases require higher-ranking leadership, a promotion was natural.

Personnel assigned to Carp came from all military ranks, backgrounds and attitudes. One of its more well-known alumnus was Corporal Lortie, the soldier who took over the provincial legislature in Quebec City in the 1980s with a submachine gun as a protest against Quebec policies. All bunkers were stocked with small arms for self-defence that were controlled by a supply technician. Since Lortie's duties at Carp included supply, he had no trouble acquiring his firearm. On the weekend in question, he simply walked out with the weapon and ammunition in his gym bag with no one noticing anything out of the ordinary. Lortie travelled to Quebec City to take over the legislature and threatened staff there by firing his weapon. Eventually, however, he gave himself up, and landed in jail. One of the unfortunate side effects to his escapade was the denial of a promotion to the current Commanding Officer at Carp.

Another story that has surfaced concerned the KL-7 cryptographic machines that every bunker possessed. One source claimed these devices were traded for newer RACE machines in the 1980s because an American spy, John Walker, betrayed them to the Soviets when he worked for the US Navy. This story is doubtful as the KL-7s were replaced at such places as Camp Borden a full two years before Walker was arrested. The KL-7s were probably disposed of because they relied on older rotor technology. This may have only been a question of the Army's communications branch trying to keep up with the times.

A few war exercises were held at Carp after its completion in 1961 but it would not be until November 1985 that another would take place. In these tests, EMO and other government departments have taken part but, given the importance of this facility, it is odd no Prime Minister ever did; apparently, only the aides have. Even during the Cuban missile crisis in October 1962, Prime Minister Diefenbaker never set foot there. The only Prime Minister ever to visit Carp was Pierre Trudeau in 1977. This is perhaps an indication of how seriously political leaders have taken the concept of government continuity.

The bunker at Penhold in central Alberta was unusual in at least one respect; it may have been the only one situated in a natural zoo. Wildlife abounds in Penhold and it was not unusual to see falcons, hawks, eagles, prairie dogs, moose and deer on the way to work or in town. At night, it was not uncommon to hear wolves howl. Apparently, some of the jack rabbits grew almost as large as greyhound dogs.

Except for a few newspaper articles in the early 1960s generated by leaks, there was never a great deal of publicity about the Diefenbunkers. The Carp bunker

The bunker at Canadian Forces Station Debert was sold in 2009 to a data firm. (Photo: Author)

was mentioned infrequently in the major local paper, the *Citizen*, and the Department of National Defence was always reluctant to talk about it, perhaps because some resented the special protection it gave to government leaders. It was not until the 1980s that DND spoke openly about it. In 1983, the Canadian Armed Forces magazine *Sentinel* described the bunker in a complete article, but there was still no mention of the other sites. While local newspapers such as the *Truro Daily News* referred to a vast underground communications facility at Camp Debert, for the most part the Canadian bunker network remained a mystery. Even after the REGHQs were listed in the publicly available *EMO National Digest* in August 1965, there was little said about them. Secrecy for the bunkers was seemingly not paramount because they were never considered 'vital enough individually to constitute a target for a nuclear weapon', according to R.B. Bryce of the Privy Council. On the other hand, according to security regulations, no one was allowed to photograph the bunkers even though one of them (the one at Penhold, Alberta) could be seen clearly from passing trains while others were clearly visible from local roads.

It is not known by the author how many and which Canadian corporations made war plans but some details have been revealed with respect to one of Canada's largest telephone companies, Bell Canada. Bell had made preparations for nuclear war as far back as the 1950s, plans that included compensation for circuit breakdowns and the automatic rerouting of telephone calls. Telephone exchanges were equipped with Line Load Control that allow selected agencies such as police, fire and EMOs priority access to circuits during emergencies. It also built, under pressure from the federal government, three underground two-storey Emergency Operations Centres (EOCs) in towns outside the target cities of Ottawa, Toronto and Montreal at Smiths Falls, Barrie and Sherbrooke respectively. These centres were constructed in the 1960s and were designed to house emergency management personnel. They had their own dormitories, dining areas, decontamination centres and offices for thirty employees and food stocks for forty-five days.

During Bell Canada's exercise 'Shakedown' held in November 1967, a simulated nuclear attack tested the company's emergency communications plan and, in a sub-exercise, security at the EOCs. The one-day drill, organized by the Office of Emergency Planning and conducted by ninety Bell employees, was considered successful since enough circuits were maintained for emergency communications. While the EOCs are no longer used by Bell, the corporation will not discuss them.

Even in a post-Cold War world, Bell Canada still maintains an emergency management office and has plans and agreements in place for any eventuality. When thirty-two guy wires holding a microwave tower serving the busy Quebec City–Windsor trunk near Williamsburg, Ontario, were intentionally blow-torched on 15 August 1987, calls were quickly rerouted via CNCP Telecommunications and even through the United States. Yet other calls were bounced off the Anik satellite. By the following day, 80 per cent of service was restored.

Alberta Government Telephones, Bell's Alberta equivalent, had similar hardened facilities in the basement of its buildings. AGT set up an Emergency Operations Centre in Red Deer for overall crisis management along with three restoration centres with network back-up capability at Vegreville, Red Deer and Lethbridge, six damage reporting stations and a Relocation Centre for company staff in Banff. As an incentive to its employees, accommodations were also prepared for dependents in AGT buildings. In total, sheltered space was reserved for 1,500. The corporation also had two senior advisory employees earmarked for the REGHQ at Penhold.

Canada's COG programme may never have reached its full potential. While many discussions and much planning had gone into government survival, weaknesses slowly crept into the system for one important reason: insufficient money. When Major-General J.V. Allard took over from Major-General Wrinch as chief of the Directorate of Survival Operations & Plans (DSO&P) in late 1963, one of his first tasks was to find economies in the system. A 1964 DSO&P update of the national survival programme showed that while many concepts had been implemented, many others were only half-completed, and some of these systems would not last very long. As the update showed, the Army was requested to 'consider alternatives within present financial and manpower policies', and this is in fact what happened.

Some of those weaknesses were found in the Nuclear Detonation and Fallout Reporting System and in the air-raid siren network. At the end of 1963, most of the Nudet Reporting Posts had only a limited operational capability, and many were located in unprotected accommodations. As for the Fallout Reporting Posts, only 50 per cent were located in protected rooms, many of which were only stocked with interim equipment. The shortage of money and interest led to the cancellation of some property lease agreements for these posts as early as 1966. By 1968, all would be vacated and most of the equipment retrieved. Similarly, only 50 per cent of the Filter Centres were set up in protected sites, and this led to a loss of interest by the Army reserve units that would have manned them. Also, while twenty national survival training sites had been planned, only seven were built and put into use.[12]

The aforementioned lack of funds was mostly a product of the new Liberal Cabinet of 1968. Besides the closure of the reporting posts, the Canadian Forces put a moratorium on the installation of new sirens. Of the 1,735 sirens that were produced for DND, 1,688 were actually installed and 47 were kept in reserve for future use. The moratorium was originally to last only three years, but by the late 1970s, it was still in place. The last forty-seven sirens were never installed.

The budget shortfall of 1968 would see another victim in the government's national survival programme. The Canadian Broadcasting Corporation had been charged with running the Emergency Broadcast System, a system designed to transmit instructions and messages of reassurance to the public. But when Cabinet pulled the plug on funding, the CBC seemed to lose interest in it. By the 1970s, the EBS was deemed 'unreliable and inadequate'. The studios at the REGHQs at Nanaimo, Penhold and Debert were useless since they were not connected to any transmitters. There are indications that the EBS function was later taken over by the federal government and renamed the Emergency Broadcast Information System.

Despite this, the COG programme would live on for a few more decades and would witness a few more changes. First, the list of public servants in Ottawa who would have relocated when the sirens started blaring was modified, as were their hiding sites. In the 1980s, the six Central Relocation Units would have housed:

Kemptville
Agriculture
Fisheries and Oceans
Labour
Employment and Immigration

Carleton Place
Transport
Energy, Mines and Resources
Industry, Trade and Commerce
Supply and Services

Pembroke
RCMP

Arnprior
Post Office Department

Smiths Falls
External Affairs
CBC
Departmental Advisers
Cabinet Secretariat
Alternate Cabinet

Cornwall
Communications
Justice
Finance
Health and Welfare
Solicitor General

Bank of Canada
Canada Mortgage and Housing
Corporation

Also, by then the list of target cities was reduced from sixteen to nine, with the remaining being the most populated and the most susceptible to attack. EMO's main focus would also change, from atomic war to natural disasters, much like FEMA's in the 1970s. By then, no one worried so much about the nuclear bogeyman.

In the mid-1980s, a federal task force was formed to examine Canada's civil defence posture. The task force noted that of the thirty-four civil defence zone headquarters, some were in poor condition, did not have an adequate store of records to continue functioning and possessed communications equipment prone to electromagnetic pulse. It also pointed out that many of the air-raid warning sirens that were part of the Army's National Survival Attack Warning System were gone, meaning that the government had no quick way to warn the population of an attack.[13] As well, the Nuclear Detonation and Fallout Reporting System had long disappeared and had been replaced with a much smaller Canadian Forces Warning and Reporting System that had detection equipment on military bases only.[14] Several recommendations to improve emergency government management were made by the task force, but soon afterwards the Cold War ended and the impetus to revitalize was gone.

With the diminished threat of a nuclear holocaust, it is understandable that these bunkers were closed. Probably as a response to the end of the Cold War, the Department of National Defence considered closing the bunker as early as 1992, mere months after the Soviet Union ceased to exist. DND did not have to wait long for a decision as the new Liberal government of 1993 saw no need for a continuity of government programme, and when they put out their first budget the following year, most of the bunkers, along with several military bases, were ordered closed. Canadian Forces Station Carp was disbanded in June 1994 and was sold to the Township of West Carleton for $213,067 two years later. Tours have since been given at the site, which have proved to be immensely popular. When it closed, though, the furniture and radio equipment had already been removed by the armed forces and sold or scrapped, this despite the wishes of the Privy Council Office that the facility remain intact. Of the four diesel generators, two are now in former Yugoslavia and Somalia respectively, while other items ended up at the Canadian War Museum. Other equipment was transferred to a new Government Emergency Operations Coordination Centre that was established on an interim basis at the Emergency Measures College in Arnprior. Prior to the bunker's sale, there had been talk of converting the Carp structure into a federal prison or a into Cold War museum. There have also been rumours of the government sealing it off permanently but, after a public protest, that idea was shelved. The bunker has been turned into a museum.

After its closure, the Richardson bunker lay quiet for a few years. The bunker was put up for sale, and bids were accepted by the federal Department of Public Works. One tour was offered to prospective buyers in 1996. Its sale was not automatic as the federal government had the right to reject any purchaser. One individual considered turning it into a winery, while another pondered converting it into a scuba-diving palace, as has been done at one ICBM silo in the United States. As of July 1997, the Richardson bunker was still up for sale

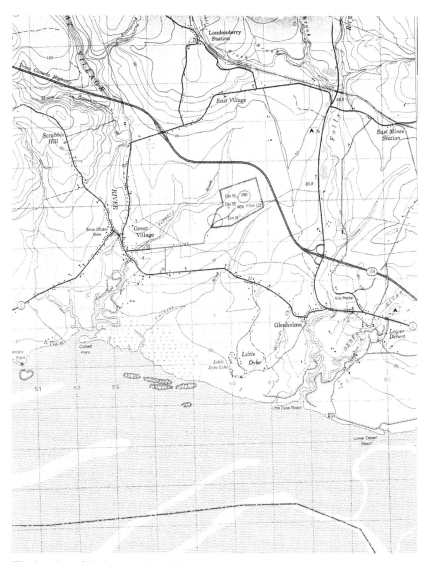

The location of the last remaining Diefenbunker in operation, outside Great Village, Nova Scotia. (© Department of Natural Resources, Canada)

but later that year the government revoked its decision, bulldozed the entrances and sealed the emergency exits with concrete. According to Public Works, concerns were raised by officials in the Solicitor General's office and by National Defence over its potential use. Some were afraid it would have been purchased by extremist groups and used for nefarious purposes. Today, the bunker is no longer visible.

As for Emergency Preparedness Canada, it still has a vital role to play in the protection of the public. As previously mentioned, its focus changed not unexpectedly from nuclear war to natural disasters during the 'Détente' period of the 1970s. It operates the Government Emergency Operations Control Centre in downtown Ottawa to monitor and report on calamities, domestic and international, and its college still offers training courses to both government employees and members of the public. It continues its public-education function through the publication of various emergencies-related pamphlets, and still maintains a list of vital points to be protected. Despite the end of COG, it still has plans 'to ensure the continued operations of the federal government following the occurrence of a disruptive natural or man-made emergency', and continues to publish useful booklets such as the *Guide to Preservation of Essential Records*. It also regularly takes part in joint counter-terrorism exercises with police and military forces as required under Canada's National Counter-Terrorism Plan. Conversely, though, the Senate standing committee for national defence has criticized it, and the federal government in general, in 2004 for not having sufficiently detailed plans for dealing with large-scale disasters. Some wonder whether the government could successfully manage a Hurricane Katrina-type event.

As for the Carp bunker, tours are still available. The private Diefenbunker Group has gone to great lengths trying to reacquire some of the furnishings sold by the Canadian Armed Forces when it was shut down. One now finds there equipment from the original CBC studio on loan from the Canadian War Museum, material that would be found in a typical backyard shelter, along with some of the radiation monitoring devices. The Emergency Government Situation Centre (previously known as the Information Co-ordination Centre) looks pretty much as it did when the bunker closed, and several other pieces of furniture that belonged in other rooms have been retrieved from various sources. The bunker has been the source of much public curiosity and has even been used by Hollywood in the movie *The Sum of All Fears* starring Ben Affleck.

As mentioned previously, six provinces were each given two bunkers, one to accommodate senior government and military staff and the other for communications crews. Alberta's main bunker at Penhold has been sold for $312,000 and its smaller shelter for $162,000 to a farmer, who seemed to be more interested in the land for his cattle than for the bunkers. The larger one has been offered for sale on the Internet but its initial asking price of $2 million was later dropped to $700,000. Arabian sheikhs and a European theatre group have shown interest, as did one individual bent on using it for military type training. After the owner received an offer from the Hell's Angels for $1.3 million (US), it was quickly bought back by the federal government for $750,000 to obviate the possibility of a sale to a criminal group. This bunker and its smaller brother have since been destroyed.

The main bunker at Valcartier remains in operation as a communication centre, as did the one at Borden until 1999. Strangely, when a request under the *Freedom-of-Information Act* was made to the Ontario provincial government on nuclear evacuation plans, provincial officers found no evidence of a plan to relocate the Premier and his cabinet to Borden. Borden's smaller communications bunker, located on the site of a Second World War auxiliary airfield at Edenvale on Highway 26, was sold, but Valcartier's smaller communications shelter a few miles south of St-Raymond remains DND property. The two bunkers on Vancouver Island, at Nanaimo and Nanoose Bay, along with the one at Edenvale have been sealed up, although the latter has since been unsealed but has an uncertain future. CBC equipment from the Nanaimo bunker can now be found at the National Museum of Science and Technology in Ottawa.

Nova Scotia's two bunkers remain. Camp Debert closed in 1996 and its bunker was offered for sale to the public.[15] One Alberta man was interested in acquiring it to grow medicinal marijuana, but that deal never took place. It was sold instead to a data storage company in 2009. Since the shelter also acted as an important military communications node – what is called the Eastern Gateway – this function is still maintained but at the remote bunker at the Great Village

The remote communications bunker at Great Village, Nova Scotia, is the only Cold War underground facility still used by the Canadian Forces. All the old radio equipment and the emergency rations are gone now. Its current transmitting equipment takes up only a small fraction of the radio room. (Photo: Author)

transmitter station a few miles west. Great Village's current Harris 25kW and 10kW transmitters allow for both military domestic and international communications and have been used to support United Nations operations. When visited by the author in 2001, the three monstrous diesel generators still lay in the power room but were no longer used; by then, the bunker was using an external generator. Many of the furnishings have been removed – including the radiation detection meter on the roof – or were no longer used. The facility does not even have a working mess hall.

Little remains at the federal relocation sites around Ottawa. The Cornwall federal building basement was gutted years ago and now serves as storage space for the local library. The basement at Carleton Place is empty, but one can still find the odd trace of its past such as wall maps, door signs and telephone connections. The old black rotary telephones were left behind but the radios were removed by the Canadian Forces. Door signs and maps also remain at Smiths Falls but gone are the two dozen cheap folding tables, chairs, office cabinets and cots. The Kemptville site is now completely gone. Emergency medical equipment was removed from the Prescott post office in 1994 or 1995 and transported to Ottawa. The Almonte TAHQ at the armoury on Queen Street is now a private residence but the sturdy basement, in which emergency equipment was stored, remains. Toronto's TAHQ in the Old York Manor in Newmarket at the corner of Yonge and Eagle Streets is gone and the property now bears a relatively new courthouse. The city's municipal bunker in Aurora now stands empty. The building that housed fallout post EO-46 in Peterborough is now used by a consulting firm.

And what of those hundreds of air-raid sirens most older Canadians remember? Those large grey blow horns that sat atop tall poles or on the roofs of various buildings for decades? A few years ago, Leslie Scrivener of the *Toronto Star* looked into one of these remaining artifacts of the Cold War that still stood in Toronto. The siren was located on the grounds of Bellwoods Park House at the corner of Dundas Street West and Shaw Street and was one of the few in Canada that had not been taken down when the federal government dismantled the network in the mid-1990s. In 2007, construction threatened to make it disappear until some citizens, including Toronto architect David Warne, decided it should remain *in situ*. Warne tried to find out who owned it, but was given the proverbial run-around by all three levels of government.[16] Eventually, he was told by the Department of National Defence to keep it, and today the siren sits happily very close to where it was installed half a century ago.[17]

Despite the cancellation of government relocation plans and the termination of the nuclear warning system, several government emergency programmes remain to this day. The Department of National Health and Welfare, now called Health Canada, still maintains an emergency division and still stores medical supplies across the country. The Brockville medical depot on Parkedale Avenue was closed several years ago but others in Cambridge, Ontario, and Shawinigan, Quebec, remain, as do stockpiles at Canadian Forces Bases Edmonton, Valcartier and Petawawa. Pharmaceuticals are no longer stored on military bases but rather on the property of the drug manufacturer under contract with stocks rotated periodically, a particularly cost effective method. Since health care in Canada is primarily a provincial matter, Health Canada maintains a close relationship with its provincial counterparts, a relationship that includes storage of federal emergency equipment on provincial government property.

For many years, Health Canada's main depot on Michael Street in Ottawa acted as the central reception and distribution centre for new supplies. The depot housed several types of pre-packaged kits along with individual items that could be required by federal or provincial authorities. In a local emergency, rescue crews would recover the injured, apply basic first aid and, depending on the level of injury, arrange the transport of some to mobile Advanced Treatment Centres and others to full-scale hospitals. The Ottawa depot stored the treatment centres as well as other items such as Casualty Collecting Units (stretchers, blankets, first-aid kits), Airport Disaster Kits, collapsible beds, transportable 'Picker' X-ray machines and Trauma Kits, and updated the equipment as technology changed. It had its own carpentry shop to build backboards and custom-made kit boxes of various sizes suitable for transport. The depot also designed portable sterilization autoclaves that became so popular they were adopted by the US Army. Civil servants may not realize that the red first-aid metallic boxes found near their offices were packaged here.

While Health Canada's Emergency Services Division (ESD) was a creature of the Cold War born out of a task force civil defence study, in the 1970s there was a shift in mandate away from nuclear war and towards natural disasters. The Division has answered the call for help several times, such as during the Edmonton hurricane, the 1997 Manitoba Red River flood and the heavy ice storm of eastern Ontario and western Quebec in early 1998. The latter case illustrates the division's role.

The 1998 central Canadian ice storm may have been one of the most taxing natural disasters for both military and civilian crews. ESD staff in Ottawa were prepared to meet the challenge and provided hundreds of generators, 85,000 stretchers, 24,000 beds and 76,000 blankets to local emergency personnel. Employees and trucking firms worked around the clock to ensure materials stocked either in Ottawa or at permanent pre-positioned sites in Ontario and Quebec reached the needy. At the local level, municipal authorities and volunteers looked after specific requirements. The division had a secondary role in that it provided advice to provincial and municipal authorities in crisis management. Even after the storm's cessation, staff still had their hands full since all the emergency equipment had to be retrieved, inspected, cleaned, tagged and stored for the next disaster.

It is of course no surprise that the events of 9-11 had an impact on emergency preparedness in Canada. By then, the main organization responsible for the protection of the public and of vulnerable points was the Office of Critical Infrastructure Protection and Emergency Preparedness. After 9-11, Parliament woke up to the threat of terrorism and increased OCIPEP's budget from $10 million to $21 million, and nearly doubled its staff, some to update the list of Vital Points, others to revise emergency contingencies and yet others to ensure 'first-responders' know what to do when faced with emergencies. Many plans have been made by this organization to deal with a variety of threats such as an earthquake in Vancouver or a terrorist attack on the communications infrastructure. Today, OCIPEP's offices and its Government Emergency Operations Coordination Centre are located in an office building in downtown Ottawa.[18]

Health Canada has also felt the effects of 9-11. Worried about possible bioterror attacks, the ministry ordered vaccines for the smallpox virus, a common biological weapon, in 2003 in sufficient quantities for every Canadian. This particular virus kills about one-third of those infected, and produces ugly facial scars in those that survive. The vaccine was ordered from Aventis Pasteur Limited of Toronto and is stored at two secret locations, one in eastern and the other in western Canada.

Every municipality in Canada now seems to have emergency plans of some sort. In Ottawa, the city had renewed its plans after 9-11 to cover practically every type of situation, from natural disasters to chemical spills. When contacted by the author about its nuclear war plan though, city staff informed him that it did not consider the scenario because if it ever happened, not much could be done.

Other Facilities

While the focus thus far has primarily been on the Diefenbunkers, there are several other underground structures scattered throughout Canada. Many exist at old wartime artillery posts on both coasts. Some of these can be found around Victoria and Yorke Island, British Columbia, while others can be seen at Gaspé, Saint John, Halifax and in Newfoundland. Several ammunition bunkers dot the countryside, such as at old RCAF Air Defence Command fighter bases at Ottawa and North Bay and at the secretive Dwyer Hill Training Centre on Dwyer Hill Road west of Ottawa. Several bunkers were drilled inside a cliff at St John's harbour in Newfoundland during the Second World War to house naval ammunition, but now are empty. At the National Research Council's complex in east Ottawa, utility tunnels exist throughout the campus, as they do at Uplands airport. And in the late 1960s, the Department of National Defence awarded a $158,572 contract to Pillar Construction to build an underground laboratory in Stittsville, a suburb west of Ottawa. Its purpose and exact location are not known by the author.

At this point, one may be left to wonder about the days before the creation of the Carp bunker. In other words, what about the 1950s? Did Parliament and the federal government have any emergency shelter plans? Were any other secret underground places considered? While a temporary relocation site for the Prime Minister and the Cabinet had been set up at Camp Petawawa in the late 1950s, were any other sites created to shelter Canadian political leaders? The answer to these questions, we find, is 'yes'.

A 1955 issue of the government's *Civil Defence Bulletin* provided details of a pre-Carp and pre-Petawawa shelter. On 17 December of the previous year, Members of Parliament and their staff carried out an evacuation drill in the Parliament buildings by relocating to 'shelters deep in the basement'. The drill was conducted by the Gentleman Usher of the Black Rod and the Sergeant-at-Arms. The article made no mention of the size of these shelters, or the time the exercise took, but it did say Parliamentary security staff made sure everyone took part by ensuring that all the rooms were empty after evacuation. The article also mentioned that the civil defence co-ordinator at the time, former Army General Worthington, also took part in the evacuation process. The author does not know if these shelters still exist.

One may also wonder if a bomb shelter was ever built under the Prime Minister's official residence at 24 Sussex Drive in Ottawa. In May 1975, it was revealed in the *Debates of the House of Commons* that such a shelter does exist. The issue only arose because some Members of Parliament questioned its cost. It is thought that this bunker consists of nothing more than a reinforced basement.[19]

Documents from the Department of National Defence's Chiefs of Staff Committee declassified in 2011 show that the Department considered building a new National Defence Headquarters in Ottawa's west end in the mid-1950s. The Headquarters would have been placed on the grounds of a sandstone mine then planned for excavation by a private company on Corkstown Road just west of the Canadian National Railway line. DND officers debated the number of buildings that would make up the new NDHQ, and whether all of it or just the operations centre would be placed in the underground mine. In one of the de-classified memos, Deputy Minister of Public Works H.A. Young suggested that General Worthington might look into the mine as a communications base. If Worthington was indeed contacted, it may very well have given him (or his successor) the idea to build the Carp bunker a few years later.[20]

NORAD

The mother of all Canadian bunkers, the NORAD 'hole' at Canadian Forces Base North Bay, was until 2006 still an active military facility.[21] The underground complex housed an air defence operations centre that was a component of NORAD, the bi-national Canadian-American organization responsible for the defence of the North American continent. The operations centre was a true creature of the Cold War with the primary purposes of surveillance and identi-fication of incoming aerial traffic and the control of air defence weaponry.

Built over a four-year period from 1959 to 1963, the complex consisted of a network of buildings forming roughly a square figure-eight shape installed in caverns 60ft to 70ft high. Its total floor area measured over 147,000sq ft. As with Cheyenne Mountain in Colorado, the structures were built independently of the cavern walls to make them impervious to earthquakes and atomic blasts. For the same reason, they are mounted on huge springs. Some of the blasting techniques were pioneered by Swedes and used in Canada for the first time here. The buildings were three-storeys high and contained numerous offices, dining hall, kitchen, gymnasium, barber shop, infirmary, Maintenance Control Centre, computer rooms, washrooms and a command post complete with four large-screen televisions. The complex was protected by a single blue 19-ton blast door. The structure's independence from the cavern walls allowed maintenance engineers easy inspection and, indeed, walkways were laid out around the complex for this reason. There were three huge 1,825kW generators, located in another cavern 500ft long, 28ft high and 50ft wide, and these were kept in constant readiness, but were rarely used since the complex normally ran on commercial power; one of these beasts alone was said to be enough to power a town of 5,000. A 6ft by 7ft tunnel running east of the power cavern discharged waste water into the city sewer system. The entire structure was designed to hold 400 and was built at a cost of $51 million.

The complex was accessible through two tunnels called the North and South Portals. The North Portal was a 6,600ft long tunnel so narrow the shuttle buses could barely pass through; pedestrians and bicycles were forbidden to use it. This gave out on the base proper very near the Military Police building. The South Portal was 3,150ft long and exited south of the base near Trout Lake. Both tunnels were lined with stabilizing bolts and fencing to prevent large rocks falling in. During excavation of one of the portals, the crew hit an artesian well partially flooding the tunnel.[22] The crew suffered no injuries, but since the water served the base the fissure required patching up with concrete.

Security at the North Bay bunker was state-of-the-art. Most of the personnel entered through the North Portal and presented their passes to the guard on

The South Portal at North Bay. (Photo: Author)

One of the tunnels leading to the underground air defence complex at North Bay.
(Photo: DND NBC 84-1371, 1984)

duty. On weekends, when there are no guards, entry was gained by having one's magnetically striped badge scanned by an electronic reader. Normally, only shuttle buses were allowed in and even these had to pass through two Sally Port fences which do not remain simultaneously open. Military Policemen could enter the tunnel through their own lift. At one time, the main portal door was kept open but after the Gulf War, it was kept closed for security reasons. The South Portal was unmanned but protected by the same card-reader and watched by surveillance cameras. All telephone calls to the facility were recorded. There was an escape hatch of sorts, which was likely in one of the ventilation shafts.

One of the in-jokes relating to the North Bay complex was that if a nuclear strike did not kill the personnel, flooding would. The bunker was located deep underground and relatively close to Trout Lake. A nuclear hit could widen any fissures in the rock and if these ran long enough, the lake could have poured into the complex. It is unknown whether or not the bunker was stocked with life preservers.

The North Bay bunker's cynosure, the operations room, has been called different names over the years. Known at one time as the Semi-Automatic Ground Environment Combat Operations Centre, it was refurbished at a cost of close to $100 million in the early 1980s and divided functionally into two halves where the Region Operations Control Centre – East monitored traffic over

Ontario, Quebec and the maritimes and ROCC – West covered western Canada. Later on, it was renamed the Sector Air Operations Centre.[23] Operational personnel were assigned to the Canadian Forces 21 Aerospace Control and Warning Squadron, while those on training, to 51 AC&W Squadron. Both units were subsidiary to the base's 22 Wing. As per the NORAD agreement between Canada and the United States, American personnel operated in the bunker; these belonged to the USAF's 722nd Support Squadron.

A look inside the early Combat Operations Centre at North Bay. Visible in this photo are the light guns that were used to identify an aircraft, and a status board listing available air defence squadrons and locations. Most of the locations are no longer active military bases. The board also lists the types of interceptors then in use: F-101, F-106, F-89J, CF-100, CF-101 and the Bomarc CIM-10B SAM. According to one source, consoles similar to those seen here have ended up on *Star Trek*. This room has been redesigned a few times since this photo was taken. (Photo: DND PL143374, September 1963)

Most of the action at North Bay took place in the SAOC. The operations centre's three main roles were the surveillance and identification of aircraft and the control of fighter responses. In radio communications with these fighters, the SAOC was known for a while by the call sign 'Irradiate'. All aircraft that approach Canadian air space are watched by radar and have their Identification-Friend-or-Foe signal verified. Minimally manned long-range radars of the Canadian Coastal Radar System operated on both Canadian coasts and, along with signals from the North Warning System in the Arctic, fed data continuously into a digital switch in the complex's computer room. This data was then inputted into an FYQ-93 computer that consisted of two dedicated machines, one of which was used for back-up; the computers decided which consoles received what data.[24] The screens could display Air Movement Data for any or all aircraft shown and, at the push of a button, could expand any particular area. The operator could monitor any individual aircraft by selecting it with a track ball and 'hooking' into it, what is really an aim and click process.[25] Flights were labelled F or S, Friendlies referring to western civilian airliners or Canadian military flights and Specials denoting foreign flights such as from the former Soviet Union and, in some cases, even from the United States. By 1993, the SAOC was identifying about 225,000 aircraft per year.

Another section of the operations room dealt with weapons control. Once an aircraft entered the Canadian Air Defence Identification Zone, a narrow airspace located off-shore, surveillance operators had two minutes to identify it, if it had not already done so. If identification was not made, interceptors were sent up to investigate. Air Weapons Controllers decided which weapons would be used and when. In yet another section of the operations centre, the ROCC-AWACS Digital Interface Link (RADIL) allowed a constant data interchange between North Bay and flying American radar aircraft, the E-3s. Data from these flying radars were processed by a GSQ-235 computer and fed into the FYQ-93 for visual display.

Throughout its existence, the North Bay underground operations centre took part in a large number of missions and exercises: when the Super Bowl was held in Detroit in 2006, it helped guard the area over the stadium. When a weather balloon lost its way in 1998, it guided interceptors towards it for destruction. When UFO sightings were made by the public, their reports were routed here before being sent to the National Research Council in Ottawa. And, naturally, every time a Soviet bomber intruded upon Canadian airspace, North Bay knew about it.

One of the newer mandates for NORAD is counter-narcotics and in this effort, the SAOC co-operated with organisations such as the RCMP and the US Drug Enforcement Administration to stem the flow of drugs into North America. If the RCMP learned a certain aircraft might be carrying drugs, it could ask NORAD for its help in intercepting the smuggler. North Bay in turn could dispatch interceptors to force the intruder down. The military officer responsible for liasing with police agencies was known as a Wing Counter-Narcotics Officer.

As mentioned above, both American and Canadian air force servicemen were found at the North Bay bunker. All major decisions were made co-operatively; even the safes could only be opened when two NORAD Safe Keys were inserted by officers of the Canadian Forces and USAF. When the Canadian Army was a separate entity, men and women from the Army were also stationed there since they and not the Air Force had responsibility for warning the population of a nuclear attack. A single Bell Telephone technician was also present on the base since air defence signals are sent along Bell lines. Since the North Warning System radar chain in the far north is operated by the civilian firm Frontec, some of the firm's personnel also worked out of the bunker.

In another room near the operations centre, Nav Canada personnel manned a civilian Flight Service Station. Originally operated by the Department of Transport, the FSS was responsible for providing assistance to pilots, be it in the form of directions, positions or emergency help. As of 1994, the FSS doubled as an Aviation Weather Briefing Station. With satellite inputs, station personnel could look at weather patterns anywhere in North America and relay this to pilots. Nav Canada, a private firm, was created when the federal government privatized air traffic services.

One of the characteristics of a decent military force is the proper training of its personnel. People assigned to North Bay were no exception and submitted to exercises on a regular basis. One of these included a 'button-down' condition, which essentially meant the bunker was sealed up and put on alert status. Although large in size, the bunker did not feel claustrophobic, yet when a drill was declared and the alarm sounded a few years ago, one of the junior female clerks panicked. The idea of being closed in was too much for her so she demanded quite hysterically to be let out. Such was her fear that she had to be restrained by several persons. After this, during 'button-down' conditions, the large door was no longer closed.

In addition to the artesian well that flooded, there would be other problems with the bunker when it was built. A project of such a size required a large manpower, and the government's contracting agency hired whomever it could. This included taking on electricians from more than one union. This mixture of staff created a serious problem since the contractors who belonged to the International Brotherhood of Electrical Workers very much resented the employment of members of the Communications Workers Union of America. Such was their level of resentment that the IBEW went on strike demanding their removal in June 1962. For support, other tradesmen joined in. This situation was settled after a secret meeting in Toronto. While details were not revealed in the press, it appears the IBEW's demands may have been met since they soon went back to work.

The North Bay facility had undergone several changes over the years. Older consoles have been replaced by newer ones as have the aircraft tracking method and the processing computers. For example, previously, an aircraft could be hooked in by an Air Defence Technician pointing a special light gun onto it on the console. To identify it, the track was fired upon with the gun and by encircling it, again with the gun, the operator could look at its movement data. This was replaced in the 1980s with a track ball. Some of the older technicians did not appreciate the new track-ball technology since they had grown fond of the guns.

The number of persons assigned to the bunker was another big change at North Bay. In its heyday in the 1960s, the bunker population numbered approximately 2,500 (working in separate shifts) but by the 1990s, only 530 worked there. This was partly due to advances in technology and partly because of decreased defence spending. The Canadian military budget has been so reduced that the Canadian Forces operate only a segment of the outside base and in fact, the military houses above have all been sold off and a number of buildings destroyed. Eventually, it was announced that the bunker would be closed as a cost-saving measure and that air defence operations would be moved above ground. Today, the SAOC can be found in a new surface building named after the only Canadian air defender to lose his life in the line of duty, Sergeant David L. Pitcher.[26] The bunker has since been declared a National Historic Site, which hopefully will guarantee it a permanent life and serve as a reminder of what could have been. Unfortunately, none of the details of any of its operations can ever be made public since the log books – all forty-one years' worth – were shamefully destroyed a few years ago instead of being sent to the Directorate of History and Heritage at National Defence Headquarters in Ottawa.

Civilian Shelters
During the Cold War, several individuals followed the government's lead and built their own nuclear shelters. One man in West Edmonton, Alberta, built his own on his property for $2,000. This one could house ten persons for ten days. Bruce Beach in Horning's Mills in southwestern Ontario near Shelburne had a more enterprising streak. He dug a large hole in a field off Mill Lane and buried forty-two interconnected school buses converted into living quarters. His complex can hold 500. Many more private bunkers exist throughout the country.

Caves, mines and federal buildings were also considered potential public shelter space, just as they were in the United States. The Emergency Measures Organization asked the federal Department of Public Works (DPW) in 1961 to conduct a nationwide survey to determine which federal facilities could serve as public shelters. The 5,000 buildings examined were listed in a directory and rated for level of occupancy and protection factor. The following year, it asked the Department of Mines and Technical Surveys to carry out a survey of all mines in Canada for the same reason. Some of the mines around Cobalt and Kirkland Lake, Ontario, were considered for this purpose. Yet another survey was carried out by DPW in 1964 of major buildings in Alberta, again to gauge the level of protection and 'to establish techniques which could be applied to a possible future national survey'. Nothing concrete came of these plans because a system of public shelters was never formally established in Canada.[27] The federal government decided that, in the event of war, the public would have to fend for itself. When Public Works and Government Services Canada, DPW's successor, was queried by the author on the national shelter survey, government officials found no copies of the shelter directory in existence.

Radioactive Waste

There was one cave built by the Canadian government for nuclear purposes which had nothing to do with civil defence or war. Atomic Energy of Canada Limited excavated a deep mine at the Whiteshell Nuclear Establishment at Pinawa, Manitoba, in the 1980s to investigate the feasibility of storing radioactive waste underground on a permanent basis. The Underground Research Laboratory consists of a deep shaft giving out to a network of tunnels for offices and geological experiments. It was the first underground facility in the world built for this purpose and its concept has since been adopted by several other nations for study. Some of its design and construction principles have found use by the mining and underground train industry. As an innovative project, the URL won an award from the Canadian Tunnelling Association. A panel of Canadians determined that storing radioactive waste underground was a safe endeavour and it remains only for Parliament to decide whether this will be done.

A New Facility?

The end of the Cold War and the closure of the Diefenbunker at Carp may not have been the last word in the chapter on Canadian continuity of government. Ottawa researcher Ken Rubin, a prolific user of Canada's Access-to-Information laws, learned in 2010 that the Privy Council Office and the Prime Minister's Office were looking to set up a secret alternate location from which they could operate during an emergency. The PCO and PMO are located in an old Ottawa landmark, the Langevin Block across the street from the Parliament, in an area wide-open to the public. The relocation plan called for the establishment of a special site from which the Prime Minister and his staff would work during a terrorist attack and, by inference (however unlikely), during a nuclear conflict. A small committee was set up for the purpose of studying the matter, and while twenty-two locations were considered for this 'PCO Alternate Site' in 2008, two years later there were only three candidates left.[28] The report did not say where those three locations were, but it did say they were already being used by the federal government. Which buildings these are will be left to the reader's imagination.

❏ CHINA

Civil Defence

As the most populous nation on Earth, China has untold miles of tunnels and countless shelters under its cities and towns. These were built after the Sino-Soviet clashes of 1968 as protection against future Russian attacks. Chairman Mao Zedong expected the entire country to adopt a civil defence mindset so that his people could survive war. 'Dig deep,' he said. Since then, the Chinese have dug.

Dr Frank Barnaby of the Stockholm International Peace Research Institute was given a glimpse of the honeycomb below Beijing in 1978. The network of tunnels revealed itself so huge that a single system under Da Sa La Street was designed for 10,000. It alone had a total length of about 2 miles, possessed ninety entrances and had an escape tunnel 6 miles long leading to the capital's outskirts. The system had its own air filters, power generators, water supply, and even kitchens, dining areas and office space. The locals were so well trained in mock nuclear attacks all 10,000 could vanish below in five minutes. Some say that the entire city is networked and that some of the tunnels run as far east as Tianjin.[1]

Typically, an underground tunnel network in China will have three levels. The first provides access, the second has living quarters, offices and an armoury and the third, the power machinery. In some cases, access can be gained from a trap door behind a shop counter or after sliding away a false upward stairway. The first level averages only 4m to 8m below ground and the third, 15m to 20m implying these have only radiation and concealment in mind, not blast protection. A direct hit over downtown Shanghai could still kill and bury thousands. In one city, Tianjin, there are not three but five levels of tunnels. A civil defence command centre is known to have been built 250ft underground at Mudanjiang.

Another example of a large underground complex is that of Dairen, a city a few hundred miles east of Beijing. Dairen's tunnels are over 60,000yd long and have sufficient room to shelter 50,000. They have apparently been built by an army of ½ million workers, such as volunteers from factories and local shops. One section of the tunnel is 4ft across, 7ft high and brightly lit and gives off to branch tunnels leading to storerooms, reservoirs and arsenals. The network consists of several rooms required for survival such as medical stations, decontamination rooms, classrooms for all ages, dormitories, assembly halls and machine shops.

A civil defence tunnel in Jiaozuo, Henan. Now, it is a tourist attraction. (Photo: Author)

It also receives a constant supply of fresh air through ventilation pumps. External security is provided through pillboxes and even inside, there is a multitude of slit trenches large enough for small arms. The primary sheltering area is 7yd to 30yd wide under the city's centre.

By all accounts, the Chinese civil defence tunnels are no longer maintained. Many, if not most, ceased to be maintained in 1978 when the threat from Russia disappeared. Many of these have since been converted for other uses. Some in Jiaozuo, Henan, for instance, have been turned into a house-of-horrors tourist attraction, while others in Hangzhou, Zhejiang, are being used as underground hotels and resorts. Part of those in Beijing are open to the public and here, one can visit various rooms, including a silk-making factory, and witness the slow rusting of ventilation pipes. One other part is used by a dealer to store wine. One Chinese newspaper article has claimed that there may be as many as 3,700 hotels and dormitories established in unused tunnels throughout the nation. The fact they are no longer used may be an admission that they would be useless during a nuclear conflict.

Several other civilian underground structures exist in China. At Hohhot in Inner Mongolia 250 miles west of Beijing, the underground is just as impressive. In 1971, a 5-mile-long tunnel leading to Great Green Mountain was built large enough for single-lane traffic, something troops could find very useful in wartime. Reinforced with concrete and steel, the 10ft-high tunnel also contains several rooms to house the city's inhabitants. Again, this is only one example. Other emergency tunnels in China, for example at Yan'an, are large enough for two-lane traffic. Smaller bunkers have also been built for the storage of emergency food. All are no longer maintained.

Nuclear Weapons

Years before the Chinese-Soviet clashes of the late 1960s, the two nations got along rather well. Forged in communist steel, their relationship existed because Russian leaders, such as Stalin and Krushchev, and Chinese Communist Party Chairman Mao Zedong envisioned a world that would live under the shadow of the red star. From the late 1930s, Mao was preoccupied with ridding his beloved China of the Japanese, and succeeded in doing so at the end of the Second World War. China was then governed by the Kuomintang government of Chiang Kai-Shek, but in 1949 the government collapsed under Mao's weight and a people's republic was officially born. Since the Japanese had ravaged China during eight long years, Mao sought help from what he then considered to be a natural ally, 'Uncle Joe' Stalin, in turning China into a modern economy.

The Russians and the Chinese would establish co-operation on many levels. The Soviet Union provided economic aid hoping it would strengthen the bonds of socialism between the two. Co-operation also came in the form of military assistance as Russia supplied artillery, machine guns and experts for defence against the United States and its 'imperialist running dogs'.[2] At the close of the Second World War, the Russian Army had troops stationed in two Chinese cities,

Lüshun and Dairen, and these were ordered to remain – at Beijing's request – in case the US attacked.[3]

The economic and basic military assistance from Russia was not enough for Mao. The Chairman had spent millions of yuans and lost thousands of troops in the Korean War, and had become no doubt nervous when President Eisenhower threatened to use nuclear weapons to end the conflict. And it did not help Mao's morale when the United States and Taiwan signed a Mutual Defense Treaty in December 1954. The Chairman had been thinking of acquiring his own A-bomb for some time, and the Washington–Taipei deal most likely firmed up his decision. He turned to fellow-communist Nikita Krushchev for assistance in the field of nuclear research as the first stepping stone in the development of his Bomb. Krushchev agreed and signed a pact with Mao. Soon Chinese students travelled to Russia to learn about everything nuclear, from isotope separation to weapons' physics. In China, a nuclear research institute was built, a test site was laid out at Lop Nur (in the underpopulated west), and weapons were planned. In 1958, Soviet weapons designers came to Beijing to share some of the secrets of their weapons research such as critical mass calculations and component designs. The Chinese had formally begun the slow process of becoming a nuclear power.

The relationship between Krushchev and Mao was not all handshakes and kisses though. On the Russian side, Krushchev, writing in his memoirs, claimed he was irritated by some of Mao's requests. The Chinese had, for instance, asked the Soviets for the transfer of their newly installed coastal fortifications at Lüshun to them for free, despite the heavy investment made by Moscow in them. Krushchev was also annoyed when, out of a gesture of goodwill that would have helped feed Chinese mouths, the offer to employ Chinese workers in Siberia was at first rejected as offensive, then accepted. The Soviets had also helped the Chinese build submarines, but after the Soviet Navy asked in return for the right to set up a radio station on Chinese soil to communicate with its Pacific Fleet, it was angrily rebuffed by Mao as he felt it was an insult to Chinese sovereignty. Krushchev was also put off by stories of Russian workers returning to their hotel rooms only to find them in a mess. Finally, in 1960, the Premier had had enough: assistance of all type was terminated, trade between the two nations fell and the advisors were recalled to Russia. The Sino-Soviet split had begun.

The loss of aid from the Soviet Union did not deter Beijing from its nuclear ambitions. Mao encouraged Chinese students to attend Western universities and to soak up all knowledge related to nuclear weapons. This they did with the strength of an atomic vacuum cleaner. When it came to missiles, the Chinese were greatly helped by a German engineer, Wolfgang Pilz, who had helped Egypt build up its arsenal in the early 1960s, and one of their own, Qian Xuesen, a brilliant physicist. Originally from China, Qian had studied at MIT and Caltech in the 1930s and was one of the creators of the Jet Propulsion Laboratory in California. At the end of the Second World War, as a colonel in the US Army, he was given the task of interrogating captured Nazi rocket scientists. Later on, he went on to work on the American missile programme. After the Korean War began though, he was stripped of his security clearance and held in virtual house arrest at Caltech. In 1955, he was deported to China, and using the knowledge he had gained during the German interrogations and during his work on American rockets, he soon went to work on Chinese missiles as director of the Institute of Mechanics in Beijing. Qian would retire years later as a national hero.[4]

The year 1964 was a landmark in the annals of Chinese nuclear history. This was the year the Middle Kingdom would detonate its first atomic bomb. A 22 kiloton device was placed on top of a tower at Lop Nur on 16 October and set off. A few months earlier, Premier Minister Zhou En-lai, Mao's deputy, ordered Chinese scientists and engineers to start building missiles that could carry these bombs, and in 1966, a rocket equipped with a 25 kiloton warhead was fired into the testing site. In the following years, more tests would be conducted at Lop Nur, many of them underground, including a 3 megaton device that was so powerful it pushed a 54-ton railway locomotive that was 3km away a distance of 18m. Further missiles would be designed, but it would only be in 1981 when its first ICBM would be deployed. The People's Liberation Army christened its missiles *Dong Feng* (East Wind).

Unlike the United States and Russia, China has not developed a massive missile arsenal. Partly for technical reasons and partly because of its policies, the People's Liberation Army (PLA) has deployed only between 80 and 130 long-range missiles. The PRC prefers to rely on the concept of nuclear deterrence to scare its opponents. Its foes are expected to realize that if a few weapons were ever to hit their territory, the consequences could still be catastrophic. Most 'sane' enemies would thus not risk attacking it. It is the same policy France has.[5]

The PLA has developed missiles in six types. These are either fired from silos or from Transporter Erector Launchers (TELs). In the former category, the *Dong Feng*-5 ICBM had a 7,400km range, used a liquid fuel and carried a 4 to 5 megaton warhead. It has since been replaced by the longer range and more accurate DF-5A, of which only an estimated eighteen exist.[6] The DF-4 IRBM has a

The China air museum is located in an old air force mountain hangar north of Beijing. (Photo: Author)

lower range – 4,750km – and a lesser 3.3 megaton warhead, but is stored in caves and would be moved out on a TEL for firing.[7] The PLA is constantly looking for ways to modernize its missile fleet and planned to retire some of its older units, such as the above two rockets, in the mid-2000s and replace them with the DF-31 and DF-31A. It is not known by the author if the DF-5A's replacement would use its silos. One of the idiosyncrasies of China's strategic missile force is that the warheads are stored separately from the rockets and that its national storage depot (described below) is directly controlled by the Central Military Commission.[8] Whether this reflects a lack of trust by the CMC towards field commanders is not known.

Very little has been revealed about Chinese missile silos, although

This bunker located at the rear end of the China air museum might have held weapons or petroleum. (Photo: Author)

Saunders and Yuan, in Bolt and Willner's *China's Nuclear Future*, claim that they are emplaced as single units, as opposed to in groups, to prevent their destruction by a single missile, and that they are shallow and not very resistant to blast pressures. They also reveal that the PLA has constructed decoy silos to keep prying eyes guessing. Some also say that the silos are covered with crops. If this is really the case, it may not be an original Chinese idea since the concept was mentioned in a 1964 episode of the television show *The Man From UNCLE*.[9]

As in Russia, the Chinese government created a new armed service for its missile force. The service would be called the Second Artillery Corps (Di Er Pao Bing), a reference to the fact that the PLA considers missiles to belong to the field of artillery, and that it is the second unit devoted to that branch, conventional gunnery being the first.[10] The Corps was officially created on 6 June 1966 and given its own headquarters north of Beijing at Qinghe. It was given control of six test sites, including Lop Nur, and an underground command centre at Xi Shan in the western part of Beijing. It has its own educational institutes such as a Command Academy at Wuhan for officers and technical personnel, an Engineering Academy in Xi'an for officer-candidates and an NCO Academy at Qingzhou. Some officers and technicians also train at the Langfang Army Missile Academy and at the Missile Academy located at the Air Force Engineering University in the eastern part of Xi'an. By 1966, the SAC had deployed its first long-range missile, the DF-2, in northern China near the border of its former ally.

Today's Second Artillery Corps consists of six major bases and several brigades and battalions. Perhaps following the Russian tradition, the units have two numerical designations: a designation and a five-digit unit number. Chinese media sources give two different unit numbers for these bases, which may be an attempt to confuse the West. The bases are:

City and Province	Base Designation	Unit Numbers	Actual Location
Shenyang, Liaoning	No. 51	80301, 96101	
Huangshan, Anhui	No. 52	80302, 96151	Tunxi
Kunming, Yunnan	No. 53	80303, 96201	Tianwei
Luoyang, Henan	No. 54	80304, 96251	
Huaihua, Hunan	No. 55	80305, 96301	
Xining, Qinghai	No. 56	80306, 96351	

The brigades carry 800-series numbers. In the 1990s, the Second Artillery had only twenty ICBMs that could reach North America, but in 2002 the CIA predicted that it would have 100 long-range missiles by 2015.[11]

The literature on the SAC suggests its men undergo training of good quality. Its mobile units practise camouflaging techniques, night movements, rapid

The North Sea Fleet's alternate command centre at Qingdao, originally built by the German army. It is now open to the public. (Photo: Author)

One of the entrances to the now-disused Yan'an military tunnel. The entrance is deceptive since the tunnel is large enough to accommodate two intercity coaches side by side. This is located behind a hotel in the western part of town. Similar tunnels exist at Hohhot and Dandong. (Photo: Author)

reaction and electronic warfare under all types of weather conditions. Support units go through exercises on intelligence-gathering, surveying and supply. Saunders and Yuan point out that the SAC's supply warehouse personnel train in the rapid delivery of missile components in the field. At silo-based units, the missileers likely practise the same message-receiving, authentication and launching drills as in the US and Russia. Some exercises have included group missile launches.

Over the years, China has undertaken steps to modernize its missiles. Its first rockets used a liquid propellant that was stored separately, but since the propellant loading time was too long, the newer missiles were designed to use a solid fuel. We also see the same accuracy–warhead balance shift that other countries have witnessed, namely that older missiles carried heavy warheads and had low accuracy, while new rockets have lower warhead yields and greater accuracy. Some Chinese officers have claimed that some of their missiles have a circular error probable of 50m, but Western analysts claim the CEP on such missiles as the DF-5A is closer to 1,000m. Either way, the use of GPS systems in the re-entry vehicles have likely given them greater accuracy. Also, newer warheads are said to have the ability to guide themselves.

China has also modernized its strategic arsenal through the use of espionage and the vacuum cleaner approach mentioned above. It has acquired nuclear secrets either through one or more spies working in an American nuclear lab or by piercing through supposedly secure computer firewalls at those labs. China has learned the details of several American warheads, such as the W62 used on the Minuteman and the W88 on the Trident SLBM, not to mention the neutron bomb. The CIA suspects that current Chinese armament makes use of those secrets. To respond to the charge, the Chinese government has insisted that it has not engaged in espionage and that it has developed its own weapons using home-grown talent.

From the open literature, much can be learned about the storage of nuclear warheads in China. By taking advantage of China's slow relaxation of censorship laws, Mark Stokes of the Project 2049 Institute was able to write a very revealing report on the SAC's network of storage depots. In his report, he states that the national depot is located in a mountain near Baoji in Taibai County in Shaanxi Province about 140km west of Xi'an. The depot is called Base No. 22 and its numerical designation is 96401. It is probably located under Taibai Mountain, which is the highest peak in China. Stokes reveals that it was built in the late 1960s to replace another underground storage facility near Xining, Qinghai. It boasts extensive security measures such as video cameras, an infrared system and fingerprint access controllers, and makes use of advanced communications and a computerized warhead accounting system. There is also an indication that the complex includes a command centre called the Hongling Command Cell.[12]

Base No. 22 is made up of several sections, each responsible for a different function. These sections consist of regiments for technology service, transportation, training, maintenance and communications. The technology service

A small food storage bunker near Jiaozuo, Henan. The bunker had no protection against blast or fallout. (Photo: Author)

The entrance to a large underground complex in Yantai. The facility is described is a 'Western Canon Position'. It is not clear if it is still in use. (Photo: Author)

regiment appears to handle the transfer of warheads to and from the complex. The base also includes an Equipment Inspection Institute (Unit 96411) responsible for warhead reliability and safety, and another institute (Unit 96412) whose function is unknown. The complex seems to be looked after by the PLA's 308th Engineering Command. The base's security battalion includes a cavalry company whose horses are better equipped to patrol the mountainous terrain.

Each of the six operational bases listed above has its own depot, all of which appear to be underground. The operating units are called Equipment Inspection Regiments. These regiments conduct warhead inspections, and may also be responsible for mating the warheads to missiles. According to Stokes, only a small number of warheads are kept at these depots, and they are only mated with missiles during times of tension or for training purposes.

Under what circumstances would China use its nuclear weapons? From the time of its first atomic test in 1964, China has vowed a 'no-first-use' policy. Simply put, this means that in a war, it would not be the first to use nuclear weapons. Some Western analysts have, however, found the policy to be wanting in honesty. One Chinese ambassador was quoted as saying that if Taiwan ever declared independence, it would be dealt with accordingly, hinting that nuclear bombs would be dropped. Furthermore, some Russian analysts predict that should China ever be invaded, it may very well use nuclear devices on the invaders (this despite the threat to its own population). This is re-inforced by a statement in a 2006 Chinese defence White Paper which stated that the PLA is committed to carrying out 'counter-attacks in self-defence', implying that it would indeed employ nuclear weapons against an attacker. And Mark Schneider in his essay on Chinese nuclear doctrine asks the question: if Bejing really has a 'no-first-use' policy, why does it keep threatening the United States over Taiwan with them?[13]

A diagram inside the entrance to the Yantai complex. (Photo: Author)

Other Facilities

Other underground bases in China include:

- For submarines at Dafudao east of Qingdao (south of the drydock), with specialized equipment to service nuclear reactors or load and unload missiles in caverns said to be twelve storeys high;
- For submarines at the Sanya naval base on Hainan Island in Yalong Bay;
- An alternate headquarters for the North Sea Fleet at Qingdao (now a museum). It is assumed East Sea Fleet HQ at Ningbo and South Sea Fleet HQ at Zhanjiang have or had similar bunkers;
- A reported SAM storage complex in Payi in Tibet;

Another large complex stood under a monument in Yantai near the 'Western Canon Position'. This was an emergency exit. The complex is devoid of any equipment or furnishings, clearly indicating it is no longer used. (Photo: Author)

- In Yantai, under a high monument in National Defence Park. The complex is no longer used and is stripped of furnishings, blast doors and light fixtures;
- In Yantai, under what seems to be an observation tower in National Defence Park. This bunker appears to be still in use; and
- At several air bases. See Appendix B.

Finally, while China possesses several anti-aircraft bases, unlike Russia these do not seem to have their own bunkers. One example of a SAM site is west of Xiamen south of the main highway and the railway line off County Road 518 near Shabancun. The site is hidden in a forest, and its network of roads seems to have a Star of David pattern that is reminiscent of older Russian SAM sites. From satellite imagery, one can barely make out truck-mounted missiles, suggesting they may be some of the S-300s bought from Russia. The camouflaged rooftops give the site away as a military installation.

❑ CROATIA

Underground facilities in Croatia include:

- A bunker under President Tito's palace at Zagreb, called Vila Zagorje. It is said to be 15m underground, and is still used by the government;
- A bunker under Mount Velebit;
- Fortifications and a naval tunnel on the island of Vis;
- Tunnels on Rab Island; and
- A mountain hangar at the Divulje air base near Split.

❑ CUBA

The website gertzfile.com quoted a US Defense Intelligence Agency report that claimed Cuba had built several underground bases on its north coast. The bases included tunnels for troops and tanks, bunkers for communications units and shelters for military command and control elements. The DIA report stated the agency had identified 400 bunkers for various government ministries, the army and the communist party.

Other underground facilities are known to exist in Cuba. For instance, when the Soviet Union installed missiles there in 1962, some bunkers were built to house nuclear warheads. One of those bunkers was at San Cristobal. A number of earth-covered hangars are seen at the Santa Clara air base. The base now seems to host a helicopter squadron.

❑ CZECH REPUBLIC

Bunkers in the Czech Republic exist at:

- Prague, near the Malostranská metro station, for the government;
- Prague, under Stalin's monument in Letna Park;[1]
- Prague, as a fallout shelter in Parukářka Park, now a music club;
- Prague, under Prague Castle, for the government. The bunker was built in the 1950s and 1960s and is no longer used;
- Outside Prague for the government. This active bunker is located in a forest and has the cover of an industrial concern. It was revealed in the Czech television show *Nova*;
- At Milovice north of Prague, for the Soviet Central Group of Forces. The CGF was formed on 24 October 1968, a few months after the 'Prague Spring' and the Soviet invasion that crushed it. Although it was to be a temporary situation, the CGF remained there until 1991. The Milovice base controlled all Soviet units in Czechoslovakia such as the 114th Fighter Regiment at Milovice proper and the 441st Missile Brigade at Mimon. The former made use of several earth-covered hangars. As in Poland for the Northern Group of Forces, the CGF had an underground command centre and most probably a backup;
- North of Milovice at three locations: two south of Lipnik and one south-west of Zelena. Some of these were probably used by the CGF;
- At Drnov east of Slany, as an air defence operations centre. This was built in the 1980s and closed in 1993. Other bunkers nearby on the same property might have housed SAMs;
- At Prelic, possibly at an old SAM site;
- In the valley of St Prokop. This facility was used to make cannons during the Second World War. The installation was turned into an army barracks during the Cold War with enough beds for 1,000 soldiers. Known as Objekt K116, it is apparently no longer used by the Ministry of Defence. In Vojtech Mastny and Malcolm Byrne's book *A Cardboard Castle?*, a 1961 resolution of the Czechoslovakian communist party central committee that required the Minister of National Defence to inspect Facilities K116 and 'S' is reproduced. It was not mentioned if 'S' was underground;
- At Vypustek Cave west of Křtiny. This was used by the Czechoslovakian Army from 1936 to 1939, by the German government from 1943 to 1945 and the again by the Czech Army from 1961 to 2000. It is now open to the public;
- A former military bunker at Dobruška, now used as a seismic detection station; and
- Near the town of Stara Boleslav. This Warsaw Pact air defence headquarters is now a Czech air force operations centre.

❑ DENMARK

Underground military facilities during the Cold War in Denmark include:

- Fort Langeland, built in the 1950s as a coastal defence battery to guard the Langeland Belt, a body of water used by ships travelling to and from the Baltic Sea. The fort consisted of four 150mm cannons and anti-aircraft guns, each of which had its own protected facility. Bunkers were also built on the grounds for a command centre and a fire control post. Approximately 400 men would have worked there during a war. The fort, which was under the responsibility of the Royal Danish Navy, also looked after the sea mine fields in the area. It closed as a military installation in April 1993, was used for a while to house Yugoslavian refugees and is now Denmark's premier Cold War museum;
- Another Cold War coastal defence battery existed closer to Copenhagen to guard the Øresund;
- Two continuity of government bunkers outside Copenhagen: one is called Regan Vest and is located at Rold Skov, and the other, Regan Ost at Helleback på Sjaelland. The latter, said to be built in the 1960s and large enough for 350 persons, can be seen on Youtube;
- NATO's Baltic Approaches Headquarters was given its own bunker at Ravnstrup, about 10km west of Viborg.[1] The headquarters includes Combined Air Operations Centre-1 whose mission is to 'plan, direct, task, co-ordinate, supervise, assess and report on air operations' in the area.[2] The bunker has sections for intelligence, current operations, operations and plans, communications and information systems, and exercises and training;
- A large surface bunker at the Karup air base. For years, it housed NATO's Allied Forces Baltic Approaches HQ until it was replaced by the new facility above. The air base was closed in 2004; and

Camp Century

The realization that northern lands might become a new battleground between East and West led the United States armed forces to bolster its assets in the far north. By agreement with Denmark, the US Army Air Force had already established a number of airfields and weather stations on Greenland during the Second World War, and in the post-war period, some of those installations were expanded primarily for the benefit of the new Strategic Air Command. One of those bases, Thule Air Base, would become the area's nerve centre and would end up hosting one of the most unusual underground bases ever.

At some point in the 1950s, the US Army decided it needed to conduct research within the Arctic Circle. The army wanted to determine if it was feasible for a group of soldiers to live underground in a new facility located in a cold environment for extended periods of time. It wanted to know what construction materials would be suitable for this type of installation, and how men would react to living there. Concurrently, the army wanted to test a new small-scale reactor as the base's power source. Nuclear energy as a source of domestic power was still in its infancy, and the scientists who designed it were keen to find out whether such energy could be produced safely and used effectively. The US Army unit that was formed to conduct this research was the Polar Research and Development Center (PRDC).

Army engineers soon set to work on the camp's design. Work crews were sent to Greenland in the summer of 1959 to a point approximately 150 miles north of Thule Air Base. The men began by building a series of trenches in the ice, within which would lay a series of pre-fabricated huts. All the huts could be accessed by a central underground thoroughfare called 'Main Street'. Added to all this was access ramps and emergency exits. All the buildings had plumbing and electricity, the latter of which was fed from an American Locomotive Company PM-2A nuclear reactor. The complex was totally self-sufficient in that it had men's and officers' barracks, kitchens, mess halls, latrines, a recreation centre, a library, laundry, chapel and a communications centre. A ventilation system ensured the walls of the trenches would not melt. For emergency power, there were also installed three stand-by diesel generators. Above ground, one could only see the access ramps, antennae and ventilation shafts. The base was dubbed 'Camp Century'.

Once built, the US Army's PRDC began conducting experiments. Tests of all kinds were carried out by the Quartermaster, Medical, Chemical and Ordnance Corps, as well as by the signals and transportation branches. Scientists and technicians conducted research on concealed SAM sites (under Project Iceworm), on the movement of ice, textiles, communications and on the use of ice – mixed with other things such as sawdust – as construction materials.[3] The small nuclear reactor was found to work so well there that the US Navy acquired a similar one for use in Antarctica. On the human side though, the camp suffered from the same drawbacks as any other bunker. The men became bored and lost all sense of time. Because of this, the army decided that a soldier could not be posted to Century for more than 180 days. By 1966, all experiments had ceased, the nuclear reactor was taken away and the camp closed.[4]

❑ EGYPT

Many sand-covered hangars and shelters are seen at air bases at al-Ghardaqah, Luxor (al-Uqsur) and to the west and northeast of Cairo (near Bilbeis and Zawantil).

Also, during the 1973 Egypt–Israeli war, President Sadat of Egypt planned to build five tunnels under the Suez to attack Israel. It is not known by the author if Sadat ever proceeded with this plan.

Finally, an air defence operations centre is said to exist in a hill somewhere outside Cairo.

❑ ESTONIA

A Soviet missile shelter at Keila-Joa west of Tallinn. (Photo: Author)

Bunkers

In Estonia, the Soviet armed forces used 1,565 different sites. These could be airfields, radar centres, SAM sites, radio stations, army barracks, supply and ammunition depots, the large naval base at Paldiski and the smaller naval station at Hara. Many of these were equipped with personnel shelters, and most of the air bases were dotted with earth-covered hangars. After the Russians finally left in 1994, forty of the sites were used by the Estonian Ministry of Defence, and the others were either converted to other uses or left to rot.

Some of the underground structures in Estonia were:

- At Kangru, as personnel shelters;
- At the Keila-Joa SAM site west of Tallinn;
- At what was apparently a radar site at Humala;

A small bunker at the Vaiatu military camp. (Photo: Author)

- At an unknown military facility on the east side of Highway 24 near Vaiatu;
- A KGB bunker underneath an ordinary looking building on the east side of Lake Paunküla southeast of Ravila. The facility was also apparently a relocation site for the Ministry of the Interior. These days, the building is used by the Estonian Police, but the bunker lies empty;
- At Vardja near Kose south of Tallinn. The bunker was built in 1964 under cover of a Youth Pioneer Camp. The cover was blown by the *Voice of America* when it revealed its true purpose, and the names of its military chief, its civilian boss and its chief of construction. The 'No Foreigners Allowed' signs also gave the game away, as did the Soviet military style radio antenna; and
- Under an artillery rangefinder tower near the village of Suurupi. The tower and a nearby coastal defence battery were closed in the 1960s.

This old wartime artillery rangefinder tower served nearby coastal batteries well into the Cold War. A bunker lies underneath.
(Photo: Author)

A missile shelter for the Soviet Strategic Rocket Forces at Rohu. The missiles would be dragged out a few yards on a transporter, fuelled and then fired. (Photo: Author)

Missile Bases

Estonia also had a number of R-12 and one R-12U IRBM sites. The R-12 was a liquid-fuelled missile that could carry a 1 or 2.3 megaton warhead to 2,000km. It was housed in earth-covered shelters and rolled out to a launching pad nearby for launch. The R-12U was placed in Dvina silo complexes. The R-12 had four states of readiness:

1. The missile was filled with fuel but not with oxidizer, its gyroscope activated and placed on its launching pad. Here, it would take thirty minutes to fire.

2. The missile was still on the launching pad, its gyroscope activated and targeting data inserted, but was unfilled with fuel and oxidizer. It would take one hour to fill it.

3. The missile slept in its shelter, but with its gyroscope and warhead connected. To get it into firing mode, it would take two hours and twenty minutes.

4. The missile lay dormant in its bunker, but without warhead and gyroscope activated. To get it into full firing condition, it would take three hours and twenty-five minutes. The rocket could be kept in this state for seven years.

The warheads were kept in the shelter in a separate room.

R-12 sites were at:

- Rohu and Kadila, south of Rakvere, used by the 304th Missile Regiment;
- Võru east of Valga, used by the 846th Missile Regiment; and
- Piirsalu, east of Haapsalu, used by the 94th Missile Regiment.

An R-12U site was at Vilaski east of Valga. It too belonged to the 846th.

❑ FINLAND

Next door to her big Russian neighbour, neutral Finland made her own invest-ments into her future in case of nuclear war. At the same time as new bunkers were established near Oslo and Stockholm, a new one was under way below Helsinki, one of at least twenty in the city.

Paralleling Swedish and Norwegian thought, the Kontula project had the dual role of sports facility and bomb shelter with a capacity for 9,500. It consists of large interconnected halls accessible through two inclined portals and two lifts. Built by hydraulic drilling and blasting, crews began by boring out a pilot tunnel from which they worked sideways to finish the halls. Since the complex was put below a built-up area, excavation was limited from 6am to 9pm. The project was initiated in 1979 and fully completed some time in 1983.

Other underground structures in Finland include:

- Operations centres for the Air Force's three geographical commands: the Satakunta Air Command at Tamperi, the Karelia Air Command at Kuopio and the Lappland Air Command at Rovaniemi;
- A car park in Espoo built in 1999. It doubles as a public shelter, as does another garage at Kluuvi, a swimming hall in Itäkeskus and a sporting facility at Kauniainen 6 miles northwest of Helsinki;
- A bunker built by the Soviets during the Russo-Finnish war on Porkkala Island west of Helsinki. The Russians remained there until 1955;
- A bunker for the Lappland provincial government at Rovaniemi; and
- A government bunker under the Senate in Helsinki.

❑ FRANCE

Civil Defence

One cannot say that France was blessed with underground structures during the Cold War, unlike its neighbour Switzerland. The French government had no civil defence bunker plans in place to protect the people, save for an inventory of potential shelters in public buildings. Many thought that purpose-built shelters would have been too expensive, that they would have been useless against an atomic assault and that a nation with such a high population density was too vulnerable. France, political leaders decided, would instead rely on its strategic deterrent.

While public shelters were indeed never built, France still invested some funds into a civil defence infrastructure. The national government established a network of seven fallout detection posts throughout the country, called the Système de prévision automatisé des retombées radioactives, to monitor radia-tion. Some of the detectors were placed at Metz, Taverny and under the Saint-Honoré market in Paris.[1] There were also 4,000 air-raid sirens installed, which were tested regularly and which were controlled by air force radar stations.

The government had also planned to create twelve Cellules mobiles d'intervention radiologique to conduct rescue and re-entry operations, but in the end only two were ever formed.

Jupiter

It is not known if Paris developed a continuity of government programme, but what is known is that it at least created a bunker under the Elysée Palace for use by the President during a nuclear war. Codenamed 'Jupiter', this is where the President would have decided the fate of the nation during a third world war. From this location, he could order fighter-bombers to take off, missiles to launch and submarines to leave port for the open seas. Jupiter came online on 1 September 1969.

Taverny

While the civilian population of France had no protection against atomic weapons to speak of, the same cannot be said of the armed forces. An old gypsum mine north of Paris at Taverny had been used by the Germans during the Second World War since its railway lines facilitated the movement of materiel and its galleries protected its occupants from aerial attacks. The mine was so large and so carefully hidden in a forest that the Luftwaffe placed its air defence operations centre there, and engineers used another part to build V-1 rockets. But once French and American troops approached Paris, the Germans left post haste and the mine became dormant.

At some point in the mid-1950s, the French Air Force decided to use the Taverny mine for its purposes. Borrowing a page from the Luftwaffe's manual, it established its national air defence operations centre there in 1957. Four years later, Air Defence Command Headquarters was installed in the mine. In 1963, the Air Force formed Air Base 921 there as the complex's management entity,

An early view of the entrances to Taverny. This photo was taken long before the installation of a metal security gate. (Photo: Service historique de la défense, Paris)

and in that same year, the COFAS – the Strategic Air Forces Operations Centre – moved into an above-ground building from Versailles. Four years later, the COFAS would relocate into the bunker. Later on, several other units would move or form there, such as an Air Radio Centre and a Special Materials Maintenance and Repair Group. In 1976, a military air traffic control directorate would also move into the mine, and in 1992 so would the Special Operations Command, remaining until 2006. In 2007, the air defence operations centre moved to Lyon (at Mont Verdun) and Air Defence Command transferred to Paris, leaving the COFAS, an air operations analysis and simulation centre, the air traffic control directorate and a meteorology centre.

Since its conversion into a national command centre, the mine at Taverny has been modified to give it protection against any threat, except perhaps for a direct atomic hit. The facility has walls lined with concrete, is proofed against a chemical or biological attack and is equipped with surveillance cameras. The entire property is patrolled by guards with dogs. The complex has its own power

Inside the Taverny command centre. (Photo: Service historique de la défense, Paris)

station, water supply and is lined with metal making it one of the largest Faraday cages in Europe.[2] Even if it was attacked, a backup centre at Mont Verdun could take over. In 2007, about 1,000 worked there.

Throughout the Cold War, one of Taverny's functions was the receipt of information on nuclear explosions and radioactive fallout. In 1964, France set up an interservice system to warn political and military chiefs of NBC attacks. This system consisted of a network of detection sites, observers and a reporting system. At an observation post, a three-man team – one officer and two men – were to report all explosions to a command centre at a nearby military base. From these bases, the reports would be forwarded to radar sector control stations that included an operational and warning cell called CEDAR (Centre d'élaboration et de Diffusion de l'Alerte à la Radioactivité) that was equipped with plotting boards and maps. Here, all explosions would be mapped and their expected fallout traced. These CEDARs in turn sent their reports to Taverny to the national CEDAR and to an alternate site at Mont Verdun (see below.) A decision would then be made to alert the public.

Despite their key role, the small observation posts were equipped with very little. Here, one did not find decontamination facilities or any modern radiation detection equipment. The three-person staff had to contend with only simple equipment such as the Model 62 manual circular radiation calculator. There was, of course, a telephone link to the nearest command centre. It was not clearly stated in the French media whether these observation posts were underground as in the UK, but the author suspects they were not.

This network of posts and the communications links are no longer in operation today.

Houilles

Another underground military command centre exists 5 miles northwest of Paris. The bunker at Houilles was also originally a mine, and was also used by the Germans during the war, this time to manufacture and repair torpedoes. Despite its high security though, the Resistance managed to infiltrate the complex and sabotage some of its works. The Germans left on 25 August 1944, and the following month the French Navy took over the facility for use by the naval engineering branch and the radio technical service as workshops and offices.

In 1960, the Navy would cease using the mine as workshops and would convert the space into a command centre, the HQ-Strategic Ocean Forces (Force Océanique Stratégique – FOST). It is here where France's submarine operations were controlled. Ten years later, the complex would be named the Commandant Georges Millé Centre after the Captain of the submarine *Protée* who was lost at sea (with all hands) in December 1943. The FOST's command centre would remain until 2002 when it moved to Brest Castle, possibly to a new bunker there.[3] In 2003, the Houilles facility became HQ-Naval Information Systems Service, but in 2008 the Service moved to Fort Kremlin-Bicêtre to become part of a new tri-service defence information service (the Direction interarmées des réseaux d'infrastructure et des systèmes d'information). Today, about 300 military and 200 civilians work at Houilles.

Mont Verdun

As mentioned above, another military bunker exists outside Lyon, France's third largest city. It was built as an alternate operations centre for the Air Defence Command. The property is called Air Base 942, and is also one of France's five radar control centres (Centre de détection et de control 05/942). It also houses a backup naval command centre tied to the main one at Brest, and a search and rescue co-ordination centre. Since 1967, the bunker has also been the location of the alternate operations centre for the Strategic Air Forces. In September 2007, it became home to the National Air Operations Centre (Centre national des opérations aériennes) which continuously receives air traffic data from civilian and military radar stations and controls air defence fighter responses.[4] The NAOC is particularly busy since France has the highest air traffic density in Europe. Its radar surveillance data is shared with neighbouring countries such as the United Kingdom, Spain, Italy and Switzerland. The bunker is located outside the village of Poleymieux-au-Mont-d'Or northwest of Lyon. The radar tower and a covered radio antenna are located across the street from the main base in an old fort.

Mutzig

Perhaps one of the most secretive underground military establishments in France can be found outside Strasbourg. The French army had long been involved in signals intelligence, having, for example, an intercept station for several years on German soil at Landau until the mid-1990s. There, its specialists eavesdropped on the Czech armed forces since they knew that, should a third world war ever take place, Czechoslovakia would have invaded France. The French unit operating at Landau was the 44th Signals Regiment (44e Régiment de transmissions), and the base itself was called the Electronic Warfare Centre (Centre de guerre électronique, CGE).

In 1994, the 44th Regiment and the CGE left Germany for a new home at Mutzig west of Strasbourg. The Centre was established inside a hill and outfitted with state-of-the-art equipment such as Thomson-CSF receivers, along with air conditioning units, new offices and blast doors. The Regiment consists of eight companies, some of whose personnel either look for and record select transmissions, or decode and analyze the catch. These intercept operators are also trained in the fine art of jamming. Translators are assigned to the Regiment, and while knowing Czech was the norm during the Cold War, these days languages such as Serbo-Croatian, Arabic and Russian are in demand. The CGE's fixed equipment, which uses an automated search function, can intercept communications within a 5,000km circle, but it also has mobile ELEBORE equipment that has been used in Africa, the former Yugoslavia, and in the Middle East.[5] The Regiment's 'catch' is shared with its parent unit, the army's Intelligence Brigade, and with the Ministry of Defence's Military Intelligence Directorate (Direction du renseignement militaire).

Drachenbronn

A few fortresses on the Maginot Line were also used by the French armed forces during the Cold War. Fort Hochwald near Drachenbronn was chosen as the site of an air defence radar station in 1952 by the French Air Force, called Air Base 901. In 1957, the base became Master Radar Station 50/921, and three years later it took on another occupant, the No. 451 Air Tactical Control Group (Groupement de contrôle tactique aérien). In the 1960s, it was equipped with the Air Force's new air defence control and reporting system, the Système de transmissions et de recueil des informations de défense aérienne (STRIDA), and for three years until France's exit from NATO served as the 4th Allied Tactical Air Force's No. 4 Sector Operations Centre. Air Base 901 later became home to the Air Commando's Training Centre and to the Air Force's radar centre 05.901. In 1998, a Rescue Co-ordination Centre was formed there.

As a radar station, Drachenbronn has the primary duties of air surveillance and fighter control. The radar operators watch all aerial traffic in the area, attempt to identify unknown airrcraft through communications or by searching flight plans and if necessary will request the dispatch of Mirage interceptors from the Dijon air base for verification. To perform its functions, the centre uses, among other things, a three-dimensional ARES radar that feeds aircraft movement data (bearing, height and speed) into the STRIDA computer. This data is shared with four other radar stations in France in case unidentified aircraft cross air defence zones. In communications, Drachenbronn is known by the call sign 'Riesling'.

Other Facilities

Other Cold War underground facilities in France were:

- In Paris under Vérines Barracks at the Place de la République as an air defence Sector Operations Centre for the northeast of France. This was closed in the 1950s when Taverny was opened;
- At Metz. Fort D'Ars was used as the Royal Canadian Air Force's 1 Air Division Combat Operations Centre from 1960 to 1966;
- At Rochonvillers, in one of the old Maginot Line forts, 6 miles northwest of Thionville. Apparently this was converted into some sort of control centre in 1980 and used until 1998;
- At Grostenquin, at an old RCAF base, as an operations centre;
- Fort Fermont, again on the Maginot Line, maintained as a gunnery post until 1964;
- Fort Molvange, apparently used by NATO for some time;
- At Metz. A fifty-man underground shelter was built by Entreprise Travlor in 1960 for the RCAF's 61 Aircraft Control and Warning

Squadron. The bunker was located on the base proper at the Chateau de Mercy south of the city;

- At Fort Jeanne D'Arc outside Metz, as a NATO air defence control centre from the 1950s to 1966. A two-storey operations room was put in Caserne 4. After France's exit from NATO, it was used by the French air force for similar purposes until the late 1990s. It was known as 'Moselle Control';
- At Brest, at the naval base at Ile Longue on the south side of the harbour. These look like ammunition bunkers; and
- At Cinq-Mars-la-Pile, southwest of Tours. One of the air force's control and reporting centres, number 07.927, is located in an old cave that apparently includes several kilometres of tunnels.

Also, Arkin and Fieldhouse in their book *Nuclear Battlefields* claim that an underground command centre was planned at Air Base 103 at Cambrai. One cannot

The old air defence command centre in central Paris, ca. 1955. (Photo: Service historique de la défense)

confirm through Google Earth if this bunker was indeed built since the area covering the active part of the base is out of focus.

Missile Bases

For over twenty-five years, the French Air Force possessed eighteen long-range nuclear-tipped missiles as part of its strategic nuclear deterrent. The missiles were placed in silos in the south of France on the Albion Plateau east of the historic city of Avignon. On a twenty-four-hour basis, officers sat in two launch control centres preparing themselves for a war they hoped would never happen.

The nuclear bug had bitten France as early as 1945. That year, President de Gaulle ordered the creation of an Atomic Energy Commission to study the peaceful potential of the atom. Perhaps prompted by the detonation of an atomic bomb by Russia in 1949, however, senior government officers proposed that France consider developing its own nuclear weapons. Politicians accepted the proposal, and soon a government committee was created to study the issue. The committee decided that having such weapons was in France's best interests, and concluded that relevant research should commence immediately. As well, some French politicians thought that during a nuclear war, the United States would not move to protect France, and this thinking provided further impetus for the development of a French 'Bombe'. Paris agreed, and in 1956 it was decided that the AEC would act as the lead agency responsible for research and development.

While details on nuclear weapons were being debated in scientific circles, the government proceeded to build two plants that would manufacture fissile material: Marcoule produced plutonium and Pierrelatte, enriched uranium. The next step was to design weapons, and this the government did at a secret laboratory in an old fortress at Villeneuve-Saint-Georges, a suburb of Paris east of Orly airport. The AEC then went on to search for a site at which to test its first bombs. It settled on the French colony of Algeria in the Sahara at a place called Reggane, far from any civilization and hopefully out of reach of foreign spies. The first device was placed on a tower on 13 February 1960 and, with great trepidation, the engineers pressed the button. The 65 kiloton bomb created a blinding flash, a heavy shock wave and destroyed the tower. On that day, France had taken the first step on the path to becoming a nuclear superpower. Other tests followed.[6]

France would end up developing a number of nuclear weapons. The first ones were gravity bombs carried by Mirage IVA fighter-bombers. The second, however, would be a newcomer to the French arsenal. French scientists had been testing rockets for various uses since 1946, but it was only in 1955 that military officers looked at them as potential weapons. In 1958, a proposal was submitted to the Defence Minister to build a nuclear-tipped rocket large enough to hit Russia – by definition an IRBM – that would form part of the nation's deterrent force. The minister, Pierre Guillaumat, with the concurrence of de Gaulle, accepted the proposal and allowed the research to begin at once.[7] A new rocket testing base was built at Hammaguir, again in Algeria, and after several tests French engineers knew what they wanted. De Gaulle ordered the missiles ready by 1968.

The 1960s thus proved a busy time for the French military aerospace industry. The Evian Accord of 1962 forced France to abandon its testing sites in Algeria by 1967, so it sought and found another one on French soil.[8] Missile testing proceeded apace at the government's new Centre d'expérimentations aériennes militaires at Biscarosse in the southwestern part of the country. At the CEAM, specialists tested solid propellants and missile guidance systems using rockets fired from a test silo. Two missile variants were tried at Biscarrosse, the S-1 and the S-2, and in the end the latter, with a range of 2,750km and a 150 kiloton warhead, was accepted for production and deployment. Partly because of the move from Algeria to Biscarrosse, de Gaulle's wish for an active IRBM force by 1968 was missed by three years.

While tests were going on in the Sahara and at Biscarrosse, the French Air Force began planning its first missile base. It had been decided in 1964 that the operational unit, the 1st Strategic Missile Group (1er Groupement de missiles stratégiques) would possess 27 missiles and 3 launch control centres, with each LCC controlling 9 units, but this was changed the following year to 45 rockets

A blast door inside the launch control centre at Rustrel. (Photo: Author)

and 5 LCCs. For reasons of cost, political leaders later settled on 18 units and 2 launch centres. There would be no question of the actual missile emplacements being underground since silos provided much better protection than surface launchers. Survey specialists began combing France for suitable silo grounds, and after looking at such places as Savoy and Corsica, eventually chose the Albion Plateau in the south because its rock structure allowed easy construction. Army engineers and contractors arrived into the area in 1966, and five years later they had finished the silos, the two LCCs at Rustrel and Reilhanette, and a support base at St Christol that included barracks, messes, facilities for dependents, warhead bunkers and anti-aircraft gun sites (and later on a Crotale surface-to-air missile installation). Together, the structures would make up Air Base 200. The 1st SMG's first operational unit was Strategic Missile Brigade 05.200, but in 1985 this was renamed the 95th Strategic Missile Squadron. The 95th's support units included Special Technical Support Squadron 15/95 and Special Munitions Workshop 11/95.

The two launch control centres (Postes de conduite de tir) would be the most secure underground facilities in all of France. Unlike American or Russian LCCs, which are relatively shallow, the French control centres were set deep inside the plateau at the end of 1.5km-long tunnels. Their depth would protect them against an enemy missile attack, and the strength and security of their entrances would prevent intrusion or sabotage. The LCCs, including their access and escape tunnels, would take an entire year to excavate. They were surrounded by three barbed wired fences – the last one electrified – and equipped with surveillance cameras and guarded by mounted patrols. Inside, one was confronted by fearless Air Commandos and a reinforced door that had weapons

Part of the very long tunnel that leads to the launch capsule. (Photo: Author)

slits. There were also offices and decontamination showers. Staff and visitors travelled down the tunnel in heavy electric carts, being careful to negotiate the sharp bends that were created to channel away a blast wave. At the end of the tunnel, one entered a concrete capsule into which one found the actual launch centre, a small pre-fabricated box hooked in with shock absorbers. An escape hatch outside the capsule led upwards, but it could only be entered once the sand, put in to protect the vertical exit tunnel from nuclear blast-induced damage, was removed.[9] The Rustrel LCC was declared operational in August 1971 and the Reilhanette LCC, in April 1972.

At 88ft, the silos were not as deep as the launch control centres, but they were just as protected. The first thing a visitor noticed of their properties was, again, the three barbed wired fences. The first was harmless enough, but the second sported a capacitance system similar to that seen at Russian silos (i.e. one that registered the approach of any object). The third fence carried a low voltage to ward off unwanted guests, but it could be charged up during crises. Once inside the perimeter, one could recognize the 145 ton silo hatch as a system that moved on rails. Near the silo door was a metal trap door which, once opened, allowed a mobile maintenance team to tie into the silo's systems without having to proceed below. Around the silo tube below ground was a two-storey space that contained communications inputs to the missile, power equipment and access to the silo hatch mechanism. All silo properties were routinely photographed from a helicopter by security staff to see if any unusual changes had taken place. The individual launch facilities were at least 3km from each other. They were designated 1-x or 2-x (e.g. 2-7), indicating which LCC they were tied to.

Even entering a silo was a task in itself. Here, one could not do so without the co-operation of several individuals. First, a maintenance chief had to open a small metal door on the launching pad with a key that only he held. Then, a guard from the Nuclear Armament Security Police (Gendarmerie de la surveillance de l'armement nucléaire) had to open a second door with a combination. The group then proceeded to the silo entry portal, which itself took twenty minutes to unlock. Even after this delay, the door could not be opened without a launch officer in an LCC turning on the power. All these measures made it impossible for anyone to gain unauthorized entry.

The S-2's command and control system was predicated on the idea that it be used in a retaliatory fashion, in other words after the enemy had struck. It is for this reason that the silos, LCCs and communications systems were built to be highly survivable. For instance, the intersilo distance precluded destruction from a single missile, and the LCCs' depth, at 450m, almost guaranteed indestructability. A direct frontal attack on the entrance to the LCCs by a nuclear bomb would have been negated by:

1. The steel-reinforced 2m-thick concrete door outside.
2. The blast door in the anteroom.
3. The dog-legged tunnels.

4. Capsules that had 3m-thick walls.
5. The shock-absorbed command centres inside those capsules.

The LCCs ran on their own power and were equipped with standby generators. In addition, batteries lay under the command centres as yet another backup system.

It was made clear to everyone that ultimate responsibility for the use of nuclear weapons lay with the President of France, with the Prime Minister as backup.[10] The President constantly travelled with a military officer who would assist him in authorizing a launch if an enemy attacked. The officer did not carry a 'nuclear football', and the President would have issued the order and the authorization codes verbally from a position equipped with a closed-circuit television camera. From the President's location, be it Jupiter under the Elysée Palace, Taverny or Mont Verdun, the order would have passed through no less than ten communications systems, such as the:

Syracuse satellite network
Transfost system for the Navy
RA-70 military telephone network
EMP-resistant RAMSES digital communications system
Syderec backup system

The order to launch could also be relayed by Transall C-160H ASTARTE aircraft (Avion station relais de transmissions exceptionelles, or Special

One of the ways the French President could communicate attack orders to the 1st Strategic Missile Group was through the Vestale tropospheric scatter radio system. The antenna remains today. (Photo: Author)

Transmission Aircraft Radio Relay), by the special Tiger military telephone system, the Vestale tropospheric scatter radio system or even by civilian radio or television broadcasting. At the launch control centres, the President's order would have been received by TERTRE equipment (Terminal d'exploitation des réseaux de transmissions extérieures) or by special orange military telephones. The two young launch officers, a captain and a lieutenant, who sat in, to quote former missileer Eric Volontier, 'improved quasi-dental armchairs', would authenticate the order and start their checks and countdown. If one LCC was inoperative, the other could assume control over the entire missile fleet.[11]

No sooner had the S-2 IRBM been deployed in the late 1960s that military officers began pondering its replacement. French intelligence had learned that the Soviets had constructed an ABM radar and missile system around Moscow. The Air Force knew that its S-2s, which was designed before the letters 'ABM' even entered the lexicon of war, was susceptible to the new Russian defences. Engineers at the Société nationale industrielle aérospatiale, then the missile's manufacturer, were ordered to build a new IRBM that would, as a cost-saving measure, be placed into the S-2's silos. The new S-3 rocket was outfitted with improved penetration aids, its warhead hardened to resist the effects of an ABM blast as much as possible and it was given a greater range since it adopted a higher trajectory to limit its travel time (and the ABM's reaction time) in Russian air

An aerial view of one of the missile launch facilities on the Plateau d'Albion. (Photo: Service historique de la défense, Paris)

space. It also had a greater punch in that its TN-61 warhead was rated at 1 megaton, and was easier to maintain. The S-3 was equipped with a larger memory so that a greater range of targets could be entered. The new missiles were installed between 1980 and 1982. Further modifications were made a few years later, such as the further hardening of silos to enhance their survivability, causing a redesignation of the missile to S-3D.

Senior military officers knew that the IRBMs had a limited life expectancy. In the 1990s, some began planning for a new S-4 rocket to replace the S-3D, but world events would derail those plans. By then, the Cold War had ended, and President Chirac wanted to cash in on the peace dividend. Chirac announced in February 1996 that there would be no S-4 and that the 1st SMG would cease operations that September. Henceforth, he said, France would rely only on Mirage fighter-bombers and ballistic submarines for its deterrence.[12]

The missileers and technicians now began the long process of de-activating the missiles and closing the LCCs and launch facilities. Targets were erased from the missile's memory, launch keys were turned in to the 1st SMG's Commander, fences were removed and sites were emptied of equipment and cleaned up. The airmen would slowly vacate the St Christol base, and in 1999 it would be handed over to an engineering unit of the French Foreign Legion. The Air Force had considered turning part of the infrastructure into a museum, but a cost-benefit analysis revealed it was not feasible to do so. At least, the missileers were glad to find out that some of their equipment, such as a launch control panel, missile and special transport vehicles, would be preserved at the air museum at Le Bourget in Paris. All would not be lost.

Today, parts of the IRBM infrastructure can still be seen. The LCC at Rustrel is now a low-noise lab available to any company wishing to do research there. The blast doors and tractor vehicles remain, but the command centre is gone and the concrete capsule is empty. The other LCC sits abandoned. The silos were either covered with dirt or filled in. When the author visited the Rustrel LCC, he was warned that the St Christol base was still being used by the Foreign Legion (and also by a signals intelligence unit), and that visitors were not welcomed. Perhaps one day historians and visitors will be able to walk where few men had walked before.

❏ GERMANY

Continuity of Government

During the Cold War, the German nation was in the unenviable position of being located in the middle of a potential major war zone. For nearly five decades, both sides had thousands of troops ready and waiting to annihilate each other upon receipt of the proper signals. The Federal Republic of Germany (West Germany) and the German Democratic Republic (East Germany) were therefore replete with military installations of all types.[1] These were controlled not only by their own forces, such as the Bundeswehr in the West and the Nationale Volksarmee

(NVA) in the East, but also by other countries such as the United Kingdom, the United States, the Soviet Union, France and Canada. All this was, of course, in addition to the infrastructures of the two multinational military protagonists, NATO and the Warsaw Pact.

Realizing their mutual threats, both sides of Germany created installations that would have ensured the continuity of their respective governments. In the FRG, the government built a huge bunker in a 1910-era railway tunnel near the town of Ahrweiler outside the then-capital city of Bonn. Used by the Nazi government during the latter part of the Second World War to build V-2 rockets, it was converted in the 1960s into the republic's alternate seat of power to be used during a nuclear war. The 2.6km tunnel was modified to include several cross-tunnels that in the end would measure a total of 17.3km. This was enough to house 3,000 persons for 30 days, which is the length of time NATO estimated a nuclear war would last. Documents show that within 893,000sq ft, 879 offices lay on the ground floor and hundreds of sleeping cubicles were established on the second. The working and support areas included offices, communications centres, conference rooms, a television studio of the West German Broadcasting Network, a chapel, a barber shop, kitchens and canteens, five security control centres, power and air filtration rooms and a small private suite for the Chancellor. The installation was so huge employees working there had to travel on bicycles or electric carts. Every detail was looked after when the facility was built, from ashtrays nailed into the tunnel walls to a payphone to call loved ones. The complex was protected by a number of unique round blast doors, called 'RollTors', that each weighed 25 tons and that were closed electrically. Several emergency exits were also put in above. Officially, the complex was known as the 'Secondary Seat of Constitutional Government', but unofficially, it was simply called the 'Marienthal Office'.[2] The bunker was built between 1960 and 1972 at an estimated cost of 4.7 billion German marks.[3]

Communications was a key function of the bunker, and in this respect much

The current main entrance to the Ahrweiler bunker. (Photo: Author)

money was spent on equipment. This included radio transmitters and receivers, telephone and teletype machines, and crypto gear, not to mention the underground cabling. Some of the transmitters were placed at a remote location at Kirspenich, while other equipment was put in at Kesseling. At the Ahrweiler bunker, antennae were placed in the woods atop Kuxberg Mountain. If these aerials were ever destroyed, a collapsible antenna could be raised from underground to a height of 16m as a replacement.

The Ahrweiler bunker may have been unknown to the general populace, but to the East German secret service, the STASI (and by extension the KGB), it was an open secret. With the hundreds of workers employed to build it, it was inevitable that the Soviets discovered it through a slip of the tongue. Another way they learned about it was through sex. In the early 1970s, a government secretary, Margret Hike, caught the attention of an East German illegal agent, Hans-Juergen Henze. Henze approchard Hike and convinced her to turn over secret information to him for a supposed thesis on neo-Naziism. The information he sought included the West German government's mobilization plans and details about the bunker at Ahrweiler.[4] Enamoured, Hike complied willingly, and the data she provided to Henze was so valuable he received the Order of the Red Star for it. Somehow, the West Germany police learned of her treachery and arrested her in 1985. She was convicted and sentenced to eight years and fined 33,000 marks.

As with many other secret places in Germany, the Ahrweiler bunker was a victim of the Cold War's end. During the 1990s, the German government left Bonn for Berlin, and public servants and politicians decided the facility had outlived its usefulness. The initial plan was to seal the bunker permanently, but many citizens had become so curious about it that they asked that it be left opened. After its closure in 1997, the German government considered selling it, but none of the sixteen offers made were accepted. It was eventually sold to a private association that was allowed to keep 203m of it as a museum. The rest is now empty.

The Warning Service

The Ahrweiler bunker was only part of the German continuity of government programme. During the Cold War, the nation had an infrastructure in place that was designed to warn people of an atomic attack. Germany already had experience with such measures during the Second World War, and it only remained to equip cities and towns with new systems and to train an appropriate cadre of personnel for a new type of battle. A warning service known as the Warndienst was created in the 1950s as a branch of the Interior Ministry and was mandated to install methods of advising the citizenry of air raids – such as sirens and radio facilities – and to build control centres in the country's ten states.[5]

The system of attack warning followed the same basic pattern as in other countries. Military radar operators at Control and Reporting Centres detected enemy aircraft and reported their movements to air force Sector Operations Centres. In

Some of the original communications equipment remains in use at the Warndienst's bunker at Krekel, not for civil defence purposes but rather for broadcasting. (Photo: Author)

the SOCs, Warndienst personnel located in a nearby operations room would mark these aircraft on vertical glass maps. A leader would then decide whether to advise the service's control centres. Also, men and women positioned throughout the country would look for the flash of an atomic explosion or measure radiation, and report such instances to the nearest control centre.[6] Such events would influence the Warning Service's decision to turn on the sirens or to transmit public emergency broadcasts.

The Warndienst's bunkers were relatively small one-storey facilities measuring approximately 9,500sq ft. Their most important feature was their radio transmission and siren control equipment. The bunkers had their own generator and battery rooms, air ventilation equipment, decontamination showers, blast doors and an emergency exit. They also had an oil supply to power those generators along with a water supply for the personnel. Outside, one found a barracks-like building to house visiting guests and a high radio tower. At such places as the Krekel bunker, the main access was gained from the basement of the personnel residence.[7]

As with Ahrweiler, the entire network of nuclear watchers and warning bunkers were closed in the 1990s. All the bunkers were sold to private individuals or companies.

State Bunkers
As the Federal Republic of Germany was a federation of states or Landen, it was deemed prudent to build relocation sites for state politicians and public servants.

The entrance to the Urft bunker was cleverly hidden in this ordinary garage. (Photo: Author)

Such places would have been needed to allow them to continue functioning during or after a nuclear war. Each of the ten states had its own bunker, and all were well concealed from public view. The sites were underground, but unlike the Warndienst facilities, they did not follow a standard design.

The bunker at Urft for the government of North-Rhine Westphalia is described as an example. From the outside, the facility is barely visible. The bunker was put in after the ground was excavated, and then covered with dirt. Its walls were of reinforced concrete 3m thick. The entrance is hidden inside a non-descript garage that is situated at the bottom of a hill. Behind it, one sees

The bunker for the Rhineland-Palatinate state government was located behind a high school on Ernst Ludwig Strasse in Alzey. The two-storey facility is no longer used as such. (Photo: Author)

what seems to be a concrete-covered stairway leading into the hill. On top, one finds an antenna hidden in the trees, a small building that houses the air intake and an emergency exit hatch in the ground. Inside the 4-storey bunker were operational and eating areas, a generator room and air filtration centre, and enough supplies for 200 persons, although only 3 worked there in peacetime. While in operation, the facility was known by the codename K704.[8]

All these Land bunkers have been closed.

Non-military Bunkers

War preparations in Germany were such that key elements of the private sector were required to maintain alternate operational sites. Such was the case for the utilities, the hospitals, the railway service and the banks. The telephone company maintained bunkers for its personnel and also for a second telephone network to be used if the main one was ever disabled. The railway company, Deutsche Bahn, had approximately 1,000 hardened facilities to shelter its personnel and its signalling equipment. The local banks were also required to build bunkers to store cash reserves.[9] Shelters were also built for water treatment plants. As well, in wartime schools would have been turned into emergency hospitals. For this reason, medical equipment was kept in their basements throughout the Cold War.

Falkenhagen

One of the more interesting East German bunkers visited by the author lies outside the village of Falkenhagen in Brandenburg north of Frankfurt-am-Oder. The bunker is part of a complex of a dozen or so buildings originally built in the 1930s by the Wehrmacht's ordnance department. The facility was established to manufacture chlorotrifluoride, a reagent necessary for the production of the nerve gas Tabun.[10] The main production centre was placed underground for security and was outfitted with a railway line that ran through the top floor. Once the tank cars were filled, the trains would travel to another facility in Poland where Tabun was made. Later on, the Falkenhagen factory also manufactured the nerve gas Sarin. Built over a five-year period, the complex was only active from October 1944 to February 1945.

The Falkenhagen chemical plant looked like any other plant in Germany. It consisted of several buildings, a network of brick roads and railway lines. It was set deep in a forest, which to a photo-interpreter might have implied secrecy. On the other hand, it might not have seemed that important since it lacked anti-aircraft protection. Also, since the railway line that ran into the bunker was set in one of the brick roads, photo-analysts would likely not have spotted these. The factory required a large amount of electricity for production, but the incoming power lines were also cleverly camouflaged.

After the war, the factory was taken over by the Soviet army. From 1945 to 1958, it served as a vehicle repair depot and as a military hospital. There is also an indication that the bunker became the Soviet's main signals centre after they learned their communications in Berlin were being tapped by the CIA. In the 1960s, the four-storey facility was transformed into the Warsaw Pact's alternate headquarters. Here, officers from all Eastern bloc nations conducted exercises and kept the bunker in constant near-readiness condition. Its new role required a massive upgrade, such as the installation of new radios and office equipment, blast doors made of lead, sleeping areas and a two-level operations centre. Approximately 400 worked there. While the installation was buried in secrecy, local residents knew something was there as helicopters were sometimes heard entering and leaving the area.

One strange anecdote of the command centre was that all non-Soviet personnel were assigned offices in a caged area on the lower floor. This section was watched over by a Russian guard. Any time one of the allied officers wanted to leave the area, he had to be escorted by a Russian. The 'cageing' of these officers was either a sign of mistrust between Soviet and non-Soviet officers, or was meant to prevent the sharing of personal details that could have influenced Russian soldiers. For instance, when comparing the life of a Soviet army soldier with that of an East German, the East German had it good. So good that a Russian unit's political officer would limit contact between the two to eliminate the possibility of jealousy and resentment within Russian ranks. When Soviet troops visited East German mess halls, they were shocked to see how well their junior comrades were fed. At the officer level, though, this compartmentalization was not possible as several NVA officers were required to travel to the Soviet Union to learn Russian. And since the East German air force and air defence force were so deeply integrated into the Soviet-dominated Warsaw Pact's structure, they too could have contaminated Soviet personnel.

The Falkenhagen complex still stands today. Tours of the bunker were given for a while, but this no longer seems to be the case. The Russian army did not leave anything behind when it departed in 1992, except for one of the officer's bath tubs. Radios, desks and telephones were taken away, as was electrical cabling and even the light bulbs. Needless to say, the guides had to resort to the use of flashlights.[11]

Zossen

Another secret underground facility with an interesting history is found in another forest, this one south of Berlin at Zossen. As with Falkenhagen, it too was built in the 1930s and served the Third Reich, and then was occupied by the Soviet army.

The Zossen bunker was installed at a time of massive Nazi construction projects. Since the government's central telephone switchboard in Berlin was a target for enemy bombardment, the communications ministry was ordered to build a new telephone network of buried landlines and switching centres capable of securely relaying traffic for the military services. Zossen was chosen as the location of one of the network centres in 1933 and was opened just in time for the blitzkrieg attack on Poland in 1939.

The Zossen bunker, codenamed 'Zeppelin', was a two-storey L-shaped struc-ture that measured 105,000sq ft (per floor). The walls were 5ft to 10.5ft thick and the upper ceiling 10ft, with much of the structure covered with tons of earth. Unlike other bunkers, it was not a self-contained establishment – since personnel ate and slept above – and had only operating and equipment rooms such as a tele-phone exchange, a transformer station, battery rooms and a communications monitoring centre. The bunker was accessed from what looked like an ordinary country residence but which was, in reality, a concrete house within a house. To enter the bunker, personnel would literally drive into the house and proceed below, after which the chauffeur would drive away. Officially, the bunker was known as Project 500.

After the war, the entire Zossen base was taken over by the Soviet army. Highway 96, the main thoroughfare in town, was closed to the public. Red army troops moved into the old barracks, new buildings were erected and a training ground was laid out in the forest on the eastern side. The Zeppelin bunker was stripped of any useful equipment. There was an attempt to destroy it as per an agreement with the Allies, but the structure was so strong only a small part was damaged. The bunker lay unused for several years, until the Soviet's regional military entity, the Group of Soviet Forces in Germany (GSFG), decided in 1960 to use it as its command centre. Known by its codename 'Ranet', this is where all Soviet attack plans for West Germany were made. New power and filtration equipment was put in, rooms were changed and radios and telephones were installed. Some walls were taken down so that part of the complex could be turned into a pistol range. The bunker came into operation the same month the Berlin Wall was erected (August 1961), and remained in use until 1994.

Ranet was not the only bunker in the area as the Soviet air force's 16th Air Army and the Soviet air defence organization, the PVO, were collocated in another bunker about 200yd away.[12] The PVO section was used as an air defence operations centre that received inputs from all sources, such as radar and satel-

The entrance to the Group of Soviet Forces in Germany command post at Zossen. (Photo: Author)

This was the Soviet air defence operations centre at Zossen. Inside was a network of rooms that included a two-level operations centre. None of the Soviet equipment remains today. (Photo: Author)

lites, and that controlled fighter responses. The heart of the centre was a two-level room where air situation images were flashed from a projector located on the second floor. Other rooms in the facility contained offices, workshops and decontamination showers. It was opened in January 1985 and closed in 1994.

Today, these bunkers are open to visitors, but the tours are anti-climactic since none of the technical equipment remains.[13]

Air Defence Bunkers
On the western side of Germany, several underground installations were erected for the purposes of air defence. Working alongside the USAF and for a while the RAF, the Luftwaffe operated several radar stations and operations centres that would track enemy aircraft and that would guide fighter interceptors towards them. The warning and control network consisted, at various times, of several Aircraft Control and Warning Squadrons, Reporting Posts, Control and Reporting Centres (CRCs), Sector Operations Centres (SOCs) and Air Defence Operations Centres, many of which were placed in bunkers.

The German air defence network at first made use of a manual reporting system where all aircraft in a given area were tracked by radar operators at an AC&W Squadron and forwarded by telephone to a Tactical Air Control Centre. At a TACC, suspect aircraft would be marked on vertigal Plexiglas boards using grease pencils, and a decision would be made as to whether fighters should be scrambled to investigate them. In the early 1960s, this manual system was computerized under the USAF's Project 412L, whereas air defence data was now forwarded electronically from Reporting Posts and CRCs to SOCs. At an operations centre a projector used light valves to flash spots of lights that represented suspicious aircraft onto the vertical glass boards. These spots were then used to guide interceptors sent to meet them. SOCs in turn sent their data to their parent-Air Defence Operations Centres. In 1984, the 412L computers were replaced by a more modern German Air Defence Ground Environment (GEADGE) system, and this newer automation saw the closure of a few bunkers such as the Reporting Post at Burglengenfeld.

Some of the CRCs were located at Börfink, Brekendorf, Brockzetel and Freising, while SOCs were found at such places as Kindsbach and Uedem. Some of the CRCs and SOCs were collocated. Many of these centres had American, German and for a while French staff.

The CRC at Börfink is described here as an example. Built in the 1960s for the German and American Air Forces, the complex consisted of a radar site on Erbeskopf Mountain, a transmitter site on Ruppelstein Mountain, a receiver station on Sandkopf Mountain and the operations bunker near the town of Börfink, all of which were about 60km northwest of Ramstein Air Base.[14] The nerve centre of the four-storey bunker was a large room with rows of seats and consoles for aircraft surveillance and identification technicians and weapons controllers. A Master Controller sat at the back in a glass cage. In a separate section called the Missile Control Center, some personnel controlled American and German surface-to-air missiles. Some of the air staff belonged to either the USAF's 615th Aircraft Control and Warning Squadron or the Luftwaffe, while some radio personnel were assigned to the USAF's 2062nd Communications Squadron. One of the bunker's radio callsigns was 'Erwin', although it was also known by the codename 'Lima'. The bunker was capable of operating in a sealed condition as it had its own messes, dorms and power plant. In 1973, it was transferred to NATO, and four years later, it was made Permanent War Headquarters for NATO's Allied Forces Central Europe. Later on, NATO formed the Central Region Joint Operational Intelligence Center there. The bunker was closed in 1994.

One of the escape hatches to the bunker. The hatch was covered with a hut to prevent foreign satellites from seeing it. It provided good security by not having an external opening handle. (Photo: Author)

Kindsbach

One of the previously mentioned Air Defence Operations Centres was found in a cave located outside Ramstein at Kindsbach. During the Second World War, the cave was used by the Germany army as its Western Front Headquarters. After the war, it was transferred to the French army, but in 1953 it was given to US Air Forces in Europe and turned into its Combat Operations Center. It was closed after the end of the Cold War, turned over to the German government and sealed.

The Kindsbach ADOC occupied a series of tunnels that could be made self-sustaining in times of war. Inside were sixty-seven rooms that included messes, offices, dormitories, a ventilation room and power centre. The heart of the facility was a three-storey operations centre where specialists watched all aerial traffic over Germany and practised air defence operations. Senior officers watched the action below from a glassed-in balcony above the back end of the room. The facility normally counted 125 staff and measured 37,000sq ft.

East German District Bunkers

East Germany was divided into fifteen administrative districts (Bezirksverwaltungen). Each district had its capital and each was given at least one underground relocation site where local Ministry of State Security staff could hide during a nuclear exchange. The bunkers were completely self-sufficient and had enough food and water for 130 persons for a few weeks. Each had offices, an infirmary, a spartan dining area, a kitchen, a workshop, communications centre, power rooms and dormitories, along with an operations centre. Some of the offices were reserved for KGB advisers. In addition to serving as relocation sites, these bunkers acted as communications intercept sites. They were all located on the grounds of a country home as cover.

The main entrance to the Frauenwald bunker. (Photo: Author)

vThis fake lamp post was one of the air intakes to the bunker. (Photo: Author)

From the air, it would have been very difficult for spy satellites to spot the bunkers. At the Frauenwald site for instance – codenamed 'Trachtenfest' – the facility was hidden under a building that was painted in very non-military pink. The escape hatches were located inside small huts, and the air intake pipes were very well camouflaged as lamp posts (that never worked). The aerials were hidden among trees. One concrete entrance could be seen near the surface building, but it too was camouflaged. As the bunker was located on the property of a resort, the presence of several cars could have easily been explained as those of guests. Perhaps the only telltale sign of anything of military significance was the presence of a tiled concrete road from the resort proper to the pink building. Such roadways were common at East German and Soviet military bases.[15]

The locations of these STASI bunkers are listed in Appendix N.

Other Facilities
Some Cold War bunkers in Germany were at:

- Altengrabow, on the large Soviet army base. There was a communications bunker and an earth-covered SS-20 IRBM storage facility;
- Baden, at the Canadian Forces Base. The bunkers were personnel shelters;
- Baumholder. A computer facility at the US Army's Smith Barracks was put below in a 26,600sq ft facility;
- Berlin. A number of public shelters were built throughout the city, but these would not have been enough for all the city's residents. By 1989, the 13 shelters could house only 26,000 persons. Some were located below car parks, while others lay in undergound stations such as Gesundbrunnen and Pankstrasse. One bunker was put under the Excelsior Hotel, while another lay under Alexanderplatz;
- Bernau, north of Berlin. The former Second World War Kriegsmarine command post was used by the Soviets later on as Objekt 17/5020;
- Blankenburg. An NVA ammunition depot had 7km of tunnels. After the Cold War, it was used as medical stores by the Bundeswehr;

The teletype room.
(Photo: Author)

The East German
government's secret
building complex
outside Berlin at
Garzau. This
building sat atop a
key bunker. (Photo:
Author)

One of Garzau's
emergency exits.
(Photo: Author)

- Büchel air base. American nuclear bombs were stored in WS3 vaults under the hangars;
- Cochem, for the Bundesbank. Until the late 1980s, the bunker kept special currency called Series II that would have been used after an atomic war. The facility could house 175 for 2 weeks. It was located on the property of the bank's recreation and training centre, which was on a hill on the left side of the Mosel River;
- Feudenheim. Used by NATO's Central Army Group;
- Fischbach bei Dahn. One of many depots operated by the US Army's 59th Ordnance Brigade, the unit responsible for the custody of nuclear warheads in continental Europe. Fischbach stored and maintained Pershing missiles, Improved Hawk SAMs and Nike Hercules SAMs. The actual operating units located here were, at various times, the 41st and the 64th Ordnance Companies;
- Fürstenberg. The Soviets kept some R-5M missiles here for a few months in 1959;
- Fürstenwalde. The former Wehrmacht bunker was later used by the NVA. Known as Objekt 16/201;
- Garzau, 6km southeast of Strausberg. Erected between 1971 and 1975, the two-storey facility was built as a government computer development centre. The bunker could operate on a twenty-four-hour basis for fourteen days and was known as Objekt 17/206;
- Geltow southwest of Berlin. Hermann Goering's command post in Wildpark was used by the NVA during the Cold War as Objekt 16/103, and then by the Bundeswehr afterwards;
- Hamburg. Public shelters were incorporated in the new rapid transit system that was built in the 1970s;
- Harnekop, east of Berlin. The Ministry of National Defence's main bunker. Known as Objekt 16/102;

- Heidelberg, used by US Army Europe;
- Idenheim, for the Mace ground-launched cruise missile. The Mace used a W-28 warhead that had a 2 megaton yield. The base was used by the USAF's 71st Tactical Missile Squadron;
- Kossa, near Leipzig. The NVA built an underground command post for its Third District in the 1970s. May also have been a command post for the Warsaw Pact;
- Lauda. The postwar Luftwaffe operated an underground Control and Reporting Centre there until 2007;
- Linnich-Glimbach, used by NATO. The 6-storey bunker was completed in 1996 and can house 500 staff for 2 months. Codenamed 'Castlegate';
- Massweiler, used by US Army Europe;
- Memmingen air base. American B61 nuclear bombs were stored in WS3 vaults located under the hangars. The USAF custodial unit was the 7261st Munitions Support Squadron from 1973 to 1993, then the 605th Munitions Support Squadron from 1993 to 1995. (The base is now closed);
- Meßstetten. As of 1994, this was the location of NATO's new Combined Air Operations Centre-4 (CAOC-4). CAOCs use NATO's Interoperable Recognized Air and Surface Information System to provide a Common Operational Picture of all military forces and activities in the area, such as ballistic missile tracks, land and naval force locations, and air situations. The bunker was closed in 2008;

This was one of the US Air Force's Mace missile bases in Germany. The missiles were stored on launching ramps and fired after huge blast doors were lowered. A command bunker lay nearby. Today, the site seems to be used by a construction firm and sports a number of solar cells. (Photo: Author)

- Pirmasens. An earth-covered vehicle shelter can be seen beside Highway 10 east of the city;
- Prenden, north of Berlin. A three-storey bunker, known as Objekt 17/5001, was built between 1971 and 1976 for the East German Premier and his government. The 150 rooms included a conference centre, switchboard room, radio centres, eating areas, dental and medical rooms, isolation ward, air filtration stations and a map room. The bunker entrance was located in one of the surface buildings. The entire property was ringed with three fences, one of which was electrified;
- Pullach, outside Munich. The headquarters of the BND, the Federal Intelligence Service, was placed partly underground there. The base had been one of Hitler's bunker properties during the war;[16]
- Ramstein Air Base. An underground facility was used by the 3rd Air Force and now houses the 603rd Air and Space Operations Center. It is now used by NATO's Air Command Europe. Also, nuclear bombs were stored in WS3 vaults under the hangars at the airfield;
- Rittersdorf, for the Mace surface-to-surface missile. Operated by the USAF's 71st Tactical Missile Squadron;
- Rothenstein, as a large 3.2 million sq ft NVA supply depot south of Jena. Up for sale in 2010;
- Ruppertsweiler, used by NATO;
- Söllichau, north of Leipzig. Here, the NVA built 6 bunkers between 1969 and 1979: 4 for the staff, 1 as a communications centre and 1 as a command centre;
- Tessin, near Rostock. The East German navy operated its command centre south of the city as Objekt 16/001. It was located in the woods off Highway L18. The bunker is no longer accessible, although antenna masts, a ventilation shaft and an entrance can still be seen;
- Üdem, south of Kalkar. (Also spelled Uedem.) NATO underground air operations centre, also used for a while by the Luftwaffe's 3rd Air Division. Had at various times NATO's Combined Air Operations Centre-1, the 2nd Allied Tactical Air Force Tactical Operations Centre, a detachment of CAOC-2 and the Joint Airpower Competence Centre. Located northeast of the town, it is still in operation as CAOC-Üdem; and
- Wüschheim. A USAF Ground-Launched Cruise Missile base was built between this town and Kastellaun in the 1980s as Wüschheim Air Station. The operating unit was the 89th Tactical Missile Squadron. Also, a bunker exists on the hill north of the town.

Bunkers were also built at Nike Hercules surface-to-air missile facilities for storage or maintenance. Some of these sites were operated by the West German army while others were run by the Belgian and American armies. Until 1966, some were also operated by the French army. The US Army units were closed in 1984 and the Belgian and German units, in 1990. All the Nikes were nuclear-

A bunker of uncertain usage near Wüschheim. This may have been a control centre for a Nike SAM battery. (Photo: Author)

tipped. Most of the bases are no longer military properties and, indeed, some have no buildings remaining. One exception is Dexheim south of Mainz. It is still US Army property as the location of Anderson Barracks, home to the 123rd Main Support Battalion and the 501st Military Intelligence Battalion.

A list of ammunition depots with earth-covered bunkers can be found in Appendix O.

Scorched Earth Policy

Had the Soviets and East Germans attacked West Germany, the armed forces of the Federal Republic were amply prepared, with their American, Canadian and British allies, to counter them. The forces of the West counted a huge array of ships, fighters, tanks and surface-to-air missiles, not to mention well-armed stay-behind networks of spies and saboteurs. The Bunderwehr had another ace up its sleeve in its 'scorched earth' policy. This included plans to destroy roads and bridges that would have been useful to the enemy. Paved rounds were equipped with either small round pits or underground chambers in which, during a period of imminent war, soldiers would have stuffed blocks of cheese-like TNT and a detonator cord. At key moments, nearby troops would have set off the charges to crater the roads. The pits were covered with ordinary-looking manhole covers, and the chambers were accessed by a small door on the side of the road. The pits and chambers were inspected at least twice a year (until 1992) and kept clear of debris and dirt by a team of soldiers in civilian clothes who drove around in innocent Volkswagen vans.

Many key bridges were also built with their destruction in mind. When new ones were erected, small chambers were put underneath into which explosives could be installed. Again, when enemy troops would have neared, the bridges would have been blown up. Both the road pits and bridge chambers were marked on special maps called Sperrobjektkarteikarten which were kept by every local military unit.

Another way the Allies planned to stop Soviet troops from pushing westward was through the use of atomic landmines. One researcher uncovered documents at the British Public Records Office that outlined a 1950s plan by the British army to plant ten large landmines in Germany that would have been set off by timers. The bombs would have destroyed key facilities (e.g. power stations) and spread radioactivity throughout the area. The British went as far as testing the bombs – without the nuclear material – but never deployed them because they were too big, too heavy and because political and military leaders were afraid of the political fallout if the Germans had learned of the plan. The weapons were codenamed 'Blue Peacock'.

The BARS Bunker

The Warsaw Pact operated twenty-six tropospheric scatter radio stations throughout Eastern Europe as a system called BARS.[17] The sites made use of the troposphere to bounce military radio signals to other sites that were 300km away. Three of those stations were in East Germany: No. 301 at Wollenberg north of Berlin near Bad Freienwalde, No. 302 at Eichental 45km east of Rostock and No. 303 at Röhrsdorf near Dresden.[18] All had barracks, an earth-covered vehicle shelter, a communications bunker, tropospheric radio scatter antennae, barracks and guard house. The vehicle bunker contained trucks that kept an emergency supply of fuel to power the transmitters, along with spare parts for the antennae and a bulldozer to clear debris after a nuclear explosion. The Eichental bunker is described as an example.

Built between 1982 and 1986, BARS Station No. 302 was placed in a wooded enclave south of the village of Langsdorf. The small base consisted of the above-mentioned buildings and a two-storey communications bunker. The latter could

The entrance to the Eichental bunker and a vehicle shelter. (Photo: Author)

A Soviet air force hangar at the Finow air base north of Berlin. Earth-covered hangars such as these were as common in Eastern Europe as prostitutes in the red light district of Amsterdam. (Photo: Author)

accommodate about thirty-five persons in times of war. It had its own power generators and control centre, air filtration equipment, water supply, sleeping areas and the key: the communications centre that had high-frequency radios, telephone links and the tropospheric equipment. As all the gear and user manuals were in Russian, the East German staff had to be proficient in the technical aspects of the language. The facility had a number of 3.5 ton blast doors, the weight of which belied the fact they could be opened with one hand. While these were made mostly of lead, all had an aluminium lining at the edge that would not melt as readily as lead during a nuclear explosion.[19] The design of these underground stations was adopted only after being tested at the Semipalatinsk nuclear test site in Kazakhstan.

The three BARS stations ceased to be used when the Berlin Wall fell. While No. 302 remained in the hands of the Bundeswehr afterwards, it was permanently closed in 1992. Today, it is now a museum.

❑ GIBRALTAR

By all accounts, the Rock of Gibraltar must be the one mountain in the world that has the highest number of tunnels. Military leaders have long recognized the Rock as having strategic value since it sits along one of the busiest maritime thoroughfares in the world. Tunnelling began here as far back as the eighteenth century for troops defending the area against Spain. The Rock's military value increased immeasurably during the Second World War when the Germans moved south into North Africa, and even today, as a British Overseas Territory, it remains an active garrison state. Eventually, the secrets of its catacombs were revealed in such magazines as *Tunnels and Tunnelling* and *After the Battle* and now the public can get an idea of what is below.

A site map of Gibraltar reproduced in *After the Battle* shows how extensive the underground network was. The diagram identified several miles of tunnels along with their purpose. Some structures were used as magazines, while others housed long-range guns, troop accommodations and hospital facilities. There were also a gun operations room, communications centres, stores and workshops, along with offices for the cable company. Many of these were connected by vehicular tunnels, some of which were almost a mile long. Every structure had its own name that often came from senior officers who had been stationed there or that were borrowed from local landmarks. The tunnels were built primarily by the Royal Engineers (by such units as No. 3 Tunnelling Group) and by such units as No. 1 Tunnelling Company and No. 2 Drilling Company of the Royal Canadian Engineers.[1]

The tunnels and chambers under the Rock were built with the help of tons of explosives and the labour of hundreds of men. Gibraltar was the first place where military engineers used diamond drill blasting. Some tunnels were built at right angles with pockets (dead ends) designed to absorb blast waves. Many were built on an incline to allow water that had seeped in to drain out. For accommodations, buildings such as the common Nissen hut were erected inside caverns, and since the caves' high humidity would have led to quick corrosion, the huts were coated with bitumen. Other structures were concrete lined. Many of the tunnels that were regularly used by troops were outfitted with either an elaborate ventilation system or with a heating system to keep them dry.[2]

The end of the Second World War did not spell the end of Gibraltar's military role. Even today, it remains an important outpost for the British government.[3] The RAF retains an airfield there for visiting aircraft, and the Royal Navy operates a naval base, HMS *Rooke*, and an air station, HMS *Cormorant*. The army maintains the Royal Gibraltar Regiment, and the UK's signals intelligence organization, Government Communications Headquarters, operates a station there. More tunnels were built after the war, with Molesend Way finished in 1968. Some of the Rock's tunnels are now open to the public as tourist attractions.

❑ GREECE

Underground facilities in Greece include:

- A bunker called Tunnel 4 in Athens behind NATO's Eastern Mediterranean Command Headquarters;
- WS3 B-61 nuclear gravity bomb vaults under the aircraft hangars at Araxos air base. (Nuclear weapons are no longer kept on the base.) The bombs were for the Greek Air Force's 116th Fighter Wing, but were under the custody of the USAF's 7061st Munitions Support Squadron; and
- NATO's Combined Air Operations Centre-7 at Larissa air base. The bunker was built between 1999 and 2004, is EMP and NBC protected and

is certified to conduct nuclear operations. It receives air surveillance data from a number of Control and Reporting Centres.

❑ HUNGARY

Underground structures in Hungary include:

- Earth-covered hangars at several air bases such as at Kunmadaras, Halásztelek and Bankhaza (the latter two being south of Budapest). Some of the Soviet air bases in Hungary had an underground reserve command post called a ZKP, Zapasniy Kommandniy Punkt;
- An Air Sovereignty Operations Centre at Veszprem. The ASOC currently conducts air surveillance operations for domestic and NATO users;
- In Budapest, as Objekt F4, a large public shelter under Kossuth Lajos Place. The entrance was hidden in a large round building in a courtyard, and the bunker could hold 2,200 persons. It ceased to be maintained in the 1990s;
- A cave under Castle Hill in Budapest. It was used as a command post by the German Army in the Second World War, then as a nuclear shelter. Its entrance is on Szentháromsag tér; and
- At two locations in the forest east of Esztergom, both of which appear to be no longer in use.

❑ INDIA

Underground facilities in India include:

- A bunker for the Nuclear Command Authority, that is the political leadership that exercises control over nuclear weapons. The weapons are assigned to the armed forces' Strategic Forces Command. The bunker's exact location has not been revealed in the media, although it is suspected of being outside New Delhi;
- Shafts at Pokhran to test nuclear bombs;
- A bunker for the Prime Minister on the grounds of his residence at 7 Race Course Drive in New Delhi; and
- A bunker possibly under or near the South Block of the Parliament in New Delhi.

❑ INDONESIA

Several years ago, police in Indonesia chased 'millionaire playboy' Tommy Suharto (a relative of President Suharto) for a property scam. The BBC Online article started that Tommy Suharto was thought to be hiding in a bunker that may have been connected to eight other underground points in the city, including one to the President's house.

❏ IRAN

Underground facilities in Iran include:

- Several tunnels and complexes suspected of being used for the development of nuclear weapons. One is thought to be in a mountain near Qum;
- A uranium enrichment plant at Natanz 100 miles north of Isfahan; and
- A former CIA signals intelligence facility at Beshahr codenamed 'Tacksman I'. It was run by American personnel to eavesdrop on Soviet communications. Built into a hilltop, it used Scientific Atlanta Pedestal Model 310 receiving equipment. The station was closed in early 1980 after the Shah left Iran, and was soon replaced by new facilities in northwestern China.

❏ IRAQ

At some point in time, Saddam Hussein must have come to the realization that he was not a very popular individual. His attempts to develop nuclear weapons and long-range guns made him a marked man, and it was perhaps the Israeli attack on the Osiraq reactor in 1981 that convinced him he should take his own protection more seriously.[1] Saddam had already surrounded himself by trusted men of the Republican Guard, but when it came to his places of residence, he no doubt wanted to feel comfortable and safe. For this reason, his eight palaces were equipped with bunkers, strongholds that could resist the 'knock-knock!' of precision-guided munitions.

Saddam's most famous bunker was located in the grounds of his Baghdad palace. The subterranean facility lay directly under one of the yellow surface buildings and was accessed from the main lobby via a narrow stairway. Inside, there were decontamination showers, a state-of-the-art air filtration system, bedroom suites, conference rooms, diesel generators, along with a medical section stocked with such items as nerve agent antidotes and bins for radioactive clothing. The steel blast doors were 2.75in thick, and some of these led to escape tunnels that extended to the Tigris River. Since American forces were not able to destroy the complex, even with powerful 'bunker-buster' bombs, they have chosen instead to offer the occasional tour. Compared with his other palace bunkers, this one was the most elaborate.

Other hardened surface and sub-surface facilities in Iraq include:

- A network of tunnels and bunkers, large enough to be considered a small city, between Tepe Zardic north of Kirkuk and Taq south of Koi Sanjaq. It was first thought to have been constructed as an ammunition depot, and later expanded to include radio and television facilities, offices and living quarters;

- A large complex under the al-Tuwaitha nuclear research centre;
- Communications sites at Ad Diwaniyah, Dabnuni and Mamia. These were attacked by coalition forces in March 2003;
- A large bunker at Karmah, 50 miles west of Baghdad. The facility included its own offices, kitchen and showers, and was found by US Marines and Iraqi forces to contain miscellaneous ordnance and night-vision goggles;
- Earth-covered bunkers at Amiriya 34 miles west of Baghdad. The bunkers were on what was believed to be an abandoned test range, although American forces were perplexed to find traces of radioactivity there;
- A records vault under the Headquarters of the General Security Directorate in southeastern Baghdad;
- Bunkers at the Salman Pak biological warfare facility;
- A munitions facility at Al Yarmook;
- A bunker in the ruins of Ziggurat;
- A depot on the hills 10 miles east of Ramadi;
- A bunker under a steel mill east of Safwan;
- A complex under the power station at Nasiriya;
- A missile depot at the Um Qasr naval base;
- A bunker at Tigrit under the Hotel Rashid. This facility was connected to the congress centre across the street;
- An alternate national command centre at the North Taji military complex; and
- A fighter interception operations centre at Nukhayb.

❑ ISRAEL

Dimona

Ask anyone what is the most famous underground facility in Israel, and the answer will invariably be Dimona. The name Dimona has long been associated with power and secrecy since it is reportedly the nation's only nuclear weapons production centre. In this facility, a reactor produces plutonium – a necessary ingredient in a thermonuclear warhead – and precision machine tools are said to manufacture warhead components. For approximately thirty years, the public knew little about the secret little complex in the Negev desert.

In a small sense, Dimona may have been a by-product of the Second World War. A Jewish nationalist by the name of David Ben-Gurion had learned of the horrors perpetrated by the Nazis upon his fellow Jews when he visited the death camps of Germany after the war. The mass extermination had so marked him that he vowed to himself that such an event would never happen again. The same year he visited the camps, 1945, the United States dropped two atomic bombs on Japan, and some people theorize that the devices gave Ben-Gurion the idea that Israel should have the Bomb. After Israel achieved statehood in 1948, as its first Prime Minister Ben-Gurion could do something concrete about his dream.

Almost from the day it was born, however, Israel seemed a nation under siege. Her Arab neighbours had threatened to send the Jews back into the sea and had built up their armies in preparation for the inevitable conflict. Egypt, Syria and Jordan therefore conspired to work together to eliminate the small nascent state. Egypt had even gone as far as obtaining Russian weaponry through Czechoslovakia and importing German scientists to build ballistic missiles. The Middle East began to heat up when Egyptian President Nasser nationalized the Suez Canal in 1956 and when Israel invaded the Sinai. Ben-Gurion requested help from the United Kingdom and France to push the Egyptians back, and London and Paris agreed, only to be pressured into calling the joint venture off by the Americans and Russians. Despite the setback, the French–Israeli connection remained strong as ever and soon that link would take Israel down an entirely new path.

In all likelihood, Israel could not have developed her atomic bomb without the help of France. Some French politicians and civil servants related well to the Jewish people, perhaps because both had suffered under the boot of Nazi tyranny. France and Israel could also relate to each other since both had enemies in the Arab camp: Algeria in the former case and, as we have seen, Egypt in the latter. France sold millions of francs' worth of armaments to Israel for her defence, and as La République began to develop her own A-bombs, it shared the fruits of its labour with Tel Aviv. Some of those fruits included nuclear reactor technology and the knowledge to produce fissile material. From this knowledge sprang Dimona.

Set in the Negev about 40km east of Beersheba, Dimona would eventually become Israel's Los Alamos. In the 1950s, Israeli scientists travelled to Paris to learn the secrets of A-bomb design. At Saclay outside the French capital, these men learned about reactors, materials and instrumentation. They later returned to Israel and help set up a new laboratory under a heavy cloak of secrecy at Dimona. From this knowledge, and with French assistance, the Dimona complex blossomed into a network of buildings ringed with a barbed wired fence. Officially, it was known as a metallurgical research laboratory, and was even called a textile plant at one time by the government, but with so many people involved in the project, the cloak of secrecy turned out to be a thin veil.

Much of the internal workings of Dimona was revealed by Mordechai Vanunu, a technician who had worked there from 1977 to 1985. Employed as a control technician, Vanunu had a pass that allowed him access to the entire facility. He soon learned about the complex's true purpose, which was the production of plutonium and nuclear warheads. When Israel invaded Lebanon in 1982, Vanunu's outlook on his nation dimmed and soon he began planning a revelation of Dimona's secrets. After his release from employment in 1985, ostensibly because of budget cuts, he travelled aimlessly throughout the world.[1] He lived for a while in Australia, and there his desire for disclosure turned into action. He contacted *The Times* of London, told everything he knew and waited to see if the newspaper would carry the article. Since Vanunu had the foresight to take fifty-seven photographs of the plant and wrote many notes, the newspaper set out to confirm his story. After having done so, it published its article on 5 October 1986. Dimona now did not even have a fig leaf to conceal itself.

From Vanunu, the world was able to learn that Dimona conists of a number of underground sections. In one 'basement' spent uranium fuel rods are coated for re-use in the reactor, and in another, chemists analyze the purity of uranium.[2] The heart of the complex appears to be Machon 2. This building consists of a surface structure under which lie six floors. On level 3, for instance, are laboratories, while on level 4 stands equipment to extract plutonium from spent fuel rods. On level 5, the extracted plutonium is shaped into spheres for use in nuclear warheads. In three other sections, lithium-6, tritium and deterium, which serve as fusion fuels to enhance a nuclear explosion, are produced. These six levels are reached by a lift that is camouflaged in the surface building. The dirt around the entire complex is regularly scanned for sign of footprints, and security teams in nearby observation posts continuously watch over the compound. If Dimona was a textile factory, it has to be the most secure such facility in the world.[3]

The United States government had long suspected that the Israelis were up to something sinister at Dimona. Slowly, word filtered back to Washington that the little complex in the Negev might not be so innocent. Prime Minister Ben-Gurion had insisted that Dimona was not being used to make bomb materials and that Western media reports that suggested so were inaccurate. One of the cornerstones of President Kennedy's foreign policy was the non-proliferation of nuclear weapons, and when intelligence reports revealed Dimona's purpose, he insisted that inspectors be allowed to investigate the site. The Israelis eventually agreed to an inspection of the surface buildings, one of which was outfitted with a dummy control room. The American inspectors found no evidence of a weapons factory and concluded that the reactor served only peaceful purposes, never knowing that Dimona's true centre of power lay beneath their feet. The deception worked, albeit only briefly since nagging suspicions remained throughout the Johnson and Nixon administrations. All this would be rendered moot when Vanunu made his revelations in 1986.

Israel has never divulged whether or not it has nuclear weapons. In 1980, the CIA estimated that it may have only 20 to 30 such weapons, but physicists employed by *The Times* to check Vanunu's facts concluded that they may have as many as 100 to 200, based on the plant's output of plutonium. Scientists at American nuclear labs suspect that the Israelis have also manufactured neutron bombs. The Israeli government was so incensed at Vanunu for disclosing state secrets that it decided to bring him to justice. The Mossad was ordered to kidnap him so that he could stand trial in Israel. Lured to Rome by a female agent and then shipped by freighter across the Mediterranean, Vanunu was arrested once on Israeli soil and sentenced to a long prison term.[4]

The Dimona plant still operates today.

Missile Bases

Some of the bombs manufactured at Dimona were produced to fit on the Jericho-2 long-range missile. The Jericho-2 is a mobile system that uses a Transporter Erector Launcher and that is reportedly based, depending on sources consulted, on either the US Army's Pershing II or the French MD-620. Some scientists estimate the missile has a 5,000km range, but in the late 1980s the US Director of Naval Intelligence claimed the 2B model could fly only 1,500km. The Jericho-2 uses an American-designed terminal guidance system, called Radar Area Guidance, which uses radar to scan the terrain below and, after matching it with images stored in its memory, corrects its course. The missiles are said to be stored in limestone caves at Hirbat Zachariyah several miles east of Tel Aviv.[5] The cave entrances are protected by earth berms to prevent damages by bombs falling nearby. Before firing, the missiles would be taken out of the tunnels and driven to pre-determined launch points, either on the base proper or at points away.

Other Facilities

Other underground bases in Israel are:

- At Nevatim air base, as sand-covered hangars and a command post;
- At Hatzerim air base, as sand-covered hangars;
- At the Ministry of Defence's complex at Tel Aviv. The bunker is known as 'The Bor'; and
- In the hills outside Jerusalem, as a new government bunker. The multi-million dollar construction project took place early in the new millennium.

❑ ITALY

In Italy, the government has built a large complex 1,400ft under Mount Moscal a few miles east of Affi for NATO.

Planning for the bunker took place between 1958 and 1960, followed by construction over a six-year period. The 140,000sq ft facility was built to accommodate 400 persons for 14 days (in wartime) and came complete with offices, dormitories, security section, infirmary, power and ventilation rooms, along with an operations centre. It had a number of water reservoirs, and the internal air pressure was kept higher than outside to prevent contaminants making their way in. The bunker's heavy equipment was shock-mounted and, of course, the entire facility was protected by blast doors. Personnel entered by one of two entrances, called Alpha and Beta, and if these were ever inaccessible, they could always use the escape tunnel. Codenamed 'West Star', it was used by NATO's 5th Allied Tactical Air Force. It was closed in 2004 and then turned over to the Italian government.

Other underground installations in Italy include:

- Ammunition bunkers at the large depot at Longare. Known as 'Site Pluto', the US Army's 69th Ordnance Company kept nuclear weapons there for years. The depot is still in operation;
- Ground-Launched Cruise Missile shelters for a few years at Comiso Air Station on Sicily. The operating unit was the USAF's 487th Tactical Missile Wing;
- In the Santa Rosa section of Rome, one of NATO Allied Forces South's subordinate units, possibly known as HQ Central Mediterranean, is or was collocated with the Italian navy's command centre;
- Verona. NATO's Allied Land Forces Southern Europe had a bunker there. In 1999, the command was renamed Joint Headquarters South and the facility was allocated to it. It was closed in July 2009;
- Vicenza. A bunker there was used by the 5th Allied Tactical Air Force and by other units. It is also no longer used;
- At Casal Palocco, in the western outskirts of Rome, a bunker is seen on the north side of Via Cristoforo Colombo in a field;
- 4km northeast of Poggio Renatico. NATO's Combined Air Operations Centre-5 is located there in a new bunker opened in 1997. In 2004, the facility was outfitted with a new Air Command and Control System. CAOC-5's area of responsibility is Italy, the Balkans and Hungary. The bunker is shared with the Italian air force; and
- In Mount Petrino north of Naples near the village of Casanova (east of Mondragone), used by NATO's Allied Forces Southern Europe. This bunker is no longer in operation.

❑ JAPAN

Tokyo's Secret Underground

In the James Bond film *You Only Live Twice*, Agent 007 travels to Tokyo in pursuit of his arch-enemies in Spectre. After linking up with the head of the Japanese secret service, 'Tiger' Tanaka, Bond is taken for a ride in Tanaka's personal underground train. Tanaka explains that the train is necessary since it would be unwise for a man of his position to travel in the streets of the city. The concept of a secret underground rail system in Tokyo may not have been entirely fictitious since a Japanese journalist has unearthed circumstantial evidence that suggests it really exists.

It all started one day when journalist Shun Akiba bought a map of Tokyo in a used bookstore. The map showed two underground rail lines to be parallel, yet in a newer map they crossed. He wondered why the change. Akiba tried to look at construction records, but the walls of silence he confronted only fuelled his suspicion. He looked further at the map and at current plans, and found other inconsistencies. By digging further, he learned of a secret complex between the Kokkai-gijidomae section of the city and the Prime Minister's residence. Also, just by riding on the underground, for instance between the

Kasumigaseki and Kokkai-gijidomae stations, he found a branch line that was not shown on maps. Eventually, Akiba had gathered so much information that he wrote a book outlining his findings, *Imperial City Tokyo: Secret of a Hidden Underground Network*.[1] The book has done well, but for some reason it had a negative impact on his career as a journalist as no one seems to want to talk to him now.

Japan's Alternate Seat of Government
Japan's alternate seat of government appears to be located in a large bunker at the old Tachikawa airfield in the western part of Tokyo.

The airfield was orginally built for the Imperial Japanese Army in the 1920s. It was used during the Second World War, then by the US Air Force until 1977 when it was returned to Japan. The bunker, reportedly below the base's housing section, serves as the government's relocation site and includes a communications centre, dormitories, a hospital, an emergency operations centre and a cafeteria. Since its return to Japan, it has been enlarged to accommodate 5,000 for up to 1 year. Above ground, the base is used to store emergency medical supplies and equipment. Today, it is still used by the Japan Ground Self-Defence Force.

Civil Defence
The organization responsible for civil defence in Japan was first known as the Central Disaster Prevention Council. Established in 1961, it is an agency that reports directly to the Cabinet and that is mandated to prepare plans to meet all types of emergencies, be they natural or man-made. It is responsible for preparing and implementing disaster counter-measures, for planning the co-ordination of relief work and for establishing disaster headquarters.[2] Each city and prefecture is also expected to maintain an emergency management organ-ization, to be headed by the mayor or governor respectively. It is not clear if the current national emergency measures office, the Central Emergency Prevention Council is responsible for continuity of government programmes or for the operation of the Tachikawa relocation site.

Other Facilities
Other underground Cold War structures in Japan include:

- Caves on Chichi Jima Island that were used to store US nuclear gravity bombs and W-5 nuclear warheads used on Regulus submarine-launched missiles;
- Radar operations centres built for the USAF in the 1950s at such places as Unishima Island, Goto Island, Abashiri, Seburiyama, Tobetsu and at the Asoiwayama Air Station north of Sapporo;
- An air defence operations centre at the Itazuke Air Base in Fukuoka located under what used to be an officers' mess;

- A complex eight stories deep under the Diet's library;[3]
- Old underground aircraft hangars at the Atsugi naval air station;
- USAF aircraft hangars near Fukuoka airport;[4]
- A personnel shelter dug into a hillside at Ashiya Air Base;
- Nike surface-to-air missile magazines at Yozadaki on Okinawa;[5]
- A communications facility at the Yozadaki missile site. This may also have been an operations centre for the US Army's 30th Air Defense Artillery Brigade;
- Nike magazines at Naganuma-Cho;
- The operations centre of the Kamiseya Naval Security Group Activity;[6]
- A USAF Air Defense Control Centre in Stillwell Park at Kadena Air Base on Okinawa; and
- A Japanese Air Self-Defense Force Direction Centre at Naha Air Base on Okinawa. This is located on the east side of the aerodrome.

❑ KAZAKHSTAN

Stepnogorsk

To people in the Western intelligence community, the mere mention of the name Stepnogorsk raised alarm bells. This was because in the early 1980s, the small uranium-mining town would host one of the deadliest military factories in what was then the Soviet Union. The factory was erected at a time when tensions between the two superpowers were high, and the products were just as lethal as nuclear warheads.

Much of what the West has learned about Stepnogorsk has come from two Soviet scientists who defected. Major Ken Alibek had been chosen by Moscow to manage the factory because of his training in microbiology and epidemiology and because of his recent experience in germ warfare at secret labs at Omutninsk and Berdsk in Russia. Alibek had learned that one of the deadliest germs known to man, *Bacillus anthracis*, had for years been produced at a secret facility in Yekaterinburg called Compound 19.[1] But when Compound 19 suffered a leak of the bacterium into the environment and people began dying, world attention was focused there. Clearly, the production of *Bacillus anthracis* could not continue at Yekaterinburg, so Soviet Premier Leonid Brezhnev ordered a new production line be established at another biowarfare facility. Enter Stepnogorsk, and enter Alibek.

Major Alibek's orders were clear: Stepnogorsk would be geared for the mass production of anthrax.[2] Out of the barren land of the area would rise a series of tall buildings that would ultimately employ tens of thousands. The property was cleared of trees for security, labs, apartment buildings, schools and shops were erected and the entire area was ringed with a high-security fence and equipped with motion sensors. To any curious onlooker, the factory produced pesticides and fertilizers, which indeed it did but in another part. Officially, it belonged to a private firm, called Biopreparat, which specialized in vaccines, but unofficially it was the property of the Ministry of Defence's 15th Main Directorate. Biopreparat and the MoD were more interested in producing weapons than manufacturing cures.

One of the key buildings at Stepnogorsk was No. 600. The large building housed an explosion test centre and animal research laboratories, as well as a vault to hold an inventory of the anthrax germ and some deadly viruses such as Ebola. In another section, strains of the anthrax bug were developed, and much tested, the most potent turning out to be type 836. In Building 221, huge fermentation vats each held 20 tons of anthrax slurry that could yield 300 tons of spores every 220 days. Every now and then, Stepnogorsk's scientists travelled to Vozrozhdeniye Island in the Aral Sea to conduct field trials. Once the bacteria in Building 221 were ready for weaponization, they were sent down pipes into a nearby bunker that contained a bomb assembly line. The bombs were filled, transported to a storage area in the bunker, and left to wait until needed. The Stepnogorsk anthrax factory was said to be, to quote Ken Alibek, as efficient as 'producing . . . Coca-Cola'.

Once the Cold War ended and the Iron Curtain was raised, former Soviet Socialist Republics such as Kazakhstan were granted independence. The Kazakh government had no need for weapons of mass destruction, so it closed missile bases, returned nuclear warheads to Russia and shut down Stepnogorsk's germ factory. Even closing the complex, or making it impotent, cost money, and this is where the United States government stepped in. The US Congress appropriated funds to dismantle the facility and to help convert it for peaceful uses. New ventures failed to mature, however, and slowly the factory's population dwindled. Today, the town remains a mere shell of what it once was.

Semipalatinsk

Kazakhstan had also long been the Soviet Union's prime nuclear testing site. The then-Soviet Socialist Republic had been chosen as far back as the 1940s to test atomic weapons because of its low population and because of its remoteness. The Soviet government established Object 905 there as proving grounds using the innocent title of 'First Mining Seismic Station' in 1947, but two years later it would become a Ministry of Defence training ground, and yet later the State Central Scientific Research Test Area No. 2. Overall, the complex would consist of several vertical shafts and horizontal tunnels where, over a 40-year period, over 400 underground tests would be performed.

The tests at Semipalatinsk were conducted in a large massif called Degelen Mountain. A total of 181 tunnels were excavated in the mountain with lengths that ranged from 1,100ft to over 3,200ft and with cross-sections of approximately 90sq ft to 260sq ft. They all had a vertical horseshoe shape, and most were reinforced with either wood or steel beams. A few were lined with concrete.

Initially, however, the atomic bombs tested at Semipalatinsk were fired off on the surface. The first test took place on 29 August 1949 under the codename 'First Lightning'. The 20 kiloton device was so strong it vaporized the tower upon which it rested and created a large crater underneath. Several more tests followed in the ensuing years, but after the Limited Test Ban Treay was accepted by both the United States and the Soviet Union in 1963, all testing moved underground. Hence the tunnels.[3]

The last test to be conducted at Semipalatinsk took place in August 1989, and the testing site closed on 29 August 1991, forty-two years to the day of its first detonation. The United States wanted to ensure it would never be re-activated, so it forged an agreement with the new Republic of Kazakhstan to seal the tunnels permanently. To close the tunnels, engineers began by removing supports, where feasible, and then setting off charges inside the tunnels. They continued by sealing them with concrete plugs, backfilling with rock, and grading to match the local topography. By 2000, the last tunnel was closed forever.

Today, passers-by (if any) would never know the awesome power the area once saw.

Missile Bases
Until the 1990s, Kazakhstan also included 104 SS-18 ICBM silos. These silos were at Derzhavinsk and Zhangiz-Tobe.

❏ LATVIA

The Soviet armed forces utilized 850 properties in Latvia during the Cold War. As in Estonia, these included air and naval bases, radar stations, missile bases, radio sites and various depots, not to mention the Skrunda ABM radar site (now destroyed) and the Ventspils satellite tracking station (now abandoned).

Some underground facilities in Latvia were:

- In Riga, as either a public and government shelter on Radio Street near the railway station;
- In Riga in Grinzikalns Park, formerly an army bunker, now a data centre;
- At two locations near Zeltini for missiles, one that had earth-covered shelters and a possible command post off Highway P34 west of the town, and the other with silos off the same highway west of Strautini, both belonging to the Strategic Rocket Forces as Unit 11664;[1]
- For the Soviet air force's 27th Air Army Headquarters at Mucenieki outside Riga;
- At Kadaga near Ādaži, east of Riga, as an air defence operations centre and for the Baltic Military District Headquarters;
- At Ogre, for the communist party;[2]
- Missile silos southwest of Vibini south of Skrunda;
- As missile shelters outside the towns of Valka and Bārta;
- As missile shelters near the town as Zālite and also near Klāvi, west of Iecava;
- Under an apartment building at 11/13 Graudii Street in Liepāja; and

- Near Lambārte, as SS-4 missile silos used by the SRF's 307th Missile Regiment.

One of the bunkers visited by the author was outside the town of Litgane. The facility was built for communist party functionaries of the Latvian Soviet Socialist Republic and civil defence staff in 1968, and placed under a resort where party officials would drop in on weekends to drink themselves silly. Its location was chosen because it was far enough away from Riga to avoid destruction, yet still close enough to be quickly accessed by helicopters and cars. The facility operated under the cover name of 'Pension House'.

The bunker lay only a few feet under the resort. Its walls consisted of 5.5ft of sandwiched concrete and lead that provided good protection against nearby blasts. To gain access inside, a visitor had to utter his name and a password into an intercom. Once inside the single-storey facility, the guests would be taken to their area of operations, be it an office, telecommunications centre or power plant. The bunker included an operations centre for civil defence staff, an alarm room that received signals from warning points throughout the country, a canteen, emergency broadcasting studio, decontamination area and enough food reserves for a three-month stay. [3] To communicate with the outside world, it used a phony television transmission tower at Sigulda. The KGB handled all incoming telephone calls, and on a tour of the bunker it is explained that when a civilian called from the outside, the operator would ask a lot of questions to the caller, and if he was not satisfied that the call was necessary, he would advise the inquirer that the phone number did not exist!

Since the bunker also acted as a civil defence control centre, it contained an operations planning room. The room contained maps for every function such as

An entrance to one of the public civil defence shelters in Riga. (Photo: Author)

An emergency exit at the communist party bunker at Litgane. (Photo: Author)

fire and transportation. Staff here would have managed the nation's food supply and would have implemented fuel rationing. Other staff would have tracked radioactive fallout by communicating with emergency staff that were located in special posts across the country. In another room nearby, an alarm information system was established to receive inputs from remote bomb sensors. It operated

Communications equipment at the Litgane bunker. (Photo: Author)

equipment that was once used at a missile launch control centre and that still had 'ПУСК' (launch) indicator lights.

Other rooms in the bunker included a suite for the communist party boss, a small library stocked with Soviet newspapers and the works of Karl Marx, and common men's/women's toilets. The power centre contained two 200kW diesel engines.[4] The motors' exhaust was connected to the resort's exhaust so that satellites would not be able to detect separate sources of heat. In another room skimpily furnished with cheap furniture, a Soviet flag and a record player, awards were presented to deserving personnel. The KGB occupied rooms 6, 7 and 8, where 6 was a crypto room equipped with protected equipment and 7 was a communications monitoring centre. The bunker also had three emergency exits.[5]

Outside, one found helicopter landing pads, an air shaft and an antenna mounting base. The base was placed between small trees, again, to make it invisible to passing satellites. Today, part of the bunker is still inaccessible to visitors as it can be used for civil defence purposes.

❑ LESOTHO

A bunker was apparently found by South African troops several years ago at the Makoanyane military base in the eastern Maseru district of Lesotho. The facility was said to be a large warren of rooms for operations, power generation and communications, and was also outfitted with decontamination equipment. The presence of luxury suites suggested it was reserved for the President and his Cabinet. Outside, one could only see entrances, ventilation shafts and escape hatches.

❑ LITHUANIA

Underground structures in Lithuania include:

- An emergency radio and television bunker deep in a forest about 15 miles north of Vilnius east of Naujasode. This was built in the 1980s. It is now a tourist attraction where visitors can briefly live through Soviet times;
- A bunker on the north side of Kaunas airport, used as a NATO Regional Air Surveillance Coordination Centre;
- An SS-4 Dvina missile silo complex in Zemaitija National Park north of Plunge at Plokščiai;
- Missile shelters on the south side of Kaunas' airport at Karmelava;
- Missile shelters at Ukmerge; and
- A series of bunkers in a fenced compound on Topoliu gatve in the Kumpiai section of Kaunas.

❑ LIBYA

Some people have suspected that Libya has maintained two underground chemical warfare facilities at Sebha and Tarhunah. This has not been confirmed by the author.

Other underground facilities include:

- Sand-covered hangars at air bases; and
- President Gaddafi's bunker under his palace outside Tripoli near al-Baida.

❑ MALAWI

Several years ago, a bunker was built in Blantyre under the presidential palace.

❑ MONTENEGRO

The entrance to what seems to be a underground naval base is seen in Boka Kotorska Bay.

❑ NETHERLANDS

During the Cold War, the Dutch government created a civil defence organization, the Bescherming Bevolking, and an elaborate system of control centres. Some of these command posts were placed in purpose-built structures, while others were located in old forts. The national control centre was established in an old nineteenth-century bunker, Fort Lunet I in Utrecht, and every province and municipality was given its own facility. Some bunkers were also built to shelter employees of the canal system, while others acted as emergency military hospitals.

Underground facilities in the Netherlands include:

- Civil defence control centres in Hengelo, Middelburg and Venlo;
- Hoensbroek. NATO Allied Forces Central Europe (AFCENT) HQ was located in an old mine;
- Brunssum. Location of another AFCENT command post;
- Volkel Air Base. Satcom bunker;
- Noordwijk, for the Royal family;
- Kloetinge, built by the Dutch Ministry of Defence in the 1950s as a four-level structure. Used by NATO until 1996 and became a private data centre afterwards;
- Olst, an underground hospital in a forest. Now a museum;
- Woensdrecht Air Base. USAF GLCM base in the 1980s. The operating unit was the 486th Tactical Missile Wing. It was activated in August 1987,

but disbanded in September 1988 because of the acceptance of the INF Treaty. While the missile shelters were built on the south side of the air base, the missiles themselves were never deployed there;

- Driebergen. Royal Dutch Air Force air defence operations centre used until November 1991. Codenamed 'Caesar';
- Bodegraven. Part of Fort de Wiericker was used as a communications centre by the Dutch Army in at least the 1970s; and
- While the Dutch armed forces used Nike surface-to-air missiles, these were not stored in underground magazines.

❑ NEW ZEALAND

The New Zealand government has established a national civil defence headquarters in the basement of the Parliament Buildings in Wellington. The government apparently does not have a remote secure facility like Mount Weather.

❑ NICARAGUA

In Managua, a bunker exists under the presidential palace.

❑ NORTH KOREA

Military Bunkers

By all accounts, it appears that North Korean government leaders have learned several things from their socialist comrades in China and the Soviet Union. When President Kim Il Sung travelled to Beijing in 1966, he had a chance to visit part of the city's underground rail system that was then under construction. Upon his return, he ordered the creation of a similar system for Pyongyang, but seemingly one geared more for the city's defence rather than for public convenience. While some underground routes were indeed designed for public usage, others were established to transport political and military officers to and from secret locations. As well, the stations were all outfitted with blast doors clearly implying their use as civil defence shelters.

Partly thanks to defectors, the West has been able to learn a few details about the Pyongyang metro. First, the underground rail system travels to a number of military facilities in and around the city. Second, an extension to Mangyongdae was (or is) considered, perhaps because senior military officers want a connection to a reported nuclear command post there. Third, the stations are very deep, giving them that much more protection from an aerial bombardment. Fourth, an underground command post at Mount Chidang in the Sosong district is already accessible by the underground rail system. And fifth, an underground road apparently connects Kwangmyong Station to Sunan airport and the Kumsusan Memorial Palace. The link to the airport is necessary if the President wanted to escape the capital. It appears that the use of the underground rail system by the public seems to have been only a secondary consideration.

The underground facility in Sosong was described in some detail by Lee Kyo Kwan in Chosun.com. This bunker was said to be huge. Close to Anhak-dong near the Rakwon Station in east Pyongyang, it is an underground square that could accommodate 100,000 persons. It is also a command post for the People's Armed Forces. Built in the 1970s, the facility had (then) modern communications and a large parking space for troop trucks. But its methods of entry were not described, and whether the facility was connected directly to Rakwon Station was not specified.

Nuclear Weapons

North Korea's nuclear ambitions were another reason underground facilities were built. Influenced by the detonation of an atomic bomb in China in 1964, President Kim Il Sung decided then that he wanted his own nuclear devices. Such weapons, he thought, would surely have enhanced his image on the world scene. Kim approached Chinese Chairman Mao for assistance in the development of these status symbol weapons that all the superpowers had, but was rebuffed, on no less than two occasions. At roughly the same time, the President had heard that South Korea was considering her own A-bombs, and this fact further pushed him into action. Kim finally succeeded in obtaining one low-power research reactor from the Soviet Union and set up a plant at Yongbyon about 45 miles north of Pyongyang to house it. The reactor, he knew, was necessary for the manufacture of fissile material such as plutonium. Kim then ordered his scientists and engineers to get to work so that he could tread the path to nuclear glory.[1]

The Yongbyon facility really began attracting the CIA's attention in the 1980s. The agency, not to mention the White House, wanted to know what was going on there. It had few in-country assets to rely on, but thanks to photo-analysts and other specialists, it was able to make several deductions. The agency learned that one particular building might have been designed as a reprocessing plant, one that could extract plutonium from spent fuel. This worried the International Atomic Energy Agency who was committed to limiting the spread of nuclear technology. The CIA had no right to walk into North Korea to inspect any facility, but the IAEA, as a UN agency mandated to prevent the proliferation of nuclear weapons, could insist upon having a look. Concurrently, several countries, including Russia, China, Japan and South Korea, pressured Pyongyang to accede to the IAEA's request, and in 1992–93, the agency was finally granted access.

It appears, however, that there was little underground activity at Yongbyon. Hans Blix, director of the agency, visited large caves under a hill there that turned out to be empty. Whether any kind of equipment or material was removed in time for the inspection is not known. US intelligence had later learned that the Hermit Kingdom had built a uranium refinery with the help of Pakistan, not at Yongbyon but at two other locations, and that a heavier reactor was put in at Taechon. Eventually, North Korea admitted to having produced plutonium and having designed nuclear weapons, and this was confirmed years later when it conducted its first underground test on 9 October 2006.[2]

What worried the West even more was that North Korea also had manufactured its own long-range missiles, the Taepodong-1 and Taepodong-2, which were robust enough to carry nuclear warheads. Developed with the help of China and Iran, the missiles had enough range to hit targets in Japan, with the second model suspected of having enough fuel to reach even Alaska and Hawaii. There are even indications that a third variant, which would consist of three stages, could hit the continental United States.[3] It is these missiles that have provided the impetus for the United States to establish a missile defence system. North Korea continues its nuclear research to this day.

Other Facilities

According to the US Department of Defense, the North Korean armed forces are the fourth largest in the world. The country spends approximately 25 per cent of its Gross Domestic Product on defence, and requires all males 17 and over to serve in either the army, navy, air force or special operations force for a number of years, first on a full-time basis, then as a member of the reserves.[4] The four services belong to the Ministry of People's Armed Forces and count 1,200,000 active troops (with 5,000,000 in reserve), which implies a huge military infrastructure.

The Korean Institute for Defence Analyses claims the North has over 8,000 underground military facilities. These are built by the Military Construction Bureau of the Ministry of People's Armed Forces, and likely consist of command centres for every military unit, communications stations, troop hideaways, storage depots and air operations centres.[5] Some underground installations that have appeared in the media include:

- A munitions factory at Kagamri in Pyongan Province. The factory was said by defector Ko Young Hwan to produce missile engines and other military hardware;
- Several other military factories;
- A missile base in Hwadae County in North Hamyong Province. This base houses Taepodong missiles, but it is not clear precisely how the missiles are stored;
- Another missile base at Okpyong in Kangwon Province;
- Tunnels for small naval ships at various places;
- Artillery emplacements;
- Bunkers at the Musudan-ri missile testing facility;
- Twenty tunnels that ran under the De-militarized Zone, some built as far back as the 1970s. These were suspected of being infiltration routes into South Korea;[6]

- A nuclear testing site at P'unggye in the east near Kilju;[7]
- Air bases with mountain hangars at Sunchon, Wonsan, Iwon, Orang and possibly at other places;
- A command centre at the foot of Mount Baekdu near Samjiyeon;
- Earth-covered hangars at the Koksan air base;
- What seems to be a single air strip that goes through a mountain south-west of Wonsan; and
- Missile development labs.

One source has revealed to the author that a bunker also exists somewhere north of Pyongyang to store gifts to the President.

If the KIDA is correct, the above list represents a very, very small fraction of the total number of underground bases.

❏ NORWAY

Norway is another country replete with underground bases. The Nordic nation has taken the survival of its people, its armed forces and its leadership as seriously as have Sweden and Switzerland, and this policy has led to the construction of all sorts of structures. Public shelters were built in every city, bunkers were erected for every level of government and several protective installations were built for the armed services and for the utilities. In addition, the Norwegian government has developed a well-organized civil defence infrastructure to help guarantee the continuity of its society.

Military Bunkers
With respect to the armed forces, there were at one time about 3,000 underground facilities. These were built for all branches of the Norwegian military, as well as for the United Kingdom, the United States, the Netherlands and Germany, by the Norwegian Defence Construction Service. When addressing a workshop on underground facilities in the United States in 1998, Arnfinn Jenssen of the NDCS revealed that defensive missiles could be hidden below ground, and that coastal surveillance is practised through retractable antennae and cameras. With so many bunkers in Norway, one may assume that every military base and station has some kind of protective structure. While few are ever revealed in the press, the following are known:

- The Norwegian armed forces Regional Headquarters North Norway has its command centre at Reitan a few miles east of Bodø. NATO also operated its Combined Air Operations Centre-3 there until 2008;
- The armed forces have a bunker in Mount Jåttå in south Stavanger. The Germany Army began building the bunker in 1943, and the Norwegian government finished the job in 1950. It was then occupied by the Air Force and by the Navy. The armed forces' Defence Command South occupied

the facility as of 1987 when it relocated from Oslo, and in 2002 it became the National Joint Headquarters. NATO located one of its sub-commands there in 1994, and as of 2003, it was used as NATO's Joint Warfare Centre;

- The Norwegian armed forces' Defence Command South was located in a bunker at Holmenkollen outside Oslo until 1987 when it moved to Mount Jåttå. The bunker included an air defence operations centre;
- The Royal Norwegian Navy's main base southwest of Bergen, called the Haakonsvern naval base, is inside rock. The base includes a unique underground torpedo launching facility for its protection. The torpedoes are launched down ramps and into the water;
- Nike surface-to-air missile sites such as at Asker and Trogstad have an underground component;
- The Bardufoss, Bodø, Evenes and Andøya air bases have earth-covered hangars. (The Evenes base is closed);
- The Bodø air base had one hangar cut into rock and one bunker at the west end of the airfield;
- On the eastern side of the Ørland air base, one sees bunkers and earth-covered hangars;
- An old Second World War coastal defence site, Karvag Fort, continued its role in the Cold War. It is now a museum looked after by the Defence Estates Agency;
- Another old coastal artillery battery, in the city of Kirkenes, was used as a civil defence bunker during the Cold War. It is also now a museum;
- A few caves are used to store American, Canadian and German war materiel under such programmes as the War Reserve Stocks for Allies and for the US Marine Corps' Norway Air Landed Marine Expeditionary Brigade. Such caves are at Bjugn and Osmarka. The Osmarka cave, 5km east of the Evenes air base, kept a mobile American field hospital until 1991;
- The Royal Norwegian Air Force's radar stations and Sector Operations Centres are probably underground. Radar stations exist (or existed) at Sorreisa, Kautokeino and Honninsvaag, and SOCs were at Reitan and Maakeroy near Oslo. The RNAF also used a number of Reporting Posts; and
- NATO's HQ Allied Forces North at Kolsås outside Oslo most likely includes an underground component.

National Bunker

From the all-knowing Internet, one learns that the Norwegian national government bunker is located near the small town of Hole on the eastern shore of Lake Tyrifjorden about one hour west of Oslo. The bunker, known as the Sentralanlegget (Central Facility), was built to accommodate 600 persons for months. Its residents would include the Prime Minister, his Cabinet, selected civil servants and the Royal Family. The facility has two entrances that lead to a network of offices, hospital, communications centre, dormitories, a cafeteria, conference room, a situation centre, not to mention power centre and ventilation equipment room. It was built in the 1960s, and has been operated by the Department for Civil Protection and Emergency Planning.[1] Since the Norwegian government has built a new bunker under its offices in Oslo in the 1980s, it is not known if the Hole facility is still being maintained.[2]

Civil Defence

Several underground structures were also built to store essential materials and to protect various industries. Norwegian emergency preparedness plans include the protection of dams and bridges, the storage of key commodities like sugar, and the protection of the news media and the communications infrastructure. Bunkers were also built outside Oslo at Røyken for the air traffic control system, to house 200 power generating stations, for a nuclear power plant and to ensure a continuous oil supply. Other underground facilities have been established for the rail authorities and for municipal governments. It is also well known that several peacetime facilities have a dual use; at Govik, an underground hockey rink doubles as a civil defence office, police station and telecommunications centre.

Where the public is concerned, about 75 per cent of the population have access to shelter space, which implies these shelters are everywhere. In Holmlia outside Olso a new public bunker was built as a gymnasium and swimming pool. At the time it was built, it was the largest sports complex in the world. Finished in 1982, the 70,000sq ft facility was designed to hold 7,000. It comprises a sports hall 45m long by 25m wide, the swimming pool next to it and another section for locker rooms. It was outfitted with emergency power generators (that have their own oil supply), a water system and air filtration equipment. When it was completed, its construction bill had reached 54 million Norwegian kroner, a high amount at the time until one considers that because it is below ground, it has lower general maintenance bills and a lower heating bill in wintertime. It had been decided to build the sports complex underground since the limited surface area above was reserved for new housing. By 1983, Norway had fifteen of these dual-use shelters.

Global Seed Vault

On Spitsbergen, there exists perhaps one of the most unique bunkers in the world. The Global Seed Vault at Svalbard was established there to keep seeds from all corners of the world. The idea was that if a natural calamity took place anywhere in the world and some species of flora became extinct, scientists would be able to replant what was lost. Svalbard was chosen because its cold climate allows the seeds to be frozen in time.

Other Facilities

Other undeground structures known to exist are:

- On Cort Adeler Street in Oslo for the government. According to Daniele Ganser in his book *NATO's Secret Armies*, it was used as of 1950 to store arms to be used by a Norwegian stay-behind network of saboteurs;
- Olav Riste, in his book *The Norwegian Intelligence Service, 1945–1970*, mentions that in the 1950s, the government ran a telephone intercept operation from a government bunker in central Oslo. From this facility, the NIS eavesdropped on foreign embassies and on Soviet shipping agencies; and
- At Loerenberg. As with Homlia, it also doubles as a sports/civil defence facility.

❑ PAKISTAN

Perhaps the most well-known underground installation in Pakistan is the nuclear test site at Ras Koh in the Baluchistan mountains. Nuclear devices were tested here in 1998.

❑ PANAMA

The US Army built a bunker in Ancon Hill in the Quarry Heights section of Panama City. It was used by US Southern Command, and included an intelligence centre. Other underground bases include tunnels at two anti-aircraft posts and a bunker at Gordo Hill between Paraiso and Gamboa which were built during the Second World War.

❑ POLAND

Legnica

One of the Soviet army's regional commands was headquartered in the city of Legnica in southwestern Poland. After the Second World War, the Soviets took

One of the entrances to the Northern Group of Forces bunker at Chocianow near Legnica. (Photo: Author)

over buildings that had been used by the German army's Eastern Forces Headquarters and adapted them for their own use. When the Warsaw Treaty Organization was created in 1955, the Soviets formed the Northern Group of Forces there. A total of 840 of the German buildings were occupied, and an additional 360 were built by the Russians. Those in the centre of town were walled off for security.

Initially, the command centre for the Soviet Northern Group of Forces was probably located in the headquarters building in the city. In the 1970s, it was decided that an operations bunker would be built at a remote location under a project named Albatross. The project really called for not only one bunker to be built but three: the main one, which doubled as a communications base, was built between 1975 and 1989 in a forest outside Legnica near the settlement of Wilkocyn.[1] The

The communications tower at Chocianow. (Photo: Author)

two-storey facility could house 100 persons for up to a year and was placed within the confines of a high-security compound. It used four tropospheric scatter and other radio antennae, and included a hotline to Moscow. It was surrounded by three fences: the first was electrified, and the second had dogs patrol in between.

A Soviet communications bunker at Trzebien. After the facility was closed, the Polish government found a small amount of radioactivity there. (Photo: Author)

One of the public shelters in Wroclaw. (Photo: Author)

Power came from both external sources and from two ship's generators put in while the bunker was being built. After the Russian army left, the bunker was used briefly by Polish forces. The Polish army was never given any information about it, such as electrical wiring diagrams and blueprints, from the Russian government.

The other two bunkers were located several miles away. One was a radio jamming station east of the village of Trzebien, and the third one, which may have been a backup to the first, was near Chocianow.

National Bunker

The Polish government's main emergency operations centre is in the Pyry suburb of Warsaw. The facility is located in a forest, but is no longer clearly visible on Internet satellite sites as it is blurred. The bunker now contains the Polish Air Force's Air Operations Centre (Centrum Operacji Powietrznych), a command post that receives input from the four radar control and reporting centres at Radiowo, Bydgoszcz, Babki and Krakow. The AOC is connected to NATO's air defence system.

Other Facilities

Other underground structures in Poland include:

The entrance to an air operations centre at the Krzywa air base in southwestern Poland. (Photo: Author)

- Under the Cultural Palace in Warsaw;
- At ulitsa wspólna 62 in Warsaw. This discotheque was apparently a Communist Party bunker;[2]
- Earth-covered hangars at all air bases;
- A two-level operations centre at the Krzywa air base. The centre was built inside two connected earth-covered hangars that made them indistinguishable from other hangars;

The entrance to the Głuchow Gorny air force sector operations centre. This and the emergency exit were well hidden by trees. (Photo: Author)

- A vehicle shelter in a park near the western Warsaw suburb of Janow. This may have been for a mobile radar unit;
- A nuclear weapons bunker at the large Borne-Sulinowo training base. When in operation, the base was known as Complex 502 and was never marked on any maps;[3]
- A Warsaw Pact air force sector operations centre at Głuchow Gorny southeast of Trzebnica. It was built in 1953 and used until 2000. Its entrance is well concealed in a country home, and its emergency exit is hidden in the forest behind the house;
- A backup command post for the Warsaw Treaty Organization at Lvov. It may have had an underground component; and
- A radar station south of the village of Raszkow. The single-storey bunker was a vehicle shelter. The station, on Wojna Polskiego Street, was closed in 1999 and now belongs to a private firm called Domex.

Warsaw's Secret Underground

The Polish government also considered building a secret underground rail system in Warsaw similar to the one in Moscow. Few details about it have been revealed, but it is known that a small part was actually built in the northern part of the city under the Vistula River. This part ran from the small theological university in the Lasek Bielanski reserve on the western side of the river to a park on the eastern side.

❏ PORTUGAL

NATO has had for years one of its underground command centres on the grounds of Fort Gomes Freire in Oeiras west of Lisbon. When the French navy abdicated its responsibility for guarding the sea lanes in the western Mediterranean, NATO formed Iberian Command Atlantic (IBERLANT) as its replacement. The command was first placed in Sintra, but after a new office building and a new bunker was built in the fort, it was moved there. IBERLANT has since changed names a few times, and today, the bunker is used by NATO's Joint Headquarters Lisbon. An aerial photo of it on the Joint Headquarters' website is no longer available, and images of it on Internet satellite sites are blurred out.

❑ QATAR

Underground facilities in Qatar include:

- A combined air operations centre and sand-covered hangars at the al Udeid air base; and
- An American ammunition depot called Falcon 78.

❑ ROMANIA

When it came to civil defence measures during the Cold War, the Romanian government followed the Soviet lead and created its own organization and adopted policies similar to Moscow's. In 1978, a law was passed by the Romanian parliament that ordered all adults (male and female) to learn certain aspects of civil defence. For instance, the public was expected to take part in exercises, to undertake training in shelter construction and to acquire their own gas masks. That same law laid out the functions of certain government ministries during an emergency: the Ministry of the Interior was to maintain traffic control and was to look after evacuation, the Ministry of Electrical Power was to ensure the proper functioning of the electrical grid and the Ministry of Public Health was to manage the supply of drugs. While it is not known by the author if the government built rural relocation sites, it is known that one bunker was built under the presidential palace in Bucharest.

Other underground facilities are seen at Mihail Kogalniceanu airport outside the city of Constanta. Here, what look like personnel shelters can be seen at the north end of the airfield near the fighter-aircraft parking areas. During the communist era, the aerodrome was called Air Base 57 and hosted MiG-29s. A few years ago, the airport was suspected of being used by the CIA for its extraordinary rendition operations. The Romanian air force currently operates an air operations centre near Constanta, but its precise location and construction is not known by the author.

❑ RUSSIA

Moscow's Secret Underground

As in a few other countries, the Russian landscape is littered with underground installations of all types. The most famous is probably the Moscow metro, first built in the 1930s, then used as an air-raid shelter by national leaders and the public, and, at the Chistie Prudy station, as an air defence headquarters during the Second World War.[1] During the Cold War, several stations were again earmarked for use as civil defence shelters.[2]

This was the public side of the metro. It has long been known that the Russian capital hides another network of tunnels underneath. In 1953, the Soviet government began constructing another underground rail system, independent of the first, which would be used to ferry politicians and selected public servants away from Moscow. Some amateur investigators have visited the network, which they call Metro-2, and have traced its paths from the Kremlin. The following is a summary of what has been revealed in the media and on the Internet:

- The first line was built in 1953–54 from the Kremlin to Stalin's dacha at Kuntsevo in the western suburbs of Moscow. The line was ordered built at a time while he was still alive and connected the Kremlin to a Second World War bunker under his dacha;
- The second line was completed in 1967 and runs southwest from the Kremlin, to a huge underground shelter at Ramenki next to Moscow State University, and then on to Vnukovo airfield. The bunker at Ramenki can accommodate 12,000 to 15,000 persons and is connected to shelters under the university.[3] Above the bunker, one sees no traces of it, save for a greenish ventilation shaft (with locked door) on Vernadskovo Prospekt. Whether this particular shaft services the regular underground rail line that runs underneath or the bunker is not known. The secret underground rail line is connected to the regular metro line between Sportivnaya and Universitet stations. After passing Ramenki, the line serves the FSB Academy, the general staff academy and the Strategic Rocket Forces base at Vlasikha. The line also serves a new bunker built for the SRF in 1986–87 2km from the old, and yet another bunker used by the space forces, with entrances apparently concealed in a small house. The terminus of this line is Vnukovo-2 airfield, which houses the nation's airborne command posts;
- The third line leads to points south of the Kremlin to military command centres at Chekhov and possibly Voronovo. The line may extend to another command post at Serpukhov. Some local residents claim they can feel trains running underneath them;
- The fourth line runs east from the Kremlin to the air defence centre at Chernoye;[4] and
- The last line was built in the mid-1990s. It runs west from the second line to a bunker possibly at Barvikha.

One source stated that some of the rail lines in these tunnels were embedded in concrete, this to allow their use by tanks or trucks in addition to trains. With respect to access, another source has entered some of these tunnels from a manhole in a public park in the centre of Moscow. Little has been revealed about the construction of these secret passageways, but what is known is that they were looked after by the KGB's 15th Main Directorate until the end of the Cold War, and that now they may be managed by the Russian Federation GUSP, a special organization controlled by the President's office.[5]

According to a private group known as the 'Diggers of the Underground World', the tunnels below Moscow are being used by various groups these days, but the presence of skulls and bones gives an idea of the kind of life it breeds. With the new Russian economic reality, many have made their homes there in conditions less than safe or hygienic. Others use the catacombs as clandestine meeting places; when the Diggers encountered several individuals dressed in monk robes carrying out some kind of ceremony, the mystery group quickly dispersed.[6]

Civil Defence

When it came to the protection of the public, the Soviet government implemented extensive measures, perhaps not as elaborate as in China, but certainly more so than in the United States. The Soviets reportedly began public shelter construction in apartment block basements in 1949 using German prisoners of war, as well as making plans for the use of the St Petersburg metro and the re-use of the Moscow underground rail system for the same reason. Civil defence was initially the responsibility of a Ministry of Internal Affairs outfit, the Local Anti-Aircraft Defence Organization or MPVO, but in 1960, this responsibility was subordinated to the Ministry of Defence and later on made a separate branch of the armed forces with its own civil defence troops. A large number of shelters were eventually built, and their construction was complemented with a strong campaign for public education, much of which was carried out by the Volunteer Society for the Cooperation with the Air Force, Army and Navy (DOSAAF). While training manuals were also prepared in conjunction with the shelter-building programme, these did not cover the effects of nuclear war until 1954, the year after Joseph Stalin's death. One author claims Stalin and his subordinates failed to consider the potential impact of atomic weapons on the population and industry, but in the closed society that was the Soviet Union, it may be that the leaders simply wanted to withhold all nuclear-related information from their own citizens. Irrespective of the reason, the Soviet government became one of the biggest spenders in civil defence in the world.

Eventually, every Russian apartment building built in the postwar period had by design its own bunker to give residents a ready place to hide. One could always tell the entrance by the blast doors lined with rubber and the exit by its stand-alone access portal. Many of these basement shelters in any given city are linked to each other through tunnels. Factories in several cities also have their own shelters usually located close by for quick access.[7] Several other facilities have been built in the sides of mountains and hills, reinforced to withstand up to 300psi of blast pressure. Each major city also had an underground food storage warehouse, apparently of immense size. Stock levels were such that both workers and live-stock had enough to last one year, but it is debatable whether these are maintained now.

The MPVO was to adopt several roles in the civil defence arena, some of which in the United States would be performed by FEMA and others by the National Guard. The basic goal of the organization was the protection of the Russian populace, planning for industrial continuity and conducting rescue work in damaged areas. Its first goal, public protection, entailed providing warnings, conducting evacuations, building fallout shelters, ensuring a food and water supply and carrying out radiation detection. To perform its second role, MPVO staff worked with key factories to ensure its personnel could be sheltered and that, if industrial production was affected, it could resume quickly. Factory managers and the plant's designated civil defence personnel were given a mandate to ensure a supply of raw materials was always on hand and that utilities could be maintained. The MPVO's third goal, rescue, required its personnel to have the ability to organize local help to rebuild a damaged site, to rescue and evacuate the injured and carry out radiation detection. To perform its duties, the MPVO could count upon the help of the DOSAAF.

The Soviet government ordered every organization to have an officer and staff assigned to civil defence duties. Every government ministry had such personnel, as did every geo-political sub-unit (such as the Soviet Socialist Republics, Krays, Oblasts and cities), factories, schools and even the collective farms. At the munic-ipal level, the civil defence bureaux had sections for communications, fire-fighting, engineering and crowd and traffic control, the latter being looked after by the local militia. There was even a section that dealt with plants and animals that would have managed the food supply and controlled meat distribu-tion. The engineering section was responsible for shelter construction.

The public shelters mandated by the government came in two basic designs: for blast and fallout. Blast bunkers were naturally sturdier than fallout structures since they were meant to protect civilians from the effects of a detonation. Fallout shelters were weaker in construction since their only role was to limit the occu-pants's exposure to radioactive dust. The blast shelters contained a combination sleeping/eating area, lavatories, a ventilation equipment room, a medical section and a storeroom for food. The entrances were equipped with blast doors and an air-lock passage. If the entrances were ever destroyed, the occupants could leave through an emergency exit that led outside. Some bunkers were equipped with a standby generator and a well, and, ideally, all were to have a telephone and a radio. Air would have been regenerated through either a sodium peroxide or potassium peroxide-filled canister that converted carbon dioxide into oxygen. Outside air was kept out of the bunkers by maintaining a positive pressure inside. Since the supply of air inside was limited, residents were forbidden from smoking or lighting candles.

Many of these structures were built in the basement of apartment buildings while they were being constructed. For older structures, some bunkers were built nearby using the cut and cover model. Some shelters were put in public build-ings such as theatres and garages, while several others were constructed near factories. The Soviet government allowed peacetime uses of these bunkers, with the proviso that they were not modified and that their use as civil defence facili-ties took precedence.

While civil defence preparations were given a back seat in the West, especially in the late 1960s, there was no such de-emphasis in the Soviet Union. In fact, the CIA learned from satellite photography and émigré reports that the ampleur of civil defence increased during the 1970s. Not only were more protected facilities built, since 1967 school children were required to take classes in the use of gas masks and Geiger counters. All residents, male and female, were obligated to take a civil defence course once every three years, training that could include building makeshift fallout shelters and providing first aid.[8] Civil defence units regularly practised civilian evacuations, decontamination and fire-fighting, sometimes using special training villages. Factory managers were similarly required to consider civil defence measures, such as the building of emergency underground facilities, the reinforcement of existing buildings and the erection of duplicate plants. To avoid industrial congestion in a city, which would have made excel-lent targets for bombers and missiles, new factories were established in smaller cities where none or few had existed before. A major advantage to the Soviet government's large-scale efforts in civil defence was that it freed regular army troops for duty in their primary role of combat engagement.

Other types of underground facilities were built in Russia during the Cold War. A 1978 CIA report on civil defence revealed that the Soviets erected 'shel-ters at critical points in the road and rail transportation system'. This indicates that bunkers were probably placed at marshalling yards for railroad staff. Also, if one looks at the website coldwar-c4i.net, one would see that a bunker was built next to a power station somewhere east of Moscow. On the other hand, while factories were encouraged to build secure structures for their staff, the CIA learned from Russian publications that their high cost proved a major dis-incentive. The implication is therefore that not all key industrial facilities were prepared to survive a war.

It appears that the end of the Cold War brought several changes to civil defence matters in Russia. Bunkers were closed, public training was curtailed, and government staffing levels were reduced. A new Russian Rescue Corps was created in 1990 to take over civil defence functions, but four years later the Corps was absorbed into a new government department with a mouthful for a name, the Ministry of Civil Defence Matters, Emergency Situations and the Elimination of the Consequences of Natural Disasters (MChS). The MChS became responsible for the State Fire Administration, the State Central Airmobile Rescue Team (known as Tsentrospas), the small vessels inspectorate and the emergencies forecasting and monitoring system. It was also given control of the Civil Defence Academy and the All-Russian Scientific Research Institute for Civil Defence Emergencies. The men and women of the Ministry train in all types of emergency situations and learn to use such diverse equipment as airmobile hospitals, remote-control robot vehicles, gas masks, hazmat suits and toxic agent detector kits. The Ministry owns its own fleet of helicopters and transport aircraft and has troops based throughout Russia. MChS vehicles are recognized by their use of military colours and the international symbol for civil defence – the blue triangle over the orange circle – laid on top of a multipoint star. Its organizational structure is very military-like as it is broken down into brigades, regiments and companies. When it was formed, the Ministry took over such places as a central command post in Ruzskiy Rayon near Moscow and a backup command centre on Bolshaya Filevskaya Street in Moscow.[9] The Ministry has its own medical clinic at 1 Vatutina Street in Moscow and its own laboratory for measurement equipment in Novogorsk outside the capital. Regular MChS troops wear blue uniforms and unit badges, and those working in the field wear orange uniforms. According to one source, some are Spetsnaz-trained and are attached to the Ministry's 271st Separate Special Operations Battalion. Some MChS staff wear sidearms for self-protection.

Government Bunkers

The other major aspect of civil defence in Russia is the protection of political leaders and government officials. According to a 1978 CIA report entitled *Soviet Civil Defense* (declassified in 1994), the survival of the political and military nomenklatura had priority over the populace, and the government spent an inordinate amount on shelters for every level of leadership. Several hardened facilities were built near Moscow, and many others were constructed in the republics, oblasts and cities, for communist party functionaries and for senior officers of key factories. Around the capital alone, there are reputed to be seventy-five bunkers for the government. The CIA report stated that some of the bunkers hold emergency equipment and food stockpiles. Many of those used as command centres have collapsible antennae.

Since the bunkers around Moscow are not clearly visible on Internet satellite imagery sites, one can assume they are located under government buildings.[10] In fact, according to a 1958 CIA report on Soviet civil defence, there were reports that basement shelters were built under government offices not only in Moscow but throughout the USSR. US Air Force General George Keegan studied Soviet civil defence bunkers through aerial photography while directing Air Force intelligence and found a network more extensive than was previously thought. Keegan claimed the seventy-five installations around Moscow were each the size of the Pentagon and several hundred feet deep. If this is the case, this would represent construction costs of astronomical proportions.

At least two government bunkers in Russia were still in use in the 1990s. When coup plotters attempted to take over the Parliament in 1993, President Boris Yeltsin learned about it while he was in a bunker at Yekaterinburg. Also, when the Literary Museum in Moscow was ordered to move from its premises, one of its new potential locations was a bomb shelter near the Bielorussian train station.

When museum staff were told the shelter was still an active property controlled by the MChS, they had to find another home.[11]

Very little information has been disclosed on the units that manage these facilities. As with Metro-2, during the Cold War they were looked after by the KGB's 15th Main Directorate. After the Cold War and the KGB's disbandment, this function was transferred to GUSP, the Main Directorate for Special Programs of the Russian Federation President, in particular the Special Facilities Service (SSO). Some of the units of the SSO bear five-digit military numbers, suggesting they really belong to the Russian Army. In 2006, a military collector's website offered for sale a number of badges pertaining to these units:

- Unit 52581, which seems to look after facilities in and around the Kremlin;
- Unit 52583, which works around the city of Chekhov south of Moscow, known location of one of the government's wartime command posts;
- Unit 45108, based in Penza Oblast, the location of another government bunker (at Chaadayevka); and
- Unit 68542 in Solnechnogorsk in Moscow Oblast. This may also be the location of another bunker.

The United States government's publication *Military Forces in Transition* states that the Russians were then (in 1991) continuing to improve and deepen the most 'important facilities in and around Moscow for the highest leavel of leadership elements, although they are already hundreds of meters deep and can hold thousands of people'. While it is not known by the author if construction for the leadership continues to this day, the Russian government announced in 2010 that new shelters would be built in the Moscow region for the public.

Military Bunkers

The armed forces of Russia were also great believers in nuclear survival. Hardened facilities were built throughout the nation for all headquarters-level formations. The CIA identified over 700 such facilities in the 1970s for the Soviet High Command, the General Staff, for all the Strategic Rocket Forces army and divisional headquarters, and for the other services' headquarters. One can assume every Military District and every senior air defence unit is similarly equipped. As well, many of these organizations have an alternate command post. Many, if not most, of these bunkers are outfitted with a buried antenna that could survive nearby blasts.

Known or suspected military bunkers in and around Moscow include:

- One for the General Staff under its main building on Arbatskaya Square;
- Chekhov, a leadership relocation site built in the 1950s and expanded in the 1970s. This is south of Moscow and is served by one of the secret underground rail lines;
- Lipetsk, a possible alternate military command centre;

- Pushkino (near Sofrino), a bunker underneath the Don-2N ABM radar;
- Chernoye, an underground air defence operations centre (this is close to Zarya and Kupavna);
- Sharapovo, a leadership relocation site built in the late 1950s and expanded in the 1970s. This facility is located on the forested property surrounded by a wide clear-cut area. Two shallow bunkers are seen on a property east of it;
- GO-42 near the Taganskaya metro. The facility, built betwen 1952 and 1956, is reputed to be twenty-two stories deep and measures 75,000sq ft. It served as an emergency national communications centre. The bunker employed 2,500 and had enough food and water for 90 days. It closed permanently in 1995 and is now a museum;
- Voronovo. This bunker is about 74km south of Moscow. One Russian source quoted in *Moscow Kuranty* stated it was built in the 1990s and that it is a component of an underground structure that permits control of vital systems;
- Veniukovskii, apparently the location of the Centre for Analysis of the Missile and Space Situation. This is located very close to Chekhov. On new maps, the town is now called Venyukovo. This bunker may be known as Serpukhov-15;
- Vlasikha, the location of the Strategic Rocket Forces headquarters. The actual underground command post may be at Perkhushkovo nearby;
- Balabanovo, another ABM radar site with a bunker underneath;
- Mityaevo, near Naro-Fominsk. The site's purpose is unknown;
- Kuntsevo, west of Moscow, at the presidential dacha;
- Solnechnogorsk, for the Third Early Warning Army command centre; and
- Kolomna, as an alternate command post for the Third Early Warning Army.

Also, an underground communications line runs from Moscow to a nuclear research institute at Troitsk southwest of the capital. The line includes bunkers at selected points for maintenance. For five years, the CIA collected information from that line through a tap. The operation ended when it was disclosed to the Russians by CIA spy Aldrich Ames.

In other parts of Russia, there are bunkers:

- At a smallpox production factory at Pokrov, 80km east of Moscow. The five bunkers were outfitted with blast doors and had all the equipment necessary for full-scale production of the virus. The plant was operated by the Ministry of Agriculture. It now produces pain-relieving pills, shampoo and animal vaccines;
- In a village hidden in a forest south of Sergiev Posad (previously known as Zagorsk, and several miles northeast of Moscow). This village may have

been the Ministry of Defence's Virological Centre mentioned in Ken Alibek's book *Biohazard*. The Ministry of Defence cultivated and stored the smallpox, Q fever and Venezuelan equine encephalitis virus there;

- On three different properties near the small town of Yuzhnorezhensk down the coast from Vladivostok;
- At Petropavlovsk, on a spit of land on the east side of the bay near the settlement of Dolinovka, and at the southwest side of the harbour at the Rybachyi naval base;
- At Chaadayevka. A leadership relocation site 650km southeast of Moscow near Penza;
- At Kosvinsky Mountain in the Urals, north of Yekaterinburg, as an alternate command post for the Strategic Rocket Forces;
- At Kaliningrad, at the western edge of a military airfield;
- At the Engels air base, on a property north of the base, and at another site a few kilometres to the southeast;
- At Kyshtym, south of Yekaterinburg, on the south side of the round lake;
- Again at Kyshtym (10 miles east). A series of three plants, collectively called called Chelyabinsk-40, exist to produce plutonium. One of those plants is said to be partly built under a lake. Construction took place in 1947–48, and plutonium was produced as of February 1949;
- At the Abez space tracking facility at Mount Narodnaya;[12]
- Southwest of Sovkhozniy (south of Yekaterinburg) on the east side of the highway west of Zeleniy Bor;
- At Teykovo, northeast of Moscow. Several properties with bunkers are seen northeast of the town. One of those properties looks like a road-mobile ICBM base. Other bunkers are seen on military reservations north and south of Krapinovo (west of Teykovo);
- At the Tatishchevo missile base, west of Saratov, in a fenced compound for the road-mobile ICBMs;
- East of Khabarovsk, east of the village of Anastas'evka;
- At Tomsk, a depot that received nuclear weapons from former Soviet republics such as Belarus and the Ukraine;
- North of Novosibirsk at four locations: on two properties east of Bibikha (one of which is a road-mobile ICBM base) and two south of the settlement of Beloyarka;
- At Koltsovo, southeast of Novosibirsk, at the Institute of Molecular Biology (codenamed Vector), for the manufacture of the smallpox virus;
- North of the Severomorsk-3 fighter base (east of Murmansk), at what seems to be an old SAM site;
- East of Kostroma, at an abandoned road-mobile ICBM base near Medenikovo;
- And again east of Kostroma, at an abandoned missile site southwest of Kuznetsovo and north of the highway;
- At Zheleznogorsk, as a multi-level extensive system of tunnels in a

mountain, used for the production of weapons-grade plutonium. This was called Krasnoyarsk-26, and may be closed now;

- Approximately 42 miles of Yekaterinburg. According to Radio Free Europe, it was used to store the nation's gold reserves while Boris Yeltsin was president;
- An old 1958 CIA document on Soviet civil defence mentions a bunker next to the administration building at a tank factory at Khabarovsk;
- North of Severodvinsk; and
- Throughout the Soviet Union at broadcasting stations.

Many of these bunkers are no longer used.

Several years ago, the Japanese newspaper *Sankei* reported the construction of submarine tunnels near Vladivostok. Imagery sites do not reveal this. Entrances to other underground naval tunnels can be clearly seen in China and the Ukraine, but no such entrances can be seen around Vladivostok. Also, Sherry Sontag and Christopher Drew in their book *Blind Man's Bluff* claim the Soviets built large underwater tunnels at the Gremikha naval base to house Typhoon submarines. Again, imagery sites do not confirm this. If such tunnels are there, the entrances are well hidden. Finally, one source revealed to the author that in the 1990s, two huge explosions took place at ammunition depots at Vladivostok, one at Vtoraya Rechka in May 1992 and the other at Novonezhino in May 1994. One of those depots was underground. The latter explosion was so fierce it damaged houses nearby.

An example of a headquarters bunker can be found in Victor Suvorov's book *Inside the Aquarium*. Suvorov was a GRU officer once assigned to the 13th Army Headquarters at Rovno. In his book, he mentions that some machine-gun casemates surround the headquarters building, and that all are linked by tunnels. He also mentions that a command post lies under the main building, and that it includes, besides the operations centre, living accommodations, a hospital, dining rooms and storerooms. While it was not mentioned in Suvorov's book, it no doubt has its own power plant. The entrance was cleverly camouflaged in the forested grounds. He also hinted that there was another underground command post, possibly a backup, but fails to reveal its location.

Moscow Air Defence

From the mid-1950s to 1993, the Moscow area was protected by a large number of surface-to-air missiles. The Systema-25 (S-25) Berkut SAM was a liquid-fuelled radar-guided rocket that was designed to destroy enemy bombers coming in from all directions. It used at first a conventional charge that would spread shrapnel upon detonation, although in the 1960s some missiles would be outfitted with a 10 kiloton nuclear warhead. Its maximum range was at first 30km, but this was increased later on in new variants to 35km, then 43km. The system included A-100 and B-200 radars to search for targets, and used the latter to track same and to control the missile. The S-25s were placed in two concentric rings around

Moscow; the first ring contained twenty-two sites that were 45km to 50km from the centre of the city, and the second, thirty-four sites between 85km and 90km from the same point.

Each site held sixty missiles and included a bunker, probably used for maintenance, and a B-200. The road network on the bases had what some people called a herringbone pattern. All were placed in wooded areas. Concurrently, the Soviet army built a small number of warhead or missile storage bases also around Moscow, each of which had a bunker. The depots were sometimes tree-lined to shield them from public view. Typical of Russian military bases, the roads to the missile and storage sites consisted of tiled concrete. Each site was manned by a separate S-25 regiment, and all belonged to the First Special Purpose Army. The two rings fell under one of four geographical sectors, Northern, Eastern, Western and Southern, where each sector, along with the army proper, had its own command centre. Some of the sites are listed in Appendix G.

Other missiles were placed around Moscow as ABM weapons. The first models were called A-350s and were installed in the 1970s as part of the A-35 system at four sites: Bereya, Solnechnogorsk, Klim and Sergiev Posad. The command centre was at Akulovo. The A-35 was replaced with a more modern A-135 ABM system that uses A-350 exo-atmospheric interceptors and 53T6 endo-atmospheric rockets. The former were placed at the A-35's four sites along with two new ones, and the latter are located at five positions around Moscow. Both types of rockets are emplaced in silos, and while they could be fitted with either conventional or nuclear warheads, some press reports claim they now have only the former. Two of the missile sites are next door to ABM radars. The command centre is reportedly at Sofrino.

Nuclear Weapons

A definitive historical account of the origins of the Russian A-bomb has never been published, but by consulting various sources a brief account can be gleaned. Only a summary can be provided here.

Research into nuclear physics had gone on in the Soviet Union as far back as the 1920s, and some scientists such as Igor Kurchatov had at the beginning of the Second World War recognized the atom's potential military application and had recommended funding for laboratory work. The war prevented such research from taking place, but when Josef Stalin heard the Americans had driven down that road, he decided Russia should follow suit. Stalin had heard from his spies working in key American labs that the research they were engaged in was ultimately to be used in an atomic weapon. But it was really only the United States government's test and only after two bombs were dropped on Japan in the summer of 1945 that the Russians began seriously focusing on their own weapons. The secrets passed onto Moscow from those American individuals greatly helped the Russians in their endeavour, and in August 1949, years earlier than the Americans had predicted, they detonated their first bomb.

The next step in Soviet weapons development was to find ways to deliver those bombs. Air dropping was the first mode of delivery, but since the bombers the Soviet air force then possessed had a limited range, other methods were contemplated. Research on rocket technology had progressed well, thanks mainly to captured German scientists and information, and tests were made with missiles that carried conventional warheads. By the 1950s, Soviet rocket technology had so advanced that by 1957, it succeeded in placing a Sputnik satellite into space. At the same time, rockets were being examined as nuclear delivery platforms, and more than a full year before Sputnik said 'hello' to the world, the first ballistic missile regiments were deployed. Within a few years, the Soviet Union's first operational rocket, the R-5M, would be supplemented with the R-7, the R-12 and the R-14.[13] The rockets then became so plentiful Soviet Premier Nikita Krushchev claimed they were coming out of the factories like sausages.

By the late 1950s, Soviet missile production was running at full speed. Rockets were being deployed on launch pads in bases throughout Russia. The missiles represented such an important element of the Soviet Union's warfighting machine that some generals thought a new and separate branch of the armed forces should be created specifically for them. At first, all rocket units belonged to the artillery corps, but eventually some were assigned to Long-Range Aviation forces and others to the Soviet Supreme High Command. On 17 December 1959, however, history would be made and the new Strategic Rocket Forces (RVSN) were born.[14] It would soon become a military service on a par with the army, air force, air defence service and navy.

The RVSN would be Russia's first line of action against the West, and in consequence it recruited the best and the brightest among Russian conscripts. Throughout its history, it would have the best facilities, the best equipment and the smartest and most loyal officers. The officers and men were treated so well that in return, Moscow expected utmost dedication from them. To expect anything less, in the Kremlin's mind, would have invited disaster.

The RVSN's organizational structure follows a pattern very similar to that of the USAF. In the United States, numbered 'Air Forces' consist of Wings and Wings are made up of Squadrons. The latter are further divided into Flights. Since the Strategic Rocket Forces were an outgrowth of the artillery corps, it adopted the army structure of numbered Armies, Divisions and Regiments. The latter are composed of Battalions where each consist of a single launcher.[15] Armies and Divisions have their own primary underground headquarters, and the Armies have apparently also a secondary command post that is airmobile. Regimental headquarters are located in launch tubes on remote properties. The missiles are either silo-based or rail or road-mobile. Following the standard Soviet practice, the various units are identified by both ordinal and five-digit numbers.[16] Some units use the prefix 'Guards' to indicate a form of eliteness. Divisions are normally numbered, although some carry names.[17] The RVSN has its own test and support sites such as the No. 4 Central Research Institute at Bolshevo in the suburbs of Moscow, and the No. 25 Central Military Clinical Hospital at Odintsovo, again outside Moscow. Training of staff takes place at military engineering institutes at Perm, Rostov-on-Don, Krasnodar, Serpukhov and at the Peter the Great Military Academy in Moscow.

In 1985, the RVSN consisted of the following six Armies:

Headquarters	Missile Army	Location
Vladimir	27th	Russia
Orenburg	31st	Russia
Omsk	33rd	Russia
Vinnitsa	43rd	Ukraine
Smolensk	50th	Belarus
Chita	53rd	Russia

It then had 1,398 missiles in service, 6,840 warheads and counted 415,000 men and women on its payroll. Today, however, only the first three armies remain, and its population is only a fraction of what it used to be. In 2008, the RVSN had 430 ICBMs in service. A relatively current partial order-of-battle is found in Appendix E.

Ultimate use of nuclear weapons is decided upon by a very small number of individuals: the President, the Minister of Defence and the Chief of the General Staff (the Nachalnyk Generalnovo Shtaba or the NGS). All three have access to a nuclear football, called Cheget or more colloquially chemodanchik, that is nearby at all times in the hands of an officer from the General Staff's 9th Directorate. According to Peter Pry in his book *War Scare*, only one person, the President, needs to issue the order. He does not need, 'in all likelihood', the consent of the other two, although he would certainly consult with them. If the President was unavailable or dead, the Minister of Defence would likely assume command, and if the Minister was incapacitated, he would probably be replaced by the NGS.[18] This line of succession seems to confirm that only one person needs to issue the go signal from the Cheget.

The Russian command and control system is predicated on the concept of 'launch on warning', which states that nuclear forces should act only when there are definite indications that an attack is under way. Orders to launch can be passed through the footballs (or from some of the underground command posts around Moscow) via a special communications network called Kavkaz, to the General Staff's and to the military services' command centres.[19] At the General Staff's bunker, the orders are transmitted via the Signal-A multifaceted communications system to the RVSN main staff, then to Armies, Divisions and Regiments. Here, they are received by special equipment called Baksan. The orders are then transmitted to the launchers by launch crews. At the same time, missile unlock codes (which are nicknamed 'goschislo') and authorization codes are passed onto the regimental command posts. One key feature present in the Russian command and control system not present in the American system is the ability of the Russian high command to bypass intermediate stages using a radio system called V'yuga and transmit orders to fire directly to launch control centres.[20] As Bruce Blair put in in his book *The Logic of Accidental Nuclear War*, the General Staff is not only the band leader but can also play the instruments.

Before the missileers shoot their loads, several steps must take place throughout the command and control system. First, a preliminary command must be sent from Moscow. The command is really generated from two parts, one that originates from the General Staff and the other from the RVSN main staff, and is then validated, combined and transmitted down the chain of command. This order can only be created after enemy launches have been detected by at least two types of sensors and only after the President has so decided.[21] Once this order is received at the regimental Launch Control Centres, launch consoles are activated.[22] Next, a permission command is generated by the same three individuals (the President, Minister of Defence and the NGS) and transmitted to the Commander-in-Chief of the RVSN. Its only role is to provide legality to the launch order. Finally, a direct command is generated in two parts, one from the General Staff and the other from RVSN Headquarters. The command is later combined and again sent down the chain of command.[23] Once received by Baksan equipment at the LCCs, it is authenticated by launch crews. The same crews then check certain computer symbols against a list kept in their safe, choose their targets (probably from a coded list) and set launch times.[24] The command also allows any missile blocking device to be disabled. It then only remains to turn the two keys. Some Russian experts estimate that launch can take place within twenty-one minutes from the time of initial missile detection. Since an American ICBM takes thirty minutes to reach Russia, this would still give a nine minute window of reaction time. On the other hand, this would prove of little comfort to Russian forces if SLBMs were fired from American or British submarines from the Barents or Mediterranean Sea.

Individual missiles contain the target co-ordinates in the memory of their re-entry vehicles. The co-ordinates are chosen from a set listed in the 'Plan of Operations of the Strategic Rocket Forces', a document that parallels the American SIOP. In the 1990s, the two superpowers agreed to de-target their missiles as a gesture of goodwill, but this is only a symbolic move as the rockets can be reprogrammed within minutes thanks to computerization. During an attack, some writers have speculated that silo-based missiles would be fired first because of their susceptibility to a first strike, and that mobile missiles, which can relocate to virtually any point, would be used in a retaliatory assault.

The command and control system in Russia has a feature that guarantees near-total reliability. Should the various communications systems be rendered inoperable, or should the human decision triad described above be unavailable, the RVSN would still be able to launch its missiles. In the early 1970s, a decision was made by Moscow to develop a system that would allow the launch of missiles if most of the human input was erased. In 1974, work began on a system that would see special UHF radio-equipped rockets take off if certain conditions were satisfied and that would automatically transmit pre-recorded voice commands to launching crews. Other missiles would then fire after a pre-set time interval.

Called Perimetr, this system was implemented to give Russian leaders an insurance policy against decapitation. This 'Doomsday Machine', as it is often called in the Western press, was declared operational in 1985.[25] It is also referred to as 'Dead Hand'.[26]

The Perimetr system operates in three stages. First, once duty officers located in a special underground radio command post receive the proper order, they must turn the system on. Second, they must determine if communications are still available with the Supreme High Command (e.g. the President). If they are not, they are to assume the leadership no longer exists. Third, the officers are to determine if any detonations have taken place on Russian soil. If all three conditions are met, they are to load a message into the radio warhead and launch the rockets, one from each end of the country. Over the next fifteen minutes, these rockets will broadcast the order to fire to the launch crews. There is apparently no way to stop the Perimetr rockets, which means the responsible officers must be sure of themselves before launching them.[27]

Automated systems notwithstanding, the value of human input in the Russian command and control system was clearly demonstrated in 1983. On 25 September of that year, Lieutenant-Colonel Stanislas Petrov was working as a missile warning officer in one of the nation's early warning facilities, called Serpukhov-15, south of Moscow. The facility received inputs from a series of detection satellites flying high over the planet. At 12.15am on the 26th, one of the warning panels in the control centre flashed the word 'launch'. It had originated from the United States.

This had never happened before to Petrov. A launch from the US required the Colonel to contact higher authorities and brace for the worst. He and others began to wonder if the United States was using the NATO exercise Able Archer which was then in process as an excuse for a missile attack. Petrov's staff began to worry and looked to him for guidance. Another indicator panel in the room showed 'high reliability'. The electronic map in front that showed all the American missile bases had one lamp turned on showing from which base the missile had come from. Petrov's duty was to alert the Kremlin and the General Staff, but he held off until he could confirm the systems were working properly and that the launch was real. He knew the system was not perfect, and he began to have doubts when the map showed only one missile launch and when the optical telescopes could not confirm that launch. Petrov's instincts told him it was a false alarm, and said so to his staff. Soon, however, the system showed five more missiles on the way. Again, knowing the system was full of glitches, he assumed it was giving false readings. Petrov knew that if the United States was to attack, it would do so with hundreds of missiles, not just five, so this knowledge served to reinforce his suspicion. He thus refused to sound the alarm, and the world was spared from a potential Armageddon.

One would think that Soviet generals would have thanked Petrov for using his judgment. Not so. A few hours after the event, senior Army officers dropped in not to congratulate him, but to berate him for not passing on the warnings. Had he done so, however, who knows what actions would have been taken by the leadership? For his actions, Petrov was soon transferred to less sensitive duties, and within a year, he would be gone from the military. Eventually, it would be learned that the warnings were generated from the sun's reflection from the clouds.[28]

When it comes to Russian targeting policy, very little has been revealed about it. What has been divulged has often been based on educated guesswork, limited military writings and, on rare occasions, on information from defectors. What is known is that during the Cold War, the Soviets' targeting plan called for the destruction of every single enemy nuclear device, preferably in one massive sweep. The most important targets were bomber airfields, submarine bases, nuclear weapons depots and strategic command and control centres. Secondary targets included radar stations and tactical air and missile bases. Other less important aimpoints would have been large army bases, conventional munitions stores and fuel depots. Civilian sites such as political centres and economic facilities (such as power stations and petroleum stockpiles) would also have been wiped out. Early Russian missiles were not very accurate, so they were likely reserved for large facilities such as air and naval bases, although when the Americans began building missile-launching facilities in the 1960s, the rockets' quick reaction time meant they too would have to be knocked out in the first wave. To ensure their destruction, some installations, such as ammunition depots (of which there were many in West Germany), could have required up to eighteen bombs to destroy because of their hardened igloos.[29] Russia therefore had a clear incentive to build up its arsenal and to increase the accuracy of its weapons.

While it was always clear that the United States and Canada were prime targets for the Strategic Rocket Forces, some have wondered how Western Europe would have fared. Some academics thought that part of the continent might have been spared the use of strategic weapons during an all-out attack for a number of reasons. First, if the Soviet Union's goal was annexation, they obviously would not want to occupy a smouldering radioactive ruin. Second, more than likely the Russians would have wanted to take over heavy industries for their own use, as they did with Germany after the Second World War. (This would have also applied to Japan.) Third, if the Russians had indeed attacked with ICBMs, normal west-to-east wind patterns and the resultant radioactive clouds would have meant that they themselves would have been contaminated. For these reasons, theorists believe the Soviets would have restricted their attacks to mostly military targets using tactical weapons only.

When it comes to actual missiles, Russia has developed a much larger array than the United States. Victor Suvorov in his book *Inside the Soviet Army* claims that one of the reasons was that the Soviet Union was not capable of manufacturing a large quantity of rockets because of the dearth of key components; it was therefore forced to produce limited runs. Whereas the United States had only two ICBMs deployed in 1975 – the Minuteman and the Titan II – the RVSN had nine models. The larger number of types was not necessarily a disadvantage, though, since one could make up for the shortcomings of another.

The year 1975 also saw three new missiles come off the assembly line; the UR-100, R-36M and the UR-100N. The UR-100N, known in the West as the SS-19, is described here as an example.

The UR-100N was a two-stage UDMH-fueled ICBM with a range of 10,000km. It was designed by the OKB-52 development facility at Reutov outside Moscow and built in two models: the first carried six independent warheads of 550 kiloton yield each and the second, a single 5 megaton re-entry vehicle. The Russians claim it had a circular error of probability (or impact accuracy level) of 350m, but in his book *Russian Strategic Nuclear Forces* Podvig claims it is 920m, which is still better than older ICBMs. The UR-100N was a leader in fourth-generation missiles since it incorporated new microprocessor technology and improved launch techniques. Some thought that the heavy warhead model was aimed at American missile silos, until it was realized too few were produced and that their high yield made them more suitable for deeper targets such as Mount Weather. Both models were manufactured at the Krunichev machine plant outside Moscow and fitted into modified SS-11 silos, such as at Pervomaysk, Ukraine, or into new silos such as at Tatishchevo. The UR-100N was also eventually put in Derazhnaya, Ukraine, and Kozelsk, Russia. When hints of the missile first appeared in the 1970s, *Jane's Weapons Systems* asserted it was hot-launched – launched from within its silo – while the US Department of Defense claimed it was raised first, then fired, or cold-launched. As it turned out, *Jane's* was right. The UR-100N was replaced with the UR-100NU in the 1980s due to its launch instability.[30]

The pattern of missile deployment in the Soviet Union seems to have paralleled, up to a point, American patterns. The rockets were either placed in earth-covered bunkers, kept on launching pads or installed in groups of silos, but later models were placed in individual silos. One of the early ICBMs, the R-7, was kept on launching pads and supported by four masts, while some of the R-12Us were put in Dvina complexes that consisted of four silos.[31] One variant of the R-14U was placed in a Chusovaya complex of three silos located less than 100m apart, while the R-16U was deployed in threes in a Sheksna-V complex of three silos forming a straight line 60m from each other. All these complexes included an underground command post. Newer missiles, such as the UR-100 and the RT-2, were placed in individual silos, and their LCCs were located separately.[32]

Russian engineers would end up devising unique ways to install and launch a missile. The R-16U, for example, was placed in a silo in a tube that could be rotated to align the missile's guidance system. The UR-100 was delivered to the launch facility in a sealed container that was simply lowered in a silo and fastened. In the case of the UR-100U, the missile and its tube were suspended from the top and stabilized at the bottom. Unlike American missiles, some Russian missiles are launched first by ejection from the tube by forced gas, followed by ignition of their motors once outside.

Where launch facilities are concerned, from satellite photos these appear simple. They are often located in wooded areas far from major highways. The properties are large and clear of nearby trees. They include a small number of buildings – one to house guards – and a square landing pad nearby for helicopters. The silo hatches are often circular-shaped and open on a hinge, unlike American silo hatches which travel horizontally on rails. The facilities are connected to their control centres by underground cable. They can be spotted relatively easily on the Internet; two of the facilities associated with the Tatishchevo base can be seen west of Saratov near Petrovo and Bolshaya Ivanovka respectively.

To say that security arrangements at Russian missile bases are tighter than in the US is an understatement. The precautions taken against enemy intrusion are more than adequate and leave practically nothing to chance, as the following shows.

Both launch and control sites are ringed with three or four coils of barbed wire, an electrified fence and in the internal perimeter POMZ-2 anti-personnel and MON-type directional mines. The first coil of wire is 200m to 300m from the silo giving guards much response time and latitude for action. The fence normally carries 800V but this can be increased to 1,600V when conditions require. In between the coils of wire, another fence responds to large objects through a change in capacitance, and the approximate point of disturbance is registered on the guards' security control panel. The entire site is kept clear of obstructions and mowed to give the greatest possible field of fire.

Inside the perimeter of a launch site, the only structure seen is a bunker for the guards. As stated above, the bunker houses intrusion detection equipment that is continuously monitored. The guards are armed with submachine guns, night vision goggles, floodlights, radios and loudspeakers. The bunkers are topped with either armoured turrets or concrete heads with small arms slits. The land mines can either detonate when tripped or be remotely activated from this position. The launch sites also include an antenna, the main role of which is to receive emergency war orders. The silos are very survivable since they can reportedly withstand thousands of pounds of overpressure.

A command post consists of much more. The property is divided into two parts where the first contains a number of buildings such as the guards' quarters and a vehicle garage, and the second, a defensive bunker, office hut, a buried LCC (called globes, or in Russian, shariki) and an ICBM launcher. A tunnel that connects the launch control centre to the guards' barracks provides protection against enemy fire and radiation. The entrance to the LCCs came in two basic forms. The older model, which is no longer used, consisted of only a round metal hatch set on a concrete pad from which one descended by way of ladder. The newer entrances are hidden in camouflage-painted buildings. The mode of descent, whether stairs or a lift, leads to a very long and narrow tunnel that termi-nates at three consecutive blast doors. The two-man launch crew, a captain and a lieutenant, sit in chairs a few feet apart at desks surrounded by consoles and indicator lights. Two of the most important features of the consoles are the launch-key slots and the square 'launch' indicator light. Working in six-hour shifts, these 'raketchiki', or missileers, routinely practise drills and continuously monitor the various systems.[33] A third man, a warrant officer, mans a communications panel. At any given time, the trio can be subject to inspections and exercises where the focus could even include armed attacks on their posts. During the Cold War, the two launch officers carried sidearms and had to surrender these to the warrant officer for safekeeping, but nowadays, they no longer carry these.[34] Also, it was the KGB, not the missileers, that armed the warheads, but again, this is no longer the case. Two of the Tatishchevo LCCs can be seen near Chernyshevka and Radishchevo northwest of Saratov.

The support bases contain all the amenities found on a typical military base. There are offices, dormitories, schools for dependents, a store, a gym and dining halls for the missileers where food is served by young women wearing short black skirts. Several missile bases are located near large cities, such as Saratov and Novosibirsk, which provide additional shopping and recreational convenience. The bases have their own motor pools that include a fleet of green trucks used to ferry launch crews to their posts. All three Missile Armies have their own aviation squadrons that use helicopters to ferry such personnel as security response teams and VIPs. Some of the helicopters can serve as airborne command posts.

Some of the key questions that have dogged defence analysts about Soviet/Russian warfighting capability regard the reliability of the RVSN. How reliable are the weapons and how dependable is the personnel? What changes are going on in the Russian nuclear world that will guarantee that the forces will work as required? Of the hundreds of ICBMs, how many will actually launch? Initially, the RVSN counted on the fact that while its missiles had low accuracy, they compensated for this by outfitting them with high-yield warheads. Nowadays, we see the opposite. Accuracy has increased and yields have been lowered. One of the early missiles, the R-9A, had a 5 megaton warhead with a maximum error of 20km, but later on, one of the variants of a newer missile, the MR UR-100, had four 550 to 750 kiloton warheads with a maximum error of 400m. The RT-23UTTH (SS-24) road-mobile missile's accuracy is even better at 200m. Also, some of the weapons in the RVSN's arsenal now have the capability to deliver an EMP pulse, which would be particularly useful in knocking out an enemy's electronic systems. On the other hand, in Soviet times some scholars estimated that during a nuclear war, perhaps only 50 per cent of the missiles would fire, and this may have been the reason why they had so many of them deployed. Bruce Blair in his book *The Logic of Accidental Nuclear War* writes that the Russian armed forces have established three tiers of nuclear forces, first echelon, operational reserves and uncommitted reserves, where the second category is meant to compensate for launch failures of the first, and where the uncommitted reserves are simply surplus weapons. What they lacked in quality, they made up for in quantity.

When it comes to the reliability of the command and control system itself, besides its high redundancy (radio, radio relay, satellite, cables), new technology developed in the 1990s was designed to enhance threat data collection and analysis. The RVSN tried to establish a system that reduced guesswork partly, no doubt, because of the early warning mishap of 1983. On the other hand, the RVSN has suffered from the same funding problems as have other military services, a situation that has sometimes put it in a precarious position. Throughout the 1990s, articles appeared in the press on the RVSN's reduced effectiveness. Not only were bases put at risk for not paying their electricity bills, some parts of the command and control system were said to still suffer because they relied on older technology or because of crime.[35] For example, the system has been known to put itself into combat mode for no reason, and thieves have been found to steal underground cables that link the LCCs to the silos for their metal. The armed forces have made up for the decline of its strength by deploying new weapons such as the EMP device previously mentioned, nuclear earth-pene-trating weapons, ABMs and precision low-yield warheads, but it is not known how they have tackled the issue of theft.[36] In the final analysis though, if the RVSN command and control system works well enough, and if the new rocket technologies it has acquired have increased firing probabilities, Russia may very well have the ability to meet its attack objectives.

Concerned about the security of its weapons, the RVSN has established its own personnel reliability programme. The missileers are tested for personality defects, not only before they enter the service, but also routinely once accepted. Membership in the 'nuclear club' is restricted to those who would turn the keys unhesitatingly and who possess no serious vices. During Soviet times, the staff was also checked for political reliability, but these days the requirement no longer exists: gone is the annoying zampolit. In the offices of missile commanders, one will no longer find the ubiquitous red star but perhaps rather a picture of St Barbara, the patron saint of the RVSN. On the other hand, Deborah Yarsike Ball writes in *Jane's Intelligence Review* that since the end of the Cold War, the Russian armed forces have seen a dramatic increase in diseases and drug abuse in its soldiers. If such individuals were to be put in charge of nuclear weapons, the West could be put at risk. Russian officers claim the West does not need to worry since those in charge of the nuclear arsenal are 'different'.[37]

For a few years following the end of the Cold War, the two superpowers enjoyed a spirit of co-operation. Both the United States and Russia sent officers to each other's country to see first hand how their armed forces worked. Both have also witnessed the destruction of each other's silos, and in 2001 a Joint Data Exchange Center was created in Moscow as a point of contact when the USAF and NASA want to warn the Russians when they are launching missiles. This spirit, however, soon disappeared when the relationship between the two super-powers began to freeze; even though its ICBMs are supposed to be de-targeted, the RVSN still conducts exercises where the main enemy is the United States. At the doctrinal level, while the Russian government has dropped its 'no-first-use' policy on nuclear weapons employment in 1993, it has stated that it would be willing to use such weapons in a conventional conflict, this to make up for the reduction of its conventional forces. Some say that if the United States began such a war and later decided to use atomic weapons, Russia would respond in kind. Both sides would then end up with a conflict no one wants.[38]

Missile development in Russia is still taking place. The new single-warhead Topol RS-12M Model 2 ICBM (the SS-27) was put into active service in existing silos in 1997–98, despite long delays and financial cutbacks, at the 104th Missile Regiment at Tatishchevo. At the same time, a road-mobile version was developed. The Topol is a three-stage rocket with a single 550 kiloton warhead and comes equipped with protection against ABMs. It is thought to have a CEP of 100m to 200m. The RVSN was expected to have 160 to 220 RS-12Ms in active service by 2005, but in 2007, only 47 of both the fixed and mobile variants were found on the roster.

Yamantau

Are subterranean complexes still being built today in Russia? For some years, the Russians have been building a large complex at Yamantau Mountain near Beloretsk in the Urals 850 miles east of Moscow. There is speculation this would be a new citadel for the Strategic Rocket Forces to replace the vulnerable command post outside Moscow. The project is thought to be controlled by the Federal Service for Special Construction, the Spetssroy Rossii, previously an independent agency but now transferred to the Ministry of Defence. Its deepness would likely make it impervious to the American's B61-11 bunker-buster bombs. Some American politicians are not pleased the Russians are spending much-needed money on this city sized facility, funds that could be used to pay troops or dismantle nuclear weapons. Peter Pry in his book *War Scare* states that this is just one of many underground facilities being built or improved in Russia.

❑ SAUDI ARABIA

Perhaps the most controversial underground facilities in the Kingdom of Saudi Arabia are the caves or tunnels that store long-range missiles. In 1985, the Saudi government bought approximately fifty DF-3A IRBMs from China ostensibly for its protection against Iran. The rockets are designed to carry a 2,200kg warhead to a maximum distance of 3,500km, a long enough range to hit Israel, Iran and even southern Russia. They are stored in tunnels at two or three locations and pulled out to a launching pad for firing.[1] The deal with Beijing included training by Chinese technicians.

When the sale to Saudi Arabia was made public in 1988, there was uproar. Everyone began to worry about Riyadh's ultimate intentions. Political leaders wondered whether the rockets were obtained for offensive or defensive purposes. Washington was so angry with the Saudis that its ambassador left, and Israel was so worried it threatened a pre-emptive attack similar to the one against the Osiraq nuclear reactor in Iraq a few years earlier. Yet, the Saudi government had only made the purchase after the United States turned down its request for Lance missiles. While the Kingdom refused to get rid of the DF-3As, it nevertheless swore they would never be outfitted with nuclear or chemical warheads. It also signed the Nuclear Non-Proliferation Treaty for good measure, and vowed not to re-sell any of the missiles to anyone else. As far as is known, the missiles are still in the Saudi government's inventory.

Other underground structures in Saudi Arabia include:

- Air defence command headquarters in or near Riyahd. One source claimed the Royal Saudi Air Force has six underground regional air defence operations centres in the country;
- A command centre five floors below the Ministry of Defence and Aviation complex in Riyadh. It includes a glassed-in upper floor where senior officers can watch the action below; and
- A number of facilities designed to hold strategic reserves of petroleum products. These products are to be used in times of crises. One of those facilities is in Riyadh.

❑ SERBIA

In 2004, Dusan Stojanovic of the Associated Press reported on the shooting of two soldiers that were guarding the entrance to a secret complex in Belgrade. The entrance, hidden among barracks in the Topcider district of the capital, led to a network of tunnels and chambers that formed a 2-mile square installation. One of the bunkers connected to this honeycomb was a six-storey facility that might have been used as a government command post. The network was said to be built in the 1960s by the order of President Tito.

Other underground facilities in Serbia include:

- A bunker at the President's villa at Dobanovac (*sic*) outside Belgrade;
- A bunker for the Ministry of Internal Affairs southwest of Belgrade;
- A military command centre at Mount Avala;
- Another military command post at Ivanjica;
- Mountain hangars at the Priština air base;
- An air defence operations centre at Strazhevica south of Belgrade. This uses a Swedish AS-84 air surveillance system; and
- Earth-covered hangars at the Batajnica air base north of Belgrade.

❑ SINGAPORE

The government of Singapore built an underground ammunition depot in the 1990s to replace an old one in Seletar East.

❑ SLOVAKIA

The communist government of Czechoslovakia built hundreds of fallout shelters for the public in Slovakia (mostly under schools and apartment buildings), and likely also for the party and the army. One in Bratislava by the white Danube River bridge has been turned into a night club, and another in Nitra has become an art gallery. Most of the rest are abandoned. There are also indications that the Soviet army had deployed long-range missiles in tunnels at Martin.

❑ SOUTH AFRICA

Underground facilities in South Africa include:

- A military command post next to army headquarters in Pretoria. According to one blog, which quoted the local newspaper *Beeld*, the bunker was built in the 1980s for the air force, and is still being used by the armed forces as an air operations centre;
- One source claimed the South African government had a nuclear shelter somewhere outside Pretoria. This has not been confirmed by the author; and
- The magazine *Tunnels and Tunnelling* reported in September 1999 that workmen discovered a network of tunnels and bunkers under the Parliament Buildings. They were thought to have been built in the 1960s during the time of President Vorster.

❑ SOUTH KOREA

One of the more well-known bunkers in the Republic of Korea is an American installation. Command Post Tango was built as a hardened headquarters for United States armed forces in Korea in the Seoul suburb of Songnam. The bunker is 307,000sq ft, contains an operations centre from which all American forces would be directed, communications equipment and power generating engines. It is NBC proof and likely contains a decontamination area. Some media have reported that the United States government was considering the sale of the bunker a few years ago and that the American armed forces would build a new facility at Camp Humphreys.[1]

Another media report mentioned that the Korean armed forces have over 170 underground installations on Pak Ryond Island.

Other United States military bunkers in Korea are at:

- Camp Walker, south of Taegu. This is called Command Post Oscar;
- Camp Red Cloud;
- Camp Howard, as a communications centre. This is near Daehong-ri;
- Yongsan, as a tactical operations centre. This is no longer used; and

- Osan Air Base for US Air Forces Korea. According to *Nuclear Battlefields*, the command post, called the 'Tree House', doubles as a combination air defence/early warning centre for the USAF and the ROK's air force. It can also receive Emergency Action Messages authorizing the use of nuclear weapons. It is debatable whether it is a surface structure or a true underground facility. The bunker's alternate is at Kwang Ju Air Base.[2]

In addition, many many tunnels were built by the allies during the Korean War at various places. One such complex was excavated by Canadian military engineers and gunners near Yongdon on the Sami-ch'on River at what was called Hill 146. It included a command post and a tunnel leading to an observation post.

❑ SPAIN

Spain has at least two Cold War bunkers in Madrid, one under army headquarters and the other under the parliament building. The latter caused an uproar several years ago when the public learned how much money was spent on it. Furthermore, some websites have reported that NATO has built a new bunker next to the Torrejon air base.

❑ SWEDEN

Civil Defence

The Cold War has undeniably had a major impact upon the landscape of Sweden. As in other countries such as Norway and Switzerland, the Swedish government has seen to it that extensive measures were taken to guarantee that it and its citizens survive a nuclear attack. It established an alternate seat of government about 250km northwest of Stockholm, built or modernized fortifications for its armed forces and ordered municipalities to build civil defence control centres. For the citizenry, shelters in apartment buildings were built and it is estimated that about 85 per cent of the population would be protected in wartime. The smart Swedes created a further advantage in some of the public facilities when they decided they could serve dual roles. At least one bunker serves as a gymnasium and four in Stockholm alone double as parking garages. Sweden has an entire industry specializing in bomb shelters and blast-proof doors, something very few nations can boast. The government has also built secret depots where essential commodities, such as oil and food, can be stored. With the end of the Cold War, many of these facilities have been closed and slowly the public has been able to learn about them.[1]

Throughout the Cold War, the organization responsible for civil defence in Sweden was the National Rescue Services Board of the Ministry of Defence. This was the service that looked after the construction of public shelters, the operation of air raid warning sirens, and the stockpiling of essential supplies mentioned above. It also was responsible for preparing plans for rescue operations. It managed local civil defence control centres, all of which were underground. After the Cold War, the NRSB's focus of operations changed to peacetime disasters, and since the government no longer felt the need to maintain the local bunkers, they were all closed.

Effective 1 July 2002, the NRSB became the Swedish Emergency Management Agency (the Krisberedskapsmyndighten or BKM), but seven years later, it, the Swedish Rescue Services Agency and part of the National Board for Psychological Defence (which provided information to the public), was combined into a new MoD organization, the Civil Contingencies Agency. One of the CCA's key roles is to co-ordinate the work of other services (e.g. police, fire etc.) in the event of large-scale emergencies.[2]

Military Bunkers

Among the major institutions of Swedish society, the armed forces were the primary users of underground installations. The underground naval base at Muskö was never really kept secret from the public, although tours of the insides were always restricted to special guests. After its sale to the marine engineering firm Kockums AB in around 2008, public visits have been allowed and the Swedish people have had access to one of the most unique military facilities in the nation.[3]

Muskö Island lies about 40km south of the capital at the southern end of the Stockholm archipelago. At some point in the late 1940s, teams of engineering specialists arrived in the area to take surveys and to draw plans for the new base. Architects decided to put the underground facility on the west side of the island. Once plans were drawn, construction crews were ordered to build a series of caves and interconnecting tunnels in the rock. The work involved the removal of 1.5 million tons of rock, the laying of tons of concrete for roads and the installation of miles of electrical cabling, not to mention the creation of a tunnel for the road leading to the island. The end product consisted of a series of four caverns, including two for docks 470ft long, which were connected by 12 miles of tunnels. The facility was so large it needed its own bus service. At the time it was finished in 1969 – after nineteen years of construction – it was most likely the largest such base in the world.

During its active lifetime, the Muskö base was home to the Royal Swedish Navy's 4th Naval Warfare Flotilla.[4] The base was also home to other military establishments such as a signals intelligence station of the Försvarets Radio Anstalt (Defence Radio Institution). It was never considered totally secret since it was featured in such magazines as the RSN's *Our Navy* and in *Tunnels and Tunnelling*. It had all the amenities to sustain itself in wartime such as its own power source, air filtration equipment, water supply and sufficient living space for its large manpower. There were, of course, a number of emergency exits.

Despite its neutrality, Sweden had long been a target for the Soviet intelligence services. Many of its military secrets were revealed by the traitor Stig Wennerstrom of the Royal Swedish Air Force, secrets such as details of missiles then considered for purchase by the Ministry of Defence and Sweden's military relationship with the United States. But since Wennerstrom may not have known much about Muskö because he belonged to the air force, the Soviets sought other ways to learn about the complex.

Espionage by the Russian navy against Sweden was revealed to the world when Whiskey-class submarine 137 ran aground near the Karlskrona naval base on 27 October 1981. It was never said clearly and truthfully why the sub was there in the first place, although some writers theorized that the captain was looking to gather intelligence or was seeking places where Spetsnaz troops could disembark during a war.[5] The Soviet government insisted that 137 was on a training mission and that its navigational equipment had failed. Moscow was falsely indignant that the sub was being held, and through the Swedish ambassador in Moscow, it demanded its immediate release. While all this was going on, intercepted radio signals showed that it was Moscow who ordered the sub's captain to use the navigational failure as an excuse. These same signals revealed that the Russians were considering a forced rescue. Even without the evidence of Soviet deceit though, Swedish military officers could never buy the story that a sub with faulty equipment could navigate through a coastal area full of islands.

It would not be the only time when Soviet subs would violate Swedish waters. One year after the above 'Whiskey on the rocks' incident, it was the turn of the Muskö naval base to be targeted. In October 1982, a number of foreign submarines were detected going through the Stockholm archipelago towards Muskö. Upon investigation, the Swedish navy determined that some of the craft were manned bottom-huggers suspected of belonging to a 'Warsaw Pact nation'. The Swedish government took the incursions into its waters so seriously it set up the Submarine Defence Commission to look into the matter, and in its report, released in 1983, it laid bare the fact that it was the Soviets who were responsible. Swedish outrage and protests failed to quell the continuing violation of Swedish territory by the Soviet navy.

Stockholm had two civil defence control centres, one at Sollentuna and the other at Lissma. This is the former. It was codenamed the 'Elephant'. (Photo: Author)

One of the entrances to the underground air base at Säve. (Photo: Author)

Stockholm Bunkers

Somewhere north of Stockholm, in the Edsberg area of Sollentuna, Swedish civil defence set up another underground installation inside a hill. Known as the 'Elephant', it was opened in 1977 as a National Rescue Services Board control centre as a small 21,000sq ft structure designed to house 220 in times of emergency. It was outfitted with its own offices, operations centre, telephone exchange, power plant, air filtration equipment and water well. The building was lined with sheet metal to reduce the effects of electromagnetic pulses produced by nuclear detonations and is so built to absorb shock waves. It had several communications connections enabling it to control and co-ordinate rescue operations, along with its own security and automatic fire-alarm systems. While its front door is concealed in the rock, it is quite visible to passers-by walking nearby. The bunker was sold to a private firm a few years ago. Today, the bunker lies under a new residential complex.

Another bunker, one that looked after the southern part of Stockholm, was placed near the suburb of Lissma. It was called 'Wolf'.

Underground Air Bases

The Royal Swedish Air Force had recognized the need to protect its aircraft as early as the Second World War. Worried about the new German threat, it began the construction of underground hangars at such places as the Säve air base in 1940. During the Cold War, the protection of its air force from the Soviets took on an even greater importance, not the least of which was because the RSAF was then said to be the third largest in the world, and because Sweden's neutrality precluded protection from NATO. More underground hangars were therefore built, and at Säve, a new deeper complex was established. Of all the underground bases, it would be the largest.

The new underground part of the base at Säve was built between 1950 and 1955. It consisted of two tunnels that lead to a network of caverns. In addition to aircraft workshops, the latter held offices, sleeping rooms, a canteen and a small air operations centre. It had its own power and water supply, communications

Inside the hangar. (Photo: Author)

links, air intakes and emergency exits leading above. The 225,000sq ft facility was located 30m below ground, and its entrances were curved to prevent a blast wave from reeking damage inside. Throughout its lifetime, its operational unit, Wing No. 9, used such aircraft as the SAAB J29 Tunnan and the J34 Hunter. The base was closed in 1969.

Today, few of the old underground hangars remain in service. Some are used as storage depots while others are empty. After the Säve hangar complex was closed, the government had considered filling it with sand and forgetting about it, until some RSAF officers and staff insisted that it remain open as a testament to the past. It is now Sweden's main air force museum. The public can now take a close look at the overweight little Tunnan fighter or the sleek Viggen interceptor. It is more than an air force museum as some of the displays pertain to the Cold War in general. Here, in addition to the aircraft, one can learn about Swedes such as Stig Wennerstrom and Stig Bergling who spied for the Soviet Union.[6]

In total, underground hangars would be built for the following Flygflottilj (Wings):

F8 Barkarby
F9 Göteborg (Säve)
F13 Norrköping
F16 Uppsala
F18 Tullinge
F21 Luleå
Arboga
Fällfors

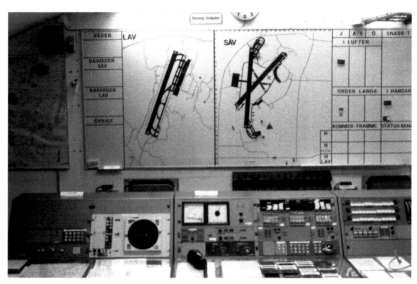

The operations centre. (Photo: Author)

At two of these bases, F16 and F18, there were also underground air defence operations centres. The F8 base, which was outside Stockholm, was also a Bloodhound SAM site.[7]

Coastal Defence
Sweden was one of the few countries in the world to maintain coastal defence sites after the Second World War. Many were built during the war and re-equipped afterwards with newer guns and made NBC-proof, while others were

The entrance to the Femöre battery was hidden in this ordinary looking building. (Photo: Author)

One of the guns.
Perhaps oddly,
these guns were set
in a park in full
public view.
(Photo: Author)

pure products of the Cold War. The Swedish Navy was mandated to protect the nation's jagged coastline, and this it did with thirty-nine artillery batteries placed at strategic locations. At Femöre near the town of Oxelösund was one such battery.

The deep harbour at Oxelösund and the steel works nearby required it to have some defences. In the early 1960s, the Swedish Navy's coastal artillery branch established a new defensive gunnery post near the Femöre lighthouse that would watch over intruders attempting to attack. Fort Femöre was built on the rocky shore as a battery of three guns and a radar. It was established as a complex of tunnels that connected the 3 guns and that could house approximately 70 men

One of the tunnels inside the battery. Tunnels such as these linked the command and support areas to the guns themselves. (Photo: Author)

The Femöre battery included a number of personnel shelters and foxholes. This was one of the shelters. (Photo: Author)

for 30 days. The installation was outfitted with living and operating facilities that included workshops, a command centre, telephone exchange, decontamination cubicles, ventilation room and emergency exits. The fort employed mostly gunners, although there were a few support personnel such as cooks, signallers and artificers. The battery belonged to a battalion with headquarters located in a bunker under a church in Oxelösund.

Fort Femöre's main equipment consisted of three Bofors Type 57 75mm guns encased in movable turrets fixed into the ground, along with a PA39 radar that had a 60km range. The guns could fire up to twenty-five rounds per minute to a range of 10km, and the shells could be either delayed action that would explode only after piercing a ship's hull, or that would spray shrapnel upon advancing troops. The gun barrels could be anchored outside to survive the effects of an atomic blast wave. The fort's entrance was hidden inside an ordinary looking brown and white house, and for added security dummy guns were placed nearby and foxholes were dug for protective troops.[8] The base ceased its operational role

All the guns in the area were commanded by a battalion headquarters in Oxelösund. (Photo: Author)

in 1975, but continued as a training facility until 1994. It was decommissioned in 1998 and turned into a museum.

Another coastal defence battery now open to the public is on Hemsö Island north of Stockholm. This installation was built in the 1950s and employed 340 men. Its armament consisted of 152mm and 75mm guns. The facility also acted as a sea mine control station.

Other Facilities

Other underground facilities in Sweden are:

- In every city, as civil defence control centres. All seem to be closed now. Many are abandoned, but at least one, in the centre of Osby on a hill, was sold to a couple and turned into a home;
- At every other coastal defence site;
- At Stromstad as an oil depot;
- At Östersund, as an air defence operations centre;
- On Skeppsholmen Island in Stockholm, as a naval command centre during the Second World War and later as a storage depot;[9]
- A Second World War air-raid shelter in White Pine Mountain in Stockholm, converted into a nuclear bunker in the 1970s, and now used by a data firm;
- The public shelter in the Katarinaberget in Stockholm;
- The public shelter in the Mariaberget in Västeras west of Stockholm;
- At Hammarby outside Stockholm, to house the national telephone exchange. This is a five-storey-high facility that was built in the 1980s;
- At Boden in northern Sweden, as a network of forts built in the early twentieth century. This garrison town had several individual gunnery and infantry forts to protect the Lulea area. The forts were closed between 1979 and 1998. One of them, Fort Degerberget, kept some of the country's gold reserves from 1941 to 1982; and
- In their book *The Royal Swedish Navy*, Erkhammar and Ohrelius state the navy built several other underground installations as command centres, radio stations, coastal radar sites and as ammunition and fuel depots.

❑ SWITZERLAND

Switzerland is most likely the one country in the world that has the largest number of underground structures. That distinction may be born from the fact that the country was defeated by the French in the nineteenth century. The defeat caused the Swiss people to adopt a strongly defensive mindset – a psychological redoubt, so to speak – from which would sprout their reputation for neutrality. From this neutralistic ideology would rise a veritable sea of fortifications.

Being neutral is one thing, but appearing to be so is another. Switzerland never joined NATO and the European Union, has not adopted the Euro as currency and until 2002 was not even a member of the United Nations. It has not sent troops overseas to fight. It has, on the other hand, sometimes deviated from its chosen path by conducting secret discussions with the French army in 1939–40 on the subject of mutual defence against Nazi Germany. During the Cold War, Switzerland purchased tanks from the Federal Republic of Germany and fighter aircraft from the United States and France causing the Soviet Union to question its neutrality. Even though the Helvetic nation pledged to take no sides during a nuclear war, the Warsaw Pact planned to ignore its neutrality by passing through its territory to attack France. Soviet intelligence agents even buried secret equipment there for use by pre-invasion sabotage units.[1] The Swiss people knew they were vulnerable to Eastern bloc threats and reacted accordingly by creating a massive army and by developing a huge defence infrastructure.[2] At the same time, their desire to burrow below gave rise to a huge tunnelling industry.

One of the chief components of Switzerland's fortified infrastructure was the bunker. Such structures were placed throughout the country to repel invasions coming from all sides, and to ensure the various levels of government could continue operating during and after an attack. Bunkers were built for the national, cantonal and municipal governments as well as for all key services such as hospitals and the utilities. The armed forces were similarly fortified with every brigade and regiment given their own bunkers. Many of these facilities were protected by the army's Festungwachtkorps (Fortifications Guard Corps).

Kandersteg
While it was no secret that Switzerland had dug itself underground, until

An entrance to a typical public shelter in Switerland. (Photo: Swiss Federal Office of Civil Protection)

recently not much was revealed about the structures themselves. The national government in Bern had its own bunker outside the city for years. Little, if anything, was ever said about it, but when the Swiss parliament decided to build a new facility at Kandersteg in the 1990s, the public got a glimpse of it. The bunker was said to be necessary as the old one had outlived its usefulness, but its hefty price tag of approximately 240 million Swiss francs shocked some politicians who failed to see its need in the post-Cold War envi-ronment. The federal government had tried to keep a lid on the subject, going

A dormitory. (Photo: Swiss Federal Office of Civil Protection)

so far as arresting a journalist, Urs Paul Engeler, in 2003 for revealing its precise location, but as the proverbial genie was out of the proverbial bottle, the battle for secrecy was lost.

The Kandersteg bunker was typical of such structures in that it included the standard assortment of offices, communications centre, decontamination cubi-cles, eating and sleeping areas and power room. It was built as two tunnels in a cliff in the south side of town near the railway line. The facility could hold 200 to 300 federal politicians and civil servants, who would have travelled there during emergencies by car or train.[3] It is also used as a backup computer centre and as the national civil defence alarm centre. The bunker's protection is assured by the presence of Festungwachtkorps troops that may be stationed at a nearby barracks.[4]

Along with the national bunker, every canton was expected to have its own emergency facility.[5] Again, very little has been revealed about them, although one source has intimated to the author that they are occupied by both civilian and military staff, and that their entrances are always cleverly hidden. In the case of the Valais canton bunker at Sion, two entrances were built, one for military personnel in a car garage, and the other for civilians in a garden shed. To get inside, a soldier would drive inside the former, close the door behind him, and proceed on foot below to get to work.[6] For added security, staff arrival times would be staggered. At the end of their shifts, the staff would exit the same way they came. One Internet site places the Bern canton bunker at Utzigen on Talackerweg.[7]

Civil Defence

The Swiss government has taken the protection of the population so seriously that it has codified the concept. Since 1964, the government has required that either new houses and apartment buildings include a shelter for their residents,

A kitchen. (Photo: Swiss Federal Office of Civil Protection)

or that citizens buy space in a communal bunker. It is very common when driving on a country road to see doors in a hill or mountain that lead to such structures. In a *New York Times* article from March 1981, the Swiss Federal Office of Civil Defence expected to have enough shelter space for the entire population by 1990.

The largest public shelter in Switzerland is located inside the Sonnenberg, a small mountain in Lucerne. The roadway tunnel was built in the 1970s as a mass shelter capable of housing 21,000 residents. From the two tunnels that pass through the mountain, doors lead to a complex of dining halls, recreation halls, a police station, air filtration centre, command post, a seven-floor hospital and even a safety deposit room. The residents would have slept in the road tunnels in bunk beds.

The bunker turned out to be less than successful in its purpose; in a 1987 exercise, for example, the giant blast doors took two days to close. According to media sources, the bunker is no longer earmarked as a major shelter and during a war, it would only house 2,000 in the command centre.

Broadcasting Facilities

Much thought has also been put into the broadcasting infrastructure. The Swiss Ministry of Defence, Public Protection and Sports includes a command charged with operating and maintaining radio, print media and television facilities during a war. The Ministry's Press and Radio Directorate is tasked with ensuring that emergency stations are operational at all times and that it has sufficient personnel to man those facilities when required. The Directorate's 1,700 men and women consist of:

- No. 10 Input Group, a unit of specialists that monitor the foreign media in fifty languages, and that translates their broadcasts into three of the Swiss languages, German, French and Italian;
- No. 20 Radio Group, a team of radio broadcasters that work in bunkered studios;
- No. 30 TV Group, staffed by announcers and cameramen that also work in bunkers; and
- No. 40 Press Group, a unit of journalists and typesetters ready to produce print media such as flyers and newsletters.

The Ministry of Defence makes it clear that the Directorate is not to be an outlet for government propaganda, but that its role is to ensure that the public is kept informed of current events at all times should the regular media be unable to operate. The Directorate's operating agency, the 1st Information Regiment, works in protected studios that can make use of collapsible antennae.

Military Bunkers

Regular underground military facilities were just as common in Switzerland. These range from small observation posts to air bases and large tunnel complexes. Most of them consist of offices, communications post, power room, munitions store and an operations centre, with entrances concealed behind some form of camouflage. They are usually hidden from public view, although local residents, many of whom belong to the militia, all seem to know where they are. At one time, the nation had approximately 21,000 such fortifications, but since the end of the Cold War, many have been closed and some turned into tourist attractions. Those that are still in use are considered military secrets.[8]

Most of these underground posts were built for the infantry and the artillery. These bunkers were so placed that they would cover all possible approaches to their area. As an example, around the town of Martigny, 100 bunkers were established to defend the area from an attack originating from Italy. The posts were placed at various heights with the higher ones designed for long-range fire and the lower ones used to repel a local attack. Every battery commander was expected to maintain maps that showed his guns' arc-of-fire and that indicated heights and locations of points of reference as such data was used to set the guns' angle.

One of the gunnery posts around Martigny visited by the author was at Champex. Originally built over a twenty-three-month period during the Second World War, the bunker was one of many that looked down upon the Great St Bernard Pass and the Val Ferret approach below and was one of three that made up Battery A46. The staff consisted of mainly infanteers, gunners and

Doors to underground military facilities in Switzerland were often camouflaged. This one is at Martigny. Behind it was one of the many artillery posts in the area. (Photo: Author)

One of the 105mm guns at Martigny.
(Photo: Author)

communications personnel who worked in three eight-hour shifts. The fort's armament included three 105mm guns and 120mm mortars, and the guns were placed not only to attack invaders below, but also other forts nearby should they be captured. The Champex fort had a camouflaged entrance, along with machine-gun slots and grenade chutes for self-protection. The embrasures in the cliff face could barely be seen as they were covered with camouflaged trap doors. The battery closed in 1988 and has since become a museum.

In Switzerland, defensive fortifications and obstacles came in all forms. The Swiss, over the years, have become very adept at blending their armament with the environment. Mortars, for instance, are set in the ground and covered with a metal hatch that can only be seen if one is close by. Centurion tank turrets are buried on the country's periphery at such places as Aigle, Buchs and Vallorbe and covered with material that makes them look like boulders in a field. The roads have innocent-looking grilles below which could be planted explosive charges, and bridges can be quickly mined to deny their use by an enemy.

Missile Bases

Other bunkers were found in Switzerland at Bloodhound surface-to-air missile sites. The BL-64 Bloodhound was accepted by the Swiss Luftwaffe in 1964 as

Bloodhounds at Menzingen near Zug. (Photo: Author)

Each Bloodhound was kept stored in an underground magazine until required. The magazines were temperature-controlled and protected by a heavy blast door. (Photo: Author)

one of the country's main air defence instruments working alongside fighter aircraft and long-range radar stations to guard the nation's air space.[9] It was sited at six locations and aimed, obviously, towards points outside.

At the time it came out, the Bloodhound was the best SAM manufactured by the United Kingdom. Built by the Bristol Aircraft Company and Ferranti, it consisted of a long cylindrical body propelled by four boosters and two ramjet engines. The second variant, which was the model adopted by the Swiss Air Force, had a 160km range in which it travelled at Mach 2.5 using kerosene as fuel. Its warhead included a 35kg RDX-TNT load and environmental sensing

Each Bloodhound site had an underground command post for use by intelligence and fire-control staff. (Photo: Author)

Each missile site also had its own radar. The transmitting equipment lay below in a sturdy structure. (Photo: Author)

devices that only allowed arming once the missile reached and sustained a force of 14Gs. The Bloodhound was guided by a ground-based T-87 continuous wave radar and was detonated by a proximity fuze.[10] To prevent early detonation by stray radio transmissions or by enemy forces using electronic warfare, the command system's receiver was equipped with a radio wave filter. The guidance system included an incidence switch that would correct the missile's path if it deviated by more than four degrees.

The six Bloodhound sites were operated by the Swiss Air Force's 33rd Air Defence Brigade (after 1986 by the 32nd Airfield Brigade), specifically by the 7th

The launch control officer's desk. (Photo: Author)

Air Defence Missile Regiment. The Regiment in turn controlled the 71st and 72nd Air Defence Missile Battalions where each operates three sites. Some sites were assigned sixteen missiles and others, thirty-two, where some were kept on launching pads and others stored in earth-covered bays. The missiles were controlled by a site's tactical control centre that was staffed by a small number of men such as the officer-in-charge, a technical officer and an intelligence officer. Each base was connected to the Air Force's national air defence centre at Dübendorf outside Zürich through the Flinte communications system. While Switzerland has four official languages, the language of usage in Bloodhound units was German.

The Bloodhound sites were at:

Bettwil
Emmen
Gübel
Laupersdorf
Schmidrüti
Torny-le-Grand

The Gübel site was also the headquarters of the 71st ADM Battalion, and the Torny site, HQ for the 72nd ADM Battalion.

The bases consisted of a small number of buildings, the hardened above-ground tactical control centre, radar, barracks and underground personnel shelters. Nearby stood a tall collimator tower for missile guidance alignment. The rockets were stored in temperature and humidity controlled magazines that were protected by heavy blast doors. The bases were ringed by a barbed wired fence, and for added security, civilians who resided nearby kept watch for trespassers and onlookers. From satellite photos, the installations could be recognized by the presence of circular launch pads.

The Bloodhound was retired from service in 1999. Only one site, Gübel near Zug, has been maintained in its original state to become a tourist attraction. Another site at Torny-le-Grand is still used by the Swiss Air Force, but as a Stinger SAM training range.

Underground Air Bases
During the Cold War, the Swiss Air Force followed the army's lead in the construction of bunkers and built its own underground structures. Caverns were

Missile magazines at the Torny-le-Grand site. (Photo: Author)

dug in the sides of mountains at several airfields for both aircraft maintenance and troop accommodation. At one air base, Meiringen, two parallel aircraft tunnels were dug out in the 1950s (which were connected to form a 'U' in the new millennium), while at Turtmann, a base that dates back to 1929, three tunnels were excavated between 1951 and 1958, two for aircraft and one for staff. The hangars are protected by heavy doors and painted in camouflage colours. Until recently, these Kriegsflugplätze (war air bases) were considered military secrets, but now the media is sometimes allowed a peek inside.

Another camouflaged entrance in Switzerland. This led to an infantry machine-gun post. The post was located in a quiet residential area of Evionnaz. (Photo: Author)

The bases with cavern-hangars were used by the Luftwaffe's air defence force. The aircraft consisted of, at various times, the Mirage, Hunter, F-5 Tiger and the F/A-18 Hornet. The bases are far from secret as they are very visible to passers-by and do not sport telltale 'No Trespassing – Defence Property' signs common to military properties in North America and the United Kingdom.[11] Indeed, Swiss fighters must cross public roads when taxiing from the runways to the hangars. The operational units, known as Fliegerstaffeln (air squadrons), are controlled by the national air operations centre mentioned above. Air bases known or suspected of having mountain hangars include:

Aircraft hangars in Switzerland were either the earth-covered or mountain type. This hangar at Wilderswil is an example of the former type. The base is no longer used. (Photo: Author)

A larger hangar at the Payerne air base. (Photo: Author)

Ambri
Buochs
Meiringen
Mollis
Turtmann

Most of these bases have closed as a result of defence cuts mandated by the Armée XXI programme, although in at least one case, Buochs, the hangars themselves remain Ministry of Defence property.[12] The Luftwaffe's main fighter school at Payerne has no cavern-hangars.[13]

By all accounts, it appears that Meiringen is the only base with mountain tunnels that is still active. The aerodrome consists of two long airstrips that parallel Highway 6 and a series of buildings and taxiways that lead to the U-shaped cavern. At the time of writing, it was home to No. 8 Air Squadron flying F-5s and to the F/A-18-equipped No. 11 Air Squadron. Both belong to the base's No. 13 Aviation Wing.[14] Perhaps strangely, the Swiss Air Force does not

This bunker at the Saanen air base was likely an operations centre. (Photo: Author)

A new bunker at the Reichenbach airfield. The bunker's recent vintage does not match that of the old Second World War hangars there. (Photo: Author)

maintain fighters on 24–7 Quick Reaction Alert, although its airspace is constantly monitored by four mountain-top long-range radar stations. Since Switzerland's air space is too narrow, it provides too little time for a scramble; the Luftwaffe relies instead on reaction by its neighbours.

Other Facilities
Other underground installations known to exist in Switzerland are:

- Near St Maurice. One of the largest underground artillery forts was dug in a mountain on the east side of the highway. It is said to have 40km of tunnels;
- St Reuenthal. This fort was built in 1937 for protection against Germany. Its armament consisted of 75mm guns. It closed in the late 1980s and has been turned into a tourist attraction;
- At Stansstad, south of Lucerne. Fort Fürigen was also turned into a museum;
- A few miles east of Vallorbe, as a machine-gun post. It is also now a museum;
- At Evionnaz. A machine-gun post was built inside rock near a residential area;
- West of Interlaken on the south side of the highway. The presence of a loading dock suggests it is a supply depot. A very similar depot is seen on the west side of the Interlaken–Lauterbrunnen road;
- South of Alpnach on the east side of the highway. A bunker entrance can be seen in the rock. The entrance is painted in dark camouflage colours;
- At every military airfield, as earth-covered hangars. These are plainly visible at such places at Alpnach, Reichenbach, Saanen, St Stephen and Wilderswil;

- Near Amsteg, a former government bunker is now used by Swiss Data Safe; and
- At Hagerbach, east of Zürich, owned by private industry as a test tunnel.

Many of the fortified gun sites were hidden inside brown and white barns. These structures were never identified as military facilities, although the presence of army trucks nearby gave a hint of their use.

❑ SYRIA

It was reported in the press that in September 2007, Israeli air force jets attacked an underground facility in Syria approximately 50km from the Iraqi border. The bunker was suspected of housing nuclear weapons that had been imported from North Korea and that could have transferred to Hezbollah. The jets were aided by ground commandos that used laser-aiming devices to guide the bombs, and by computer experts that shut down the Syrian air defence system. The Syrian government claimed the facility was only part of an agricultural research centre.

Other bunkers in Syria apparently lie under a mountain near Misyaf and under a radar station in Chenchar.

❑ TAIWAN

The small country of Taiwan, otherwise known as the Republic of China, has the unenviable distinction of being located next to an enemy superpower. The island, once part of China proper, owes its status as a sovereign nation to the 1940s civil war on the mainland. During the conflict, future Premier of the People's Republic of China (PRC), Mao Zedong, battled with Kuomintang leader Chiang Kai-shek for control of the Middle Kingdom. The war did not bode well for Chiang, and his defeat forced him to relocate elsewhere.

The entrance to the underground harbour at Mount Zhai on Kinmen Island. Inside are tunnels only large enough for patrol boats. (Photo: Author)

Another underground harbour on Kinmen Island. This one was by the ferry to Little Kinmen Island. (Photo: Author)

Chiang decided to make the island of Formosa into his new home. The island had long been Chinese territory and was occupied by the Japanese army during the Second World War. When Chiang fled China in 1949, he created, with the help of the gold reserves he took with him, the Republic of China there which would eventually become a relatively liberal democracy and rely upon a market economy and foreign economic ties for growth. Taiwan, as Formosa came to be called, has since followed its own path to self-realization always ignoring calls by Chairman Mao for re-unification. Mao and his successors have never recognized Taiwan's sovereign status and have always fought attempts for it to claim total independence, and it is this state of tension that has made the region into one of the world's flash points.[1]

The regional Cold War between the PRC and Taiwan has caused the latter to seek American aid, to create a strong armed force and to burrow below.[2] The main island, along with remote properties such as Quemoy (now called Kinmen Island) and Matsu, is honeycombed with underground structures of all types to protect military forces, the political leadership and the civilian population. Lying approximately 2km from mainland China, Kinmen Island is especially vulnerable to the PRC's armed wrath and as a consequence of its position has witnessed first hand attacks from Chinese artillery.[3] It therefore became what is probably one of the most heavily fortified islands on earth.

An article written by Sean Boyne for *Jane's Intelligence Review* in 1997 was very revealing of Kinmen's defences. At the time, military forces on the island belonged to the Kinmen Defence Command. Headquarters for the KDC was located under Tai-Wu Mountain in the centre-east of the island. The Command was composed of four sub-units, three on the island and the fourth on Little Kinmen Island to the west. Boyne writes that KDC Headquarters were built in the late 1950s after the Chinese army shelled the island and after the army realized how vulnerable it really was. It remains today as Kinmen's centre of military operations.

An earth-covered
artillery post.
(Photo: Author)

The Tai-Wu facility is probably the largest underground installation on Kinmen. It includes a vehicle tunnel approximately 4km long, an auditorium that can seat hundreds and is built in extremely solid granite. The complex is self-sustaining and is NBC proof. From Tai-Wu, the armed forces are connected by telephone to other underground military installations such as observation posts along the coast (for instance in the northeast at Mashan and in the northwest at Kuningtou), the Huagangshi Hospital near the centre of the island, various 155mm and 240mm artillery positions and defences around the joint military/civilian airport. For years, it also operated two underground harbours, a small one near the Shuitou Pier at the western end of the island, and a larger one in the southwest under Mount Zhai. Similarly, on Little Kinmen Island, the navy had an underground base in the southwest. On both islands, the public has its own shelters at several points.

Another Taiwanese island, Matsu, is just as fortified. The large Andong tunnel in Dongyin, built to hold 1,000 troops, consists of a network of tunnels that end at several seaside observation posts. Another installation, Tunnel 88, was excavated as a storage depot for tanks and as troop barracks. The Beihai tunnel, on the other hand, was built to house small ships.

Despite the occasional threat from Beijing, the Taiwanese armed forces have reduced their manpower levels on Kinmen, Little Kinmen and Matsu Islands. Places once considered secret have been written about, have been turned into tourist attractions or have simply been destroyed. Tunnel 88 on Matsu was later used to store wine, and bunkers on all three islands are now open to the public. Visitors are now welcomed in the underground harbour at Mount Zhai on Kinmen or in the Beihai tunnel on Matsu. Tourists can walk freely through a few civil defence tunnels, but at least one on Kinmen at Hepingshin Village no longer stands as it has been destroyed. The armed forces nevertheless maintain a strong presence on the islands even today, and indeed the Ministry of Defence still has the right to use some of these facilities.

The entrance to a public shelter. The tunnels beneath will only fit very skinny people. (Photo: Author)

On Taiwan's mainland, several other underground installations exist. Some were built to protect the public, while no doubt others were laid out to protect politicians and civil servants. When the Chinese armed forces conducted exercises near Taiwan in 1996, government officials considered re-opening large public air-raid shelters that had slowly fallen into disrepair. The government also considered re-opening an underground emergency control centre outside Taipei. Together the control centre and the bunkers are said to be able to hold 4 million people.

Other underground facilities in Taiwan include:

* Mountain hangars at the Chia Shan and Taitung City air bases. The hangars at Chia Shan were built between 1985 and 1994; and
* Nike SAM shelters at four locations west and north of Taipei. The sites were first under control of the US Army's 71st Air Defense Artillery Regiment, then managed by the Taiwanese armed force's 1st Missile Battalion, headquartered at Shu Lin Kou Air Station. The Nikes were installed as a response to the heavy Chinese artillery shelling of Kinmen in 1958.[4]

❑ TURKEY

As a member of NATO, Turkey hosts a number of international military facilities. The Combined Air Operations Centre-6 west of Eskisehir at Fidanlik Garrison may very well be an underground installation, as may be war headquarters for the 6th Allied Tactical Air Force at Izmir. An air defence operations centre at Sirinyer may also be underground.

❑ UKRAINE

The Soviet Strategic Rocket Forces maintained the 43rd Missile Army in Ukraine at Vinnitsa. The Army consisted of the 19th Missile Division at Khmel Nitskiy, which had, in the 1980s, 9 UR-100NUTTH (SS-19) regiments, and the 46th Missile Division with 4 UR-100NUTTH regiments and 5 RT-23UTTH (SS-24) regiments around Pervomaysk. Some reserve ICBMs were stored at

A silo hatch at the Pervomaysk ICBM base. (Photo: Lars Hansson)

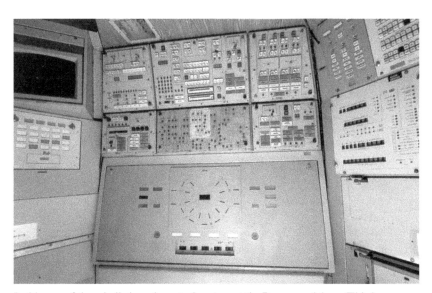

Inside one of the missile launch control centres at the Pervomaysk base. This is now a tourist attraction. (Photo: Lars Hansson)

An entrance for vehicles at the Balaklava submarine base. (Photo: Robin Ware)

Mikhaileni. The 43rd Army had an underground command post and is now a museum. The two divisions also likely had their own command centres.

One of the most fascinating places in Ukraine lies on the southern coast near the town of Balaklava. Here, the Soviet navy built one of its few underground bases. Constructed as Objekt 825GTS from 1957 to 1961, it could hold 7 submarines and house approximately 3,000 persons. The base included a house nearby with windows that were painted on the walls. By the mid-1990s, all the subs had left for Russia and today, the base is a popular tourist attraction.

Other underground installations include:

- Earth-covered structures along the coast near Sevastopol; and
- An unfinished naval command centre at Balaklava.

The submarine entrance. (Photo: Robin Ware)

Inside the sub base. (Photo: Robin Ware)

❑ UNITED KINGDOM

Within easy reach of Soviet missiles, it was imperative for the United Kingdom to have its own underground installations during the Cold War. When the concept of sheltering against atomic weapons was proposed by military and civilian planners, Britain had an edge over North America in that it had already experienced rocket attacks from Germany and fully understood the importance of civil defence. It had another edge in that, unlike the United States and Canada, many underground structures from the Second World War were still in existence. Since Britain had plenty of old gunnery posts, underground factories, radar sites and fighter control centres, the government only had to re-equip them to fight a new kind of war. This chapter begins with descriptions of military bunkers and continues with civilian facilities, both of which were plentiful in Her Majesty's kingdom.

The ROTOR Network
In the early part of the Cold War, British military leaders knew that if the Russians were ever to attack, they would most likely begin with an aerial onslaught. Long-range bombers would be flown from western Russia and from Warsaw Pact countries reaching the British Isles from either the north or east, and possibly even from the west following a circuitous route. During the Second World War, Britain had established a network of Chain Home, Chain Home

Low, Chain Home Extra Low and Centimetric Early Warning radar stations along its coasts to detect the Luftwaffe. After the war, most of the network was made dormant, but when tensions rose between East and West the RAF convinced Whitehall this network was still needed to protect the nation, and that some savings could be achieved if some of the old stations could be re-activated instead of building new ones. Whitehall agreed, and so the ROTOR radar network was born.[1]

ROTOR possessed several similarities to the wartime network of radar stations. Reporting radar posts, such as the Chain Home or Chain Home Low stations, were charged with detecting oncoming aircraft and with passing their co-ordinates to Ground-Controlled Intercept (GCI) sites for a fighter response, or to Anti-Aircraft Operations Rooms for gunnery action.[2] The co-ordinates were also passed on to Sector Operations Centres (SOCs), whose personnel would show movements on large plotting tables, as was done in Fighter Command operations rooms during the war. The reporting stations, the GCI sites and the SOCs were all linked by telephone cables, which was a more secure way to communicate as it prevented enemy radio jamming. The operational sections were located in either buried bunkers or surface blockhouses. The first 'edition' of ROTOR became fully operational in 1955, and in total, there were sixty-three stations and six SOCs then in service.[3] The various reporting and control stations were about 30 to 40 miles apart.

The radar equipment used by the RAF in ROTOR consisted at first of used Second World War and new American systems. The wartime equipment consisted of the Type 14 search radar and the Type 13 height-finder. Some stations were given newer Type 54 or American AN/FPS-3 search radars.[4] For low-flying aircraft, Chain Home Extra Low stations were resuscitated with either Type 14 or Type 54 equipment. GCI stations used the same equipment, less the FPS-3, and a few sites used the Type 7 Mark II or the Type 11. The Type 7 could track aircraft flying at 20,000ft at 90 miles, or those flying at 50ft at 10 miles.

No sooner had the ROTOR system come online that the Marconi Company developed a better radar. The Type 80 would outclass all its wartime predecessors with its greater range (200–270 nautical miles) and the ability to negate enemy jamming. The radar antenna consisted of a huge rectangular shovel-shaped metal lattice that worked in the S-band at approximately 3GHz. Its new display equipment, along with Kelvin Hughes situation-imaging projectors, quickened aircraft reporting. GCI sites given the Type 80 were also given American AN/FPS-6 height-finders. The greater ranges of these two radars caused the closure of many stations.

The ROTOR system was broken down into six air defence sectors. The controlling entities within those six areas were the Sector Operations Centres. In the operations rooms – the nerve centres – aircraft were plotted and fighter and gunnery responses were co-ordinated. If any aircraft crossed a sector line, the next SOC was advised. Ops room personnel also maintained a tote board that indicated airfield status and fighter squadron readiness. The location of the six

The bungalow
entrance to the
Kelvedon Hatch
bunker. (Photo:
Author)

SOCs were Barnton Quarry, Shipton, Kelvedon Hatch, Bawburgh, Box and
Longley Lane, with the first four established in new structures and the last two,
in wartime bunkers. All the SOCs were connected to Fighter Command's
national bunker at RAF Bentley Priory.

As the radar antennae were visible to passers-by and eventually to aerial spies,
their locations were never truly secret. A typical station had, in addition to the
telltale antenna, a security fence, a car park and communications antennae. At
stations on the west coast, one could clearly see the operations centre as a concrete
surface windowless blockhouse. In aerial photographs, specialists could sometimes detect these stations by the fact their grass looked different from the local
crops. One could never rely, on the other hand, on Ordnance Survey maps since
they rarely marked military properties as such, unlike in the United States and
Canada.[5]

Those radar station closest to Eastern Europe – thus on the eastern and
southern coasts – had their operations buildings underground. CEW and CHEL
stations possessed one-storey bunkers, and GCI stations, two. The building
types were labelled R1, R2 and R3 respectively. Sector Operations Centres were
equipped with R4 bunkers that had three floors. All were outfitted with blast
doors, air filtration and power plants, telephone switching section, offices and
lavatories. All also had stairways that led to emergency exits. The bunkers
contained an operations room that had plan position indicator consoles, equipment racks and an air cooling duct. At GCI sites, the nerve centres were two levels
high, the lower with aircraft plotting tables, tote boards and radar consoles, and
the upper, enclosed in glass, with more consoles, sections for fighter controllers
and space for a fighter marshal. The air-conditioning plant was also located on
this floor. All the bunker types had outer walls that were 10ft thick and inner
walls that varied from 6in to 2ft. They were built to a depth of 22ft to 65ft, and
designed to resist a 2,200lb armour-piercing bomb dropped from 26,000ft. The
R3 bunkers cost approximately £500,000 each.

The same type of bungalow as Kelvedon Hatch is found at the Anstruther bunker. (Photo: Scotcrown)

SOCs contained the same types of rooms as found in other bunkers – i.e. power plant, lunch room, lavatories etc. – but with a difference. The operations room was a large three-storey affair with, again, tote boards and a plotting table on the first floor, and staff working in two mezzanine levels to control fighters and missiles or to liaise with the radar stations. SOCs had no radars associated with them.

The method of entry into these bunkers was deceptive. Many could only be accessed by presenting oneself to guards on duty in what looked like sixteenth-century bungalows. These houses were never meant to fool anyone since the presence of a radar antenna nearby gave the station away. On the other hand, they were by themselves deceptive as they were built of reinforced concrete for protection, to which was added an innocuous exterior made of brick or stone. The idea of hiding the bunker's entrance in this manner was not totally original since the Germans used the same principle at their underground facility at Zossen-Wunsdorf before the war.

Over the years, several changes were made to the ROTOR network. Some of the radar stations and the six SOCs were closed due to technological progress. The new radars coming out of the factory, the Types 84 and 85 search radars and the HF200 height-finder, were more powerful and thus more resistant to jamming. The Type 85 could operate on more than one frequency, giving it extra protection against jamming. The Type 84 could operate in three modes, early warning, fighter control and general surveillance, which led to the closure of uni-functional stations. Other equipment called 'Winkle' was introduced at four sites to, again, counter Soviet jamming. This new 'Linesman' programme reduced the number of stations to a handful, and by the early 1970s, the RAF counted only six radar sites, with another two under NATO control.

Today, there are only two principal radar stations operated by the RAF; these are the Control and Reporting Centres at RAF Boulmer and RAF Scampton. Since 2006, RAF Boulmer has been the hub of the UK Air Surveillance and Control Systems (ASACS) Force. Replacing the old IUKADGE air defence system, ASACS operates on the same basic principle of its predecessor by first having identification officers look for unusual flights, and then having weapons controllers send up Quick Reaction Alert aircraft from such places as RAF Coningsby or RAF Leuchars to meet them. If the 'bogeys' happen to be Russian bombers, they are escorted out of British airspace (either with a wave or with another appropriate gesture).

Besides receiving data from the two CRCs, the ASACS gets air traffic data from the civilian air traffic system and from RAF Remote Radar Heads at Neatishead, Benbecula, Brizlee Wood and Saxa Vord. ASACS's information is regularly shared with NATO partners since an unusual aircraft's path will often cross NATO–UK boundaries. In addition to being the ASACS hub, Boulmer is home to the RAF School of Aerospace Battle Management (previously known as the School of Fighter Control) and to the ASACS Force Command Headquarters. The CRC still operates in the original R3 bunker, although it was modified in the 1980s to include decontamination cubicles and a larger power plant. Its two-level operations room has been changed into two one-level units.

The bunker at Neatishead is also still being used to this day. The RAF station had originally been built in the early 1940s as a GCI site, and during the early part of the Cold War it became a member of the ROTOR network and was given a two-storey bunker. There, it collected radar signals and forwarded these to the Air Defence Operations Centre at RAF High Wycombe. By the 1970s, RAF Neatishead was one of the few surviving stations of the original ROTOR network and by then had become a Control and Reporting Centre using Type 84 and 85 radars and later, a Type 91. In 2005, it ceased its role as a major radar station and became a remote facility reporting to Boulmer. It currently uses a Type 93 radar that is actually located at Trimingham. The bunker is only used for communications purposes.

Another ROTOR bunker that will be described here was on the south coast.

RAF Ash had its beginning during the early part of the Cold War as it was built as a GCI station to cover the southern approaches. It used several types of radars over its brief lifetime, the Types 7, 13, 14, 79 and 80 and one AN/FPS-3 and two AN/FPS-6s, and was given a two-level bunker. The operating entity was then the RAF's No. 491 Signals Unit. In 1956, the station counted 27 officers and 395 men and women. It closed in 1958 during the ROTOR modernization programme, and in 1965 it was transferred to the Civil Aviation Authority for £1. The CAA used a 264 radar for about two decades, but the bunker was not used and fell into disrepair. During the RAF's air defence radar modernization programme in the 1980s, Ash was returned to the RAF, this time for £250,000, and refurbished. Some of the changes included the addition of surface bunkers on top of the bunker to house water tanks, new power machinery and a new pedestrian entrance. Ash was not made operational, but it did become a reserve reporting centre. It also contained an Operational Conversion Unit for the RAF's then-new air defence system, the Improved UK Air Defence Ground Environment. It was also used for about two years as home to the RAF's

The bunker at RAF Holmpton is now a museum. This was a military command centre.
(Photo: Author)

Ground Environment Operational Evaluation Unit to test equipment used in CRCs. The station closed on 31 December 1995 and was sold in 1998 to A.L. Digital Limited for use as a secure data facility.

High Wycombe

Perhaps one of the most important bunkers ever built for the RAF lies near the quiet rural town of High Wycombe in Buckinghamshire northwest of London. Sensing war was imminent in the late 1930s, the British government authorized the RAF to build a rural headquarters for Bomber Command, away from a threatened London and far from prying fifth-column eyes. The Air Ministry signed a contract with John Laing and Son in 1938 for an air station that would include everything except a runway and hangars. The heart of this new station would be an underground operations block.

The bunker at High Wycombe was set at what was called Site No. 1 on New Road northwest of the town proper past Naphill. The structure was built 50ft below ground and was afforded great protection through a 5.5ft concrete roof covered with ballast, then by another 2ft slab, 4ft of earth and yet another concrete slab designed to absorb a bomb hit. The complex was then covered with earth and grass. Since staff walking outside also needed protection, tunnels were built that linked the bunker with the Command's administration building and to an officers' mess nearby.

It was in this bunker that RAF Bomber Command conducted its operations during and after the Second World War. Cold War games involving the

V-bomber force and Thor IRBMs were no doubt held here. When Bomber and Fighter Commands were amalgamated into Strike Command in April 1968, the new Command's operations centre was put in the bunker. Strike Command's responsibilities increased when it was given control of a new NATO unit in 1975, UK Air Forces. UKAIR looked after the air defence of Britain and managed offensive and re-inforcement assets. It could make use of fighters, bombers, tankers, early warning aircraft and surface-to-air missiles. Again, the control centre for the new outfit was the old wartime bunker, which by now was known as 'Broad Shield'.

By the 1980s, the High Wycombe bunker began to show its age, and by doing so revealed some of its limitations, one of which was its low protection factor of 300psi. Also, the facility's dual RAF/NATO functions required more personnel and equipment and more space. A contract was let out by the Ministry of Defence for the construction of a new underground block nearby that would hold not only an operations room, but also a new computer centre, dormitories and a canteen. The 75ft-deep 4-storey structure was designed for an occupancy level of 600 and was given modern NBC protection. This new UKAIR Primary Static War Headquarters, which Chief of Air Staff Peter Harding said had 'high protective qualities and [a] comprehensive array of communications', opened in the late 1980s. The old Bomber Command bunker then fell into disuse.

Very little has been disclosed by the Ministry of Defence or the RAF over the precise layout or usage of either bunker. However, by consulting various journals and historical publications, one can get a glimpse of the workings of the old bunker. It was no great secret that Bomber Command continued using the operations block during the Cold War, i.e. to order bombers into action or to conduct exercises. What few outside the government knew was, during a nuclear conflict, what the bombers' targets were and how attacks on Eastern Europe would have been carried out. Writing in the *Journal of Cold War Studies*, Ken Young revealed that the RAF had at first chosen to target Russian cities, as the USAF initially did, but after the Americans decided it made more sense to cripple the Soviet war machinery, both Air Forces geared up for attacks on bomber, missile and air defence installations. In the late 1950s, for example, the RAF was at first assigned 106 targets that included 69 cities and 37 military bases, but within a few years the balance would change to 16 cities and 82 bases.[6] Young claims the emphasis had shifted due to the 'population avoidance' policy of US Secretary of Defense McNamara.

A few details have also been revealed on the communications infrastructure of the early Cold War period. During the research for their book *Planning Armageddon*, Stephen Twigge and Len Scott learned that control of Britain's nuclear deterrent would have been exercised, not surprisingly, by the Air Ministry. Orders to attack would have originated from the Ministry's operations centre in the basement of its offices on King Charles Street in London. This basement was too shallow to protect its staff from a nuclear bomb, so a deeper basement bunker called 'Montague' was constructed at the 100ft level.

'Montague' was connected by telephone lines to a special GPO exchange called 'Kingsway' located under Furnival Street.[7] Through this secret exchange, the Ministry could talk to Bomber Command HQ at High Wycombe, as well as to other military organizations such as Bomber Command Group HQs, Fighter Command HQ and the USAF's Strategic Air Command. The infrastructure included a backup radio relay network.

The telephone and radio systems installed in the 1950s were all well and good for a few years, but when the Soviets launched Sputnik in 1957, Whitehall knew that it would have even less time to react if missiles were suddenly fired towards the United Kingdom. This new threat gave the government the impetus to devise new ways either to communicate with foreign leaders or to pass 'go codes' to Bomber Command. After the Air Ministry was absorbed into the new Ministry of Defence in 1963, a new Air Force Operations Centre was established in Whitehall from which the order to attack would be sent. From this AFOC, those orders could be passed by telephone, telegraph or radio to High Wycombe, and from High Wycombe through similar methods to attack units. Twigge and Scott wrote that the RAF could then not afford a communication system totally impervious to a nuclear attack, but this did not matter as long as the initial order to bomber crews was sent. On the other hand, they say, if the system did not survive a Russian assault, there would be no way to recall the V-bombers if the situation changed. A change of mind by Whitehall without a way to talk to pilots and bombardiers could have led to disastrous results, on both sides.

The RAF also worried about the effects of an electromagnetic pulse, which could disable much or all of the communications equipment, including the telephone system. When the communications infrastructure was reviewed, it was decided that bombers would be equipped with several modes of communications, such as HF, VHF, UHF radio and HF telegraphy. This redundancy would have helped to ensure that messages from Command got through. Furthermore, if High Wycombe was ever disabled, the bomber Groups then at Bawtry and Mildenhall were equipped to assume respective control of their forces. High Wycombe and the two Groups were also connected to all the bomber bases and the dispersal airfields, so that any of the three headquarters could take control of the entire force. The telephone network linking all three components was considered survivable since if one leg was cut, calls could be re-routed through other legs, just like in the civilian system.

Today, the old bunker is no longer used, but the new facility is still active. It has served as the nerve centre for the Improved UK Air Defence Ground Environment, that is the system for the national control of defensive fighters, and continues as the National Air and Space Operations Centre. Until its disbandment in 2008, it was also NATO's Combined Air Operations Centre-9. The new bunker is also used by the RAF's No. 1 Group, which is responsible for strike forces, units in Germany and for providing support to NATO troops, and by No. 38 Group, which handles air-to-air refuelling and transport operations. Recently, it has become the operations centre for the RAF's new Air Command, and the control centre for the new Joint Forces Air Component Headquarters.[8]

Daws Hill

Another bunker that was found in the High Wycombe area was at Daws Hill. This one was built for the US Army Air Forces after their entry into the war to serve as the operations centre for its VIII Bomber Command.[9] The bunker was located on the grounds of a girls' school called Wycombe Abbey, which had been expropriated by the Air Ministry. The entire base became known as Station 101, and sometimes also as Camp Lynn. It, or the bunker specifically, was codenamed 'Pinetree'. The base was so hectic that by the end of the war, 12,000 men and women were stationed there.

Construction of the bunker itself began in 1942. The three-level facility measured 23,000sq ft and cost almost £200,000. Its roof consisted of 10ft of concrete overlaid with 20ft of earth. It was built as a building-inside-a-building to protect it from bomb blasts. The structure had an emergency power and water supply and was protected from gas attacks by air-tight doors. It lay in the centre of the expropriated property just to the north of Daws Hill House. At first, the bunker was occupied by the RAF, then jointly by the British and the Americans, but eventually it became an American-only establishment.

After the war, Wycombe Abbey was returned to school authorities, but the RAF retained use of what was called the 'Protected Area', i.e. the bunker.[10] In 1952, the Americans returned to Daws Hill, and the bunker was occupied by Strategic Air Command. It was used by SAC's 7th Air Division from 1958 to 1965 to control SAC assets in the United Kingdom. The base, then called High Wycombe Air Station, was managed by SAC's 3929th Air Base Squadron, and later by the 7520th and then the 7563rd ABS. Communications were handled by the 485th Communications Squadron. After the 7th Air Division disbanded, the Air Station was transferred to US Air Forces in Europe's (USAFE) 3rd Air Force. In 1966, it became headquarters for Military Airlift Command's 322nd Air Division, but only until December 1968 after the Division stood down. The bunker itself ceased to be used in 1970, and in 1993, the property was transferred to US Navy Activities-UK. The entire base was then known as RAF Daws Hill. The bunker's exact use at this time is unknown by the author. The station closed in 2007, but was soon re-activated for use by yet another country, Canada. Part of it is now used by Canadian Forces Support Unit-Europe.

Northwood

Northwest of London, in Northwood, Middlesex, lies another military bunker. Very little has been written about this facility, although it is known that it was built in the early 1960s as the Royal Navy's Fleet Headquarters operations centre. It and the surface buildings were called HMS *Warrior*. Since its construction, the bunker has also been used as headquarters or operations centre for the following:

The RAF Strike Command's No. 18 (Maritime) Group
The RN Flag Officer Submarines
NATO's Eastern Atlantic Area
NATO's Channel Command, later called Allied Command Channel
NATO's Regional Command East
NATO's Submarine Forces Eastern Atlantic Area
NATO's Maritime Air Eastern Atlantic Area
NATO's Allied Maritime Air Force Channel
Tomahawk Land Attack Cruise Missile Support Centre

Royal Navy and RAF staff in the Joint Ocean Surveillance Information Centre also monitor the activities of the world's navies with the help of a Fleet Operations Command System, and have the ability to provide its data to outside users through secure channels. Since April 1996, the bunker has been used as a Permanent Joint Headquarters, a tri-service installation designed to control joint military operations. Among other things, in the 2000s, the PJHQ ran operations in Qatar, Iraq, Afghanistan, Oman and in the Falkland Islands.

The BBC reporter David Shukman was allowed to visit the facility in 2001, and in his subsequent article he revealed, besides the heavy guard presence and the bullet-proof glass, that some suites were used for intelligence briefings and some for special operations planning. At the time of his visit, the three British armed services were working on the Kosovo crisis, but the charts in use were covered with plastic sheets because of the presence of journalists. Shukman also disclosed that Northwood was *the* primary link between the Prime Minister and British forces in the field.

Pitreavie Castle

Another bunker of the Cold War period stood on the grounds of Pitreavie Castle outside Dunfermline, Scotland. This Area Combined Headquarters at RAF Pitreavie was used at various times as or by:

The RAF Strike Command's Northern Maritime Air Region HQ
The Rescue Co-ordination Centre-North
A NATO Integrated Communications System Telegraph Automatic
    Relay Equipment (TARE) post
The Royal Navy Flag Officer Scotland and Northern Ireland
The Air Officer Scotland and Northen Ireland
HQ NATO Northern Sub-Area, Eastern Atlantic Command
HQ NATO Northern Channel Command
An alternate headquarters for the RN at Northwood

The bunker is located under the base's tennis court. A Second World War-era plan showed it to be two levels with teleprinter, map room, stores, battery and air-conditioning rooms, telephone exchange and lavatories on the upper level. After a refit in the early 1960s, there was also a galley, a bedroom for admirals, a communications centre, decontamination area and sleeping cots here. Some of the offices were used by intelligence, mine counter-measures, submarine liaison and logistics personnel. Also, the operations centre was located here. On the lower floor was British Telecom equipment and the NATO TARE facility. The bunker was used until the end of the Cold War, and its entrances and emergency exits were destroyed by the Royal Engineers in 1996.

RAF St Mawgan

One bunker that still remains active is the one at RAF St Mawgan in Cornwall. Very little has been publicly revealed about it, other than the fact it is used as a Joint Maritime Facility where British and American personnel track ships and submarines. Input is received from both reconnaissance aircraft and from the SOSUS system. Also, it is known that for many years, the base stored American nuclear weapons that would have been used by Dutch P-3s and by RAF Nimrods. Since 2008, however, all military flying has ceased here.

RAF Alconbury

RAF Alconbury has long been known as a reconnaissance base that was used by both the RAF and the USAF. In the late 1980s, a large avionics and reconnaissance interpretation centre was built by the American government as a two-storey earth-covered bunker. Inside was an area were radiation airplane pods were brought in for examination. The pods would say if a nuclear test had occurred, and what types of isotopes were involved. The operating unit there was the USAF's 17th Reconnaissance Wing.

The bunker also contained a decontamination section for personnel and an air ventilation system below that was used to keep positive pressure inside. The structure was unofficially known as the 'Magic Mountain'. One source claimed it cost $69 million to build. The base closed in the 1990s and the bunker now sits unused. As it has been declared a historic site, it will not be destroyed. One

The 'Magic Mountain' at RAF Alconbury. (Photo: Author)

Inside the USAF bunker. (Photo: Author)

rumour has it that English Heritage is not too happy with the lack of co-operation over the facility from the United States government as it has refused to provide drawings of it.

RAF Sopley

One of the many bunkers built for the ROTOR radar network lay under grass north of Sopley, Hampshire. The property had been used during the Second World War, first to house a mobile GCI unit, then a fixed radar station that included a brick surface bunker called a Happidrome. After the war, the station became a combined GCI/Sector Operations Centre. It remained an Air Force radar station in the 1950s, at which time it was given a two-storey underground operations block. For a few years, the RAF School of Fighter Control was located there. The station became a joint military-civilian air traffic control centre in 1957 operated by the RAF's No. 15 Signals Unit. RAF Sopley also had the Joint Air Traffic Control Area Radar School as of 1960. It remained a joint ATC facility until 1974 when a new air traffic centre was opened at West Drayton.

The Sopley bunker remained in military hands afterwards, first used by a Royal Signals unit in 1975–76, then by a unit of 2 Signals Brigade. Renovations were made to it in the 1980s for use as a UK Land Forces wartime headquarters, but these seem not to have been finished. The bunker was sold to a data storage company in 1993 for £150,000 and has since been re-sold many times. It is apparently still being used as such.

Cruise Missiles

Some of the most famous bunkers to be found in the UK were those that housed a new type of weapon. The arms race between the two superpowers demanded that both sides develop instruments that would outwit each other's defences. Perhaps as a realization that ICBMs, whose locations were long known by the Soviets, would be the first target in a nuclear conflict, the USAF decided to build a weapon system that would be hard to detect and difficult to destroy. At the same time, the weapon could act as a counterweight to the new Soviet systems that were deployed all over Eastern Europe such as the SS-20 missiles.

The new weapon that would be based in the United Kingdom (and in other countries) was the BGM-109G Gryphon Ground-Launched Cruise Missile, better known by its initials GLCM. The Gryphon was a small but formidable weapon that used a terrain matching computer to guide it following an algorithm that moved ailerons depending on the obstructions ahead. The missile was 21ft long, 21in in diameter, flew just under Mach 1 and carried a W84 warhead that may have had a variable 2-150 kiloton yield.[11] It was first boosted by solid fuel for thirteen seconds, then propelled by a Williams International F-107 turbofan engine. The Gryphon's range was 1,500 miles and had the best circular error probable of all the Air Force's missiles at approximately 100ft. It was designed to be fired from a special vehicle, called a Transporter Erector Launcher (TEL), whose mobility was the key factor that made the weapon hard to locate and destroy. The missile was equipped with Category F Permissive Action Link, an electronic lock system that required a twelve-digit number that, once entered, completed the internal firing circuit and allowed the weapon to be armed.[12]

To house the missiles, the USAF built special earth-covered bunkers. These large structures contained crew shelters, the TELs and sixteen GLCMs each. Some of the bunkers also housed launch control trailers. They were equipped with heavy doors to shield the personnel from the effects of a bomb blast. The areas containing these shelters were called GLCM Alert and Maintenance Areas or GAMAs, and were ringed by three barbed wired fences. One source claimed that if a trespasser crossed the first fence, he'd only be given a lecture by the security staff. If he crossed the second one, he would be detained for forty-eight hours and issued a stern warning. A jump over the third fence would earn the intruder a bullet.

The usage of a Ground-Launched Cruise Missile required deployment of the squadron's convoy to one of several pre-surveyed launch points. A convoy consisted of four TELs, two control trailers and sixteen vehicles for the commanding officer, maintenance crews, medical tech and security staff. Once these vehicles reached their firing points, they would be camouflaged and ringed by an intrusion detection system. The commanding officer would then wait for the order to fire.

Having GLCMs deploy to a remote location for firing gave American forces a great measure of survivability. Once the Gryphons had left their GAMAs, there would have been nothing left for the Russians to destroy. But what the USAF gained in survivability it could have lost in control. Former Defence Minister Heseltine once remarked that when the GLCM convoy was getting ready to move, the British government was in a position to exercise an effective veto by its ability to block roads. If for any reason Whitehall did not want the Americans to fire, it could have simply cut off its access to the road network. The Americans

One of the cruise missile shelters at Greenham Common. (Photo: Author)

could have tackled this problem by firing from the bases, but if they did so they would have lost that element of survivability.

Two GLCM bases were established in Great Britain. RAF Greenham Common outside Newbury had been a bomber base for years, having been used by the RAF and the USAAF during the Second World War, and after the war by SAC bomber units on short-term deployments. The bombers were gone by 1964, and the base was then used as a military post office. All this would change in the 1980s when the Department of Defense chose it as a cruise missile station. Construction crews then moved in to convert the bases's ammunition dump at the west end of the runways into a GAMA. There, 96 GLCMs would be stored – 64 in 4 bunkers and 32 in reserve in another 2 bunkers – to be used by the USAF 501st Tactical Missile Wing's only operational unit, the 11th Tactical Missile Squadron. RAF Greenham Common may have been chosen because its runways were long enough to accept transport aircraft.

The second GLCM base was located a few hundred miles to the east in Cambridgeshire at RAF Molesworth. This was another USAAF base during the Second World War, used by such units as the 303rd Bombardment Group. Some time after the war, the runways were destroyed and in the 1980s, a GAMA was established on the west side. Its four bunkers kept sixty-four missiles that were assigned to the USAF 303rd Tactical Missile Wing's 87th Tactical Missile Squadron. The Squadron formed in December 1986, but its installation never reached full operational status due to subsequent political events.

Unlike the Minuteman III and the Titan II, the Gryphon would have a very short life-span. The missiles were first placed at Greenham Common in December 1983, and in less than ten years all would be removed, not because of obsolescence but because of politics. On 8 December 1987, President Ronald Reagan and Soviet Premier Mikhail Gorbachev negotiated an historic treaty that banned medium-range weapons from Europe. The Intermediate Nuclear Forces (INF) Treaty outlawed the deployment and use of those weapons that had accelerated the arms race to too high a degree and that, on the Western side, had caused much protest. The USAF thus retired its GLCMs, the US Army its

Pershing IIs and the Russian Strategic Rocket Forces their SS-20 Pioneer MRBMs. According to David Hoffman in his book *The Dead Hand*, it would be the first time the two superpowers would agree to eliminate an entire class of weapons.

Today, Greenham Common is no longer an air base. The operations area is now an industrial park, and the residences are now used by the public. The runways were destroyed years ago, but the GAMA lies untouched and unused, although still surrounded by a barbed wired fence. According to the INF Treaty, the Russians have the right to inspect the facility at any time to ensure it has not been re-activated. RAF Molesworth, on the other hand, remains an active military base. Its GAMA is also not being used, but the rest of the base remains in operation as home to such units as US European Command's Joint Analysis Center. The JAC produces intelligence summaries, regional assessments, threat assessments, orders-of-battle, indications and warnings reports, and exercise analyses for any military or intelligence service. It has supported peacekeeping operations in former Yugoslavia and has provided counter-terrorism reports to various stakeholders.

Other Facilities
Other Cold War bunkers in the United Kingdom include:

- An Air Defence Operations Centre at RAF Bentley Priory at Stanmore, Middlesex, outside London. The bunker was first built in 1939–40 for Fighter Command, continued being used after the war, but was replaced in 1982 by another underground facility nearby. The base closed in 2008;
- The wartime Fighter Command's No. 11 Group bunker at RAF Uxbridge, west of London, used then as an operations centre, and after the war as an air traffic control centre. The bunker was closed in 1958 and the entire base in 2010;
- A Royal Navy Armament Depot at Coulport on Long Loch west of Glasgow;
- A RN underground fuel depot at Inchindown a few miles north of Invergordon, Scotland, used until the 1990s;
- Another naval fuel depot, to the west of Fort Southwick, which is north of Gosport, Hampshire. Two entrances were at the end of Hillsley Road and another was off Crooked Walk Lane. The depot was closed in the 1990s;
- A wartime underground block for HMS *Badger* at Harwich, used after the war as a customs depot, re-opened in the 1980s as a naval emergency port control centre for the area and closed in 1994;
- A bunker used as a control centre at the RAF's missile testing facility at RAF Spadeadam, Cumbria;
- The Manod Quarry at Blaenau Ffestiniog in Wales, designed to store British art treasures under Operation Methodical;

- The Westwood Quarry, 15 miles west of Corsham in Wiltshire, also to be used as an art repository; and
- A Sector Operations Centre at RAF North Weald outside London. This surface blockhouse was built during the Second World War, used by the RAF until 1964, transferred to the British Army, and finally closed as a military facility in 1977. It is now Epping Forest District Council's emergency operations centre.

Regional Government Headquarters

Numerous underground facilities were also built as civil defence control centres and for the purposes of government continuity during the Cold War.

The end of the Second World War saw the closure of many military installations and the abandonment of the system for Air Raid Precautions due to a desire of the national government for a return to peace. The United Kingdom had just gone through six long years of war, not to mention the Depression before that, it now looked forward to a time of prosperity. Its desire for peace was soon curtailed, however, when the Soviets blockaded Berlin and after they had detonated their first A-bomb. Based on their recent wartime experience, some in Whitehall pushed for the creation of secure structures from which civil defence could be managed.

In the 1950s, the first set of those secure facilities would be established and would be called Regional War Rooms. The United Kingdom was broken down into twelve regions – more or less as in the Second World War – where each contained an RWR with personnel tasked with with various emergency functions such as the co-ordination of fire, police and medical services, the distribution of food and the restoration of electricity.[13] From these buildings, staff would have done their utmost to minimize the suffering of the public. A secondary role to these Regional War Rooms was that of government continuity, where representatives of ministries would continue, on a much reduced scale, the business of government. Each RWR would have been run by a Regional Commissioner, and each would have been able to act independently if the central government was disabled. The network of war rooms was run by the Home Office's Civil Defence Department.

The Regional War Rooms were all located in windowless concrete surface buildings. They all had two storeys where the lower floor had offices, toilets, a canteen and dormitories, and the upper floor, more offices. In the centre of the building lay an operations room where personnel would perform such duties as tracking radioactive fallout, keeping in contact with outside forces and planning rescue efforts. The room was two storeys in height where the second floor lay behind glass so that its personnel could see what was going on below. Overall, the building measured 90ft by 75ft, and was protected by heavy blast doors. On the roof stood ventilation ducts and antennae.

As well as building secure facilities, the Home Office provided training to civil defence staff at three schools. The purpose of this education was to train individuals, such as from the army, police and even from the Women's Volunteer Service, as future trainers of emergency personnel. The schools' curriculum was broken down into two parts, with the first teaching the students general subjects such as civil defence organizations, fire fighting, missiles, atomic warfare and protective measures. The students then continued their training in rescue subjects where hands-on instruction was provided in specially constructed bombed villages. Exams naturally followed. The three schools were at Falfield, Gloucestershire, Easingwold, Yorkshire, and Taymouth Castle, Perthshire. The Falfield 'Civil Defence Technical School' took up 4 square miles in Eastwood Park.

With respect to the Regional War Rooms, the Home Office soon recognized that they suffered from one major handicap in that they only offered some protection to their occupants. In the 1960s, the RWRs were supplanted by new structures that reflected a greater understanding of nuclear war. By then, government planners realized that if London was ever obliterated, the regional centres would have to be given greater powers, to the point of near-absolute authority, what Nick McCamley in his book *Cold War Secret Nuclear Bunkers* called 'Whitehall(s) in microcosm'. Larger and better protected facilities were therefore needed to house staff that would have attempted to bring order and stability to damaged areas. Thus was born the concept of Regional Seats of Government (RSGs).

Having accepted the new plan, the Home Office began in earnest looking for suitable sites. A few of the Regional War Rooms were retained for this use, some like the one in Nottingham doubled in size, and others placed in army camps or in disused underground ROTOR sites. A further two were placed in underground wartime factories. Most of the structures were completely refurbished to give them more office space, to provide a section for the Ministry of Defence and the armed forces, and to create an area for the BBC for its public announcements. The RSGs were designed to hold 450.

One of the most unusual Regional Seats of Government was that which was

The ROTOR bunker at RAF Hack Green was built as a two-level structure with both located within this blockhouse. It was later used as a government bunker. (Photo: Author)

Regional government communications equipment inside Hack Green. (Photo: Author)

built for Region 6. RSG6 was placed in a disused chalk mine at Warren Row northeast of Reading that had been converted into an aircraft component factory during the war. One of the mine entrances, hidden in a clearing on Warren Row Road, led to a series of irregular tunnels into which were fashioned several sub-units that contained offices, sleeping rooms, an air-conditioning plant, lavatories, decontamination cubicles, conference rooms, a telephone exchange and dining areas. Near an emergency exit, one found water tanks and a switchroom. At most places in the tunnels, the height was 15ft.

RSGs were much larger than Regional War Rooms because not only were local forces represented (i.e. police and fire), but most government departments would also have been found there. Space was reserved in these bunkers for the Ministries of Agriculture, Labour, Housing and Transport, as well as for the Post Office, HMSO and the BBC. Some areas were also allotted to the armed forces and to communications staff. As with the RWRs, there was also an operations centre full of desks, maps, charts, filing cabinets and plotting tables. Quarters were created for the Regional Commissioners and his deputy, called the Principal Officer, and telephone connections were established to other bunkers, including the one for the central government at Corsham, Wiltshire. The facilities had enough food and water for thirty days, and were stocked with a small number of firearms for self-defence.[14]

As in other countries, the army was given several roles during and after a nuclear conflict. On the home front, it would have provided aid to police and to fire services, shepherded and fed the homeless, evacuated casualties, guarded vital stocks, distributed essential supplies and controlled transport. Its Corps of Signals would have fixed or maintained communications, while the Engineers would have helped restore roads and railway lines. Some troops would have managed camps for displaced persons and internees. The Territorial Army might have shared some of the above roles, and would have operated a number of mobile Austin K9 communications trailers to maintain links between the bunkers and military forces in the field.

British civil defence preparations included a scientific intelligence network scattered throughout the Isles assigned to make technical assessments of threat and damage conditions during an emergency and to report their findings to senior government staff. The network was made up of teams equipped with chemical, biological and radiological detection instruments which were ready to move within their assigned districts after an attack. They could communicate their information via buried GPO telephone circuits or through backup radio links. The Home Office's Civil Defence Department had its own scientific advisory committee codenamed LONGSTUD (previously, JIGSAW) which consisted of the Home Office's Chief Scientific Advisor, the chief science advisors to the three armed services and other scientists from the Ministry of Defence to provide advice to higher echelons on all matters scientific pertaining to nuclear war.

During a nuclear conflict, and until such time as would have been needed, the bunker chiefs – the Regional Commissioners – would have possessed a large amount of power, a great deal of autonomy and immense responsibilities. These individuals' roles were to maintain law and order, allocate resources and ensure services would have been returned to normal. They were empowered to take such measures to keep or restore the economy and to maintain modes of travel. The Commissioners also had the important duty of reassuring the public by dis-seminating messages through the BBC studios. Lesser known, and more controversial, was their right to order the shooting of looters.[15] The individuals selected to be Commissioners were Ministers of the Crown; at RSG6, it would have been the Minister of Public Buildings and Works.

The Regional Commissioners' authority would have been nothing without an underlying legal framework. The Home Office wanted to make sure that what-ever emergency measures were proposed, there would be a corresponding law to support it. One of those laws was the *Emergency Powers (Defence) Bill* that, once enacted during a crisis, would have given the Prime Minister the right to rule through Orders-in-Council (what Americans call Executive Orders). These OCs would have allowed the Prime Minister to act quickly without the need for a debate of legislation in Parliament. The Bill had a provision for passing the same authority to Regional Commissioners, with exceptions since the central govern-ment kept its jurisdiction on such things as foreign affairs and the conduct of the war. Both the Prime Minister and the Regional Commissioners would have also given themselves the right to control the media, property and banking, the latter to ensure the economy did not collapse. The *Emergency Powers Bill* was kept secret from everyone except a small number of senior government officials.

The entrance to RSG6 at Warren Row. (Photo: Author)

While emergency powers legislation remained secret for years, the bunkers that would have been used for continuity of government were made public in 1963. Since the start of the Cold War, there have always been in Britain those that oppose nuclear war and the secrecy it generates. The Campaign for Nuclear Disarmament had been established as early as 1957 with the purpose of ridding Britain of its nuclear monsters. While most of its members engaged in letter-writing campaigns or took part in peaceful protests, one of its splinter groups, Spies for Peace, would go one step further. In 1963, this group had learned about one of the secret Regional Seats of Government, RSG6, and wanted to peel away its veneer of secrecy. Its members broke into the bunker in April to find secrets, probably knowing that such facilities were normally vacant in peacetime (except perhaps for security guards). By rifling through maps and files, they were able to learn about the entire British COG network. Once back in safe territory, they produced a pamphlet describing RSG6, its structure, location and purpose, along with a list of other RSGs and their telephone numbers. It also listed the names of those who would have worked there during a war – for example, D. Osmond, Chief Constable for Hants, Air Commodore J.B. Cowerd and Rear-Admiral F.E. Clemitson – along with university professors who would have acted as scientific advisors. Spies for Peace also learned that RSG6 had been used during exercises, and that those exercises revealed shortcomings in the COG programme that the government probably did not want the public to know about.[16] The Spies for Peace pamphlet was sent to local councillors, politicians, famous scientists and members of anti-war movements. It was also sent to the Prime Minister and to the head of MI5 in the 'hope it will make them cross'. The Spies were never caught.

Even though the proverbial cat was out of the bag, the national government continued its nuclear war planning. In the 1960s, it replaced RSGs with a new regional government structure that included protected facilities in what were called 'sub-regions'. Now, instead of only one RSG per area (often for two or three counties), each county would have some sort of bunker, and these new facilities, called Sub-Regional Controls (SRCs), would report to new Sub-Regional Headquarters (SRHQ). Financial constraints, however, forced the government to modify this ambitious plan in 1968, and in the end, the RSGs were simply renamed SRHQs (and three new ones built), and a handful of SRCs were established in existing accommodations such as disused ROTOR bunkers, Anti-Aircraft Operations Rooms, emergency food stores, in the basements of public buildings, or in old ammunition bunkers. The main advantage to these SRCs was that they all now had better protection than the RSGs since they were underground.

Following the new trend that ran against the political complacency that had infected Western governments in the 1970s, international events provided the impetus to Whitehall to re-new its commitments to civil defence and government survival. Soon after the Conservatives gained power in 1979, the Home Office ordered a review of the government's emergency plans and concluded that a boost of financial testosterone was needed to make things work. The UK Warning and Monitoring Organization (of which more below) was modernized, as was the Wartime Broadcasting System. Money was also given to local councils to upgrade their emergency government infrastructure. There would also now be less secrecy than before with the publication of books such as *Emergency Planning Guidelines for Local Authorities* and *Protect and Survive* for the public.

The UKWMO national bunker on Langley Lane in Preston. It was originally built as an RAF Sector Operations Centre as RAF Longley Lane. (Note the misspelling.) It also housed the ROC's No. 21 Group Control. This was one of three bunkers in the area. Another one to the west down a country lane was a communications facility, and the other was used as a filter centre and was on the south side of Whittingham Lane a few miles to the east. All three bunkers remain. (Photo: Author)

The trend towards rejuvenation was repeated in North America where Canada and the United States injected more funds into their own programmes.

One of the most expensive changes to civil defence during the Thatcher era was the creation of new emergency government facilities. In 1984, it was decided to modernize the bunkers and their communications networks, and build new structures where they were lacking. SRHQs now became Regional Government Headquarters (RGHQs), as did many Sub-Regional Controls. The main bunker in a region would now be identified as RGHQ x.1, and subsidiary facilities as RGHQ x.2 and RGHQ x.3.[17] If the primary bunker was incapacitated, the secondary or tertiary one could take over. Entirely new bunkers were built in the late 1980s, for instance in Crowborough, Sussex, to replace an old one under Dover Castle, or were converted from disused facilities such as the ROTOR bunker at Hack Green, Cheshire.

No sooner had the new RGHQs been built that geopolitical events would cause their demise. The death of the Soviet Union in December 1991 provided a large peace dividend that had a major impact on British defence-related spending. After the issuance of the defence White Paper announcing the end of the Cold War, the government closed the RGHQs in 1993 and began offering them for sale to the general public. Many were indeed sold, including some that had been built only a few years before, but with the proviso that they be returned to the government in wartime. Today, some still exist, but as museums, data storage warehouses or as private dwellings. Others have been destroyed as victims of progress. The United Kingdom of today no longer has much of a civil defence system. A list of the RGHQs can be found in Appendix H.

The UKWMO

The RSGs, SRHQs and RGHQs were only part of the civil defence story. The government needed a way to warn the populace of a nuclear attack and set up the United Kingdom Warning and Monitoring Organization as a consequence. The UKWMO was established to receive warnings from BMEWS radars at RAF Fylingdales and from NORAD and to activate the network of air-raid sirens. It was also charged with advising the public of approaching fallout. The Organization was geared to supplying information on nuclear bursts (obtained from Royal Observer Corps posts) to military forces at home and abroad. The UKWMO's headquarters was located in a bunker outside Preston, Lancashire, at Goosnargh.

The sequence of warning was thus: BMEWS receives information that a missile attack is under way. The information is sent to the RAF's national Air Defence Operations Centre. A signal is sent from the ADOC to the UKWMO, and from there to 250 Carrier Control Points in major police stations throughout the country. The chief constable activates the air-raid sirens at the CCP. Simultaneously, at the UKWMO messages of warning are broadcast to the public advising them to take cover. Once the missile strikes, Royal Observer Corps monitoring posts record the blast's location and intensity, and transmit this data to their Group Controls. Group assesses the data, correlates it with that received from other other posts or other Groups and passes it on to their Sector Controls, the central war headquarters at Corsham, and to the RGHQs. Fallout would be tracked, and again everyone would be advised, including the public. Then would begin the long and arduous task of re-building the damaged area.

As with the UKWMO headquarters, the ROC posts were also located in bunkers. These 20ft by 7ft structures were scattered approximately 8 miles apart throughout the United Kingdom. Each was outfitted with special equipment and facilities to sustain a two or three-man team. The technical equipment consisted of at first a Radiacmeter for measuring radiation levels and a Ground Zero Indicator camera to detect the location of a nuclear explosion, but these were replaced later on with a field survey meter and a Bomb Power Indicator respectively.[18] The posts also contained, in addition to a telephone and radio to communicate with their respective Groups, sanitary facilities, bunks and batteries along with supplies of food and water. From the outside, one saw only the access hatch, air intake and a white can that housed four small cameras making up the GZI. Each post cost approximately £1,250, and throughout the Cold War, a total of 1,560 were built.[19]

The Group Controls were somewhat more elaborate affairs in that they were built to house a much larger staff. Also located in hardened facilities, they were staffed by sixty or so members of the Royal Observer Corps along with a number of scientists who would have made the decision as to when and whom to contact during an alert. In a two-storey operations centre, some personnel manned the telephones, others plotted fallout and yet others marked tote boards with such

The ROC No. 20 Group Control at York, now a museum. Note the collapsible antenna in front. (Photo: Author)

The ROC No. 6 Group Control at Norwich. This building was opened in 1961 and used until 1991. It was demolished in 2008. (Photo: Author)

items as detonation type (e.g. air burst or ground burst). All staff were unpaid volunteers, except for the Commandant and the Duty Officer. Telephone communications were first processed through manual switchboards but in the 1980s, these were replaced with Mitel SX200S switches that took a lot less room. Some Group Controls contained Atomic Weapons Detection Recognition and Estimation of Yield (AWDREY) instruments to record nuclear bursts and Directional Indication of Atomic Detonation by Electromagnetic Means (DIADEM) equipment to show the location of an attack; both instruments worked through triangulation. Other rooms in these structures contained a standby generator, decontamination showers, beds and food stocks. They were also equipped with blast doors and possessed an emergency exit. Most of these Group Headquarters were built as semi-buried bunkers and identified by the presence of a collapsible antenna.

The Central Government War Headquarters
The central war headquarters alluded to above had perhaps one of the most secretive histories of any of the government's Cold War 'citadels'. For decades, mining was common in the hills of Wiltshire. Limestone was so plentiful that a few thousand acres of land was bored out to collect it. In so doing, the miners ended up forming several underground galleries. Eventually, production ran out, or was too costly, and the galleries fell eerily silent. The Second World War would change all that.

When war appeared on the horizon, Whitehall decided to make use of some of the largest of these formations, Tunnel Quarry and Spring Quarry. The former was converted into an army ammunition depot and the latter, modified for use by the Bristol Aeroplane Company as an engine factory. A small section connected to the north side of Tunnel Quarry was also converted into Fighter Command's No. 10 Group Headquarters. A huge amount of money was spent on the Bristol factory, which in the end produced only a few Centaurus engines. By the time the plant closed, the government had invested over £20 million in it.

At some point in the postwar period, the government decided that, with the advent of nuclear weapons, it needed a home away from London. Whitehall had every intention of surviving a nuclear exchange and secretly began developing plans to that effect. One of those plans was to establish two bases that would be used as relocation sites: Spring Quarry and Drakelow. Spring Quarry was accepted as a relocation site by the Prime Minister in September 1955, although there are minor indications it was considered for such as early as 1946 and 1947.[20] The new Central Government War Headquarters (CGWHQ) would house 4,000 civil servants, including ministers and senior military officers, with a 3 : 1 ratio of men to women. Any government information about it was classified 'Top Secret-Acid'.

In 1956, construction crews began building ventilation shafts, lift housings and spiral staircases. One escalator was obtained from the London Underground and installed beside Westwells Road, and two passenger lifts and one goods lift were also put in. Much of the primary construction was done by 1962, work that included the installation of internal partitions, blast doors giving out to an Admiralty depot next door, kitchen equipment, an air-conditioning plant and several two-level operations centres, and eventually communications equipment was put in. Office space for this new facility, initially codenamed 'Subterfuge', amounted to 1,000,000sq ft. Part of it lay below the Box railway tunnel.

The Central Government War Headquarters at Spring Quarry was divided into twenty-two areas, all linked by a network of roadways that had been created long ago by the mining company. Each area contained a particular function. In the late 1950s, Area 2 had office space for such organizations as the Board of Trade and HMSO, and Area 22 was reserved for the Colonial Office and the Foreign and Commonwealth Office. Other sections were used by the armed services, the BBC and by ambassadors of certain friendly nations.[21] There were rooms for conferences, the ventilation equipment, food storage, water treatment and for dining and sleeping. Several tanks were installed that could hold a large supply of water for the residents and fuel for the standby diesel generators. In total, there were 584 working rooms.

The nerve centre of the Corsham facility was found in Area 14. This is where the Prime Minister's office and bedroom were located. Area 14 also contained offices for various Ministers, the War Cabinet Secretariat and the Ministry of Defence. Ministers and senior military officers would have worked in their own operations centres that overlooked their own map rooms. There were also sections for the Secret Intelligence Service, the Security Service, Government Communications Headquarters, a CIA liaison officer and for clerks and typists. One room was reserved for the mysterious London Communications Security Agency. Occupants in the various rooms could communicate by way of a Lamson tube system or by messengers.

Subterfuge's primary goals were to act as a national civil defence control centre and as a relocation site for the Prime Minister and public servants.[22] As previously discussed, much power was devolved to Regional Commissioners in the SRHQs, and the CGWHQ would have been limited to international affairs, the conduct of the war, the control of essential supplies (food and fuel) and matters of civil defence of a national nature. The role of the staff in the bunker was therefore to provide broad policy direction to the Regional Commissioners, rather than conducting day-to-day life-saving activities. Lines of communications were established with every SRHQ and the military commands (not to mention NATO), and for this reason a huge telephone exchange was put in by the GPO. There were rumours that the facility would have housed the Royal Family, but while no solid information to back this up has been forthcoming, there are strong indications that they would have been quartered in Area 17.

If war appeared likely, the Prime Minister and public servants would have travelled to Corsham two ways. The former would have probably embarked on a helicopter with some of his staff, and the latter would have initially taken coaches that would have been leased for the occasion. The route taken by the coaches to the bunker would not have been direct, but rather first to a rural spot, and then after transferring to other coaches, to Corsham. Later on, the civil servants would have gone to Kensington Olympia station to catch a special train for the journey west.

When it came to the security of the Corsham facility, the British government took great pains to ensure it. Those civil servants who were earmarked to work there were not told of it and were not given any kind of training. They would have been informed only the day before their movement through a 'First Information Slip'. Even then, they were not told where they would go, and were only ordered to report to certain transport collection points. Once at Corsham, this staff was highly restricted and were forbidden to make outgoing calls, and could not travel to Areas outside their own. Where the public and the press were concerned, if they began asking questions, the government prepared a number of cover stories (which seemed to change every few years) such as it was a post office communications centre, a naval storage depot, an RAF signals centre or a standby regional government headquarters. When British journalist Chapman Pincher planned to write an article that would have mentioned a 'huge underground facility', he was fed disinformation by the government and as a consequence omitted reference to it in his article.

Along with the regional bunkers, the CGWHQ went through a period of modernization in the 1980s. By then, the facility had lost its civil defence role, much of its floor space and remained only as a relocation site. It was, on the other hand, given new kitchens and new diesel generators. Its emergency government staff was also reduced, from 4,000 to 1,000. It was transferred to the Ministry of Defence in 1991, renamed Site 3, barely maintained and officially declassified in 2008. Today, while it sits idle with the telephone equipment and the stationery gathering dust, one hopes this fascinating place will be turned into a national museum.

Drakelow

While this book's focus has been on underground bases built during the Cold War, some with origins in the Second World War are either so large or mysterious they deserve to be mentioned. An example of this is Drakelow.

The Cold War facility at Drakelow had its beginnings after the outbreak of the Second World War. At the behest of the Ministry of Aircraft Production, Rover, among other automotive firms, was asked to manage a small number of shadow factories in environments hidden or protected from the Luftwaffe. One of those factories, an engine parts manufacturing establishment, was built inside rock on the Blakeshall estate in northern parts of Herefordshire and Worcestershire. The government began construction there in the summer of 1941 and by early 1943, full production capacity was achieved by Rover.

Rover's No. 1D site (D for dispersal) at Drakelow consisted of a huge network of caverns giving a total usable floor space of 284,931sq ft. The installation had several entrance adits leading to dozens of criss-crossing tunnels and bays up to 18ft in height forming a large grid. Each section housed a separate functional unit such as cylinder machine shops, tool stores, grinding section, polishing division, canteen, offices and in one section, RAF stores. A games room, several bars and a concert hall were added for recreational purposes. The employees lived in barracks nearby on Sladd Lane or in neighbouring villages and commuted to work every day; all had to pass by a time office recessed in the entrance adits to check in. Above ground, the establishment included several ancillary buildings such as a boiler house, oil and coal stores, storage tanks and various other shops. One of the plant's more picturesque components, an old school dating from 1855, housed the local ARP detachment. Although thousands of Pegasus and Mercury engines were made by Rover during the war, it is not known how many actually came from No. 1D.

As the war came to a close, parts and engine production decreased at Drakelow. The factory was then used for the storage of machine tools but some

One of the
entrances to the
Drakelow complex.
(Photo: Author)

work was performed there on the Meteor tank engine. Now known as the Drakelow Depot, it continued its storage role until 1958 when the Home Office decided it would be converted into a nuclear bunker as a Regional Seat of Government. The Drakelow RSG was designated backup to the other RSG at Swynnerton.

Modifications were made in the following years for Drakelow to fit its new role. There was the addition of a BBC studio, communications and cypher equipment, conference rooms and, since extended stays were now envisaged, dormitories. Offices were allocated to many government ministries – such as Health, Treasury and Customs and Excise – and to the armed services and the Post Office, which then controlled the telephone network. Overall, only half the original underground complex was used and about 350 men and women were slated for occupancy. For a number of years in the 1950–60s, it was considered as an alternate seat for the national government under the codename 'Macadam', one that would serve as a backup to Corsham, but this never came about.[23]

As time went by and as the threat of nuclear war rose and fell, change in Home Office policies impacted on Drakelow. In the 1980s, the renamed Regional Government Headquarters 9.2 was given new equipment to replace the old, such as computers, telephone switch and newer diesel generators, but by then, only 25 per cent of the original wartime establishment was now in use. A total of 140 spots were reserved for the following: Commissioner, support staff, civil servants, military representatives, scientists and communications and BBC personnel. Drakelow kept up with the times with new office equipment and furniture. Just before the Cold War was officially pronounced dead, the RGHQ was moved into a hardened UKWMO post at Church Lawford, Warwickshire, and the secret factory-cum-nuclear shelter was shut down.

Since its closure in 1992, Drakelow has seen little activity. It was offered for sale by W.S. Atkins, a company responsible for selling off surplus government properties, and one tour was offered to the public. In 1994, it was sold to owners who prefer not to be named. At the time of publication, it was not being used and some tours were offered by volunteers.

Pindar

At this point, the reader may wonder, are there any other bunkers not mentioned above still being used by the British government? Has there been perhaps a replacement established for the CGWHQ?

Besides the bunkers at High Wycombe, Northwood and RAF St Mawgan, there is at least one more in operation. Below the Ministry of Defence's building at Whitehall, a new facility was built during the late 1980s and early 1990s. The bunker, known as 'Pindar' but officially called the Defence Crisis Management Centre, is a three-level structure that is designed to act as the government's main emergency control centre in times of crises. Little has been revealed about it, but it is known that it cost £126.3 million, that it is continuously staffed by about

100 individuals and that it can be self-sustaining for 3 months. It is also known that it was built in the shell of an old Second World War communications centre that had remained active after the war. The bunker, and some sections of the Northwood facility, make up the government's Defence Crisis Management Organization.

❑ UNITED STATES

Continuity of Government

In the 1964 film *Seven Days in May*, Burt Lancaster plays a right-wing Chairman of the Joint Chiefs of Staff bent on taking over the United States government from what he considers to be a weak-kneed White House. His plan is to lock up the President in a bunker built to house senior government staff in case of nuclear war at a time when the White House staff was to be relocated there briefly for a nuclear drill. The film was based on a novel of the same name by Fletcher Knebel and Charles Bailey and was possibly the first time anyone outside the government mentioned the possibility of such bunkers. This inevitably gave rise to speculation about whether such facilities really existed.

It is no longer a secret that the United States government has in fact built several bunkers around the District of Columbia to house personnel during a nuclear war. The role of this personnel is to provide continuity to government. It was revealed years ago that if the panic button was ever pressed, senior American government officials, including the President and White House staff, Cabinet secretaries and Supreme Court judges, would have quickly relocated to a large bunker at Mount Weather near Bluemont, Virginia. From this secret post, which was codenamed 'High Point', democracy would supposedly have continued.

The secret Mount Weather facility was built in the 1950s by the US Army Corps of Engineers as a small city in its own right. Essentially, it consists of two major sections: an above-ground town and the bunker, known as Areas A and B respectively. The latter was built as a set of buildings inside caverns that house dormitories, cafeterias, hospital, an operations centre and various offices. The bunker was built to withstand 50psi of pressure, although studies have shown it could still be disabled by a small number of 10 megaton bombs. Every item imaginable is stored there: large stocks of food, government stationery and even birth control pills. A medical lockup with padded walls was even built for those who would not be able to stand the strain. To repel those trying to force their way in, security personnel in the bunker keep several firearms on hand; even relatives of bunker occupants would be scared away. At 200,000sq ft, the entire shelter can hold approximately 1,000.[1] During emergencies, personnel would travel to the complex by cars or buses or, if they were senior enough, by helicopter. In addition to calling the complex 'High Point', government documents have also referred to it as the 'Special Facility' and the 'Western Virginia Office of Controlled Conflict Operations'. Nowadays, the entire property is known as the Mount

Weather Emergency Assistance Center and is run by the Federal Emergency Management Agency (FEMA).

How would High Point swing into action during a war? Government officials designated to live there during and after an attack have their movements tracked on a daily basis so that when the call is sounded, all could be contacted and ordered to report to the bunker, dependants excluded, following procedures outlined in the Joint Emergency Evacuation Plan. The President's original taxi service, the USAF's 2857th Test Squadron at Olmsted AFB in Harrisburg, Pennsylvania (and later at Dover AFB, Delaware), was kept on stand-by twenty-four hours a day by a specially trained crew equipped with, among other things, radiation protection gear. These days, the President would not relocate to Mount Weather but would board a special 747 airliner outfitted as an airborne command post. His successors (e.g. the Vice-President, the Senate leader etc.) would relocate to various command centres, including Mount Weather, with teams of special personnel under a plan called 'Treetop'. The fact the President will no longer move to High Point during a war may be because at least one President, John F. Kennedy, has been quoted as saying he would not have gone there and leave his family behind if the Soviet Union ever attacked, or it may be because the facility is so well known that any President relocating there would be a sitting duck.

With a grid of sensors located across the country, technicians at Mount Weather can tell from an electronic map in the 'Bomb Alarm' room where nuclear detonations take place and can respond accordingly. Fallout can be tracked through V-781 Aerial Survey Meters deployed across the country. After the Secretary of the Army was designated the chief civil defence support officer, it befell the Army to form support detachments ready to aid with communications and bunker security. Every facet of modern civilization was considered in the war plan: the mail, the banking system, utilities and the press. The church is relied upon for mass burials and, in rural areas with no civil defence organization in place, for damage control leadership.

What goes on at Mount Weather regularly? Some of the 240 or so staff frequently conducted war games on computers during the Cold War in preparation for the real thing. Missile strikes were planned and fallout patterns were predicted to see how best the government should respond. In the 1960s, there were 63,000 radiation monitoring posts set up on public buildings throughout the nation which were capable of giving a good idea of how radiation would travel. Once the fallout track was predicted, cities and towns that were located downwind could be warned and appropriate forces prepared.

Among other activities carried out by Mount Weather, even in our post-Cold War world, are continuity of government (COG) exercises. These continue to be run throughout the Washington area. Some have used the following codenames:

Flash Burn:	presidential exercises
Nine Lives:	presidential exercises

Snow:	first word for presidential exercises (e.g. Snow Fall)
Southern Pine:	presidential exercises
Surf Board:	presidential exercises
Title Globe:	for interagency communications

Emergency procedures have been tested during some of the above exercises, but apparently have only been used twice in real situations at Mount Weather; during the urban riots of the late 1960s and during the large power outage in the northeast in 1965.

The amount of emergency government planning that went on, and that may still be going on, at Mount Weather was huge. Its computers maintain all sorts of records useful in postwar recovery: medical and educational institutions, military bases, television stations, grain silos, population statistics, communication and transportation networks, and manufacturing centres. A list of mines and caves that could be turned into shelters is also kept on file as possible relocation sites. In his highly revealing article on the facility, 'The Doomsday Blueprints', Ted Gup of *Time* stated that the author of the *Federal Register* in the 1980s, Martha Girard, was expected to rush to the bunker if the Soviets attacked and continue publishing the document as the *Emergency Federal Register*.[2] She was instructed to keep with her a special identification card that listed her biographical statistics and that declared she was an essential government employee of the federal government, and that she be allowed unrestricted movement. In his article though, Gup claimed Girard did not have much hope for life after doomsday.

Much more planning was put into COG than the above suggests. As in bunkers in other countries, the federal government had pre-recorded audio tapes that would broadcast messages of reassurance to the public. These tapes would have been played over the Emergency Broadcast System, but only upon presidential approval. In the 1950s, the voices used in those recordings were those of President Eisenhower and a well-known celebrity of the time, Arthur Godfrey. In addition to this, selected members of the news media would have been allowed in the bunker during a war to broadcast news to the public. Of course, the newsmen could never reveal anything of the bunker itself since they were sworn to secrecy.

The bunker's existence was kept from the public for several years until the mid-1970s when a writer learned about it through Senate sub-committee hearings and after conducting discrete interviews. Others caught wind of it after an airliner crashed nearby in 1974. What the writer discovered was that Mount Weather is the nexus to nearly 100 other facilities scattered throughout neighbouring states – most being only hardened office-building basements – and that it acts as the focal point to the entire emergency federal government. The base is so sensitive many hikers who have gotten too close have had their cameras confiscated and when the Russians tried to buy adjacent land for a country estate, the

State Department disallowed the purchase. It was never even marked as government property on topographical maps.

Above ground, the Mount Weather complex consists of over two dozen buildings that make up the Emergency Assistance Center. The EAC consists of dormitories and cafeterias that are used by students and guests for law enforcement and disaster management conferences. In 1997, over 23,000 attended various courses and seminars there such as in riot control and rescue planning. Other buildings in the complex include a Veterans Administration-run health centre, fire department, guard house and storage and vehicle depots. At one time, Mount Weather's fleet of 149 vehicles consisted of buses, maintenance trucks and ambulances. A firearms range is used for practising by law enforcement and security students. The antennae seen on the grounds belong to the agency's own radio network, the FEMA National Radio System. Rules at Mount Weather are strict and guests are told not to bring in firearms, except for official purposes, pets or cameras; everyone is subject to search. Jogging is prohibited at night and hiking is discouraged because of the presence of poisonous snakes. Gambling and smoking in any building or vehicle are also prohibited.

In addition to COG, Mount Weather's manager, the Federal Emergency Management Agency, was and is the primary unit responsible for the physical protection of the public. Most of the countries that were threatened during the Second World War had had a civil defence agency in place. After the war, these organizations were either disbanded or held in abeyance, but as the Cold War gathered speed, some began calling for their return. In the United States, the *National Security Act* of 1947 created the National Security Resources Board as the planning body for civil defence. The lack of immediate threats and the United States' atomic monopoly, however, caused then-President Truman to deny the Board any real power, so it stuck to planning. But Truman would have a change of heart after the Soviet Union detonated its first atomic bomb and after China fell to the communists in 1949. The President ordered his staff to plan for a new civil defence organization, and in January 1951 the Federal Civil Defense Administration was born. Its director would be a civilian officer who reported directly to the President. Construction soon began on Mount Weather.

Since the 1950s, the FCDA has been renamed so many times it could make one's head spin. It was known by its first name for only a few years since it was redesignated the Office of Civil and Defense Mobilization in the late 1950s. It was still under civilian control as its chief still reported to the President, although some claim generals and admirals resented having a civilian direct defence activities. This perhaps why the OCDM was later split into the Office of Emergency Preparedness and put under White House control, and the Office of Civil Defense placed under Department of Defense control. The OEP in turn eventually became the Federal Preparedness Agency and the OCD, the Defense Civil Preparedness Agency. In 1979, these two outfits, along with the US Fire Administration, the Federal Disaster Assistance Administration and the Federal Insurance Administration, were consolidated into the present-day FEMA.

Not quite a 'Get out of jail free' card, this Federal Civil Defense Administration emergency identification card from the 1950s gave the holder access to areas hit by nuclear weapons or devastated by natural disasters. A large red vehicle marker with the letters 'CD' also allowed quick passage. The marker and card were issued to any federal personnel who had civil defence duties, save those from the military services.

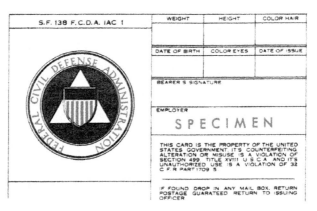

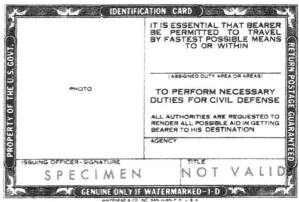

After Mount Weather opened in the mid-1950s, President Eisenhower ordered a nation-wide nuclear drill to see how well citizens and the government would respond. The President was spirited to a secret facility in 'a wooded area' in Virginia and 15,000 public servants made their way to relocation points. Everyone in a designated target area was ordered to take cover and those that refused, such as pacifists or a salesman in New York City who refused to leave his truck, were arrested. The press was given no hints of the presidential facility's location other than the fact Eisenhower's ride took six hours and five minutes from the White House. If Bluemont, which is only 45 miles from the centre of Washington, was indeed this facility, the ride length may have been disinformation.

In addition to geographical and demographical data, FEMA computers keep data on thousands of Americans. In 1960, the point was raised in a top-secret presidential executive memo to the National Security Council that a sufficient number of persons should be kept on file to fill key government posts in times of war should regular staffers be unavailable. Created by Executive Order, the database, known as the National Defense Executive Reserve, is a list of persons from the public and private sectors who would be willing and able to fill positions in the many emergency agencies that would have arisen. The candidates were selected on the basis of their technical or managerial qualifications and accepted only after passing a security screening. But not just anyone could be chosen since applicants were excluded if they served in one of the armed services, if they were elected officials or whether they were already assigned an emergency government function at any level of government.

James Bamford reveals in his book *A Pretext for War* the names of several of the selected civilians who expressed willingness to serve in this Executive Reserve. One of them was Aksel Nielsen, head of the Title Guaranty Company of Denver. An old friend of President Eisenhower, Nielsen was asked in 1958 to direct the Emergency Housing Agency if war with the Russians had ever broken out. The President was pleased when Nielsen accepted. Others who also accepted at that time were Pierce Baker of the Harvard Business School and Frank Pace Jr of General Dynamics. It is not known by the author if the Executive Reserve still exists.

Yet another FEMA function, perhaps one that is lesser known, is the management of strategic materials that would be used primarily for defence purposes. Since 1939, many minerals and elements are kept stored at various sites throughout the country to be used if natural supplies were ever contaminated or if their importation was ever threatened. That year, Congress passed the *Strategic and Critical Materials Act* that orders the government to maintain supplies of those materials sufficient for a three-year period. This new National Defense Stockpile first began with six elements, and by the 1980s, counted sixty-one materials and minerals that were valued at about $13.7 billion. The NDS is a dynamic concept since materials are acquired on the basis of necessity and often disposed of when substitutes are found. FEMA's roles are to decide what materials to stockpile and in what quantities. The actual purchasing of these materials is done by the General Services Administration, and the protection of the stockpile is the responsibility of the US Marshals Service.

The biggest threat to the NDS and, up to a point, to the American economy comes from those foreign nations hostile to the United States. The main purpose of the stockpile is to maintain a supply of those materials that would be hard to come by if a global war ever occurred. Those countries whose locations or political bent preclude the guarantee of delivery could place an unwanted stranglehold on the economy. When Count de Marenches, head of the French secret service, visited President Ronald Reagan in the 1980s, he pointed out that the Soviet Union was the exporter of eight critical minerals, such as germanium and titanium, and that this fact put the United States in the unenviable position of a reluctant beggar. Partly because of de Marenches' warning, Reagan soon ordered the creation of a government committee to examine the stockpile's supply weaknesses.

To give an idea of the uses of the NDS, we look at two ores: bauxite and chromite. Bauxite is a primary source of aluminium. This metal finds widespread uses in consumer goods and, more importantly where national security is concerned, in bombers, fighters and tanks. One of the major sources of bauxite is Jamaica, which means the US government has an interest in keeping sea lanes between that country and Gulf of Mexico ports open, and in ensuring its industry remains viable.

Another critical ore is chromite. This is one of the chief sources of chromium, which is incorporated into stainless steel and nickel alloys. This metal is again found in fighting vehicles, as well as in jet engines and in some projectiles. Much of the world's chromite is mined in Russia and Albania. If either nation ever refused to sell to the United States, weapons production would be seriously hampered and jobs lost. The federal government therefore has a serious incentive to maintain adequate supplies of this ore.

While FEMA decides which materials should be purchased and the GSA does the actual purchasing, another branch of the government is involved in the NDS: the Department of Defense. It is DoD that does the actual storing. The main office responsible for this is the Defense National Stockpile Center at Fort Belvoir, Virginia. Actual storage takes place at at least thirteen locations, such as in Baton Rouge, Louisiana, and Binghamton, New York. Over the years, however, many of these locations have been closed for budgetary reasons; the Memphis Defense Distribution Depot is but one example.

The United States stores several other items in case of war. A 1950s-era map showed FEMA (or rather its predecessor, the Federal Civil Defense Administration) stored medical and engineering equipment such as power generators at dozens of locations across the country, many of which were military bases. This equipment would have been used for such things as clearing rubble in bombed cities and providing temporary sources of electricity to those in need. Some of the engineering warehouses were located at McMinnville, Oregon, and Bastrop, Texas, while some of the medical depots were at Pueblo, Colorado, and Anniston, Alabama.

Chemicals and pharmaceuticals are also stockpiled at various locations for a variety of uses. Opium, for one, is or was stored for a time at West Point, New York. In 1998, the Nuclear Regulatory Commission, another player in the stockpile game, approved the acquisition of potassium iodide by the federal government. This compound prevents radiation being absorbed into the body, which could happen if there were nuclear disasters similar to Chernobyl. In 2000 CBS's *60 Minutes* programme revealed that the federal government then had eight drug warehouses throughout the country, the locations of which and storing agency are secret.[3]

On some occasions, purchases for these stockpiles have been affected by political considerations. In 1983, the acquisition of a sedative, morphine sulphate, was delayed since the government did not want to give the public the impression it was preparing for a nuclear war. This, oddly enough, seemed contrary to the stockpile's purpose.

Another function of FEMA's computers is to store post-attack survival data. The computers can tell by probabilities what industries would be destroyed given such and such a blast given such and such weather patterns. One of the software programmes has the ability to respond to specific queries such as, for example, how many television stations would be left after five missiles hit Los Angeles. In addition to damage assessment data, the same computers can prepare population relocation plans and even design protective structures.

While some groups have decried FEMA's excessive secrecy and potentially unlimited power during an emergency, the Agency does have a public face. As the main disaster control service, it issues detailed booklets describing who should do what during an emergency. During a major catastrophe, FEMA is the agency mandated to co-ordinate emergency services, meaning fire, police and medical help. In the 1960s, it funded the hardening of public radio stations against atomic blasts and in the 1970s, gave them protection against electromagnetic pulses that result from nuclear detonations. With predictions of staff shortages during wartime in mind, it signed an agreement with the Salvation Army in 1973 for co-operation in assisting the displaced. It also administers the Chemical Stockpile Emergency Preparedness programme and offers funds to those communities close to chemical weapons depots where accidents could occur.

During a major conflict, FEMA would run its national operations from Mount Weather and perform other functions at a bunker in Olney, Maryland, that is called a Federal Support Center. Olney is one of the central warning points that would send an attack signal to state and other federal facilities if and when the enemy struck. It also houses the agency's National Computer Center, which first used Control Data computers, but were later replaced by a more powerful UNIVAC 1100. Communication with the outside world is through two 10kW and three 1kW transmitters. Physically, the bunker is a 67,000sq ft two-storey facility built on top of an old Nike surface-to-air missile site. Construction was in 1964 and cost, building and equipment included, over $9.4 million. It normally houses over 100 staff but in emergencies, it can take in over 400.[4]

FEMA regional operations are controlled by Federal Regional Centers, Olney being one of them. Most of these are underground and all were built in the 1960s. The FRC in Bothell, Washington, was constructed to look after FEMA operations in the northwest. It is located at 130 228th Street South West also on the site of an old US Army anti-aircraft missile base on a plot, incidentally, still owned by the Army. The two-storey shelter was built for almost $1.9 million in 1968 and consists of dormitories, offices, an operations centre, an independent water supply and dining facilities along with food stocks for thirty days. In wartime, it would house 300. Typical of nuclear bunkers, the facility was outfitted with equipment designed to block electromagnetic pulses. Today, Bothell houses thirty-five employees ready to assist and co-ordinate disaster relief operations in the northwestern United States and Alaska.

Another Federal Regional Center at Maynard, Massachusetts, looks after

The Maynard
Federal Regional
Center. (Photo:
Author)

relief operations in the New England area. This one was built from scratch by the US Army Corps of Engineers and had been planned for Harvard and then Acton, Massachusetts, but its final location was set for Old Marlboro Road by the Army's Natick Laboratories southwest of Maynard. As with other FRCs, the Maynard bunker contains the regular assortment of offices, dormitories, dining and sanitary facilities, operations centre along with its own power supply. Some people have been known to call it the 'mushroom factory'. All disaster-related calls in the area are routed to the operations centre in the bunker, which is attended twenty-four hours a day.

By the 1980s, it was realized that Mount Weather and the entire continuity of government infrastructure was falling into disrepair and needed a massive facelift. Millions of dollars secretly began to be spent on the modernization programme in what would become unofficially known as the 'Doomdsay Project'. Some of those millions, some would claim, would end up being lost as the technology the government bought was of questionable use. Also, government investigators found that the contracts for the new system may have been unjustifiably inflated. It was during government probes and during House Armed Services Committee hearings that much would be revealed about COG.

The impetus to revive doomsday planning came from President Ronald Reagan. The President considered nuclear war 'winnable' and ordered a review of the COG programme under the auspices of his National Security Decision Directive-55. After examining the entire programme, his staff recommended a total revamping, especially of its weakest link, the communications infrastructure, which was then still relying on 1950s and 1960s technology. A new organization was created in the White House to manage COG, the National Program Office (located in a separate building in Washington), and another outfit was created to plan the changes, the Defense Mobilization Planning Systems Agency. Within a few years over $3 billion would be tendered out in contracts. The programme was called Project 908 and was implemented by the US Army's Information Systems Command.

Steven Emerson of the *US News and World Report* would write one of the most revealing articles on the Doomsday Project in 1989. In it, he claimed that since COG staff assumed the Soviets knew about Mount Weather and other major underground command centres, a series of new bunkers were secretly built that could act as 'emergency White Houses'. By doing so, Emerson wrote, the person in charge, whether it is the President, Vice-President or the Speaker of the House, could play a shell game that would prevent the Russians from knowing where the current seat of government was really located. In fact, the Reagan White House had conducted secret COG exercises to test the Doomsday system by having not one but three teams relocate to secret sites and having one of them assume the functions of the Presidency. The teams consisted of senior government officials familiar with national security affairs, such as representatives of the Departments of State and Defense, the CIA and other agencies, along with a single member of the Cabinet who would act as President. The exercises tested the ability of the Cabinet member in becoming the de facto government.

Another major aspect of Project 908 was the establishment of new secure and reliable mobile communications systems that would keep all the different branches of government connected and that would be used for other things such as issuing missile launch orders. The systems were housed in specially built tractor trailers. Some of these new vehicles included decoy trailers that would have been used to deceive prying Soviet satellites.

Emerson also revealed in his article that much waste took place during the COG upgrade. Many of the contracts were awarded to Betac Corporation, a firm that specializes in command, control, communications and intelligence systems. Betac's financial bottom line grew better every year with Army contracts jumping from $316,672 in 1983 to $22 million by 1988. Working for Betac was so attractive that several Army personnel who had worked on the COG project resigned from the government and returned to do the same work for the firm at much higher wages. But, as Emerson wrote, just trying to review Betac contracts was problematic in itself. When an Army contracting officer, Gicola Thorndike, tried to do so repeatedly, she claims she was forced out of her job.

The lucrative contracts awarded to Betac were not the only problem. Some of the equipment that was designed for the new and improved COG system did not always work as it should have. Quoting intelligence officials, Emerson stated that some of the computers used by the various stakeholders of Project 908 could not communicate with each other. The solution came in the form of special modems, but these too caused problems in that they interfered with the transmission of data. Also, when the new mobile command posts were ordered, no one thought to check to see if they would have cleared road bridges. As a result, during testing in rural Virginia, one truck got wedged under a highway overpass. Meanwhile, the House Armed Services Committee investigated, but within a few years, the end of the Cold War would kill Project 908 and the National Program Office, and none of it would matter.[5]

Possibly even today, every federal government department has a set of plans and procedures in place ready to be acted upon should the alert ring. Regular departments and agencies would continue their business at alternate sites and several temporary organizations would rise to begin certain functions. The civil defence organization of the 1960s, the Office of Civil and Defense Mobilization, had four units in place at the national level ready to take over certain segments of society:

- The Telecommunications Office would have reviewed frequency assignments and ordered the closure of telecommunications facilities or authorized their use by any federal agency;
- The Transportation Office would have controlled all domestic transportation and port facilities along with aircraft except for those used by the military services. It would have also ordered the construction of any required road;
- The Economic Stabilisation Office would have controlled prices, wages, rents and the distribution of consumer goods; and
- The Censorship Agency would have requested 'the voluntary censorship of the domestic press, radio and television'. (The Agency was also known at one time as the Office of Censorship.)

These offices had their basis in Resource and Telecommunications Directives. Some examples are:

- Resource Directive 2 gave the office the right to requisition private property and allow its use by any federal agency;
- RD 7 authorized the General Services Administration to release strategic and critical materials;
- Telecommunications Directive 5 ordered the Federal Communications Commission to close amateur radio stations, except those that were part of the Radio Amateur Civil Emergency Service; and
- TD 8 ordered the FCC to extend its wartime monitoring system in the United States.

These directives are still on the books today.

To illustrate the wartime role of a government department, one can examine the Department of Health, Education and Welfare. HEW is responsible for looking after the public's well-being through agencies such as the Food and Drug Administration and the Public Health Service. In peacetime, the PHS monitors common food items such as milk but during a nuclear war, it would suspend normal operations and switch gears to co-ordinate emergency health services and provide health supplies to civilian bodies. Some of the Washington staff would have relocated to Mount Weather but most would have moved to a secret facility codenamed 'Spark'.

One of the most controversial aspects of war – perhaps just as much as the weapons themselves – is the loss of freedom individuals endure at the hands of their elected leaders. Wars often bring out the worst in governments since they will arrogate much power claiming either necessity or supposed public support. In the case of the Cold War, there were plans made by the government to censor every form of media to prevent the publication of any fact that could be useful to the enemy if it ever attacked, including such mundane things as weather reports. During COG planning in the 1950s, President Eisenhower oversaw the development of a Censorship Code that staff would follow during a nuclear war when members of the media wondered whether or not to print or broadcast a story. If the alert was ever sounded, eight men that made up the United States Office of Censorship would report to their relocation site at Western Maryland College in Westminster, Maryland, and begin issuing censorship instructions to field offices throughout the nation. If a newspaper editor hesitated on publication on national security grounds, he or she could submit the article for review to any of these offices before printing. The system was supposed to be voluntary, much like it was during the Second World War, but few editors and producers were expected to violate the Code. The plan was so secret only the White House, the Office of Civil and Defense Mobilization, the chosen eight and a few members of Congress knew about it.

The idea of censorship has always been anathemic to liberal democracies such as the United States. Eventually, the plan for wartime censorship was leaked out and people began asking questions. Some wanted to know who the eight men were who would have run the Office at Western Maryland College. Organizations such as the Office of Emergency Preparedness (as the OCDM was later called) and the White House declined to reveal their names, but this proved useless as some were leaked to the *Washington Star* and all were published in David Wise's book *The Politics of Lying* in 1973. James Bamford points out in his book *A Pretext for War* the irony that it was a senior member of the media, the then-vice-president of CBS Theodore Koop, that would have directed the Office of Censorship. Wise also revealed in his book that the outfit was renamed the Wartime Information Security Program in the 1970s to make the program 'sound more palatable'. No matter what it was called, it still carried the same mandate.

As far as the author knows, the programme still exists.

Perhaps not surprisingly, the events of 9-11 reminded the government of the need for continuity planning. Having airliners crash into key buildings served as a wake-up call to the President and Cabinet of the importance of the survival of the executive branch of government. In 2001, the *Washington Post* wrote that President Bush had created a shadow government poised to take over if key leaders were killed. One hundred or so men and women lived and worked outside Washington on a rotational basis ready to continue government operations. The *Washington Post* later revealed that COG exercises have since been held by FEMA in 2004, 2005 and 2006, under the names of 'Forward Challenge '04', 'Pinnacle' and 'Forward Challenge '06' respectively. The latter exercise required thirty-one agencies and departments to relocate and to be prepared to provide truly essential services to the nation.

Culpeper

The Federal Reserve System was another organization with its own secret facilities throughout the nation. Its main one was a 140,000sq ft three-storey bunker opened in 1969 at Culpeper, Virginia, as the federal wartime bank and relocation centre for the bank's seven governors and staff. As the US Mint in Washington was suspected of being one of the main Soviet attack targets, Culpeper kept a huge sum of neatly wrapped cash on hand in a 23,500sq ft vault ready to restart the economy. The vault was so well organized different cash denominations were segregated in separate cages. The bunker was set west of Washington – which meant protection from blast effects over the capital – but was no great secret since it could clearly be seen from the access road.

In addition to cash storage, FRS personnel at Culpeper had the capability to monitor major financial deals through an electronic transaction monitoring system. With its own offices, water reservoirs, uninterrupted power supply, cafeteria, large shower/bathrooms, communications centre and nurse's station, the bunker was well suited to run on its own during a nuclear attack. It was designed to house 540 for 30 days and while most would have slept in multi-bed dorms, the governors would have been quartered in pairs in separate rooms. Security was extremely tight and centralized in a separate unit with the guards even having their own internal pistol range for practising.

An aerial view of the Culpeper bunker. (Photo: Federal Reserve Bank of Richmond)

The emergency exit
at Culpeper.
(Photo: Author)

The bunker's primary role of emergency relocation and cash warehouse was terminated in 1992 and since then, it served as the Federal Reserve's main communications centre and as a backup data processing facility. Thanks to a grant from the David and Lucille Packard Foundation of California, it is being converted for the storage of films, videos and records by the Library of Congress. The building, to be known as the National Audiovisual Conservation Center, will act as a central depository to replace several storage depots now in use.

White Sulphur Springs

Even in wartime, the President's actions would still be monitored by an independent House of Representatives. War brings several dangers to a democracy, the principal being that the suspension of democratic rule and the granting of extraordinary powers inexorably lead to tyranny. To therefore ensure continuity in democracy, Congress had a huge secret facility buried into a hillside for its survival at the world-famous five-star Greenbrier Hotel at White Sulphur Springs, West Virginia.

The Greenbrier resort had long had a strong relationship with the United States government. What began as a place of elegance and relaxation near the popular sulphur springs turned into a military hospital during the Civil War. It was later bought by the Chesapeake and Ohio Railway and expanded, then later taken over as an internment centre during the Second World War for German and Japanese diplomats. In 1942, the federal government purchased the resort outright and converted it again into an army hospital. Six years later, the C&O Railway bought it back from the government and once again carried out modifications. The upper class then began flocking back to the popular resort for a pleasant stay of rest, golf or swimming in the springs. It was so well known it was even alluded to in the film *Seven Days in May* when General Scott (Burt

Lancaster) suggested to his aide Colonel Casey (Kirk Douglas) that he take a few days off there.

Then came the Cold War. The President and the Department of Defense began planning their secret relocation sites and eventually, every government branch would have its own. President Eisenhower expected Congress to continue its business outside the capital during and after a nuclear exchange and began wondering where this hideaway should be. He eventually settled upon the Greenbrier, one of his favourite vacations spots, which by coincidence was then planning on building an addition, the West Virginia Wing. A proposal to build a bunker at the same time for Congress under the wing was put forward and soon plans were drawn and the sod was turned.

The Greenbrier bunker, codenamed 'Casper' but also known as Project Greek Island, was one of West Virginia's best-kept secrets. It was officially never talked about and only a handful of Congressmen knew about it.[6] When the hotel's new manager took over his duties several years ago, he could not account for the many additional expenditures until someone informed him of the establishment's second purpose. The fact that one of the hotel's auditoriums held 470, nearly the same as the number of Congressmen, never sparked any curiosity.

As with Mount Weather, Casper was self-sustaining. The bunker consisted of dormitories with enough beds for every Congressman, a dining hall, decontamination centre, an infirmary and dental clinic, a communications centre with secure lines to High Point and even a crematorium. It had its own air purification system and generators capable of supplying power for over forty days. The walls and ceiling range from 36in to 60in thick and the entire shelter lies under 20ft of dirt. Overall, it measures 112,000sq ft and could house over 1,000. It was kept stocked with sixty days worth of food, which personnel replaced regularly.

As mentioned, the bunker was built under cover of the West Virginia Wing's construction, which took place between 1959 and 1962. It was so cleverly incorporated into the resort as a regular component that guests and employees

The West Virginia Wing at the Greenbrier. Few knew about the bunker that lay below. (Photo: Author)

A blast door.
(Photo: The
Greenbrier)

never realized what its real function was.[7] As the bunker belonged to the hotel, the federal government was billed $25,000 for it in rent per year until 1979 when the fee doubled. One of the ironies of Casper was that during its construction, Deputy Secretary of Defense Roswell Gilpatric delivered a speech in October 1961 to the Business Council at the hotel challenging Soviet Premier Krushchev's assertion of nuclear superiority. Given his rank, Gilpatric probably knew of the shelter close by and the protection it offered against a Russian attack, a fact he could not have shared with his audience.

Mosler Safe was contracted to build four doors for the site, the two largest of which were so big they had to be shipped by train from the company's plant in Hamilton, Ohio. At 28 and 20 tons respectively, the doors were so delicately balanced and carefully hinged they could be opened manually. Locks were installed on the inside only to prevent unauthorized entry in times of war. The two heaviest doors were fitted to a vehicular entrance while the third, for pedestrians and the fourth, as an escape hatch. The bunker is invisible to outsiders but

The all-important US Congressmen would have been stuck sleeping in dorms during a nuclear war. (Photo: The Greenbrier)

two of its emergency exits were camouflaged behind 'Danger – High Voltage' doors, which remain.

During its lifetime, the Greenbrier bunker was operated by Forsythe Associates, ostensibly a television repair and service provider. For decades, it was quietly manned and maintained by a staff of only a dozen. The bunker remained unknown for decades and would have continued as such had Ted Gup, writing for the *Washington Post*, not stumbled upon it. What real use Casper would have been is questionable since many members of Congress would not have gone and left their spouses behind if war had been declared. These days, the bunker is opened for tours.

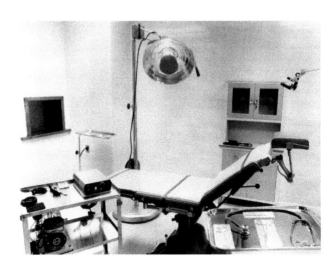

Everything was considered when the government built the bunker, from the mail to dentistry. (Photo: The Greenbrier)

The emergency exit to the bunker. The 'Danger-High Voltage' sign was a phoney. (Photo: Author)

The back door to the bunker. (Photo: Author)

The White House

Yet more Cold War subterranean workings can be found under the White House. Ronald Kessler in his book *Inside the White House* mentions a secret tunnel originally planned as a bomb shelter that 'extends from the basement of the Treasury Department into a subbasement of the White House under the east wing'. The tunnel is sometimes used by persons wishing to avoid outside onlookers, including from the press.

Another facility found under the White House is the President's Emergency Operations Center or PEOC. As its name implies, this is a control centre that would be used during emergencies by the President's staff, and perhaps even by the President himself. It is not known by the author when it was built, but it may very well be the one that Secretary of Defense Robert McNamara proposed to President Kennedy in early November 1963. The proposal called for the construction of a Deep Underground Command Center that would have been impervious to weapons in the 200–300 megaton range then predicted to be developed by the Soviets. The DUCC was suggested because it was feared that reaction times to reach High Point or for the Emergency Airborne Command Post to reach safety were too long.

Geographically, McNamara proposed putting the DUCC 3,500ft below somewhere close to the Pentagon. It was envisaged the command centre be accessed by lifts from the Pentagon, White House and State Department and connected by horizontal tunnels and rapid transit systems to facilitate movement from the latter two locations. Two bunker models were put forward; au austere 10,000sq ft bunker would have housed 50 while the larger 100,000sq ft model, 300. Construction costs for the austere facility were estimated at $110 million over forty-seven months and $310 million over sixty-six months for the larger bunker.

McNamara's memo stated that the proposed DUCC had 'a unique capability in terms of accessibility and endurance to the President and key military and civil advisors'. In other words, the chief advantages were the quickness of access and the high protection factor. Another argument was that the 'fixed sites of the present system . . . are not very survivable' and would have been less so if the Soviets did manufacture bombs in the 300 megaton range. It was never intended that the DUCC project be classified since its construction would have warned the Soviets the United States was still in a position to retaliate if attacked. As the memo put it, there was a 'desire to convey an image of national will and determination during crisis and tension by making realistic provisions to fight if necessary'. Secretary McNamara recommended funding be approved immediately and that construction begin in Fiscal Year 1965 on the austere model with possibilities of expansion to the larger model in the future. The DUCC may very well have become the PEOC.

Richard Sauder in his book *Underground Bases and Tunnels* mentions the existence of an underground complex deep under the White House. Sauder claims this complex was possibly built during the Eisenhower era and is reached by a lift that travels at least seventeen floors below. Since these same lifts could have spirited White House staff to access tunnels leading to the DUCC, something that logically should have been mentioned in McNamara's top-secret 1963 memo, the author doubts it was really built during the Eisenhower presidency; rather, it was probably installed during Lyndon Johnson's period in office. It is not known if President Kennedy ever saw or considered the memo as he was assassinated two weeks after it was written. It is interesting to point out that in the film *Failsafe* when the President descending below the White House in a lift tells his Russian translator that 'It's a long way down', it is not known if the script writer knew something the public did not, or if he was making a statement allegorical to a descent into political hell.

Site R

One of the largest bunkers built during the Cold War would belong not to the White House or FEMA, but rather to the Department of Defense. DoD's alternate Pentagon is east of Blue Ridge Summit, Pennsylvania, in an underground facility called 'Site R'. In official jargon, the base is known as the Alternate National Military Command Center but unofficially it is dubbed 'Harry's Hole' after Harry Truman, the President who ordered its construction. Site R is a poorly kept secret since a large amount of information can be found about it on the Internet and it is mentioned in several books on the Cold War.

The ANMCC was built in a mountain called Raven Rock by Parsons Brinckerhoff, a world-renowned New York engineering firm with much experience in large-scale projects (including Cheyenne Mountain in Colorado). As part of its planning, the firm sent engineers to Sweden, Germany and France to visit other underground works and to incorporate some of their techniques into it. Construction began in 1951 and by 1954, the complex was in operation. It is also known as the Alternate Joint Communications Center.

Overall, Site R measures 265,000sq ft and consists of a series of buildings inside caverns that include the same types of rooms as found in other bunkers such as dorms, offices, operation centres and dining facilities. Along with offices for the Secretary of Defense, all three major armed services have their emergency operations centres there. Site R has communications connections with several other COG installations in the Washington area, along with several military facilities in the United States, Canada and Europe. It is fully able to dispatch Emergency Action Messages to nuclear forces should the National Military Command Center in the Pentagon be obliterated.[8] The complex's power room consists of six 1,000kW generators, and the water reservoir can hold millions of gallons. The base is so large it even has its own chapel, barber shop and conve-

One of the portals
to Site R. (Photo:
NARA SC-618318)

EXCAVATION IN CONNECTION WITH COMMUNICATION CENTER, FORT RITCHIE, MARYLAND
View toward Portal of Tunnel A from Junction with Tunnel B, showing Completion of Reinforcement
Photo 24 January 1962

One of the tunnels under construction. (Photo: NARA SC-408759)

nience store. In the 1960s, it was hardened to withstand 140psi of pressure. Upon its opening, it was made a lodger unit of Fort Ritchie but with the Fort's closure in 1997, it is now a sub-unit of Fort Detrick. Most of the personnel reside at Fort Detrick and are shuttled in by bus daily.

A blast door. This led to a series of lettered buildings. (Photo: NARA SC-622562)

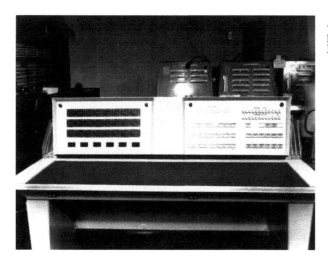

A telephone control panel. (Photo: NARA SC-622553)

In the 1980s, 350 were said to work at Site R, but with the end of the Cold War, this number was reduced after it stopped operating on a twenty-four-hour basis. Many of those who work there belong to the US Army's 1111th Signal Battalion, whose motto of 'Masters of the Rock' gives a clear idea of the kind of installation they work in. Other staff include naval, Air Force and Marine Corps personnel, along with sundry civilians. The ANMCC is fully connected to Mount Weather as the latter was designed to serve as backup to the former if it was destroyed.

From access roads, one sees only fences and an antenna on top of Raven Rock. There are absolutely no signs announcing Site R's presence, save a small green one by Route 116 describing a small building nearby as 'Site R Wastewater Treatment Plant'. A sign by the rear exit on Cove Hollow Road identifies it as

The back door to Raven Rock. (Photo: Author)

the AJCC and warns that persons making sketches or taking photographs will be detained. The author's requests for information from DoD on this facility were ignored, and similar requests for photos from Fort Detrick were rejected for security reasons. In some places, Cold War secrecy is alive and well.

Other Facilities Near Washington, DC
Other emergency government relocation sites around Washington were:

- For the Department of State, at the Department of Agriculture's research station at Front Royal, Virginia (now the location of the Smithsonian's Conservation and Research Center);
- For the Department of the Interior, at the National Parks Service's training centre at Harper's Ferry, West Virginia;
- For the National Archives and Records Administration, at the Randolph-Macon Women's College at Lynchburg, Virginia; and
- For the NATO Standing Group at Norfolk, Virginia, at Mount St Mary's College in Emmitsburg, Maryland.

Yet another bunker, or special basement, exists under the National Defense University at Fort McNair, in Washington. This one is used for exercises as a War Games and Simulation Center. And below the Pentagon, one finds the army operations centre, the air force operations centre and the National Military Command Center.

Also, Vice-President Joe Biden accidentally revealed in 2009 that a new bunker was built for him at his official residence at the US Naval Observatory. After Biden revealed the secret, his office was quick to deny it.

As the sands of history pass, it was inevitable that remnants of the Cold War would become items of curiosity, much like artillery fortresses of the First and Second World War. Nowadays, the public can look at an old bunker and wonder why it was built and for whom. Some will even go as far as taking steps to preserve those concrete skeletons and the accoutrements they possesed. When an old public civil defence shelter was discovered in the basement of 3801 Hudson Manor Terrace in the Riverdale section of New York City, almost every one was surprised. The large room in the basement was still stocked with old metal bins that contained crackers, cardboard toilets with instructional manuals and yellow radiation detectors. The superintendent thought nothing of these relics, until some knowledgeable resident recognized them for what they were and requested to keep some as souvenirs. As it happens, the apartment building in Riverdale was only one of 15,500 in New York City that had the familiar yellow and black fallout shelter sign. How many more basement shelters exist in the United States, and how many more civil defence kits can be found in them? Probably more than we think.

Strategic Air Command

One of the most important underground military posts in the United States is that which is found at Offutt AFB outside Omaha, Nebraska. Early on during the Cold War, the USAF's Strategic Air Command realized it needed a strong command centre from which to launch its long-range bombers. The post had to be tough enough to withstand the kinds of bombs the enemy was then thought to have, if not through a direct hit, then at least through a near miss. And to make it that much more difficult for the enemy to get at, it was sited in the country's heartland.

The SAC command centre was built as two parts. The surface structure looked like a typical office building, which indeed it was, but the below-ground building was where the real power lay. The bunker was built as a three-storey structure that had yet more offices, along with eating and sleeping areas, and a huge operations rooms with status boards and maps in front, rows of communications and other equipment for the battle staff and a glass-enclosed area above and behind for senior staff. Overall, the complex initially measured 14,000sq ft and was connected to the surface building by a ramped tunnel. It was also accessible from emergency exits on top. Construction began in 1955 for both the above and below ground buildings, and by January 1957, the underground centre was occupied. The total cost was then $9 million. In the late 1980s, a 16,000sq ft addition to the complex was built.

SAC's underground operations centre, especially the operations room, could very well have been designed by Hollywood, and in fact at least one film was inspired by it, *Failsafe*. But whereas the operations centre in *Failsafe* used aircraft movement images that were more-or-less updated in real-time, in real life the command centre used at first status boards and maps that were updated manually by airmen on cherry-pickers using long sticks, somewhat akin to the airwomen in the wartime United Kingdom who similarly updated table maps in

STRATCOM's headquarters at Offutt AFB. (Photo: LOC HAER NE-9-M-7)

operations rooms. This activity in the Omaha bunker was televised so that images could be seen in other places such as the Pentagon.

This manual data display technique would be replaced within a few years by more modern equipment. The status boards and maps would disappear, and in their place large 16ft screens would show such things as SAC aircraft locations or weather conditions around the world through slides fed by classroom-type overhead projectors. Further refinements were made later on with the help of computers. The operations centre's other key equipment consisted of red telephones that were used to keep in touch with every SAC unit, with every fleet submarine headquarters and with command centres in the United States and abroad. These telephones and their associated network made up the Primary Alerting System. Naturally, SAC could get in touch with the Pentagon and the White House at all times.

The underground building at Offutt AFB consisted of several other departments that supported SAC. The Intelligence Operations Center monitored foreign strategic forces and political events, and the Weather Support Center tracks weather patterns since they could have major effects on missile and bomber flights. The Force Status Readiness Center does as its name suggests, that is it monitors the conditions of United States strategic forces, and the Alternate Processing and Correlation Center keeps a constant lookout for foreign missile launches. Finally, the Image Generating Facility produces the maps and charts that are displayed on the large screens in the operations room. The bunker goes through annual performance assessments called 'Praetorian Guard' to check staff utilization of nuclear attack and response procedures.

In 1992, when the Strategic Air Command was replaced by a unified command of the Department of Defense, Strategic Command (STRATCOM), the Omaha bunker was transferred to it. The dropping of the word 'Air' from SAC was a reflection of the fact the United States' attack force includes submarines, and it was pressure from the US Navy that STRATCOM should be answerable to the Joint Chiefs of Staff and not to the Secretary of the Air Force.[9] At the same time, the USAF formed the Air Combat Command to take over the operational assets of SAC, namely 6 missile and 21 bomber bases, although since the end of the Cold War these have been reduced to 3 missile wings at Minot AFB, North Dakota, Malmstrom AFB, Montana, and Francis E. Warren AFB in Wyoming, 2 B-52H bomber wings at Minot AFB and Barksdale AFB, Louisiana, and the lone B-2 wing at Whiteman AFB, Missouri. These days, the missiles and bombers are controlled by a new Air Force organization, the Global Strike Command. Exercises that involve all nuclear forces are conducted under the codename 'Global Thunder'.

Next to the delivery vehicles, Strategic Command's most important feature is the plan it would follow if war was ever declared by the President. As the number of bombs and bombers grew during the early Cold War period, military leaders realized that eventually an attack upon the Soviet Union would require co-ordination of forces. At the end of the Second World War, the bombardment of

Japan was a simple affair of dropping two atomic bombs on two separate cities, but with the American's growing arsenal in the 1950s, factors such as sequence of bombing and timing had to be taken into consideration, lest waves of bombers interfere with each other. The problem became more acute when new weapons platforms such as ICBMs and submarines entered the picture and as more knowledge was gained on target hardness.

Strategic bombing plans were made by SAC as early as 1945. One of the first plans, called 'Dropshot', envisaged having bombers drop 300 atomic bombs and 20,000 tons of explosives on Soviet industrial areas. The logic of this campaign was to deny the Soviets any industrial capacity, that is to prevent the manufacture of ships, planes, tanks and guns, rather than attacking military bases. This meant primarily the destruction of the electrical power grid (necessary to run those factories), iron and steel plants, and oil refineries. The following decade, when SAC's inventory grew many-fold and when the Russians began their military build-up in earnest, military planners began considering government and communist party control centres and military targets, which at the time meant mainly long-range bomber bases and naval facilities. Plans were formed and maintained separately by each United States military regional commander (e.g. the Supreme Allied Commander-Europe). By the late 1950s, the number and sophistication of Russian military assets had grown even more, and when in October 1957 the Soviet Union launched its first Sputnik rocket into outer space, the Pentagon immediately realized that the Russians would adapt these rockets for military use and that the American war plan would now have to include attacks on missile fields. It also realized that the disparate plans that then existed within each regional commander's office would not have led to the efficient bombing that was then desired, and that perhaps they could have even been counterproductive. The Joint Chiefs of Staff thus formed the Joint Strategic Target Planning Staff (JSTPS) in 1960, the main role of which was to develop a comprehensive set of war plans for efficient attacks on the Soviet Union and its allies. This set would be known as the Single Integrated Operational Plan (SIOP).

The SIOP was the bible of American nuclear warfare. It told missile and submarine crews what weapons to launch against what targets, and specified what routings bomber crews should take and what their positive control points were. The development of these attack plans begins with the collection of potential targets by the Defense Intelligence Agency and Air Force Intelligence to form the National Strategic Target Database, and continues with refinements that ultimately yields the National Strategic Target List, the former listing every single potential target and the latter, only those that would be actually attacked.[10] The NSTL would include such priority items as missile launch control centres, airfields, nuclear warhead storage sites and command posts. The SIOP is one of the most secret documents in the United States armed forces and has the high Top Secret security classification of ESI-Extremely Sensitive Information. It also carries the label 'Noforn', designating 'No Foreign Distribution', although exceptions have been made in the past for those European allies that possessed nuclear weapons, such as France, Britain and Germany. These nations maintained officers at Omaha (until they got rid of their weapons or, in the case of France, after it dropped out of NATO), and today only the Royal Navy remains as a guest since it still carries nuclear missiles aboard its submarines and would most probably take part in a NATO attack on Russia. The SIOP is usually updated annually.

Besides obvious information such as geographical co-ordinates, each target in the SIOP contains other information. This includes the hardness of attack aimpoints, which helps to determine the type and quantity of weapons that would be used against them. The level of hardness is rated by Vulnerability Number, e.g. 11P1, where the first two numbers show the hardness level or the 'peak overpressure or peak dynamic pressure corresponding to a 50 percent probability of achieving the designated level of damage', the letter indicates whether the 'damage probability should be calculated using peak overpressure or peak dynamic pressure' and the last number – called the K-factor – refers to the target's sensitivity to blast wave duration, with 0 indicating high susceptibility and 9 indicating high resistance.[11] A relatively weak object such as a parked aircraft could have a K-factor of 0 while an SS-19 missile silo has a K-factor of 8.

Another key consideration in the choice and number of weapons used is the accuracy, especially when it comes to missiles. One of the most important characteristics of an ICBM and SLBM is its 'circular error probable', which is defined as the distance from the designated ground zero which 50 per cent of the missiles would reach. In ordinary terms, it is a simple measure of accuracy. When the JSTPS compiles its target database and decides on weapons allocation, CEPs are taken into account for maximum effectiveness. A low accuracy suggests that more than one weapon may need to be used against a target.

The type and hardness of an objective will also decide the weapon to be used. If the target was an airfield and the intent was to damage its runway, accuracy may not be critical because of its large surface. An underground command post, on the other hand, requires a high-yield weapon with relatively good accuracy. Current Russian missile silos, which by themselves are very small objectives that can withstand thousands of pounds per square inch of overpressure, would require an even more accurate weapon. To destroy these, the JSTPS would either assign a very accurate missile, such as the Trident-II sea-launched ballistic missile carried by Ohio-class submarines, or plan for a two-missile strike. To give an example, when it came to the ABM system around Moscow, a system that included long-range radars and short-range missiles housed in underground silos, the USAF and the USN planned as far back as 1968 to use 64 ICBMs and SLBMs against its 8 complexes.

Other factors are considered when the SIOP is planned. For instance, a weapon is chosen based on its probability of kill. The W88 warhead carried on the Trident-II SLBM has a single-shot probability of kill of between 0.44 and 0.69 against an SS-18 silo. Using a second missile increases the probability range to 0.69–0.90. Also, since wind and rain can affect a missile's trajectory, the SIOP takes average monthly weather patterns into account. The SIOP will also state whether the weapon should be detonated as an air burst, ground burst or, if two warheads are used, as a combination of both. Finally, consideration has also been made with respect to the mobile ICBM systems used by Russia. SAC has conducted some targeting experiments on mobile systems in the Ottawa National Forest in Upper Michigan in the 1980s under the codename 'Gifted Eagle' in order to learn how best to destroy them.

The first SIOP was developed in 1960–61 and became effective at the beginning of the 1962 Fiscal Year; it was therefore called SIOP-62. It set out targets destined to be hit by SAC bombers and missiles, by Tactical Air Command aircraft in Europe and by RAF Bomber Command aircraft and IRBMs. In the early 1960s, it was estimated that SAC and TAC could together deliver 18,000–20,000 megatons to the USSR within twenty-four hours. As new targets were discovered (not only in the Soviet Union but also in China) and as new aircraft and weapons – such as the Polaris SLBM – came off the assembly line though, revisions were made.[12] In the late 1960s, the plan's nomenclature changed whence it now included only an edition number instead of the Fiscal Year (e.g. SIOP-5). In 1980, the National Strategic Target Database had no less than 50,000 targets, but when China was removed from the Plan in 1982, the number dropped.[13] In the 1990s, the Department of Defense reverted to the old format (e.g. SIOP-93), but soon after, the name 'SIOP' was dropped and the plan became OPLAN 8010-08, where the last two numbers again refer to the Fiscal Year. As of January 2009, the United States had 2,702 warheads in service (gravity bombs, ICBMs, SLBMs, ALCMs and SLCMs) and approximately another 2,600 in reserve that would be used against opportunistic countries, like China, who would be willing to capitalize on a Russian–US nuclear battle. The number of active warheads is more than enough for the estimated 2,500 targets in the SIOP.[14]

The SIOP would see several revisions over the years, not only in the targeting list and weapons mix but also in its basic premise. President Eisenhower and his military commanders had always assumed that the SIOP should be based on a policy of massive retaliation and that all 1,459 nuclear weapons then on alert, out of a total of 3,423, would be used. In other words, all the active bombers and missiles would be mobilized and used against all 654 targets in the Soviet Union, Eastern Europe and China. SIOP-62 was based on this concept. This policy of massive retaliation was considered too inflexible by President Kennedy since he thought the United States armed forces should be allowed some leeway when attacking its enemies. Some asked why China should be attacked at all if it was not involved in the conflict, and others wondered why the tiny state of Albania, which had broken away from Moscow's domination, should be wiped out. As well, Kennedy and Secretary of Defense McNamara rejected their predecessor's emphasis on cities and thought that adopting a counterforce policy – that is attacks on military bases only – made more sense. They also thought it a good idea not to launch all the missiles and bombers in one large salvo but rather keeping some in reserve as a bargaining chip if the Russians continued their attack. Newer SIOPs issued by the JSTPS were subsequently modified to reflect the new administration's wishes.

When President Nixon was given a briefing on the SIOP in January 1969 at the Pentagon, he was told that if the Russians attacked, he would have to choose one of three options. If he chose option Alpha, the armed forces would set out to destroy urgent military targets. If he selected Bravo, they would attack secondary military objectives. If he chose Charlie, industrial and urban areas would be bombed. From these three taskings, the armed forces, in 1974, were to use one of the following four SIOP options:

Major Attack Options
Selected Attack Options
Limited Nuclear Options
Regional Nuclear Options

The Major Attack Options were those meant to be used during an all-out attack on the Soviet Union, China and their allies. There were then four MAOs in the SIOP where MAO-1 consisted of a strictly counterforce attack (e.g. against missile, naval and air bases, warhead storage sites etc.) against the Soviets and their Eastern European allies, and MAO-2 increased in scope to include urban, political and non-nuclear bases. Major Attack Option-3 was aimed at Chinese military targets, while MAO-4 included the same along with economic targets necessary for postwar recovery. At one time, MAO-1 listed 1,000–1,200 aimpoints which, given the less than perfect probability of weapon effectiveness, would have required more bombs than there were targets. All the options took attack times into account to avoid what is called fratricide, i.e. the destruction of bombers or missiles by one's own forces. If an ICBM was fired on the Engels air base to crater its runway, one would not want to send in a B-52H beforehand to drop gravity bombs on the bomb storage depot located close by on the eastern side of the base.

Selected Attack Options were just as their title states. They were aimed at specific segments of the Soviet or Chinese armed forces. Option 1 saw the destruction of all Soviet nuclear assets that threatened the United States, and Option 4 was to be used against Soviet conventional forces aimed at NATO. Some Options were specifically designed to disable civilian and military command centres.

The Regional Nuclear Options would be used for small-scale conflicts controlled by regional military commanders. Such situations could include battles with North Korea and Iran. In the case of North Korea, submarines of the Pacific Fleet could fire their SLBMs and SLCMs, and B-52Hs from Guam could drop a series of B-61 bombs. As for Iran, B-52Hs and B-2s could be flown into the Middle East using Saudi Arabia as a staging base, or depart from the Diego Garcia base in the Indian Ocean, and submarines could launch their SLBMs from the Arabian Sea.

Recognizing that a major attack would at times be unnecessary or even undesirable, SAC and the Joint Strategic Target Planning Staff adopted new options in 1974 that reflected the acceptance of limited warfare and 'controlled escalation' as one of the current doctrines. This concept followed a policy enunciated by President Nixon in his National Security Decision Memorandum 242 that wholesale attacks on civilians be avoided if at all possible. The new Limited Nuclear Options incorporated into the SIOP assumed a nuclear war would begin with a small attack that carried the potential for an increase. By providing only measured responses in the beginning, the United States armed forces hoped they could prevent all-out war by allowing flexibility that could range from a limited assault of a few weapons to perhaps a few hundreds. The goal would be to stop theatre conflicts before they escalated into something more serious. LNOs thus allowed for early war termination and had the potential to circumscribe the amount of damage or the number of casualties. According to the NRDC, the SIOP had about sixty-five of these options.

The basic premise of LNOs is questionable. The Options are based on the idea that both sides would show self-restraint during a small-scale attack and seek to destroy only a few of the opponent's military assets. On the American side, limited strikes would send a message to the Russians that although it has a strong arsenal, it may be willing to stop its attacks if the Russians cease theirs. This flies in the face of military logic since, during such a conflict, both sides would normally want to destroy each other's nuclear stockpiles as soon as possible to prevent their use. There would therefore be a great incentive to use as many nuclear weapons as possible early on in the exchange, and thus limited attacks would quickly become all-out attacks. Fortunately, the LNOs have never been tested in combat.

By the new millennium, the new SIOP, or OPLAN 8010-08 as it is now called, had drastically changed. Where the old plan considered nuclear strikes only, the new programme now includes the use of conventional weapons. Such devices include Tomahawk SLCMs, 'bunker-busters' and the Hellfire missiles carried by unmanned aerial vehicles. A clear advantage in the use of such weapons is that they will not leave a lasting radioactive impression. OPLAN 8010-08 still includes nuclear attack options, however, but these have been re-designed to fit a post-Cold War world. In a 2010 Federation of American Scientists Brief, the FAS lists the current warfighting menu as:

Emergency Response Options
Selected Attack Options
Basic Attack Options
Directive Planning/Adaptive Planning Options

Details of the various options are understandably classified, but it was revealed in the FAS Brief that the size of an option could vary from a few to hundreds of warheads. The major targets are still Russia, China and North Korea, although there are hints that one non-state actor – probably al-Qaeda – is also included. It was also disclosed in the Brief that each option could be exercised in stages, as opposed to fully, giving commanders that much more flexibility in action.

Adaptive Planning Options were a relatively new addition to the SIOP. Created during the Clinton administration, these options allow STRATCOM quickly to change its plans to meet rapidly emerging threats. Hans M. Kristensen, a nuclear weapons expert with the Federation of American Scientists, stated that the system could allow changes to targets to be made daily (or, some say, even within eight hours), instead of waiting weeks or months for a SIOP amendment, and that instead of focusing on specific scenarios or aimpoints, the options use generic targets. As an example, a strike commander could be ordered to destroy all chemical and biological warfare plants in Libya instead of just known sites such as the underground chemical factory at Tarhunah.

Another major alteration to the SIOP is that which took place in 1991, the same year Russia underwent its own drastic change from a 'worker's paradise' to a relatively liberal democracy. That year, Secretary of Defense Dick Cheney ordered SAC to cut down the number of targets by 2,500, which was a major reduction. This required SAC to analyze its targeting priorities, that is the number of aimpoints, number of active weapons, number of reserve weapons, sequence of missile launches etc., so that only the most important facilities would be hit. The analysis became known as the Phoenix Study as it used the same word as its security clearance codeword.

The Phoenix Study was revealing in a number of ways. The declassified portion gave details that were hitherto not made public. For instance, it showed that, on the average, a delivery method required an average of twenty warheads to reach eight targets, giving a mathematical ratio of 5 : 2 warheads per target. This is what was needed to ensure a weapon's probability of arrival. A table was included in the report showing that for a level of 3,500 warheads, 1,400 aimpoints could be targeted based on that ratio. The number of aimpoints could also be calculated by combining a weapon's probability of arrival with characteristics such as target hardness and nearness to other targets. The report also gave other details such as the fact that bombers were three times more vulnerable to enemy action than missiles. The Phoenix Study had a direct impact on START II force levels as well as on both the 1994 and 2001 Nuclear Posture Reviews.

Another change that took place in the 1990s was the creation of a new unit that would perform miscellaneous tasks related to nuclear warfare. The 625th Strategic Operations Squadron was formed to find, analyze and evaluate strategic targets, and to train and supply personnel for the Air Force's Airborne Launch Control System. It also runs the Strategic Automated Command and Control System. It is not clear, however, how the 625th STOS interfaces with the Air

Intelligence Agency or the Joint Strategic Target Planning Staff in target identification. The Squadron is based at Offutt AFB.

Next to the weapons, people and delivery vehicles, the communications systems used by the National Command Authority (NCA, i.e. the President or his designate) and STRATCOM are of major importance. These are used primarily to pass and authenticate launch orders, to recall bombers, control escalation and even to communicate with the enemy to settle the conflict. The systems also have the useful purpose of allowing a change in attack plans midway into a battle if new information became available. The entire infrastructure for command and control is built with redundancy in mind to ensure that control is maintained under all conditions. The systems are tested every quarter by STRATCOM under the codename 'Polo Hat' to ensure functionality.

Quoting Dr Dineen, Assistant Secretary of Defense for C3I systems under the Carter administration, Desmond Ball in his 1981 essay *Can Nuclear War Be Controlled?* wrote that the United States armed forces had at one time no less than forty-three communications systems in place that could be used during a nuclear war. Other systems were created afterwards in the 1980s in response to President Ronald Reagan's National Security Decision Directive-12, a Directive that called for better systems after weaknesses were exposed. Yet others were adopted to take advantage of new technology. Whatever the reason for their implementation, the systems would be particularly useful during the employment of Limited Nuclear Options as they allow for the cessation of hostilities before things get worse.

While a comprehensive list of those forty-three systems has never been published by the Department of Defense (as far as the author knows), a partial list is provided below, along with some of the newer ones. Note that while all of these were used for command and control, some could also be used for intelligence dissemination or attack warning. Also note that many are no longer used.

- The World-Wide Military Command and Control System, a network of computers located in twenty-seven command centres in the United States and abroad to pass all kinds of military messages (created in 1962 but replaced in 1996 by the Global Command and Control System). It included, as of 1970, the Minimum Essential Emergency Communications Network, used mainly for SIOP execution and termination. The MEECN comprises, among others:
- The Survivable Low Frequency Communications System, also known as Project 487L, a network of teletypes with receivers at bomber and missile bases and on submarines for the transmission of Emergency Action Messages (EAMs);
- The Emergency Rocket Communications System (also known as Giant Moon and Project 494L), a group of ten radio-equipped Minuteman IIs at Whiteman AFB that could remotely launch ICBMs (shut down in 1991);

- The Air Force Satellite Communications System (AFSATCOM), later replaced by MILSTAR satellites;
- The Ground Wave Emergency Network (GWEN), a group of unmanned EMP-resistant Very Low Frequency radio relay sites established throughout the continental United States to pass EAMs through a process called packet switching. The towers were 299ft high and carried a beacon light for aviation safety. In the late 1980s, there were fifty-six units in operation. The network was shut down in 1998; and
- The ICBM Launch Control Center EHF-VLF-LF radio system (ILES), a replacement to the Survivable Low Frequency Communications System.

Other systems include:

- The Defense Satellite Communications System, now being replaced by the Wideband Global Satcom network;
- The Defense Communications System, which included:
- The Autovon military voice telephone system, which used non-secure dedicated telephone company lines to pass military messages of all types (operational as of April 1964, but replaced in the 1980s by the Defense Switched Network);
- The Automatic Digital Network (Autodin), which was a system that also used telephone lines, but that used punched cards, paper tapes or teletypes as input devices. The system was also created in 1964 but replaced by the Defense Data Network in the 1980s; and
- The Automatic Secure Voice Network (Autosevocom), which used dedicated lines to carry scrambled conversations;
- The Mystic Star system, an HF-Single Side Band radio system used by the National Command Authority in Air Force One and other command aircraft when they are out of range of other links;

A Looking Glass aircraft at Offutt AFB. (Photo: LOC, HAER NE-9-B-1, Clayton B. Fraser)

Inside the communications section. (Photo: LOC, HAER NE-9-B-10, Clayton B. Fraser)

- Combat Ciders, a frequency division multiplexing system on Air Force One used to tie into the Autovon network;
- The Green Pine UHF radio network (Project 488L), used to pass messages to bombers flying in the northern hemisphere (created in 1962 and shut down in 1987);
- Giant Talk, a USAF HF radio network (replaced by Scope Signal);
- The Primary Alerting System (Project 465L), the red telephones used by SAC to communicate with its numbered air forces and with bomber and missile bases;
- Verdin, the navy's VLF-LF Digital Information Network, another system used for message handling;
- The Airborne Launch Control System, communications equipment used in special EC-135 aircraft that could remotely launch ICBMs;
- The Hardened Intersite Cable System, a network of underground cables linking silos and Launch Control Centers (no longer used);
- Clarinet Pilgrim, a system using Loran-C stations to broadcast messages to ballistic submarines;
- Commando Escort, a Pacific Air Forces HF-Single Side Band radio network;
- The Post Attack Command and Control System, previously a group of modified Boeing 707s called Looking Glass that were capable of initiating

The command centre. (Photo: LOC, HAER NE-9-B12, Clayton B. Fraser)

an attack (presumably once authorization has been received), replaced in 1998 by navy E-6B TACAMOs;

- The Nuclear Planning and Execution System, which is used to provide information to the National Command Authority;
- The Fleet Satellite Communications System (FLSATCOM);
- Flaming Arrow, a UHF communications network linking all the bases in Europe that stored nuclear weapons;
- Regency Net, a radio communications network in Europe used for the transmission of EAMs;
- The Digital European Backbone, a microwave relay network linking US European Command bases in the UK, Germany, Belgium, the Netherlands and northern Italy. In the 1990s, it was capable of transmitting at 1.54Mb per second, although this has probably been increased since;
- Bright Dawn, an HF radio network used by NATO;
- Last Talk, another HF network used by NATO;
- The Single Channel Anti-jam Man Portable (SCAMP) system, which is equipment that uses improved technology to communicate with bomber and missile crews (and which replaced the GWEN network in 2000);
- TACAMO (Take Charge and Move Out) aircraft of the US Navy, specially outfitted E-6B aircraft that can relay messages to submarines;
- The SACCS, Strategic Automated Command and Control System, which since January 1968 has been the primary system used to transmit

EAMs from the National Command Authority to Omaha to missile and bomber wings. SACCS is also used to provide other information such as intelligence, force status, warnings and operational monitoring data and damage assessments;

- The Joint Chiefs of Staff Alerting Network, a dedicated telephone system that allowed the various command chiefs to talk to each other;
- The Emergency Action Teletype System, no longer used;
- The previously mentioned Project 908, a mobile communications system used for continuity of government and strategic communications, created in the 1980s;
- The President's Emergency Satchel, otherwise known as the 'nuclear football', which contains a black book that lists responses to nuclear attacks (once called the *SIOP Decision Handbook*), a list of classified relocation sites, instructions for the use of the Emergency Broadcasting System, satellite communications equipment and a plastic-coated presidential verification code card;
- The Military Affiliate Radio System, normally used to send non-military messages to the dependents of troops, but that can also be used to transmit EAMs; and
- The Coordination of Atomic Operations Communications Network which, when active, was run out of a Joint Coordination Centre at the Alternate National Military Command Centre near Fort Ritchie.

According to Dr Dineen, even the civilian telephone network could be used to pass EAMs, if all else failed.

The Department of Defense and the US strategic forces created this large mix of systems for two very important reasons: reliability and survivability. The NCA needs to know that Emergency Action Messages will reach attack crews as quickly as possible. Even more importantly, the NCA wants to ensure it has the capacity to cancel its orders if the situation changed (which, in wartime, it can in a flash). Defense also understands that communications are the weakest link in a command and control system since they are the most susceptible to various forms of interference. Any radio or microwave signal can be jammed, satellites can be destroyed by an anti-satellite weapon and any cable, whether above ground, underground or underwater, can be severed. The United States armed forces have already experienced several such setbacks, for instance when in 1965 a farmer in Finland accidentally cut the Moscow–Washington 'Hotline' cable that passed through his farm. The systems are also prone to EMP since military engineers have learned from the Starfish Prime nuclear test of July 1962 that when a 1 megaton device was exploded 248 miles over Johnston Island in the Pacific Ocean, high-frequency communications between Australia, Hawaii and San Francisco were affected for twenty minutes. A similar burst over the central United States would create EMP strong enough to affect communications in most of North America. All this begs the demand for survivability and, at the same time, redundancy.

And if this is not enough, there are Presidential idiosyncracies to worry about. Ronald Kessler revealed in his book *Inside the White House* that President Jimmy Carter absolutely refused to have the nuclear football near him when he went on vacation to his home at Plains, Georgia. Whenever he travelled there, the armed forces (or the White House Military Office) asked to station a trailer on his property nearby so that the football would be accessible 24–7, but the President adamantly refused. The officer carrying the football had to stay in a nearby town, Americus, about 10 miles away. If a nuclear attack had taken place, Carter's insistence would have lost him several precious minutes of decision-making time. The former President, through his lawyer, denied everything in Kessler's book.

The Omaha bunker was not the only one built for SAC. In addition to it, the USAF managed several others throughout the country. Many were built on Air Force Bases to house bomber alert crews, what some people dubbed 'alert cities', at such places as Minot AFB in North Dakota and Plattsburgh AFB in New York. In the late 1950s three other command bunkers were laid out at Westover AFB in Massachusetts, Barksdale AFB in Louisiana and at March AFB in California as backup posts if the main operational centre at Omaha was ever obliterated. The Westover bunker at Amherst, Massachusetts, was built for the Eighth Air Force and was the only one of the three that was constructed as an independent bunker.[15]

The Amherst bunker was built in stages. Its basic design was completed in July 1958, but additions were made from November 1961 to April 1962 and from April 1962 to September 1963. When finally completed, it measured 44,500sq ft,

The Amherst SAC bunker, now owned by Amherst College. (Photo: Author)

covered three storeys, had five underground wells that could hold 800,000 gallons of water and a fuel tank that could hold 20,000 gallons of diesel oil. The walls and ceiling were made of concrete reinforced with steel.

The bunker's heart was the two-level operations room with projection screens and a raised glassed-in balcony for senior officers, much as is found at Omaha. In another section lay a backup war room. One of the offices on the second floor had a bull's eye on the tile floor. The facility included a storeroom for cots and C-rations, a darkroom, encoding and decoding centres, and after 1962 a separate shower room for women. The escape hatch lay directly on top of the bunker and was accessed by ladder. The facility was a maze of corridors and small offices so compartmentalized some were not aware what lay around the corner. The building's cover was that of Westover Air Force Base's Communications Annex No. 3.

News of the bunker came to light when it was put up for sale in 1992. One newspaper advertised its sale for $250,000, and it was Amherst College's bid of $510,000 that won the day. The sale price included 27 acres of land and the radio tower on Mount Barre in the Holyoke Range behind it. The bunker had been decommissioned by SAC in 1972 due to its perceived vulnerability and had been transferred to the Federal Reserve Bank of Boston, which used it for record storage and as an emergency relocation facility. For twenty years, the operations room lay unused. When it was acquired by the college, only the original air system, generators and plumbing remained. One of the backup power generators was sold to an electric company in Argentina while another is now used by a travelling circus. After some remodelling, the bunker was converted into the college library book depository. Amherst College does give tours there on occasion.

One of the few times Mount Weather, Site R and the Strategic Command bunkers were fully activated was during 9-11, according to James Bamford in *A Pretext for War*. As soon as President Bush was notified of the attacks, he took off from his Florida location in Air Force One and began making phone calls to keep abreast of the situation and to let others know where he was. He called Vice-President Cheney at the White House bunker, which then was also occupied by the Secretary of Transportation Norman Mineta and National Security Advisor Condoleeza Rice. It was while Cheney was in the bunker that Bush gave him the authorization to order the shooting of any airliner that strayed off course. At the same time, continuity of government plans were activated and federal public servants were ordered to their relocation sites. Cheney quickly moved to Site R, followed later on by Deputy Secretary of Defense Paul Wolfowitz. As for Bush, he landed at Barksdale AFB in Shreveport, Louisiana. Bamford suggests that Air Force One chose to land there because the runways were large enough (and secure enough) to receive one of the President's airborne command posts, although another reason may be that its underground command post was still an active facility. From Barksdale, Bush addressed the nation, then flew off to Offutt AFB for a brief stay in STRATCOM's bunker. Hours later, he flew back to Washington.

Atchison

Among the largest underground facilities operated by the United States government is an old quarry under Jackson Park in Atchison, Kansas. Billed as the world's largest one-level storage facility, it was originally excavated by the Kerford family in 1886 as a major source of limestone. Its 127 acres were first leased to the federal government in 1944 and the Department of Agriculture kept food stocks, such as vegetables, butter and eggs, in cooled portions of the mine. These stocks would have been released to the public in times of shortage. Then, as of 1951, the US Army Ordnance Corps began storing machine tools that would have been required during a war under the Production Equipment Readiness Program. At the same time, the Army installed electric lights, paved some of the floors and built loading docks. It was then also renamed the US Storage Facility-Atchison Cave. In 1955, the complex was bought by the government for $1.325 million, a number that is co-incidentally close to the facility's usable area of 1,295,270sq ft. Eventually, the contract to manage it was awarded to Page Airways of Rochester, New York.

Over the years, several other alterations and additions were made to the cave. A dehumidification system was put in to maintain a humidity level of 42 per cent. Large fans were also installed for air circulation. The mine's ceiling was coated with gunite to seal any cracks, and in the 1960s thousands of rock bolts were put in to stabilize the formation, as has been done at many other underground complexes. Finally, a power generator was installed in case the outside power ever failed.

In September 1963, the Ordnance Corps transferred the cave to the Defense Supply Agency.[16] The complex became the Atchison Storage Facility and the machine tool warehouse component of it, the Defense Industrial Plant Equipment Facility. The food stocks eventually disappeared and the complex was mainly used to store and repair machinery under the Department of Defense's General Reserve programme. All are kept covered with fire-resistant nylon parachutes. Other miscellaneous military items were later stored there such as medical equipment, uniforms, boots and blankets. In 1974, the DIPEF was employing 138 persons, mostly under contract, and was storing 7,224 different industrial items. The amount of machinery has, however, decreased over the years and by 1999, only 300 machines remained.

One of the Atchison facility's newer mandates is that of record-keeping. Part of the mine is used by the Army Materiel Command to store duplicate records of such places as arsenals and ammunition plants. These documents consist of technical publications and drawings, circulars and supply catalogues along with research and development data. Slowly though, the paper collection will disappear as everything will be put on tapes or CD-ROMs. The AMC units responsible for this collection are the Master Duplicate Emergency Files Depository and the Technical Data Repository.

Today, the Atchison facility is managed by the army reserve's 88th Regional Support Command.

Kunia

Under the pineapple fields of Hawaii lies perhaps one of the most secretive bunkers in the United States. For years, the National Security Agency and the three major armed services operated a listening post in an old Second World War aircraft plant near the town of Kunia 15 miles west of Honolulu. There, the eavesdroppers would tune their radios to everyone who operated in or near the Pacific.

The Kunia bunker had a dynamic history. While it had been built to manufacture war planes in the Second World War, it was never used as such. Instead, the US Army's 30th Base Engineering Battalion used it as a map-making and photographic centre. After the war, the complex was transferred to the Air Force, but was not used until 1953 when the US Navy acquired it to store ammunition and torpedoes. In the 1960s, it became a fleet operations centre used by the Commander in Chief-Pacific Forces, and until 1971 it was also used as a Joint Coordination Centre to co-ordinate atomic operations. In 1976, it was again mothballed, but four years later, the US Army regained control and began using it as a radio intercept station calling it the Kunia Field Station. Redesignated the Kunia Regional SIGINT Operations Center in 1993, it would host a number of intelligence units over the years such as the Army's 703rd Military Intelligence Battalion and the USAF's 324th Intelligence Squadron. The Navy would call its detachment there a Naval Security Group Activity.

When originally built, the Kunia bunker consisted of a large three-storey building upon which was dumped tons of earth. It is equipped with a large air-conditioning and ventilation system and with protection against chemical, biological and radiological attacks. There are three lifts on service there, two for heavy machinery and vehicles and one for passengers. There do not seem to be any living quarters there as the airmen, soldiers and sailors live on a nearby base, Schofield Barracks. The bunker has 250,000sq ft feet of usable space.

NORAD

One of the more well-known underground installations in the United States is the NORAD/Space Command complex at Cheyenne Mountain Air Force Station near Colorado Springs. It is one of the worst-kept secrets in the US military – perhaps intentionally – since from its birth, the base was so well publicized it became an instant target for Soviet ICBMs. Daniel Ford in his exposé of DoD's command and control system, *The Button*, posits that since the complex is only 1,500ft below the mountain's peak, it could be obliterated by high megatonnage rockets.[17] It was, on the other hand, at least safe from saboteurs.

Planning for an underground air defence centre had begun as early as 1956, at roughly the same time the ANMCC at Raven Rock was being built. Site investigations and plan design for the NORAD complex were prepared by Parsons Brinckerhoff, the same firm that designed Site R. Cheyenne Mountain was chosen over other local sites because it seemed the most stable. Construction began in June 1961 by Utah Mining and Construction under supervision of the

US Army Corps of Engineers, and with shifts working six days per week around the clock, the three-part access roadway, called North, South and Central Access Tunnels, was completed in three months.

From the Central Access Tunnel, a series of chambers were excavated into which several interconnected buildings were erected. Test borings had revealed cracks in the underground rock formation, but by rotating the entire complex, the caverns were aligned with the rock joints. By 1964, a series of 600ft-long, 60.5ft-high chambers were completed, across which another series of caverns 335ft long and 56ft high cross-connected. Other chambers were built for the power plant and for water and fuel storage. One of the unique characteristics of the complex was the 100ft concrete shell built under a fault zone for protection against weak rock; the shell allowed loads to be transferred along its surface. There were two pedestrian tunnels, called adits, bored, one connecting the Central Access Tunnel to the complex and the other, to the power plant. An escape hatch also gives out to the central tunnel. Yet another tunnel was excavated diagonally upward for the communications cables connected to antennae on top, but this was filled with concrete once the connections were made and tested. By 1966, excavation and equipment installation was completed with the total cost exceeding $142 million. Operations began on 20 April of that year.

The entire complex at first consisted of eight buildings inside the mountain but with new construction in the 1970s, this was increased to fifteen. Total floor space measures 270,000sq ft and total acreage, 5 acres. The Cheyenne Mountain 'city' employed over 1,000 American and Canadian personnel and had sufficient stocks of food and diesel fuel for a thirty-day buttoned-down status. It had everything expected of a small town such as its own police force, fire department, barber shop, convenience store and chapel. Under normal conditions, the complex operated on local power but in an emergency, it could have relied on its

The entrance to the Cheyenne Mountain Complex. (Photo: NORAD)

own six diesel generators. Air intakes were outfitted with filters capable of preventing the passage of radiological, chemical and biological contaminants, and their closure valves were actuated by blast sensors located at the North and South Portals. If the complex was ever destroyed, NORAD had an alternate command post set up at Peterson AFB nearby ready to take over.

The Cheyenne Mountain Complex was accessed by the main pedestrian adit protected from blasts by two heavy hydraulically operated 25 ton doors 50ft apart. Most buildings within were three storeys high and all were independent of the cavern walls for safety and ease of access. The effects of vibrations caused by earthquakes and nuclear hits were considered from the outset and after considering several shock-absorption methods, machinery was installed on huge 4ft-high springs. The tunnels themselves were stabilized with thousands of 6ft to 32ft long rock bolts and protected by a wire mesh. All the buildings were shielded against electromagnetic pulses by low-carbon steel sheets welded together. At the North and South Portals, huge steel ribs lined with concrete were installed to prevent loose rocks from falling in. Fences lining the outside roadways were topped with concertina to give protection against ground attackers.

The heart of the Cheyenne Mountain Complex was always the Combat Operations Center (COC). It is here where data was received from all sources and from which air defence operations were conducted. Initially, the COC used three Philco 212 computers to receive and process information from radar stations and flying radar platforms. This combination of computers was called 425L, so numbered after the Air Force contracting project number. Later on, when the Space Defense Center opened, it used its own 496L computers to process satellite-based information. Between the 425L and the 496L, there were sub-systems for the detection of sea-launched ballistic missiles, the warning of approaching aerial forces, and the detection of ICBMs. The COC also made use of the NORAD Attack Warning System – also called the '10A' – to warn fighter and missile bases (through NORAD Regional Headquarters) for possible action. As well, the Combat Operations Center controlled the short-lived Safeguard ABM system that was established in North Dakota.

Since it began operations in 1966, there have been several changes and re-organizations at the Cheyenne Mountain Complex. One of the biggest changes was in the computer equipment. Perhaps in recognition of the growing Soviet ICBM and space-based threat, a plan was proposed by the USAF to replace the 425L and 496L systems with a new higher capacity computer as early as 1968. After years of study and testing, the new system, called 427M, was declared operational in 1979. It used the Honeywell HIS 6080. Also, the COC's increasing range of functions caused the complex's population to augment from 1,100 in the 1960s to 1,400 by the end of the 1980s. In 1987, the CMC would be redesignated as Cheyenne Mountain Air Force Station and would thus become an independent military establishment.

Recently, one found the following eight major divisions in the complex:

The Command Center
Air Defense Operations Center
Missile Correlation Center
Space Control Center
Operational Intelligence Watch
Weather Center
Domestic Warning Center
The Systems Center

Since the complex was established as a bi-national American-Canadian air defence centre, staff from both the USAF and the Canadian Forces are stationed there.

The Missile Correlation Center had the responsibility for detecting both long-range missiles aimed at North America and short-range missiles aimed at American troops overseas, what are called strategic and theatre threats respectively.[18] Foreign ICBMs were tracked in the MCC by the efforts of Defense Support Program-647 satellites. These carried large infrared telescopes that picked up strong heat sources and which mirrored them onto an array of lead sulfide cells. The pattern of cells hit gave an indication of the heat source's origins. The satellites carried other sensors to detect nuclear explosions, electromagnetic pulses, gamma radiation and X-rays. All DSP signals were processed by an on-board computer and downlinked to stations in Australia and Colorado for transmittal to the MCC and to Strategic Command at Omaha.

The Missile Correlation Center received further inputs from Pave Paws long-range radars that operate on both coasts to sense sea-launched ballistic missiles, and from huge UHF antennae of the Ballistic Missile Early Warning System in Alaska, Greenland and the United Kingdom. During the Gulf War, the MCC received data from satellites that were modified just before Desert Storm that were used to detect Iraqi SCUD launches. Once processed by Cheyenne

The NORAD Air Center at Cheyenne Mountain. (Photo: NORAD)

Mountain, the data was used to help programme Patriot surface-to-air missiles to their targets.

A typical alert at Cheyenne Mountain might have looked as follows. One of the USAF's satellites detects the heat signature of an ICBM launched from Russia. Staff in the Command Center have mere minutes to decide whether to advise Washington and Ottawa. A voice loop is established between the Command Director in the Command Center and other centres in the complex, and their discussions and analysis quickly begin. One officer rules out the possibility that a sun burst caused a false reading. The Pentagon and the National Defence Operations Centre at National Defence Headquarters in Ottawa are advised of the launch. An intelligence specialist in the Operational Intelligence Watch reveals that the launch is indeed of an ICBM, but one on a training exercise that is due to fly from Tyuratam to the Kamchatka Peninsula. Long-range radars confirm the track. The missile soon lands as predicted, and the threat disappears.

Another key operational division at the Cheyenne Mountain Operations Center, the Space Control Center, tracked everything in space. Its database cataloged every rocket flight and debris, predicted positions and estimated times and locations of re-entry. As of 10 June 1998, there were 2,489 satellites, 24 space probes and 6,222 items of debris indexed by the SCC, the large majority being from the United States and Russia. The command's Tracking and Impact Prediction computer programme monitored re-entering objects that could mistakenly be categorized as hostile missiles. Object positions were also used by space shuttle computers for collision avoidance.

In the Air Defense Operations Center, later known as the Air Warning Center, all flights entering North American airspace were closely watched until correct identification was made. Aircraft were colour-coded on the display screens to show status: yellow/red signified an unknown, green a special flight and red, a hostile. In 1994, 880 aircraft flying into North America were categorized as unknown with 10 to 15 per cent later identified as narcotics smugglers. Personnel in the AWC included surveillance and identification specialists, as well as weapons controllers, an Air Battle Management officer, a Northern Command Domestic Events officer, a Federal Aviation Administration representative and fighter control operators.

Among other units at Cheyenne Mountain, the Weather Center kept constant watch on the weather. At one time, maintenance of facilities and food preparation was looked after by the USAF's 4604th Support Squadron. The 47th Communications Group and the Defense Information Systems Agency were also found there. In addition to the FAA officer, other civilians worked in the complex were from FEMA since that agency operated its Domestic Warning Center there as the main civil defence warning site.

One of the things that kept Cheyenne Mountain staff busy was the exercises. These varied from actual or simulated B-52 or B-1B strikes coming in from the north or over the coasts, missile attacks from Russia or as aerial threats to

American troops overseas. The bi-annual Amalgam Warrior series of exercises, for example, tested the personnel's response to an attack coming from Russia that consisted of a series of bombers armed with cruise missiles and using various forms of jamming and penetration tactics. The staff at Cheyenne Mountain were tested for their proficiency in detecting the intruders and directing fighter inter-ceptors. Yet other exercises, such as Amazon Condor, tested battle staff in command post exercises.

Many alert conditions have arisen at Cheyenne Mountain over the years, but these have always been due to false alarms. In the early days, rocket test flights, computer malfunctions and even natural phenomena could trigger an alert. On 10 November 1979, a technician loaded a war game tape to test the computer and through some error, the game data was fed into the sensor system. The warning operators dispatched 10 interceptors to verify the attack – 2 from Kingsley Field, Oregon, 2 from KI Sawyer AFB in Michigan and 6 from CFB Comox, British Columbia – only to recall them minutes later. The alert was taken sceptically since the Cheyenne Mountain crew did not believe the attack was real. While other bases were put on low alert, there was no widespread response and, indeed, no B-52s were launched.

One of the largest transformations to take place in NORAD occurred in 2005. That year, a new above-ground command centre was opened nearby at Peterson AFB to replace the Cheyenne Mountain Complex. To 'accommodate the expanding homeland defense mission . . . as well as to provide better situational awareness', as the NORAD press release put it, the new facility was outfitted with a larger war room. New large screen displays and workstations were put in by a long-time defence contractor, Lockheed Martin. The main purposes of the new control centre were to accommodate the larger staff that was needed to monitor and identify aerial traffic and to operate the new National Missile Defense system. The Cheyenne Mountain Complex was vacated but remains on stand-by as an alternate command post if the new command centre was ever disabled. Just to make sure the old operations centre can still function, staff carry out relo-cation exercises there on occasion.

Other Facilities
In addition to Cheyenne Mountain and Omaha, several 10,000sq ft to 12,000sq ft underground transmitter facilities were built by Parsons Brinckerhoff across the United States for the Office of Civil Defense's Decision Information Distribution System, a network used for strategic communications. These small shelters consist of generator and transmitter rooms, bunk rooms, dining facili-ties and storage areas, and are equipped with blast doors and shielding against radioactivity. Their locations have not been disclosed.

Other government bunkers have been revealed over the years. Jim Schnabel in his book on secret government psychic experiments *Remote Viewers* described how one trainee during a mind viewing session identified a subterranean facility called 'UBG' at the National Security Agency's listening post at Sugar Grove,

West Virginia, a station so sensitive the trainee himself, who held a high security clearance, was investigated as a possible foreign agent when he tried to confirm what he saw.

Another bunker apparently exists north of Warrenton, Virginia, according to the book *Nuclear Battlefields* by Arkin and Fieldhouse. The bunker is supposedly a relocation site for an unnamed government agency. The sign by the property's Bear Wallow Road entrance identifies it as US Army Warrenton Training Center Station B, NCS. NCS is the National Communications System, a network of government communication systems managed by the Defense Information Systems Agency (DISA) designed for interoperability in times of conflict. The NCS ensures various radio and data networks from such diverse departments as State, Treasury, Transportation and Justice along with agencies such as the CIA, NSA, FCC and FEMA can talk among themselves during wartime, this to solve a shortcoming discovered during the Cuban missile crisis. The NCS also includes the 'Hotline', officially known as the Direct Communications Link, that connects Moscow and Washington.

DISA will give no information on the bunker itself, or even admit there is one there, but it will say the Training Center was first established in 1951 as a 'Department of Defense Communication Training Activity'. It was transferred to the Army Security Agency – the Army's signals intelligence service – in 1973 and returned to DoD in 1982 and now 'is a communication training and support facility' that employs personnel from the various NCS signatories. One might assume Warrenton is either a central node or junction for the NCS member networks or some kind of testing centre. It is not known what the house called 'Brushwood' on the base's west side is for. Whether there really is a bunker on this property is debatable since nothing about it is visible from satellite imagery.

Other federal underground installations include:

- A generating station used to power a radar installation for the now-defunct Safeguard missile system at Malmstrom AFB, Montana. The power station and radar facility were linked by a tunnel;
- Portions of Los Alamos National Laboratory in New Mexico;
- Research facilities at Rosamond, Hellendale and Llano, California, used by Northrop, Lockheed and McDonnell Douglas respectively;
- Part of National Security Agency headquarters at Fort Meade, Maryland;
- Munitions bunkers at:
  - Pine Bluff Arsenal, Arkansas;
  - Hermiston, Oregon;
  - Tooele, Utah;
  - Air Force Bases;
  - The Yorktown Naval Weapons Station in Virginia;
  - The Strategic Weapons Facility-Pacific at Bremerton, Washington; and
  - The Strategic Weapons Facility-Atlantic at King's Bay, Georgia;

- In Monticello, Iowa, as a former Air Force communications site that has been turned into a data centre;
- In Florida, on Peanut Island, near the Coast Guard station, for President Kennedy;
- In Oregon, 8 miles east of Bend off Highway 20 and Dodds Road. Here, a bunker was built in the early 1980s ostensibly as a communications site. This may have been one of the Project Doomsday bunkers;
- In Tennessee, near Clarksville, to house nuclear weapons. The depot was known as National Stockpile Site Charlie and was built in 1948. The caves ceased to be used in either 1965 or 1969;
- In Hawaii. Batteries Arizona and Pennsylvania were used as civil defence command posts in at least the 1950s and 1960s;
- In Pennsylvania, on Route 97 between Wakeford and Union City. A bunker lies quietly under a non-descript building on the south side of the road; and
- In California, outside Edwards AFB between Boron and Barstow off Highway 58. An unknown bunker was discovered by locals a few years ago. This one seemed to be out-of-use for years.

Then there is the very large underground nuclear weapons depot outside Albuquerque, New Mexico, presently known as the Air Force Nuclear Weapons Center. Built between 1992 and 1994 to replace a mountain complex in nearby Manzano (itself built in 1949–50), the base stores approximately 2,000 nuclear warheads and cruise missiles in an area reported to be the size of 40 football fields. The operating unit at the AFNWC, the 898th Munitions Squadron, is a sub-unit of the 498th Nuclear Systems Wing of Kirtland AFB. Another unit, the 377th Air Base Wing, looks after the depot's security and staff training. The *Air Force Times* reported in 2010 that both Wings failed a nuclear surety inspection because of problems in 'personnel reliability, maintenance operations, and nuclear weapons security'. While precise details were not made public, the article quoted Brigadier-General Everett H. Thomas, head of the AFNWC, as suggesting some personnel were not properly screened before being employed there.

State and Municipal Bunkers
During the Cold War, many states followed Washington's lead and built their own relocation and command centres. States are responsible for providing different services to the public than the federal government, e.g. drivers' permits and birth records, so they too had an incentive for developing plans to continue functioning during a nuclear war. Many went on to build reinforced concrete structures that were either located underground or that were made an integral part of some government building. Often, these structures would be called Emergency Operations Centers (EOCs) and were controlled by state civil defence organizations. These EOCs also often doubled as alternate seats of

The Massachusetts state bunker at Framingham was never a big secret as it lay in full public view. (Photo: Author)

government. Following the change in focus from nuclear war to disaster assistance in the 1970s, state civil defence units were renamed Emergency Management Agencies.

Massachusetts' state bunker would be one of the few that would be built as a stand-alone facility. It is a single-storey structure with offices, a small emergency control centre, power room, communications room along with separate male and female dormitories that is located next to State Police Headquarters at 400 Worcester Road in Framingham. The entrance hallway was built at right angles to negate the effects of a blast wave. The bunker sits on a plot so small its parking area was put on top. When visited by the author in 1998, some of its personnel were getting ready for a nuclear accident exercise.

Much more extensive than the Framingham bunker is New York State's combination underground emergency operations centre and alternate seat of government under State Police Headquarters on Washington Avenue in Albany.

Desiring of protection against a Soviet attack, Governor Nelson Rockefeller

The New York state bunker was under State Police Headquarters in Albany. (Photo: Author)

followed the federal lead and began preparing plans for the continuity of his government in the early 1960s. The plan's linchpin was a 2-storey complex with every amenity capable of sustaining 750 for 14 days. By the time it was completed in April 1963, the 77,000sq ft structure cost $4 million – with half paid by the federal government – and could withstand the blast from a 2 megaton device 1.3 miles away or a 20 megaton hit 2.8 miles away.

Regular entry to the Albany bunker is gained from the main floor of police headquarters. The first floor contains decontamination rooms for men and women, offices, the operations room, an assessment and evaluation centre and a well-equipped communications room. In wartime, the regular civil defence staff would be moved out and the offices taken over by personnel from the various government departments: finance, taxation, corrections, health, public works, agriculture and Attorney-General etc. The lower level contains a mini-hospital complete with pharmacy, ward, operating room and morgue, kitchen, a lunch counter and in the power room, three 375kW generators, one for backup. Initially, most of the dormitories would have housed men, and many jokes were made of the fact that the single small women's dorm was located next to that of the Governor's staff. The entire structure is protected from radiation with 20in of concrete roofing and tons of earth. Normally, less than 100 men and women work there.

In times of emergency, civil defence personnel at the bunker would perform several duties. Since states have primary responsibility for disaster assistance, it would be them who would issue warnings of attack and fallout, allocate resources and set up emergency hospitals. Co-ordination of state-wide rescue efforts would be carried out there. The bunker possesses instruments that can warn of radiation and equipment that protects its occupants against it. A battery operated radiation detector sits on the roof of police headquarters. Air intake and exhaust closure valves are equipped with pressure and light sensors that can be triggered by an atomic blast. Much of the furniture and equipment inside is shock-mounted for stability, and pipes and electrical conduits are fitted with barco ball joints that can move when the bunker is shaken.

Other state bunkers are:

- In Iowa, at Camp Dodge under the state national guard armoury;
- In Colorado, for several years, as Building 120 at Camp George West in Golden;
- In Florida, just outside Fort Pierce;
- In Nebraska, at 1300 Military Road in Lincoln;
- In Virginia, as a small 2,500 sq ft facility under the state police academy;
- In Oklahoma, under the grounds of the state Capitol in Oklahoma City;
- In Ohio, 8 miles northwest of Columbus on Granville Road in the basement of a Ohio State Police dispatch office; and
- In Hawaii, in an old military complex called Birkhimer Tunnel near Diamond Head Crater.

Many cities and counties also had their own emergency command centres. Some of these were:

- In Portland, Oregon, in the southeast part of the city in Kelly Butte Park;
- In Baltimore, Maryland, under a fire station 5 miles north of the city centre;
- In Volusia County, Florida, as a surface-type bunker off US Route 92;
- In Decatur, Alabama, for the 911 centre;
- In Cincinnati, Ohio. Part of the never used and never completed underground rail system in the downtown area was converted into civil defence office space during the 1950s;
- In Dallas, Texas, under the Health and Science Museum's outside patio in Fair Park;
- In Los Angeles, for many years under City Hall East. The city had considered building an underground communications centre on Mount Lee in the 1950s but never proceeded with its plan;
- In Burlington County, New Jersey, in an old Nike surface-to-air missile magazine in Marlton;
- In Montgomery County, Maryland, under the council office building in Rockville;
- In Elmhurst, Illinois, in Ben Allison Park; and
- In Clermont County, Ohio, at 2279 Clermont Center Drive, for the county's EOC.

At the height of the Cold War, even educational institutions would fall victim to the Soviet scare. The bunker craze prompted a school board in New Mexico to build a new school in 1962 for one to six-graders in Artesia below ground. While all classrooms, offices and cafeteria were built underneath, the kids enjoyed recess on the basketball court on top. The rooms were all provided with good lighting and coloured walls, and were equipped with a movie screen and audio/video equipment. The temperature control system guaranteed a constant temperature without which the heat would become unbearable. The structure also has its own diesel generator and emergency fuel supply if normal power was ever interrupted. The school normally accommodated 550 and could house 2,100 during an emergency.

Nevada Test Site

The Nevada desert contains possibly the largest underground testing facility in the world. Until the cessation of nuclear tests in 1992, atomic bombs were detonated at Area 12 of the Nevada Test Site within Nellis Air Force Base in chambers built especially for this purpose. Since the 1950s, over 800 detonations of varying magnitude have taken place there under the auspices of the Department of Energy and the Defense Nuclear Agency. Area 12 is only one section of the test site and it alone consists of five general sections that have over

40 miles of tunnels. If other areas also have underground passages, the total tunnel length would be staggering. In 1993, the test site employed 11,000–5,000 on a full-time basis – and operated on a budget of $1 billion.

One of the roles of the Nevada Test Site in the 1950s was to test structures for resistance to atomic blasts. An entire town was built in 1953 to determine the level of damage it would sustain if attacked. Survival City, or Doom Town as some called it, came complete with residential and industrial buildings, a power grid, radio station, appliances and mannequins. One of the tests conducted that year used a 29 kiloton device, the blast from which may have had disastrous effects on the mannequins but little on sheltered props proving that even a small amount of protection was better than none.

At least one of the Nevada tests has had near lethal consequences. One 20 kiloton blast in 1984 that took place 1,168ft below the surface near Rainier Mesa created fissures and caused monitoring vehicles above to fall 10ft to 30ft below. While no one died, fourteen scientists and engineers required medical attention.

Yucca Mountain

More recently, an intricate nuclear Exploratory Studies Facility was built under Yucca Mountain, Nevada, near Las Vegas. The US Department of Energy excavated a system of tunnels and ramps 10 miles long to study the feasibility of storing nuclear waste underground. DOE is presently conducting geological, hydrological, engineering and geochemical research there.

Corporate Bunkers

Since many large private firms also had their own underground shelters, it was still possible for corporate America to work after the 'Big Bang'. At the height of the Cold War, several companies sprang up offering shelter space to firms eager to survive the holocaust. Iron Mountain Atomic Storage bought an old iron mine by Mount Tom 5 miles south of Hudson, New York, on Columbia County Road 10 in 1951 for use as a corporate documentation depot for rent. After the mine's acquisition, Iron Mountain refashioned into it 150 vaults of various sizes from 6sq ft to 15,000cu ft and began offering space to any firm that sought to continue operations after an attack. For a fee, Iron Mountain rents out vault space to companies either wishing to store records or wanting emergency accommodations for executives and staff.

The entrance portal to the Hudson facility looks like a huge white railway tunnel entrance sealed up. Once inside, a guest passes through three heavy doors that eventually lead to a comfortable and secure complex. The mine walls and roof are covered with concrete, and a constant room temperature and humidity level is maintained. The complex includes its own power generators, food plant and for short-term guests, a motel. Shell Oil, one of its corporate clients until 1975, had a 4,400sq ft facility ready for forty-four persons, complete with dining and sleeping facilities, a lounge, a medical station and a kitchen. Other organizations hid valuable art treasures or stamp collections there. The Hudson facility

Many firms have been created over the years to offer secure storage space to corporate America. This is Archival Solutions at Pepperell, Massachusetts. (Photo: Author)

was only one of many in the United States as Iron Mountain owns other underground vaults at secret locations.

Another example of a mine serving a new role is the Carey salt mine in Hutchinson, Kansas. Since Kansas had so many strategic military assets at one point, the state made for a good target. After the salt was removed from the mine, management wondered what to do with the large network of tunnels. Some were sold to Underground Vault and Storage and, as with Iron Mountain, were converted into office space and accommodations for lease. Some of the leasors have included the Federal Reserve Bank of Kansas City, Cessna Aircraft, Pizza Hut and Mobil Corporation. Metro-Goldwyn-Mayer stored some of their old film negatives there. The tunnels' depth of 650ft gave its occupants more than adequate protection against a nearby blast.

More impressive than the Hutchinson salt mine is an underground city in Kansas City, Missouri. A huge limestone cavern was also converted into an office

Another document storage company was located on Branchton Road in Boyers, Pennsylvania. One of its current customers is the National Archives and Records Administration. (Photo: Author)

complex but this one is even more well developed. Known as the Great Midwest Underground, the cave is a huge network of roads, offices and warehousing facilities capable of accommodating thousands of workers. As of 1982, there were 18.5 million sq ft mined out, and while most of it is leased out as storage space, smaller percentages are used for manufacturing and offices. The complex includes several loading docks as well as over 3 miles of roads and 2 miles of railway tracks. The cave's facade is attractively framed by a natural tree line and a series of flags over the entrances. One of its corporate clients, Brunson Instruments, found the environment sufficiently stable for its precision manufacturing operations. Another advantage for an underground complex of this type is the constant temperature, which means no heating system or insulation, but the drawbacks are the same as living in a bunker: lack of sunlight and disorientation upon exit. The cave can be accessed from Underground Drive off Interstate 435.

As late as the 1980s, much of the private sector lacked an emergency war plan. AT&T was one of the few firms that had detailed plans that included several underground hideaways. The corporation had (or has) a National Emergency Control Center under a non-descript building in Netcong, New Jersey. Normally, the centre acts as a relay point for long-distance communications but in wartime, sixty key individuals would be told to report there. The massive telephone switching units are so anchored to absord shock waves.

Another AT&T underground facility exists at Ellisville, Florida, a small town off Interstate 75 about 35 miles north of Gainesville. The site consists of a surface building atop a two-storey bunker, various antennae, two chain link fences and a closed-circuit TV camera. Inside the building lies a combination of new telephone equipment and vintage racks, along with the standard assortment of rooms found in bunkers such as a decontamination cubicle, power and filtration rooms, offices and a bathroom complete with spring-mounted toilets. There are enough supplies for 150 persons for a month. During a war, staff would be allowed to bring their families in for shelter, otherwise, one employee claims, nobody would show up if the bombs began dropping. This facility is suspected as being one of the sites that provides secure communications to the presidential plane Air Force One under a programme called 'Combat Ciders'.

Other AT&T bunkers were built at such places as Fairview, Kansas, and Lyons, Nebraska, in the Midwest. These act as ground entry points for communications originating from flying Air Force command posts to missile launch control centres, communications that could include Emergency Action Messages or nuclear attack orders. The aircraft, the previously mentioned modified Boeing 707s called Looking Glass, fly around the entry points daily with a crew ready to assume strategic control if Washington or Offutt AFB was disabled. AT&T also had twenty bunkers throughout the nation to handle Autovon communications. One of those bunkers, in northeast Bates County, Missouri, was up for sale in 2009. Some of the corporation's bunkers in Maryland and Virginia may still be in use. A few more are listed in Appendix D.

Among other firms:

- US Steel had a 16,000sq ft underground facility several hours from Pittsburgh;
- National Underground Storage occupies an old mine south of Boyers, Pennsylvania which, at one time, counted 125 clients such as Westinghouse, the Social Security Administration, US Investigations Services, the National Archives and Records Administration, Universal Studios and Warner Brothers.[19] It too has furnished apartments and kitchen facilities; and
- Another major corporation, Standard Oil of New Jersey, bought an old convalescent home 30 miles from midtown Manhattan as a relocation site and fashioned a records vault below.

Some caves also performed similar roles. One in the Ozarks in Arkansas was so huge someone from Colorado converted it into his home. Spurred on by the ABC drama about a third world war aired in 1983, *The Day After*, the man had heard about the cave and quickly bought it up for several thousand dollars. Part of it was tastefully redecorated to make it habitable. To prevent water dripping on the tile floor, the walls were covered with eleven coats of epoxy. One of its main drawbacks was the impossibility of television reception so the family had to make due with videos. The home had one of the biggest backyards around, a 2-mile-long pitch black cave, complete with salamanders, crickets and un-welcomed bats.

Civil Defence

Where the protection of the public was concerned, it would be a very different matter. There would not be any huge public shelters built anywhere in the United States like those built in Switzerland or Sweden. While he was President, Eisenhower never eschewed the idea of developing a system of mass shelters, and in that respect, Congress agreed with him. Neither wanted the state to interfere with American individuality, and Congress was also very fearful of the potential for waste. Several American politicians also disliked the regimentation that a civil defence programme would likely have entailed. Judging by the lack of public demand, both Eisenhower and Capitol Hill realized there was no public support for it. Government involvement would be limited to public education through the Federal Civil Defense Administration and the media. The public was encouraged to build their own basement or backyard shelters and to stock them with suitable supplies under what would be termed a 'self-help' policy. Those that would not or could not build their own bunker would rely on evacuation.

All this would change when John F. Kennedy assumed power in 1961. While Kennedy had originally been lukewarm to the idea of mass shelters, the sudden erection of the Berlin Wall reminded him of the delicate times he was living in. Kennedy began thinking more and more about nuclear war and the protection of the American people. Politicians such as New York Governor Nelson Rockefeller, who went so far as creating his own tax-funded shelter programme in his state, along with Attorney-General Robert Kennedy began extolling the virtues of the programme to the President. This was enough for President Kennedy to go to Congress to request $695 million for civil defence.

Congress would not, however, share Kennedy's vision. The amount requested represented a huge sum at the time, and in the end it only authorized $80 million. Huge complexes would not be built for the public, as the new President had hoped, but at least basements of public buildings such as city halls and court-houses would be turned into shelters. These would be stocked with emergency food rations, water, blankets, a radiation meter and a radio, along with several cots and folding chairs. Once a warning was declared over the Emergency Broadcasting System, the public had the option of either staying at home and covering themselves, or running to the nearest fallout shelter and huddling with their neighbours. These shelters were clearly marked as such with yellow and black signs. American society would never have a civil defence programme that matched that of the Swiss.

Then, there are those thousands of private shelters that were erected in the 1950s, 1960s and even in the 1980s across the United States. One of the larger ones was built by a relative of the President of Taiwan, Chiang Kai-Shek, Ling-Chih Kung. The bunker was set under Kung's Westland Oil building on Highway 105 near Conroe, Texas. It was apparently large enough to accommo-date 1,500 for 90 days. After Kung died, the building and property were sold to West Hills Joint Venture, and the bunker was leased by the new owner to the Jarvis Entertainment Group to be used as a network operations centre.

ICBM Bases

The second category of American underground structures discussed here is that which houses staff and weapons that would be on the front lines of a nuclear exchange. During the early part of the Cold War, the United States borrowed a page from the book of German research on unmanned weapons that could travel long distances to deliver a deadly payload, i.e. missiles. Some military planners and designers saw in the missile a potential for great firepower at reduced cost since it could deliver a then-new potent invention, the nuclear bomb, without the need for flight crews and the maintenance of expensive aircraft. A missile also had the advantage of speed since it could reach the Soviet motherland in minutes while bombers took hours. Research into ICBMs had begun as far back as 1946 by Consolidated Vultee under a USAF contract, but it would take years, new technology and information on the Soviet Union's progress before any signifi-cant headway would be made.

Serious funding for an American ICBM programme only came during the Korean War. Rocket engineers had tried to keep track of developments in Soviet rocket research and came to the conclusion that their efforts were well ahead of those of the United States. They travelled to the Pentagon to meet senior Defense staffers and to impress them with their findings. These staffers, along with a newly formed Strategic Missiles Evaluation Committee, eventually convinced higher-ups and Congress to approve massive funding for ICBM development. Such funding materialized, and by the late 1950s spending was in the order of $3 billion, an astronomical sum at the time.

The first ICBM on the drawing board was Convair's Atlas.[20] The Atlas was a fat 75ft-long missile that used a kerosene-based RP-1 fuel that burned with liquid oxygen. Its warhead had a 1.44 megaton yield. To keep its weight to a minimum, its airframe consisted of only dime-thin stainless steel; there would be no supporting internal beams. As such, it was considered just one large inflated balloon. The missile had to be constantly kept full of helium gas to prevent it collapsing on itself. While Convair had been the main contractor, it really represented the productive output of other aerospace giants, such as Boeing and Douglas, as well as over 200 other contractors and subcontractors. In official military literature, it was designated SM-65.[21] On a test launch at Vandenberg AFB – the US's ICBM testing and training site – on 9 September 1959, an Atlas travelled 4,300 miles at 16,000mph. Operational missiles would have a range of 5,500 miles. With respect to its targets, the Atlas' first priority was enemy missile launch sites and the second, to quote Harry Stine in his book *ICBM*, 'to be able to put one through the window of the men's room at the Kremlin'.

The Atlas was deployed in three models: the D, E and F. The D variant was housed in a surface coffin where the missile would remain horizontal under a heavy door. After turning the appropriate keys, the door slid sideways and the missile was raised, fuelled and launched within fifteen minutes. The Atlas D used a combination of command (i.e. radio) guidance and all-inertial guidance to control its thrusters. Four squadrons of this model were formed at the following bases: Francis E. Warren AFB in Wyoming, Offutt AFB outside Omaha, Nebraska, Fairchild AFB, Washington, and Vandenberg AFB in California. Deployment patterns varied from base to base: at Warren AFB, for instance, Google Earth shows that its two squadrons of three missiles each were placed close to each other at the launch site several miles north of the base and west of Interstate 25. All the Atlas D Strategic Missile Squadrons had an underground Launch Control Center (LCC) near the missiles.

The Atlas was the first American ICBM to enter service. This model stands in front of the National Museum of Science and Technology in Ottawa, Canada. (Photo: Author)

The Atlas D only appeared to be a

stop-gap measure rushed into production to keep the Russians at bay. Even before the first squadrons were set up, Convair was working on the E model. This new variant made use of a major technological advance in electronics in the form of the transistor, a revolutionary device that would impact on everything from home electronics to computers. In the field of missilery, the transistor impacted on the guidance system to such a large extent the Atlas' circular error probable dropped from several thousand feet to 910ft. With its 3 to 4 megaton payload, any object located within its destructive footprint would have suffered great damage.

One of the Atlas D's main disadvantages was its vulnerability to attack. In 1957, President Eisenhower formed a Science Advisory Committee to look into the nation's defences against an atomic attack and the deterrent value of its strategic assets. In its report, the Gaither Commitee, as it came to be known, recognized that until missile-carrying submarines were produced SAC would carry the entire responsibility for an attack on Russia. The Committee recommended that SAC forces be increased and that ICBMs be based in sturdier structures. The USAF and the Department of Defense listened and began planning those structures.

To destroy Atlas D coffins, Soviet missiles did not require a great deal of accuracy. Even a near miss with a heavy megaton weapon would have sufficiently damaged the structure to make it inoperable. When the E model was designed, the USAF heeded the Gaither Committee's recommendation and modified the coffins to give some blast protection to the missile. Atlas Es therefore slept in partly buried coffins officially rated to withstand 25psi of pressure. As with Atlas D sites, crews were similarly put underground in capsules that were connected by tunnels to the coffins. Each Atlas E unit had nine missiles deployed singly in what was called a 1 x 9 pattern. Each launch site cost $4 million to build with responsibility for construction vested in the Army Corps of Engineers. The squadrons were located at Warren AFB, Wyoming, Forbes AFB, Kansas, and Fairchild AFB, Washington.

Soon after the E model was deployed, it was realized these coffins were still too vulnerable to enemy attack. Newer Strategic Missile Squadrons were therefore equipped with the F models, what were really Es modified to fit in underground silos 180ft deep and 52ft wide. Each F site still had independent underground control and living facilities, but the squadrons had a 1 x 12 dispersal pattern, three more than the E. The silos themselves were officially rated to withstand 100psi of pressure. During an alert, an Atlas F would have been filled with a hydrocarbon/liquid oxygen/helium mixture in its silo through a Propellant Loading System, and raised on a platform for launch within fifteen minutes, except for those rare occasions requiring immediate firing when a missile would blast off from within.

A typical Atlas F site consisted of a small plot of land with the silo and its two steel doors, two large quonset-type buildings, an access portal, escape hatch and an underground Launch Control Center. The LCC had living spaces, kitchen,

Blast doors at the Elizabethtown, New York, Atlas site. (Photo: Author)

shower and sanitary facilities on one floor, launch console and communications equipment on another and power room below. Although the missile was located approximately 30ft from the LCC, the crew was protected from the missile's exhaust by two separate heavy blast doors. An emergency exit was included, but it could not be accessed on a regular basis since it was kept filled with sand that would act as shock absorber if a bomb had dropped nearby. Each Atlas F site cost approximately $3.6 million to build. The squadrons are listed in Appendix J.

The Atlas was not without disadvantages. One of its primary drawbacks was its use of liquid oxygen as oxidizer, lox being easily prone to combustion. Both its requirement for low temperatures and absolute purity made it a hazard. Since newer missiles then being developed used either a liquid fuel with long-term storage capability or a safer solid propellant, the Atlas was retired. The squadrons were disestablished in 1964 and 1965 and their silos sold off.

The actual Atlas missile silo locations were no great secret. Local newspapers often carried articles and photographs of their construction, and when the

Every Atlas command centre had its escape hatch. This one is also at the Elizabethtown site. (Photo: Author)

missiles were brought in, they aroused much curiosity from local residents. These may have been the only times when a civilian would get close to a nuclear weapon. As for the launch sites themselves, they could easily be spotted since all looked the same.

Not surprisingly, the Russians showed keen interest in the American missile programme and soon began efforts to pinpoint individual sites. In 1958, a long-term Russian agent by the name of Kaarlo Tuomi was dispatched to the United States to gather as many secrets as he could. Many of these were of a military nature useful for conversion into attack targeting data. Besides building up his legend, one of Tuomi's assignments was to determine the exact location of two of Plattsburgh AFB's missile sites, one near Lewis, New York, and the other near Swanton, Vermont, used by the 556th Strategic Missile Squadron.

By driving around, Tuomi did in fact find the two sites. Unbeknownst to him, however, he had been trailed by the FBI the moment he set foot on American soil. The FBI watched his every move for over four years and eventually confronted him. Aghast that he had always been under surveillance, Tuomi avoided a prison term when he agreed to work for the Bureau and act as their informant. He was allowed by the G-men to send the missiles silos' locations to the Soviet Union by secret message – the KGB would have found them out by other methods eventually, such as by consulting topographical maps – only to be rebuked for uncertain reasons. Soon after, Tuomi's FBI handlers warned him that they had reason to believe he would be recalled home and not be allowed to return to the United States. He was given the choice of returning to Russia or staying in America, and since by then he had grown fond of life in the West, Tuomi chose to stay.

The USAF was not content to adopt only one ICBM. At the same time the Atlas was being designed, the Glenn L. Martin Company was contracted to build a second missile, the Titan I, in case the Atlas did not work out. The Titan I differed from the Atlas in several respects, including a greater height, a two-stage design, a robust self-supporting airframe and a more powerful 4 megaton warhead. It could fly its 5,500-mile range in thirty-three minutes. In one test flight, a Titan came to within 0.8 nautical mile (4,860ft) of its target. It had some of the same drawbacks as the Atlas in that it still needed to be raised before launch – always a time-consuming process – and that it still relied on the hazardous RP-1/lox fuel mixture. It had the added disadvantage of a copper-aluminium airframe, which was extremely difficult to weld, although by using a new tungsten gas welding process, reliability in construction was assured. While in development, the missile was designated SM-68, and after deployment, LGM-25A. The Titan I was built in a brand new plant erected by the Martin Company southwest of Denver.

It was first considered to place Titan Is in a 9 x 1 pattern, meaning the nine missiles would be located on a single property controlled by a single launch centre. As this made them susceptible to a single burst, the deployment pattern was changed where the nine rockets were divided into three sites at three per site.

Each site had its own underground Launch Control Center as well as maintenance and living facilities, all interconnected by up to 2,000ft of tunnels. Water could be stored in two 30,000 gallon tanks and diesel fuel, in two 67,000 gallon tanks. A complex could house personnel for thirty days and was hardened to 100psi.[22] Crews worked in twenty-four-hour shifts. The silos themselves were 160ft deep and 44ft wide and protected by two 125-ton doors. Titan I squadrons were located at Lowry AFB, Colorado, Mountain Home AFB, Idaho, Beale AFB, California, Ellsworth AFB, South Dakota, and Larson AFB, Washington. At Lowry AFB, the first Titan I base to become active, there were two squadrons.

With the Atlas and Titan I, there was always the nagging worry over the hazardous fuel they used. RP-1 was highly toxic, and as mentioned above lox required absolute purity. Both liquids could only be pumped in just before launch, and the fifteen-minute loading period created a window of opportunity the Russians could have exploited. Even before the Atlas and the Titan I were deployed, Aerojet-General had developed a propellant that could be stored in an ICBM on a long-term basis, an unsymmetrical dimethyl hydrazine/hydrazine mixture. The two compounds were so stable they could be kept in a missile for years. Having it and its oxidizer, nitrogen tetroxide, stored in the missile saved precious minutes in the launching process. Since the Atlas and Titan I could not make use of the new fuel, both were retired and in their place would rise Titan II.

The fuel-oxidizer combination was not the only advantage of the Titan II. The

A Titan I site under construction at Lowry AFB, Colorado. (Photo: NARA SC-162766)

high cost of ICBM development pushed some Pentagonians to consider budget reductions. Force levels were one way to decrease expenditures, but another was on the infrastructure of the new missile. Someone suggested that in-silo launching be looked at. If an ICBM could be fired from within its tube, the lift used to raise it to the surface could be eliminated. A 1/6th scale test silo was built by Aerojet-General in California in 1959 and, after thirty-six tries using a scale model of a Titan airframe equipped with Nike-Ajax surface-to-air missile engines, the company knew what the silo should consist of for a successful 'hot' launch. The USAF adopted Aerojet-General's concept and in-silo launches became a reality.

The Titan II would become the most powerful nuclear weapon in the United States inventory. Partly due to the advantage of a silo launch, it had a quick launch time of fifty-eight seconds. The two-stage configuration gave it an acceptable range of 5,500 nautical miles, although one source claims the range was more like 8,100 nautical miles. It had a lower CEP than the Atlas, 0.785 nautical miles (approximately 4,800ft) versus the Atlas's 910ft, but this was made up by its whopping 9 megaton W53 warhead. It was estimated that the Titan II's powerful warhead could create a crater 1 mile wide and 200ft deep, start a 2-mile wide fireball and kill everyone within 3 miles. Its Mark VI re-entry vehicle carried, in addition to the warhead, mid-course and terminal penetration aids, including chaff (thin strips of foil), and since the Mark IV re-entry vehicle on the Titan I was equipped with replica warheads for deception, one might assume the Titan II carried the same. Never revealed by the USAF were the targets programmed into the onboard computer. The Titan II was so deadly that, to borrow another line from Stine's book *ICBM*, one could have called it the 'where did everybody go?' weapon.

One of the things that worried Strategic Air Command and the Pentagon (not to mention the White House) was the security of its nuclear weapons. The government and the public trusted the USAF to do everything it reasonably could to ensure the weapons would not be misused. This insurance came in the form of a thorough Personnel Reliability Program investigation to weed out misfits, the construction of an entrapment area in the LCC's entrance, and the requirement to authenticate launch orders. With respect to the missile itself, it was outfitted with a special lock, called a Coded Switch System, which prevented an unauthorized launch. The CSS consisted of two locks that could only be opened by selecting letters on six thumbwheels in a Butterfly Valve Lock Control panel in the Launch Control Center. (The sequence of letters was provided to the launch crews through Emergency Action Messages.) If the correct code sequence was entered, both the first and second locks would also open. If an incorrect sequence was entered, after the seventh attempt the Butterfly Valve Lock would close and a warning message would be transmitted to wing headquarters. One might then expect a visit from the air police. If anyone tried physically to bypass the first lock, a small explosive charge in the second lock would disable the system. As an added precaution, the CSS plates were painted with a special coating to prevent drilling.

Each Titan II site utilized a crew of four: two officers, the Missile Combat Crew Commander (MCCC) and a Deputy Missile Combat Crew Commander (DMCCC), and two enlisted men, the Ballistic Missile Analyst Technician (BMAT) and a Missile Facilities Technician (MFT). The MCCC was responsible for, in addition to the actual launch of the missile, site security and operations, systems testing, malfunction isolation and the movement and control of visitors. The DMCCC looked after the communications equipment, air quality and, when required, some of the Commander's duties. He was also, of course, responsible for turning one of the launch keys. Both had the duty of authenticating Emergency Action Messages. For a while in the 1970s and 1980s, the MCCC was also responsible for obtaining the codeword that was needed by other members of his crew to enter the complex. Both officers carried firearms in case one decided to act unilaterally.

The two technicians had different functions. The BMAT monitored the missile's status and corrected, as far as he could, whatever problem that appeared. He watched over the missile fault locator like a hawk. If an error correction was not possible, he was usually in a position to recommend a course of action to the two officers. The MFT performed the same monitoring function but with respect to the complex, that is ensuring the ventilation, water and electrical systems were working. If the 'Explosive Fuel Vapor-Launch Duct' or 'Launch Duct Temp Low' light would turn on, he was the one who would investigate. Collectively, the four-person crews were given designations that consisted of one letter and three numbers, e.g. S-117.

A Titan II crew's most important function was the launching of a missile. The launch sequence would begin with the receipt of an EAM, its authentication, the breaking of the small seals over the launching key switches and the insertion of the two launch keys. The BMAT would then enter the CSS code to unlock the butterfly valve. The two officers would then turn the two keys simultaneously one quarter turn, and hold them for five seconds (or until the Launch Enable light lit up). They watched for certain lights to turn on, such as 'Batteries Activated', 'APS Power' and 'Guidance Go'. A further quarter turn launched the missile, and in case the crew did not feel it, they knew it was gone by the 'Lift-off' indicator light. As previously mentioned, all this would be done within one minute.

A Titan II complex consisted of the following: one silo 147ft deep and 55ft wide, an access portal, two air intake pipes and a control centre three storeys high and 42ft wide.[23] The control centre housed bunks and a kitchen on the first floor, the launch control console on the second, and communications equipment on the third. The silos were nine levels deep and were lined with exhaust ducts and deflector vanes. They were capped with a single 758-ton door. The silos were more secure than those of the Titan I since they could withstand 300psi of blast pressure. The sites were equipped with an AN/TPS-39 short-range radar surveillance system to detect intruders.[24] There were 57 of these complexes with 18 each at Little Rock AFB, Arkansas, McConnell AFB, Kansas, and Davis-Monthan AFB, Arizona, and another 3 for training purposes at Vandenberg

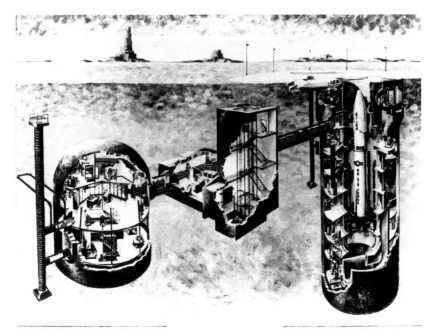

A diagram of a Titan II site. (Photo: USAF 175135 via David Stumpf)

AFB. Where organization was concerned, each of the 3 bases had a Strategic Missile Wing that consisted of 2 Strategic Missile Squadrons of 9 missiles each. A Wing also included a Security Squadron, a Fuel Training Squadron and a Missile Inspection and Maintenance Squadron.

Despite its awesome power, the Titan II was a relatively safe weapon. The USAF had procedures and checklists to be followed for everything from launch, to inspections, to maintenance and transport. When it came to maintenance, the procedures called for the use of specific tools, such as a torque wrench and socket to remove a pressure cap from the missile's upper stage. On 18 September 1980 at the Damascus, Arkansas, silo, some maintenance technicians had arrived to repressurize the second stage. As the men forgot the torque wrench in their truck, they decided to use a ratchet that was connected by a spring-loaded cable to the decontamination area wall in the silo's upper level. The technician who retrieved the tool failed to notice that a socket was not firmly attached to the ratchet. The socket fell approximately 80ft and punctured the skin on the missile's first stage. When the men saw fuel being released, they called the Launch Control Center. The maintenance crew wisely left the silo closing the blast door behind them. In the LCC, several indicator lamps began to light up: 'Fuel Vapour Launch Duct', 'Fire in Engine' and 'Oxidizer Vapour Launch Duct'. Inside the silo, water was sprayed to dampen the escaping fuel. Just to be on the safe side, the launch control crew and everyone else were ordered out of the area. A few hours later, at 3am, there came a huge blast.

The whole top of the silo was destroyed. The blast was so strong the silo door flew off into the woods. The warhead was found next to the site's access road. One airman was blown 150ft and another, 50ft. A third man, Senior Airman David Livingston, was found only several minutes later and immediately sent to a hospital, as were twenty others. The squadron's security staff quickly established a cordon around the site. The press soon picked up the story and reporters flocked to the site. Some of the news accounts would be less than accurate with, for example, the *New York Times* claiming a large crater was formed when in fact there was no such thing, as photos later showed. Truth was not the only casualty to the event as Airman Livingston would die in hospital a few hours later. At first, the USAF would not confirm that there was a nuclear warhead involved even though everyone knew there was. Some fears were later allayed when the Air Force reassured the population that the warhead could not have detonated since its mechanism only allows arming when the missile is in re-entry.

It is widely believed that the Damascus explosion led to the demise of the Titan II. Not only was the missile becoming increasingly expensive to maintain, the 1980 explosion was its fourth major mishap. At Rock, Kansas, serious oxidizer spills occurred in November 1964 and August 1978, the latter resulting in two fatalities. And at Searcy, Arkansas, a silo fire in August 1965 resulted in the loss of fifty-three lives. With the new MX Peacekeeper in development, some politicians thought funds would be better used there. The Reagan administration thus decided slowly to eliminate the Titan II from the USAF's inventory, and by August 1987, the last missile had been removed and the last silo destroyed. According to David Stumpf in his book *Titan II*, the missile had exceeded its life expectancy by fourteen years.

Today, the Titan II lives on, in a way. Some Air Force missileers wanted to keep one of the missiles and a launch complex intact. They wanted to remember the weapon that absorbed their lives and be able to show to future generations what is was all about. These missileers contacted the Tucson Air Museum Foundation and convinced them to adopt one of the launch complexes that belonged to Davis-Monthan AFB. The Foundation accepted the proposal and formed the Titan Missile Museum at the Green Valley silo (south of Tucson) in 1986. In 1994, the complex was declared a National Historic Landmark. To date, the museum has been visited by hundreds of thousands of people.

At the same time the Atlas and Titan were being developed, some of the major rocket companies were conducting research into solid propellants. What the Air Force ideally desired was a missile that could hold its fuel for extended periods of time. A solid fuel would reduce the propellant loading hazard and perhaps even reduce the missile's overall weight. Companies such as Boeing, Thiokol and Aerojet-General worked together to design such a missile, and within a few short years, their research would pay off.

The SM-80 Minuteman was the product of that research.[25] It incorporated many advances that had been discovered while the other missiles were being built and tested. The Minuteman's major advantages over other ICBMs were that its propellant could be kept stored internally for years, did not require constant cooling, and did not corrode the missile's fuel tanks. The rocket consisted of three stages: the first used a mixture of synthetic rubber, powdered aluminium and ammonium perchlorate, the second polyurethane and ammonium perchlorate, and the third, a composite ammonium perchlorate propellant in a glass fibre filament-wound casing. To spread government funds around, the three stages were built by different contractors, Thiokol, Aerojet-General and Hercules respectively. The Minuteman also had the advantage of an in-silo launch – thus saving precious minutes during an attack – and because it packed more fuel power per unit weight, it had a greater range. It also had the added advantage of swivel nozzles that could control its direction. The missile was also one that could be mass produced. Generals at the Pentagons were elated since they realized this was *the* weapon that could narrow the so-called 'missile gap'.[26]

This new Minuteman wonder-weapon would eventually come in five models that some writers call IA, IB, II, IIIA and IIIB. The IA was only used for thirteen years (1961–74). It had a limited range, was limited to one target and did not have as much firepower as the Titan since its W59 warhead was only rated to approximately 1 megaton. The Minuteman IB had the same characteristics except that its W56 warhead was rated at 1.2 megaton and that its second stage body was made of titanium instead of steel. These two variants were based at Warren AFB, Wyoming, Malmstrom AFB, Montana, Whiteman AFB, Missouri, and Grand Forks AFB, North Dakota. Some Minutemans were kept in silos at Vandenberg AFB for testing and training purposes; these were operated by the 394th Strategic Missile Squadron. While the USAF had wanted to deploy 3,000 missiles, the Kennedy administration would settle for 1,000. This number remained fixed until the 1990s.

The Minuteman II had a few improvements over the first model, chief of which was the greater range. It could travel over 700 miles more than the Minuteman I. It also had a more powerful second stage engine, a more accurate re-entry vehicle and defences against ABM radars. It had the advantage of having a memory into which could be programmed eight possible targets over the I's single aimpoint, and could be fired singly as opposed to in squadron-level salvos, another drawback of the first model. The Minuteman IIs were based at Whiteman, Grand Forks, Malmstrom and Ellsworth AFBs, in some cases until the 1990s.

The Minuteman III would be very different from the other two models. Research into rocket technology had so advanced in the 1960s that missiles were now being considered as multiple warhead delivery platforms. Avco had designed a re-entry vehicle that could house a number of weapons where each could be used against separate targets. The conical warheads were placed on a round platform called a bus and were released at a predetermined height to follow a path to their target. Such a system was called Multiple Independently-targeted

Re-entry Vehicle, or MIRV. While some buses were tested with up to seven warheads, the Minuteman III carried only three. The warheads were the W62 on the Minuteman IIIA and the W78 on the Minuteman IIIB, but more recently (2006–7), the W62s were replaced with W87s in Mk21 re-entry vehicles obtained from decommissioned MX Peacekeepers. Eventually, the Minuteman III would be converted to carry a single warhead as per START II. The missiles were deployed at Malmstrom, Minot, Warren and Grand Forks AFBs as of 1970 and are still found at the first three bases. If absolutely necessary, some could be deployed at Vandenberg AFB in training silos.

Missile	Warhead	Yield	Launch Probability	Detonation Probability	Range (miles)	CEP (nm)	Number of Warheads
MMIA	W59	1Mt			4,300		1
MMIB	W56	1.2Mt			6,300		1
MMII	W56	1.2Mt	.9	.8	7,021	0.34	1
MMIIIA	W78	335Kt	.9	.85	8,200	0.10	3
MMIIIB	W87	300Kt	.9	.85	8,200	0.10	1

The Minuteman III's range was confirmed by test launches conducted in 2006.

As technology progressed, especially with respect to computerization, Boeing and the Air Force have tried to keep up with the times. For instance, in the early Minutemans, to set up a target in the guidance system's computer, a technician needed to open the missile's re-entry vehicle and manually install a tape that contained the aimpoint, a procedure that took up to thirty-six hours. In the mid-1970s, tapes were dispensed with and in their place came a Command Data Buffer System. The CDBS allowed a missile officer to set the missile's target electronically from a keyboard in the Launch Control Center. Re-targeting of all missiles under the control of a launch officer now took approximately twenty minutes.

This system was further changed in the 1990s when the Minuteman's target could be reset within just a few minutes with new Rapid Execution and Combat Targeting (REACT) equipment. The rationale for REACT was to replace 'logistically unsupportable' electronic components, to consolidate crew positions at a single LCC for greater efficiency and to improve crew responsivity to EAMs. REACT equipment included EHF satellite communications terminals that allowed connectivity with the Air Force's new Milstar satellite. The new equipment makes use of computers that use Windows-like screens to receive EAMs and to enter targeting information.[27]

Other changes to the Minuteman were caused by defects that unexpectedly appeared. For instance, when chips in the on-board computer started burning up due to their long periods of inactivity, all had to be replaced.[28] It was also found that the small amount of radiation emitted by the warheads wiped out the memory in the guidance system. This necessitated modifications to the missile.

Among one of the most closely guarded secrets STRATCOM possesses are the targets assigned to the Minuteman. STRATCOM will not say where those aimpoints are, not even for retired missiles such as the Titans and the Atlases. Such targets can, however, be deduced by inference, an exercise Martel and Savage performed in their book *Strategic Nuclear War*, and the Natural Resources Defense Council (with McKinzie, Cochran, Norris and Arkin) in *The US Nuclear War Plan. A Time for Change*. Martel and Savage claim the Minuteman IIIA is designed as a 'hard target' weapon since its lower CEP and higher yield (than the Minuteman IIIB) makes it ideal to smash silos, shallow bunkers or even Launch Control Centers.[29] They also say that given its less-than-unity probability of functioning properly, two warheads might be needed to destroy one silo. The Minuteman IIIB might, on the other hand, be used against soft targets because of its lower yield. In reality though, both Minuteman III versions might be required to hit Russian silos because of their sheer numbers.[30]

Martel and Savage also theorized that the Minuteman II was designed as a countervalue weapon, that is one capable of destroying unhardened targets such as large factories or nuclear weapons production complexes, because of the missile's relative inaccuracy and high yield. These same characteristics made the missile good for blasting sprawling naval bases. The point is now academic since the Minuteman II is no longer in the USAF's inventory.

The Natural Resources Defense Council agreed with Martel and Savage in the choice of targets for the Minuteman III. Russian silos would most effectively be destroyed with high-yield weapons, and the greater the number of warheads assigned to a target, the higher the probability of its destruction.[31] Since a Russian silo can be used more than once, its destruction would necessitate quick action. Gravity bombs would not be used against launch facilities because of the time a B-52 or B-2 would take to reach Russia. Missiles are therefore the obvious choice.

Another aspect of the Minuteman that is much classified is its counter-measures. Very little has appeared in print on the subject, but what is known is that it uses chaff. Even though a Minuteman re-entry vehicle travels at great speeds, chaff used in the terminal phase of an attack might be good enough to blank out an ABM system. In addition, the Minuteman may use aerosols to reflect infra-red light if the enemy was using plume infra-red detection methods. There have also been hints that powered inflatable conical decoys of the same size as actual warheads are used to, again, foil ABM radars. These decoys may be painted or coated to make them look like the real thing. It has not been revealed whether the Minuteman is equipped with electronic jamming equipment.

With respect to the launch of a Minuteman, a number of safeguards were put in place to prevent unauthorized firings. As part of the missile launch procedure, the crews receive a six-letter code in their Emergency Action Message. The code needs to be authenticated before launch. To verify it, two Launch Control Officers – the Missile Combat Crew Commander and his Deputy – must retrieve a plastic-coated code card from a locked box in the Launch Control Center and check to see if that code matches the one in the EAM. Also, an eight-digit number needs to be entered into the launch enable panel to unlock the missile.[32] This is

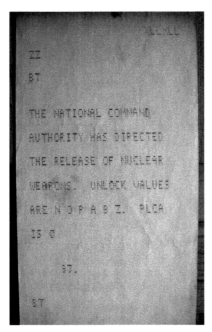

A sample Emergency Action Message. It reads 'The National Command Authority has directed the release of nuclear weapons. Unlock values are N O P A B Z. PLCA is 0.' Such paper tapes are no longer printed at Launch Control Centres; the EAMs now come in by computer. (Photo: USAF via John Clearwater)

still by itself not enough to carry out the launch since another crew in another Launch Control Center must also receive its authoization and must turn their two keys. If this second crew, whose location is always unknown to the first, does not receive this authorization, they can flip an 'inhibit launch' switch to prevent the firing. A third LCC crew can over-ride the inhibit action of the second crew. Yet another safeguard exists at the policy level in that the missile crews do not have any pre-delegated launch authority; if a higher body such as the wing or STRATCOM Headquarters were destroyed, the missileers would not, in theory, fire.

Minuteman crews also have the added protection of duress words. These are words that, once uttered in a radio or telephone conversation, would signal their capture. The idea was adopted from those special agents sent behind enemy lines during the Second World War who risked being caught by the Germans. If they had been captured, inclusion of these special words in a radio message would have warned home base that any transmissions they made should be ignored. Presumably, once those words are mentioned by missile crews, squadron or wing headquarters could disable the particular Launch Control Center and send a security force to investigate.

As with the Atlas and Titan, the Minuteman required land for its Launch Control Center and silos. But where the Titan and Atlas had their LCCs co-located with the launch tubes, the Minuteman would have its control centres located several miles from the missiles. Most of the time, the LCCs and the launch facilities were placed in the American Midwest in the middle of wheat fields or grass lands away from large population centres and far from easy reach of Soviet missiles.

The Launch Control Centers are located on properties called Missile Alert Facilities. The MAFs are small establishments that provide support to launch, security, caretaker and maintenance crews. They include a support building, a vehicle garage, antennae, chain-link security fence, sewage lagoons, floodlights and a helicopter landing pad. The fence dons a large brown sign showing the

A Minuteman Alert Facility in Missouri. (Photo: LOC, HAER MO-87-5, Arnold Thallheimer)

site number, which always consists of a military phonetic word followed by the number '1', and its location in white (e.g. Juliett-1 at Peetz CO). Not quite visible is a buried cylinder about 21ft in diameter and 50ft deep that contains a high-frequency antenna that could telescope to 120ft, part of a radio system that was deactivated in the early 1970s. The support building houses electrical machinery, quarters, a kitchen and the entry to the LCC underneath. Also found is the security control centre placed in a bay that gives guards a clear view of the main gate. Anyone heading for the LCC has to pass by it. MAFs occupy 6.4 acres of land, 1.85 of which is inside the fence.

The Launch Control Center's small size belies its importance. Built in the shape of an egg – and often referred to as such – it is in a sense a small building inside a building. The outer structure is 54ft long and 29ft in diameter and made of reinforced concrete lined on the inside with ¼in thick steel for EMP protection. Inside the shell is a small 28ft by 12ft rectangular building that is the actual Launch Control Center. The LCC is suspended inside the egg with chains and pneumatic cylinders that allow movement if a blast occurred nearby. It is

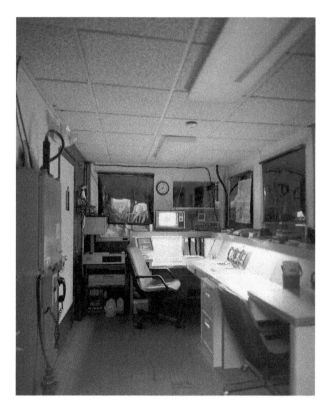

The security control centre at a MAF in South Dakota. (Photo: LOC, HAER SD-50-A-50, Robert Lyon)

accessed by descending a ladder or taking a lift from the security section 45ft down and by walking down a short tunnel past 12 ton (some say 8 ton) blast doors 8ft high, 7.5ft wide and 21in thick. Typical of such doors, they are so well designed they can be opened with one hand.

A typical Minuteman III complex has a Launch Control Center controlling ten missiles 3–15 miles away. Since a squadron consists of fifty missiles, there are five LCCs per squadron. The Launch Control Centers were at one time inter-connected by landline so that if one was disabled, another could fire its missiles.[33] As mentioned above, under normal circumstances the two Launch Control Officers (LCOs) in one LCC need a green light from another LCC to fire – this to prevent a conspiracy – although this system can be overridden if all other possible inputs were destroyed.

There is not much to an LCC. On one side stands a number of racks, such as for power or communications, and near them, the two launch and missile status control stations. The two LCOs sit in high red airline-type seats that rest on rails for easy movement and that are located approximately 15ft from each other to prevent one LCO turning both keys. At one time the two officers carried sidearms, ostensibly for their protection, but this is no longer the case. The LCC

The Oscar-1 Launch Control Center at Whiteman AFB in Missouri. (Photo: LOC, HAER MO-87-29, Robert Lyon)

also contains a single sleeping section for those times one of the officers wants to rest. It also contains compartments under the floor that hold survival equipment, emergency batteries and a generator that would kick in if the outside power grid ever failed. The walls and ceilings hold sound-absorbing material. Most of the equipment is painted light green, a colour some crews have apparently learned to dislike.

The launching of a Minuteman missile is an easy task that crews practise countless times during exercises or competitions.[34] The procedure is very similar to the Titan's in that an Emergency Action Message is first received and decoded. It would normally state that the National Command Authority authorized the use of nuclear weapons and includes an authentication code and a two-digit Preparatory Launch Command number that is used to select targets and timing delays from a set that was pre-entered into the missile's memory. As mentioned previously, the authentication code consists of six letters that has to be verified with a document stored in a red steel box located above the Deputy Missile

Some of the communications equipment at an LCC in South Dakota. (Photo: LOC, HAER SD-50-C-40, Robert Lyon)

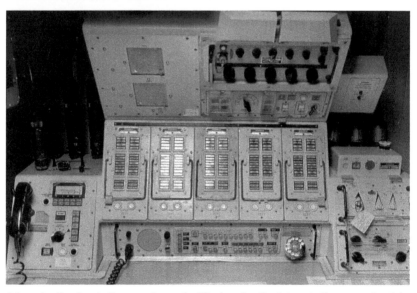

A launch officer's missile control console. The key that fired the missile was on the right and can be seen in this photograph. (Photo: LOC, HAER MO-87-32, Robert Lyon)

A closer look at the key to Armageddon. Also visible here is the 'Inhibit Launch' switch. (Photo: LOC, HAER MO-87-33, Robert Lyon)

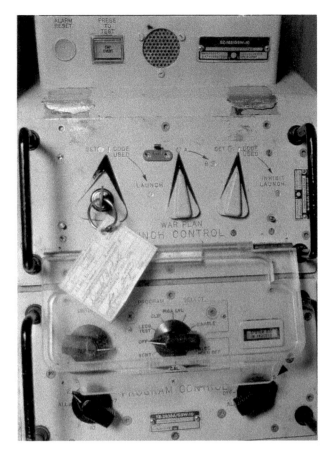

Every capsule had its escape hatch in case the main doors were damaged or destroyed. (Photo: LOC, HAER SD-50-A-84, Robert Lyon)

A missile door.
(Photo: LOC,
HAER MO-88-5,
Robert Lyon)

Combat Crew Commander's console. Once the message is authenticated, the launch officers retrieve their respective keys and insert them into the switches. One of them then enters the two-digit PLC number. One of the officers then keys in an eight-digit control number into the Launch Enable System, and both then turn their keys simultaneously and hold them in place to start the countdown.[35]

The access hatch to
a Minuteman
launch facility in
South Dakota.
(Photo: LOC,
HAER,
SD-50-C-23,
Robert Lyon)

Once another crew in another LCC perform the same action, the missile is fired. Back-up missile fire control equipment, called the Airborne Launch Control System, is found in the Looking Glass aircraft. This has the capability to fire a squadron's inventory, but only if all the LCCs were disabled or if one of the launch crews turned on a 'hold-off' switch to give the plane access.[36] Since the missile has no command destruct mechanism, there is no way for a crew to change or abort its flight once fired. As for the launch crews themselves, once their job is done, they can either wait for the enemy's missile to hit them, and hope to survive, or leave quickly for safer grounds.

With systems as complex as those found in ICBMs, engineers and designers have put in sufficient safeguards to prevent accidental firings. Despite this, it is still possible for a false attack order to be transmitted. This happened once in 1974 at one LCC. Somehow, the order to fire was received by launch officers but, as there were then no international threats, they quickly grew suspicious and requested confirmation. The check did in fact reveal an error. If anything, this episode demonstrated the wisdom of having humans control machines.

Despite the destructive potential of a Russian missile, much thought was put into the launch crew's survival. If a detonation occurs nearby, a blast valve in the air intake would instantly seal the capsule from the outside. The generator and batteries would keep the electrical systems running for some time. The crews would then use a hand pump to regenerate oxygen. If the main access tunnel was damaged, the two officers can use an escape hatch to reach the surface, but only after digging the sand out from the escape tunnel. Rations are kept in the LCC for extended stays.

A typical Minuteman launch facility also consists of a small piece of land but here, there is even less than at a Missile Alert Facility. On the surface, one sees only the security fence (which bears the site number), antennae stubs, an intrusion detection system, floodlights, the heavy 90-ton concrete silo cover and its sliding rails, and a round personnel entry hatch. The fence carries a sign warning trespassers that deadly force is authorized. While such force has never been used by security staff (known as Alert Response Teams) even against protesters who have tried to damage silo door rails, this unofficial 'no shooting' policy was changed after 9-11 to allow security forces to shoot first and ask questions later.[37] Perhaps unusually, since May 1975 the missiles have been escorted to and from launch facilities not by the Air Force security police but rather by the US Marshals Service under its Missile Escort Program, perhaps because the Marshals have the power of arrest and the military guards do not. Further security to the missile and its maintenance crew is provided during transport by armed Air Force security staff riding in menacing green armoured trucks equipped with solid rubber tires impervious to bullets. Also, the USAF has apparently a policy in place that disallows the planting of trees near silos since they could hide snipers.

The launch facility's real power lay underneath. This is where the missile rests, along with the power source necessary to run the installation. The launch tube itself is 25ft in diameter and about 80ft deep. Around the upper part of the silo is a two-level equipment room which contains such things as power surge arrestors, an actuator to open the silo hatch, an autocollimator that is used to align the missile's guidance system, and batteries. Electricity is used to operate lighting, to control the temperature and humidity in the silo, to activate the silo hatch and to initiate missile launch. The equipment room also contains stainless steel tanks that hold sodium chromate used to cool the missile's guidance system. The launch tube contains motion sensors that would 'freeze' a guidance system's alignment if a large explosion occurred nearby. It is also equipped with electronic filters that would detect EMPs and that would shut off the electrical system very briefly until the pulse had passed.[38] Finally, shotguns are kept on site in case maintenance crews need to defend themselves.

Missile technicians belong to a wing's maintenance support squadron. These men and women look after such things as a silo's air-conditioning system, the back-up diesel generators and the missile's guidance system. When working on a missile, the crews are required to perform a radio check every fifteen minutes to let security officers at the MAF know they are fine. As with the LCCs, the launch facilities are 'No Lone Zones' that do not allow people to work alone there at any time. Each silo cost about $500,000 to build – much less than the Atlas's $3.6 million – since it used prefabricated components and standardized plans. The USAF built 1,000 of these silos, along with a few at Vandenberg AFB to be used for instructional purposes, and one at Cape Canaveral AFS in Florida for tests. One of the few times a Minuteman was fired from an operational silo was on 1 March 1965 at Ellsworth AFB to test the launch facility.

For a maintenance crew to gain access to the silo, they first have to open a heavy round hatch. This will only happen if the accompanying security team dials a combination into what is called an A-circuit lock. Once the hatch opens, the maintenance crew dials another combination into another lock called a B-plug that will lower a ladder. This takes several minutes, a delay intentionally created to prevent quick access by an intruder. Neither the security team nor the maintenance crew know each other's combination. On those rare occasions when a B-plug fails, the only way in is to jackhammer the silo hatch, a process called 'forced entry'.

The B-plug, one of a launch facility's many security devices. (Photo: LOC, HAER, SD-50-C-26, Robert Lyon)

When ICBMs were adopted as strategic weapons, senior Air Force officers had at least one personnel issue on their hands. The missile sites require men who would be willing to wait patiently for an order everyone hoped would never come, men who would know what to do if the President ever ordered a launch and who would react without hesitation, and men who would be willing to live underground without seeing their families for days.[39] The men chosen for this profession had to possess a combination of patience and dedication, and an ability to work closely with an extremely small number of individuals. Before being accepted as a missileer, an officer must submit to a personnel reliability check to ensure his loyalty and lack of serious vices that would detract from his mission. Drug users, alcoholics and rebels are therefore not welcome in this 'family'.[40] Afterwards, the officer has to go through four months of Initial Qualification Training at Vandenberg AFB where he must absorb such things as the verification checklists – called Technical Orders – along with Emergency War Orders and Codes, and must then endure the stress of a Missile Procedures Trainer. Only then can he be assigned to a missile squadron.

One of the biggest changes to the manning of a Launch Control Center was the introduction of women. In the 1970s, women were more and more encouraged to enlist in the armed services since many politicians on Capitol Hill saw in

A Minuteman II being loaded onto a transporter erector. (Photo: LOC, HAER SD-50-C-18, Robert Lyon)

them potential soldiers, airmen and sailors that could be just as capable as their male counterparts. Women had enlisted in the administrative and medical trades for years, but, slowly, more occupations were made available to them. In 1978, the world of the missileer changed forever when the first woman LCO was accepted. Women thus began by serving in female-only launch teams, until 1988 when these teams became of mixed gender. In the Launch Control Centers, the only change required was the addition of a curtain to the lavatory.[41]

Women in Minuteman crews were not always welcomed though, since some were afraid they would lead to sinful temptation. One launch officer, Lieutenant Ryan Berry, did not feel comfortable working with a woman in a capsule because of his religious teachings. Berry was afraid that even the appearance of sin would make him look bad. Senior officers at his base, Minot AFB, at first accommodated his desire to work only with men. However, when he switched squadrons other officers began complaining, and Major-General Thomas Neary of the Air Force's senior missile organization, the 20th Air Force, ordered Berry's exemption cancelled. Berry then received a negative personnel evaluation, which he thought was an excuse for the Air Force to deny him future promotions. This being the United States, a lawsuit was the result, with the conclusion that his negative report was removed from his service record. It is not known by the author if Berry is still in the Air Force.

On a daily basis, what do the launch crews do? The answer is, practically everything. They first perform their Daily Shift Verification to make sure everything is in proper working order: communications and power equipment, missile status boards etc. Any malfunction is attended to immediately. Launch officers also test standby diesel generators, and sometimes will receive VIPs. During quiet times, they might play cards, do crosswords or read. Education was (and is) a big thing in the Air Force and the crews are encouraged to continue their studies for a degree through various institutions such as the Air Force Institute of Technology. Having the government fund a missileer's post-secondary education was seen, from the outset, as an excellent way to boost morale and increase retention of staff. Many have gone on to earn Masters or PhDs. One launch officer, Bruce Blair, went on to graduate from Yale University with a doctorate and has written extensively on strategic weapons.[42]

Both launch and maintenance staff are subject to constant inspections to exceedingly strict standards. Strategic Air Command long had a unit dedicated to ensuring launch crews were up to par, the 3901st Strategic Missile Evaluation Squadron. The 3901st consisted of two major sections where one, Operations, tested crew proficiency in codes, Emergency War Orders and weapon systems, and the other, Maintenance, looked again at weapon systems, but also at warheads and support equipment. After usually giving a missile squadron some notice of their visit, the 3901st SMES would select twelve launch crews and put them through the Missile Procedures Trainer (located on the support base) using scripts and checklists to check every aspect of a missileer's function. Those who failed were expected to take remedial training. At one time, a visit from the

Squadron would involve 120 evaluators, each having his or her own specialty. Their visit lasted two weeks and ended with a formal briefing in a large room such as the base theatre.

The 3901st SMES was not the only unit the crews worried about. SAC had its Inspector General ready, again, to check up on its personnel. The IG's Operational Readiness Inspections, conducted without advance notice, also looked at missile readiness, communications, launch and maintenance procedures, security and support facilities. They could also examine the helicopters that were operated by the Wings' Rescue Flights. ORIs, which at one time were codenamed 'Giant Fox', occured once a year. At times, the Secretary of the Air Force's own Inspector General would take part to see how well the SAC IG did. Readiness inspections were so strict a failure could have resulted in a Wing Commander's dismissal.

When it came to the warhead, it too was scrutinized. SAC routinely conducted full and limited Nuclear Surety Inspections on anything related to the weapon, from transport, to storage, security, maintenance and personnel reliability. Whenever one of the devices needed to be moved, an NSI officer was surely not too far behind. These same officers tested security police response at a silo or inspected the truck used to transport the warhead for defects. The entire programme of evaluations and inspections created, as former SAC officer Charlie Simpson said, a stressful atmosphere that demanded perfection. By doing so, he wrote, SAC was fully ready to carry out a mission everyone hoped would never be executed. Conversely, the exercises were the only way the Pentagon could test the missile force's readiness short of an actual launch upon an enemy.

As indicated earlier, Strategic Air Command no longer exists. It has been replaced by STRATCOM and a new operational Air Force sub-unit, Space Command. Since 2010, however, missileers now belong to a newer unit, the Air Force Global Strike Command. The difference between STRATCOM and the Global Strike Command is that the first creates war-fighting policy, and the second carries it out. At the same time SAC was renamed, Strategic Missile Squadrons and Wings were stripped of their 'Strategic' title. Missile forces have been greatly reduced since the advent of the Strategic Arms Reduction Treaty and the end of the Cold War. The United States armed forces are down to three missile wings that control 450 ICBMs, which represents half of its 1970s-era strength, and the 2010 Nuclear Posture Review saw that number reduced to 400–20. The Minuteman III is scheduled to remain in operation until at least 2030; with life upgrades that have taken place since the late 1970s, it will have lived more than fifty years. While it will eventually disappear from the Air Force roster, some missileers can take comfort in the fact that a few launch sites and LCCs will remain in existence as museums. These can already be found in South Dakota and Missouri. Another may eventually be opened in North Dakota.

For approximately twenty years, the USAF had another ICBM on its books. The MX Peacekeeper had been developed as a mobile missile and as a potential replacement to the Minuteman, but funding limits and political wrangling would delay its deployment for several years. No less than forty basing methods were considered such as: placing them underground in a series of looped tracks, inside mountains, on trucks roaming the nation's highways, on shallow-water submarines, in a tightly packed network of silos that would be used as a shell game, mounted on surface ships, launched from aircraft or in Titan II silos soon to be decommissioned. In the end, the Air Force adopted what was probably the cheapest option and placed them in fifty existing Minuteman silos at Warren AFB. The first missiles were installed in December 1986 and the last, two years later.

Unlike the Minuteman, little has been written about the Peacekeeper. What is known is that it was a four-stage missile with a range of about 6,800 miles. It had a CEP of about 400ft and carried ten W87 330 kiloton warheads in a Mk 21A re-entry vehicle. The W87 was an improvement over other weapons because its plutonium pit – the part where the actual nuclear detonation takes place – was fire resistant and was insensitive to high explosives. In its silo, the MX was encased in a canister. To launch, it was ejected by pressurized gas, and after 150–300ft its motor ignited. During the missile's terminal phase, the ten warheads would separate from the warhead bus and travel along their pre-programmed individual trajectories to their designated aimpoints.

It was originally intended to house 100 missiles at Warren AFB, but after the first 50 were declared operational, Congress insisted the other half be made more survivable. Planners decided to base the remaining fifty on trains that would be headquartered at Warren AFB and that would travel around the country to other SAC bases during times of tension.[43] After exercises and tests were made, the Pentagon ordered the USAF to proceed with the development of this new Peacekeeper Rail Garrison. The end of the Cold War, however, saw the cancellation of the Garrison, and the Air Force retained only the fifty silo-based missiles at Warren AFB's 400th Strategic Missile Squadron. Since the START II treaty called for the phase-out of all MIRV-capable missiles, the Peacekeeper was taken out of service, this in 2005.[44]

What exactly remains of these sites? There are as many answers are there were silos. Unused Minuteman and Titan II launchers were blown up, as required by START, but as the Titan I and the Atlases were retired prior to the treaty, their launch sites remain. Some were still listed for sale on the Internet by a California real estate agency as recently as 1997. Atlas silos ranged in price from $64,500 to $232,000. One Kansas underground complex was repainted in pleasing colours and became a public school, while others throughout the western states have become residences, research facilities or, in one case, a light aircraft manufacturing plant. In the case of the Atlas sites around Plattsburgh, New York, some serve as garages and others are used for storage. At least four of them, Ellenburg, Chazy Lake, Mooers Forks and Alburg, have flooded undergrounds making inspection impossible. The site near Lewis north of Elizabethtown has been sold to an Australian entrepreneur and was restored. The one at Chazy Lake is owned by the town and used as a municipal garage. One of the missile maintenance huts

The entrance to the
Chazy Lake, New
York, Atlas site.
(Photo: Author)

at Harrigan, New York, is now a residence. Most of the Au Sable Forks site has been dug up and the Swanton, Vermont, site is now a machine shop owned by a drilling company. Not surprisingly, many silos were never marked on any maps, not necessarily because of secrecy but rather because they only existed for a few years.

Experimental Tunnel

Finally, there was one unusual tunnel that was built for the US Air Force during the Cold War. The magazine *Tunnels and Tunnelling* reported that in the late 1970s, the Air Force built a very long concrete tunnel at the Yuma bombing range in Arizona as a testing structure to house missiles. The idea was to store the weapons underground on a long-term basis in tunnels capped with a layer of earth that would have made visual or satellite detection impossible. The article reported that the Air Force had indeed succesfully fired a missile from this structure. Despite this success, this basing method was never used. The tunnel was reported to be over 22,000ft long.

SAM Sites

Many bunkers are also found at old surface-to-air missile sites around major cities and certain military bases. These bunkers were built in the early Cold War period to house weapons that would defend given areas. The importance of area defence was made apparent during the Second World War after the bomber showed what massive destruction it could wreak. During the war, some American cities were ringed with anti-aircraft guns, but technological advances afterwards gradually made them obsolete. One of those advances was the rocket.

The concept of a surface-to-air missile had sprung up in the later stages of the Second World War when First Lieutenant Jacob W. Schaefer first proposed it as an area defence weapon. Among other things, the advantages of rockets were their longer range, higher explosive power and the ability of ground crews to control their direction. Army Headquarters accepted Schaefer's proposal and awarded a development contract for Project Nike to Bell Telephone Laboratories in 1945; Bell in turn had its manufacturing partner Western Electric design the electronics and the servo controls, and Douglas Aircraft manufacture the new missile. The specifications called for a rocket that could hit bombers at 60,000ft flying at 600mph and that was capable of performing evasive manoeuvres at 3Gs at 40,000ft. Douglas and Western's end result consisted of a two-stage 33ft rocket that would look much like an extended dart.

The Nike surface-to-air missile was a truly complex instrument made up of 1.4 million parts manufactured by 1,300 suppliers. It was controlled by ground radar and equipped with three Composition B high-explosive charges wrapped in pieces of square metal that acted as shrapnel when the charges went off. The first stage (which fell off after use) carried a solid propellant made primarily of nitrocellulose and nitroglycerin by the Goodyear Tire Company, while the upper stage was fuelled by a liquid mixture of Inhibited Red Fuming Nitric Acid and JP-4 jet fuel catalyzed by unsymmetrical dimethyl hydrazine. The rocket had a range of 30 miles, a ceiling of 60,000–70,000ft, a speed of Mach 2.3 and a flight time of just over one minute. Its three explosive charges were detonated by ground command that was either sent by the guidance computer or by the battery commander in a control van.

The Nike missile relied on three separate ground radar systems, one to acquire the target, one to track it, and another to guide the missile. The Acquisition Radar worked like any other early warning system in that its sole purpose was to detect aircraft. The Target Tracking Radar (TTR) followed the aircraft and fed co-ordinates to an attack computer. It had electronic counter-counter-measures built in to foil jamming, and since crews trained on continuous wave and noise-modulated jamming, one can assume the Nike system possessed equipment capable of defeating both. The Missile Tracking Radar (MTR) guided the rocket to its victim using those co-ordinates received from the TTR, and included a

Nike-Ajaxes at Fort Barry, California. (Photo: NARA SC-461960)

safety feature that caused the weapon to self-destruct if the rocket–MTR link was interrupted for more than two seconds. The Nike may not have been the best weapon for the job, though, since one Canadian declassified document stated it only had a probability of kill of 0.3. Over 15,000 Nikes were built at a cost, at peak production, of over $19,000 each. It became known as the Nike-Ajax only later on.

In 1951, the new Nike-Ajax was successfully tested at White Sands Proving Grounds in New Mexico and three years later, the rocket was deployed. The first operational site was at Fort George G. Meade in Maryland outside Washington, DC, and belonged to the 36th Anti-Aircraft Artillery Missile Battalion. A theoretical Ajax site had separate Integrated Fire Control, launch and administrative areas, but in practice, the control and administrative areas were often located on the same lot. The control base sported communications and radar equipment of various types along with a generator building and maintenance and supply shops, and the adminstrative area had barracks, offices and a mess hall. A typical battalion had about 440 men.

A Nike launch area had launching racks, a warhead mating building, fuelling station, sentry post, pump house, barracks hall and underground missile magazines buried below the launching pads. The magazines – also called pits – were small square structures with personnel access doors, a crew shelter, main storage area, a lift to raise the missile and an escape ladder and hatch. They were painted

Nike-Ajax site T53L guarding Travis AFB, California. (Photo: NARA SC-567712, July 1959)

The Montrose Nike site was in the northern part of Chicago by Lake Michigan. (Photo: NARA SC-575386, October 1959)

light green and white inside which, co-incidentally, were the same colours some-times found inside Soviet missile bunkers. Normally ten rockets were stored and maintained in these magazines, and raised by lift during crises or for training and maintenance purposes. With so many sites involved, the Army's missile lift order was then the largest order ever. A single site often had two or three bunkers, but in some cases sites were twinned resulting in as many as six magazines. In the original site design, these underground missile shelters were not contemplated, but when cost estimates were made and public pressure grew over land expro-priations, some felt that storing missiles below would reduce land requirements. A single Nike battery usually required a total of 40–50 acres of land.

In a typical firing scenario, the Integrated Fire Control's surveillance radar first picked up the target. With a range of 125 miles, this gave a few short minutes for the crew to react. A battery commander would then call out a two-word code (which changed daily) for the rest of the team to assume battle stations. The missiles were taken out of their magazines, and some men would then perform a quick electrical check with a cable called a 'squib'. If everything appeared nominal, they would remove safety pins that would prevent the missile from firing. A section chief would then proceed into a magazine and turn a key, which would flash a green light in the battery control trailer's launch panel to signal a 'go'. Once the missile was fired, the shorter range Target Tracking Radar fed co-ordinates into a computer, and these in turn were used by the Missile Tracking Radar to guide the interceptor. Missiles on the lifts were fired first, since this

Inside a Nike missile shelter at Farmington, Minnesota. The site was one of four that protected Minneapolis. (Photo: LOC HAER MN-100-64, Andrew Baugnet)

would allow a new missile to be raised from below, followed by those on the outside rails.

The Ajax was, however, to see only short service. Rushed into production because of the Korean War, it was no sooner deployed en masse that the US Army began considering its replacement. Some of the missile's shortcomings were the liquid-fuelled second stage, its limited 30-mile range and its restricted explosive power. The low range, for one, gave battle commanders too little time to manoeuvre, especially against the faster planes then being developed by the Soviets. As for the fuel, it was so hazardous personnel had to wear a special suit when refuelling and work near showers to wash off any propellant. The tracking radar system itself was of limited use since it was unable to track an individual aircraft in a formation and thus unable to home a Nike on a single plane. Bell Labs and Douglas Aircraft were thus asked to work together to develop a new radar system and a better missile, one that could at least offer a big enough punch to destroy that formation.

Some of the disadvantages of the Ajax were remedied in its successor, the Nike-Hercules. The Hercules had better performance with a range of about 90 miles, a ceiling of at least 150,000ft and a speed of about Mach 3.5.[45] It could be outfitted with a conventional T45 HBX-6 high-explosive warhead or a W31 nuclear load with a 2–40 kiloton yield which could be set manually. Those missiles equipped with a nuclear warhead could only fire after a numerical code was entered in a combination device called Permissive Action Link.[46] Since the Hercules's AN/MPQ-T1 training simulator could produce such electronic

One of the few Hercules missiles left in the United States is in front of the Fort George Meade museum in Maryland. (Photo: Author)

counter-measures as false radar echoes and noise, pulse, square wave and continuous wave jamming, the operational equipment probably possessed the ability to defeat all. Furthermore, since the nuclear warhead required tritium gas to work, gas leakage detectors were installed in the magazines as a safety measure. The rocket also had the added advantage of a solid propellant in the first and second stages, which obviated the need to work with hazardous liquid compounds, and the incorporation of solid state electronic components, which reduced power requirements. The Hercules had another advantage in that it could be employed against low-level threats and also as a surface-to-surface missile. Each cost $55,200 to build.

The Ajax-to-Hercules conversion began in June 1958. One of the advantages to a nuclear payload was its greater punch; fewer Hercules were therefore needed and several Ajax bases were closed. At those sites being converted, the lifts were modified to accommodate the heavier Hercules, but because of the rocket's larger size, only six could be stored in a pit. Some Ajaxes did remain active but were turned over to National Guard units who were only too pleased to adopt a role in the nation's air defence. By 1964, the Ajax was gone from the Army's inventory and remained active only overseas in such places as Denmark and Turkey.

A Nike-Hercules battalion consisted of five batteries, four operational and one headquarters, with each battery having its own launch site. At the Nike programme's peak in 1963, there were 134 Hercules and 77 Ajax batteries operational in the United States. Nike sites consisted of a varying number of rockets which could total up to thirty Ajaxes and after conversion, eighteen Hercules. Those with the larger inventories had two batteries co-located. The conversion

A warhead mating building at Dorseyville, Pennsylvania. This is where the warhead was attached to the missile prior to its storage in the magazine below. The site protected Pittsburgh. (Photo: Author)

to Hercules spawned the construction of several new sites, although in at least one case, the sites around Walker AFB in New Mexico, these were never declared operational. At the same time the missile conversion began, the US Army redesignated its SAM units as battalions and regiments (e.g. 2nd Missile Battalion, 51st Artillery Regiment).

The Hercules fire control system was similar to that of the Ajax in that the target was first picked up by an Acquisition Radar and then followed by a Target Tracking Radar. The rocket was controlled by a third radar, the Missile Tracking Radar, that sent two pulses to control its flight; different MTRs used different pulse separation widths to control their respective missiles, this to prevent interference. Later, improvements to the Nike system were made by the addition of a General Electric L-band High Power Acquisition Radar (HIPAR) for longer-range (175 miles) scanning, the addition of an Alternate Battery Radar for use as a backup and the inclusion of a new Target Ranging Radar that could work on different frequencies in the K-band in case of jamming. The greater range of the HIPAR gave battle commanders a few extra precious seconds of decision-making time. Other additions included a Low Power Acquisition Radar (LOPAR) and the deployment of co-ordinating systems to control several batteries: the AN/GSG-5(V) Battery Integrated Radar Display Equipment (BIRDIE) for instance could control 4 to 16 missile sites, while the AN/FSG-1 Missile Master, up to 24 sites. BIRDIEs were therefore used to protect small sites such as air bases and Missile Masters, large urban centres such as New York City and Los Angeles. The Nike Hercules was so popular many were sold to NATO members, Japan, South Korea and Taiwan. There were also rumours it was briefly considered for deployment in Newfoundland, Canada, to protect air bases at Goose Bay and Stephenville, but this never came to pass.

Over 300 Nike sites were built by the Army in the 1950–60s in the United States, 145 of which were used by the Hercules. Each consisted of administrative, launch and fire control areas, and each launch area had underground rooms measuring approximately 50ft by 60ft. As previously mentioned, the missiles

Part of the Nike launch site at Gaithersburg, Maryland, outside Washington, DC. After the Nikes were taken out, there were rumours that this site was used for special operations training. Indeed, the makeshift building from which this photo was taken may have been used for urban assault exercises. Today, the property is identified only as 770 Muddy Branch Road with no user agency. A small sign nearby reads 'Sprinkler Research Lab' suggesting it may be used by the Consumer Products Safety Commission, as is the associated control site. (Photo: Author)

were only raised to the surface for maintenance, training or for public display, although they were actually put on alert during the 1973 Arab–Israeli war. At some bases erected in the 1960s, fallout shelters were added. Each Hercules launch site had sentry boxes, launch control trailer, an electronics building, generator hut, a warhead building and between two and six underground

An escape ladder in a missile magazine. (Photo: LOC, HAER MN-100-70, Andrew Baugnet)

An escape hatch at the Dorseyville launch site. Entry is not possible since the hatch is welded shut. This is just as well as the magazine is flooded. (Photo: Author)

magazines. For recreational purposes, some sites had baseball diamonds or mini-golf ranges. Since guard dogs were used from 1958 to improve night security, kennels were included.

A Nike site was coded to show the Defense Area covered, site number and use. The site number normally represented co-ordinates along a 100-point imaginary circle where 0 was due north of the centre of the defense area and 50, due south with the numbering sequence working clockwise. To illustrate an example, site SF88L at Fort Barry, California, signified: San Francisco Defense Area, site 88 (northwest of city centre), Launch area. SF88A was the administrative area and SF88C, the integrated fire control section.

In general, the Nike missiles were relatively safe weapons. For instance, all were armed with safety devices that were removed only before launch or during drills. Also, despite the corrosive liquid used in the Ajax's second stage, there were few known fuel mishaps. Accidents were few and far between but one of the more serious took place in April 1955 when a rocket suddenly took off its launcher at Fort Meade, Maryland. The exhaust burned a nearby crewman, Sergeant Stanley Kozak, but the missile caused no casualties since it crashed harmlessly onto the Washington–Baltimore expressway after its fuel ran out. Thankfully, the warheads did not detonate, and the debris that fell onto the expressway caused no accidents. After a thorough investigation, it was concluded that an electrical short caused by rain had taken place in a junction box on a missile control trailer.[47]

In another more lethal incident, when a trigger mechanism was being replaced in an Ajax at Leonardo, New Jersey, in May 1958, the rocket blew up. The explosion was so fierce it killed 10, destroyed 8 Ajaxes, a missile assembly building and 2 trucks. A subsequent court of inquiry determined that a ruptured detonating cap was the cause. When one considers the number of Ajaxes and Herculeses deployed and their length of service though, especially the Herculeses, this is still a good safety record.[48]

The Nike air defence programme had the unique characteristic of being controlled by two services, the Army and Air Force. This dual command line led to some acrimony since services normally guard their powers fiercely. Manning and training was looked after by the Army but since the missile's effectiveness required integration with the US Air Force's radar defence network, operations were controlled by the latter. The individual units were first known as Anti-Aircraft Artillery Missile Battalions, but were later subsumed under Air Defense Artillery Regiments (and eventually, Brigades) and subordinated under Defense Areas controlled by the Army. These Areas were in turn controlled by USAF Air Defense Command sector headquarters. From 1950–57, defensive army units were managed by the Army Anti-Aircraft Command and from 1957 on, by the Army Air Defense Command (ARADCOM).

The threat of a Russian attack itself naturally brought home to many the fears of a nuclear exchange. In an attempt to show the public the government's commitment to continental defence, Nikes were put on display by the US Army across the nation. Missiles could be assembled and disassembled relatively easily so it was not uncommon to find them in lobbies of department stores and hotels or featured in local parades and other public venues. When Columbia high school student and up-and-coming actress Sharon Tate vied for the title of Queen of the Atomic Frontier Days at Camp Hanford, Washington, publicity photos were taken of her riding an Ajax.[49] The Nike also made some guest appearances on television and in movies. In the 1964 Hitchcock film *Marnie*, starring Sean Connery and Tippi Hedren, one sees two shrubs or bushes shaped into Nikes at an Atlantic City racetrack, and in one early episode of the 1960s sci-fi show *Voyage to the Bottom of the Sea*, several Nikes are being prepared to shoot down a UFO.

One of the most controversial aspects of the Nike that has already been alluded to was the land it required. As mentioned above, two parcels of land were needed for each battery, one for fire control and the other to house the launchers and

Personnel entry doors at the Hamburg, New York, launch site. (Photo: Author)

The Rehoboth, Massachusetts, control site is now used by the state National Guard. None of the radar towers remain. (Photo: Author)

magazines. Purchases of terrain varied from easy to outright difficult, the latter because the owners did not want to cede their land or because they were afraid the missiles' boosters or their shrapnel would fall upon them. In Los Angeles, Mayor Norris Poulson was extremely reluctant to sell land near the international airport for a battery, and in the negotiating process he called Army staffers in Washington 'bullheaded'. One Army general replied by saying that if the Russians ever attacked, there would be more than just boosters falling down on the city. In this particular case, a compromise was reached and the Army was allowed to set up a battery nearby at Playa del Rey.

In the end, the Nike-Hercules would live less than twenty years. The disbandment of ARADCOM and the Nike units was due to the Department of Defense's view of a perceived shift in the Soviet Union from bombers to missiles, that ICBM attacks on urban areas would incapacite the Nike and that ECM-equipped bombers that would have been employed in a follow-on attack would have rendered them ineffective. This ignores the fact that *some* of the Herculeses could have been used against *some* of the bombers, and that their removal from service left cities wide open to aggression. Also, if the Nike was good enough to be kept in Europe until 1990, it should have been good enough for the United States. Irrespective of arguments, most of the units were closed in 1974, and the following year, ARADCOM disappeared.[50]

To date and as far as the author knows, only one Nike site has been well maintained and opened to the public. Closed in 1996, Fort Barry in Sausalito, California, had been an Army post since 1897 and was the location of one of the Nike batteries protecting the San Francisco area since 1955. While battery headquarters were at Fort Baker next door, Barry contained the business section and a 30-acre launch area with two pits and eight launchers. Bits and pieces of the fort have been transferred to the National Park Service since 1974 and today, the entire property is part of the Golden Gate National Recreation Area. Other Nike sites throughout the United States are now used as schools, by police forces, municipalities, Army Reserve and National Guard units, or have simply vanished under urban sprawl.

Missile Defence

The newest underground facility built by the United States government is that which houses a new type of weapon. Worried about those small nations that might harbour less than friendly intentions, President Clinton authorized the Department of Defense to develop a missile system that could knock down long-range missiles aimed at the United States and its allies. This Ballistic Missile Defense System consists of a number of missile types, one of which is a Ground-Based Interceptor (GBI) housed in silos. The programme was generally known for a while as National Missile Defense, and is being implemented by a new DoD outfit, the Missile Defense Agency.

This new GBI is a four-stage missile that destroys its target not through an explosive warhead, but rather by simply slamming into it. The interceptor uses a multi-dimensional basis of operation that begins with foreign missile launches detected by satellites, tracking by long-range radars and guidance of the GBI by a battle management computer in Colorado Springs, Colorado. Once in space, the GBI is guided towards its prey both by ground radar and by its own infra-red sensors. Once close enough to the target, the missile releases an Exo-atmospheric Kill Vehicle (EKV) that slams into the enemy weapon at 15,000mph, much like, to quote one General, slamming one refrigerator into another. The rocket's current official designation is 'Ground-based Mid-course Defense', a title that reflects the fact it performs its task during an enemy missile's mid-course phase.[51]

As part of the development of this Ballistic Missile Defense System, millions were spent on the detection and communications infrastructure. Foreign missiles are detected in a number of ways, as they have always been, but now by using upgraded technology. Monies were expended on the upgrading of the old BMEWS radars at Fylingdales, United Kingdom, and Thule, Greenland, and on the Cobra Dane radar at Shemya, Alaska. Also, the old Defense Support Program satellites now in use will soon disappear and will be replaced by a new space-based infra-red system. One new detection method included in the BMDS involves having large planes detect foreign launches using lasers. The Department of Defense makes no secret of the fact that the BMDS was designed to counter the North Korean and Iranian threats, and for this reason it has installed X-band AN/TPY-2 radars in Japan and Israel to detect launches from their unpredictable neighbours.

As of the time of writing, the GBI was deployed mainly at Fort Greely, Alaska in 2 sites: 1 having 6 silos and the other, 20. There were also four operational silos at Vandenberg AFB. The Department of Defense has presently decided to leave the inventory at thirty missiles. The twenty-six weapons at Fort Greely are managed by the Alaska Army National Guard's 49th Missile Defense Battalion, a unit that is controlled by the US Army's 100th Missile Brigade, which is head-quartered at Colorado Springs, Colorado. The missileers' training is also given at Colorado Springs.

One of the ways to guard against a multiple warhead strike is to use a large number of missiles against it. Indeed, at one time, National Missile Defense was to consist of 125 rockets in Alaska and 125 in North Dakota. These would have been more than sufficient to counter the North Korean threat. This projection has since been greatly reduced, as we have just seen, and the Missile Defense Agency has opted instead to deploy other types of weapons in addition to the GBI, such as the Aegis on warships and new Patriot SAMs. This is just as well since it introduces deployment flexibility into a system that could see threats emerge from other states that use different types of missiles.

One of the biggest challenges that faced the Missile Defense Agency is knowing the types of decoys enemy missiles may carry. One Army officer was quoted as saying that building a missile is a relatively simple affair that practi-cally any nation can do, but that its effectiveness is very much dependent on the defensive measures it employs. One group of experts called the Union of Concerned Scientists has published a report describing the types of counter-measures foreign missiles may use. For instance:

- An enemy missile could be equipped with replica warheads of the same size, shape and flight characteristics as live warheads making it very diffi-cult for the EKV to decide whom to attack;
- Since the EKV has infra-red sensors, reducing the infra-red signature of the warhead could reduce EKV reaction times or detection ranges;
- An enemy could use 'signature-diverse' devices where all, including the live warhead, act slightly differently making it impossible for the EKV to discriminate against the dummies;
- Using old-fashioned chaff would work against the ground radars;
- Hiding the warheads in metallized mylar balloons, which are impervious to radar waves, and launching several during the mid-course phase of the flight would prevent a radar from tracking them; and
- Hiding chemical or biological agents in small devices called submunitions. If a single missile can be made to deploy hundreds of those devices, an EKV would be near useless, unless it acted before the submunitions' release.

To counter some of the above tricks, the Missile Defense Agency could do two things. One, it could ensure the EKVs act before the warheads and decoys are released from their re-entry vehicle bus. If the entire assembly can be destroyed, none of it would reach American soil. The second choice would have been to arm the GBIs with nuclear warheads, just like the Russian ABMs around

Moscow. If a warhead of sufficient strength was detonated near an enemy missile, even after the warheads and decoys were released, the entire array of devices could be destroyed without having to worry about finding the live bombs. According to Bradley Graham in his book *Hit to Kill*, this approach was not adopted by the Department of Defense for two reasons: the nuclear explosions would have intefered with the radar systems, and they would also have 'unnerved populations on the ground'.

The greater questions one asks at this point are: Is the Ballistic Missile Defense System necessary? Are these rogue states – North Korea and Iran principally – really valid threats? Would a nation such as North Korea really risk incurring America's wrath with a missile strike? Since North Korea has a well-developed missile industry and is strongly suspected of having nuclear warheads, the Department of Defense sees it as a credible threat. Not only does it manufacture its own rockets, it has even exported some to Iran, Syria, Egypt, Libya and Vietnam, some of whom could threaten the United States in the future. A report released by the Canadian Security Intelligence Service in 2001 stated that the Democratic People's Republic of Korea was then testing a new missile, the Taepodong-2, which would have enough range to reach North America. This and the fact the DPRK has thrown nuclear inspectors out concerns some in Washington in terms of the country's ultimate intentions. Others worry less since they do not think the North Korean Premier would ever risk a good retaliatory flogging from the United States by launching an attack. One is left to assume that the Ballistic Missile Defense System was created to be just one big insurance policy.

❑ VIETNAM

In their book, *The Tunnels of Cu Chi*, Tom Mangold and John Penycate describe elaborate tunnel systems dug by the Viet Cong outside Saigon in the Cu Chi district. Sources interviewed for their book claimed that tunnels began during the French occupation were, by the 1960s, expanded into a 200km network that American forces would nickname the little IRT (after the New York underground rail system). The system ran under the Ho Bo Woods and the Fil Hol Plantation a few short kilometers from the South Vietnamese army base at Trung Lap and the US 25th Infantry Division camp at Cu Chi respectively. The complex included two local military headquarters, one for the Saigon/Gia Dinh and the other for the Cu Chi Military Districts, and the Saigon/Gia Dinh District political headquarters. A Viet Cong manual captured by members of the South Korean 28th Infantry Regiment in 1967 stated that the tunnels' roles were 'the strengthening of combat vitality' and the protection of military and political units and of the public. Through search and destroy missions, American forces would eventually find howitzers, large stocks of captured ammunition and even one of their M-48 tanks inside. At other underground facilities nearby, one in the Bo Loi forest and one near the Thi Tinh River, American soldiers would also find signals intelligence stations. Despite several attempts, the tunnel complexes were never destroyed.

Other underground facilities in Vietnam are:

- Under the presidential palace in Saigon; and
- Along the former Demilitarized Zone as American radio intercept posts.

As well, the North Vietnamese government had its command centre under the Kinh Thien shrine in Hanoi. The bunker complex was built in 1967 and was used to plan such operations as the 1968 Tet offensive. Today, it is a tourist attraction, although much of it remains off-limits to the public. According to press reports, the current Vietnamese government's command centre has since been moved to another location.

❑ APPENDIX A – Canadian Bunkers

There were two types of Canadian bunkers: a relocation site for politicians, military staff and civilian personnel, and a transmitter station for Army radio technicians. The two bunkers were always twinned and were always located on military properties. In Canada, large properties are called Canadian Forces Bases (CFBs) and smaller sites, Canadian Forces Stations (CFSs). The American analogies are Air Force Bases and Air Force Stations. The national bunker was at CFS Carp outside Ottawa, and its associated transmitter site, called CFS Carp-Richardson Detachment, was outside Perth, Ontario.

Province	Main Bunker Location	Transmitter Station
Alberta	CFB Penhold	Penhold
British Columbia	Camp Nanaimo	Nanoose Bay
Manitoba	CFB Shilo	Camp Hughes
Nova Scotia	CFS Debert	Great Village
Ontario	CFS Carp	Perth
Ontario	CFB Borden	Edenvale
Quebec	CFB Valcartier	St-Raymond

❑ APPENDIX B – Chinese Air Bases with Mountain Hangars

The following is a list of Chinese air bases with mountain hangars. These are characterized by very long taxi strips that lead away from the main runways.

Location	Province or Area	Comments
Anqing	Anhui	North of the city
Chifeng	Inner Mongolia	Nearest city is Ulanhad
Datangshan	Beijing	The hangar is now the China Aviation Museum. The rest of the base is still active
Feidong	Anhui	Near the town of Shitang
Jinzhou	Liaoning	
Le Dong	Hainan Island	Has very long runways
Qingyishanzhen	Liaoning	Outside the city of Kuan Dian. No longer used
Yantai	Shandong	May no longer be used
Yinchuan	Ningxia	West of the city
Yiwu	Zhejiang	Northeast of Jinhua
Yongningzhen	Beijing	North of Beijing

❑ APPENDIX C – Chinese Second Artillery Corps Order-of-Battle

The Corps consists of a headquarters and six major bases (jidi) commanded by Major-Generals. Each base has two or three missile brigades (lü) that are called in Chinese Basic Combat units (jiben zuozhan danwei) and that are run by Colonels. Brigades are made up of Basic Firepower Units (jiben huoli danwei), known in the West as battalions. Each battalion has six or nine missiles. The SAC is thought to have about 100 missiles.

During a war, communications of launch orders would come from the Chairman of the Central Military Commission – probably from his command centre under Yuquan Mountain in western Beijing – and proceed to the PLA's Central Emergency Command Centre under Xi Mountain in Beijing, to SAC HQ, to a base, brigade and battalion. The SAC uses the same two-man rule to verify launch orders and to turn the launch keys (as in the United States and Russia). Orders pass through microwave, high-frequency radio and landline systems. The messages are encrypted.

The following list of brigades was taken from the book *Modernizing China's Military*. It is not complete. Furthermore, the 806th Brigade at Hancheng, Shaanxi, was listed as being under both Base No. 51 and Base No. 56. Since it is much closer to Luoyang, home of Base No. 54, it may actually be one of its units. For a while, the brigades had 400-series numbers.

Base No. 51
810th Brigade   Dalian
816th Brigade   Jinchang
818th Brigade   Tonghua

Base No. 52
807th Brigade   Shitai
811th Brigade   Qimen
815th Brigade   Leping
817th Brigade   Yingtan

Base No. 53
802nd Brigade   Jianshui
808th Brigade   Chuxiong

Base No. 54
801st Brigade   Lingbao
804th Brigade   Luanchuan
813th Brigade   Yiyang

Base No. 55
803rd Brigade	Jinzhou
805th Brigade	Tongdao
814th Brigade	Huitong

Base No. 56
806th Brigade (?)	Hancheng
809th Brigade	Datong
812th Brigade	Wulan

❑ APPENDIX D – AT&T Bunkers

The following is a list of some AT&T bunkers. The corporation had about 100 of these at one time, although only about 20 held such things as Department of Defense AUTOVON switches.

City	State
Windermere	Florida
Chesterfield	Massachusetts
Littleton	Massachusetts
Clarksville	New York (on the west side of County Road 312)
Tully	New York
Chatham County	North Carolina
Winston-Salem	North Carolina
Pottstown	Pennsylvania
Neersville	Virginia
Buckingham	Virginia

❑ APPENDIX E – Russian Strategic Rocket Forces Order-of-Battle, 2009

The list of units is not complete.

	Rocket type
27th Guards Missile Army, Vladimir	
7th Guards Missile Division, Vypolzovo	RT-2PM
41st Guards Missile Regiment	
510th Guards Missile Regiment	
14th Missile Division, Yoshkar-Ola	RT-2PM
290th Missile Regiment	
779th Missile Regiment	
108th Independent Helicopter Squadron	
28th Guards Missile Division, Kozelsk[1]	UR-100N
74th Guards Missile Regiment	
168th Guards Missile Regiment	

373rd Guards Missile Regiment
38th Independent Helicopter Squadron
54th Guards Missile Division, Teykovo   RT-2PM
  235th Guards Missile Regiment
  285th Guards Missile Regiment
  365th Guards Missile Regiment
  60th Independent Helicopter Squadron
60th Missile Division, Tatishchevo   UR-100N, Topol-M
  104th Missile Regiment
  687th Missile Regiment
  10th Independent Helicopter Squadron
98th Independent Mixed Aviation Squadron

31st Missile Army, Orenburg (Rostoshi)
  13th Missile Division, Dombarovskii   R-36M
  42nd Missile Division, Nizhniy Tagil   RT-2PM
  102nd Independent Mixed Aviation Squadron

33rd Guards Missile Army, Omsk
  35th Missile Division, Barnaul   RT-2PM
  39th Guards Missile Division, Novosibirsk   RT-2PM
  51st Guards Missile Division, Irkutsk   RT-2PM
  62nd Missile Division, Uzhur   R-36M
  105th Independent Mixed Aviation Squadron

A regiment normally consists of six to ten launchers. Each has its own underground command post in a silo-shaped structure. Very few regiments have been identified in the press. The aviation squadrons have helicopters to ferry personnel (e.g. security response teams and VIPs) to and from support bases, launch facilities and LCCs. Some are equipped to act as airborne command posts.

❑ APPENDIX F – Nuclear Weapons Storage Sites in Russia

The US-Russia Cooperative Threat Reduction Program states that there were, at least in the 1990s, 123 such storage sites. These were operated either by the navy, the air force, the Strategic Rocket Forces' (RVSN) 6th Directorate or the Ministry of Defence's 12th Main Directorate. In the case of the RVSN, they had twenty-three, while the MoD had fifty. Others may belong to the navy. This list below was taken from a May 2002 edition of *Kommersant Vlast*. Some of these sites may no longer be used today.

Location	Nearest Largest City	Purpose	Operating Entity
Bataisk	Rostov-na-Donu	Maintenance	RVSN
Berezovka	Saratov	Storage	MoD
Bolon	Komsomolsk-na-Amure	Storage	MoD
Borisoglebsk	Voronezh	Storage	MoD
Bryansk	Bryansk	Maintenance	RVSN
Chebsara	Vologda	Storage	MoD
Dodonovo	Krasnoyarsk	Storage	MoD
Golovchino	Belgorod	Storage	MoD
Karabash	Chelyabinsk	Storage	MoD
Korfovskiy	Khabarovsk	Storage	MoD
Kryzoly Tovy	Yekaterinburg	Storage	RVSN
Lesnoy	Yekaterinburg	Storage	MoD
Mozhaysk	Moscow	Storage	MoD
Nizhnyaya Tura	Yekaterinburg	Storage	MoD
Olenegorsk	Murmansk	Storage	MoD
Perm	Perm	Storage	RVSN
Pibanshur	Izhevsk	Storage	RVSN
Trekhgornyy	Chelyabinsk	Storage	MoD
Zhukovka	Bryansk	Storage	MoD

Security at these depots has been called less than perfect. According to a 2002 report by the US National Intelligence Council that quoted an anonymous military officer on Russian television, the sites lacked sufficient guards, and the alarms sometimes worked only 50 per cent of the time. The MoD closed one site in 1997 after the employees went on a hunger strike (because they were not being paid). Military staff throughout the RVSN were also not being paid regularly, and housing for the personnel of the 12th Main Directorate is limited.

There have been reports that twenty-three warheads were stolen from the Komsomolsk-na-Amure site in 1992. Russian officials insist that the stockpile is safe, but no one knows for sure if the count of nuclear weapons is really correct.

❏ APPENDIX G – Moscow S-25 SAM Sites and Storage Depots

There were twenty-two operational sites along the inner ring road, and thirty-four sites along the outer. Each had sixty launchers and included one bunker. The sites began to be decommissioned in 1989, and by 1993 all S-25s had gone. At some sites, they were replaced by new S-300P SAMs. At least two of the old properties are now residential communities. The site at Vasil'chinovo south of

Kubinka no longer has its bunker, but now sports a number of radomes. This list is not complete.

Location	Purpose
Aksin'ino	SAM
Bereznyaki	SAM
Bortnevo	SAM
Deshino	SAM
Dmitrovo	Storage
Dobrino	SAM
Domodedovo	SAM
Domodedovo	Storage
Golovinka	SAM
Karabanovo	SAM (?)
Kashino	SAM
Kholubenovo	SAM
Kobyakovo	SAM
Kobyakovo	Storage
Lupanovo	SAM
Lytkino	SAM
Mar'ino	SAM
Nikiforovo	SAM
Plaskinino	SAM
Sazonki	SAM
Sivkovo	SAM
Svatovo	SAM
Svatovo	Storage
Vasil'chinovo	SAM
Verevskoye	Storage
Voskresenskoye	SAM
Zakharovo	SAM

❏ APPENDIX H – British Cold War Regional Government Headquarters

RGHQ	Village or City
2.1	Shipton
2.2	Hexham
3.1	Skendelby
3.2	Loughborough
4.1	Bawburgh
4.2	Hertford
5.1	Kelvedon Hatch
6.2	Basingstoke/Crowborough

❑ APPENDIX I – Earth-covered Ammunition Bunkers in the United Kingdom

Many of these bases are now closed. This list is not complete.

RAF Alconbury
RAF Bentwaters
Chelveston
RAF Chilmark
RAF Coningsby
HMS *Gannet*, Prestwick
RAF Gaydon
RAF Greenham Common
RAF Honington
RAF Lakenheath
RAF Leuchars
RAF Lossiemouth
Machrihanish
RAF Marham
RAF St Mawgan
Salisbury (Dean Hill)
RAF Sculthorpe

A bunker at the nuclear bomb store at RAF Alconbury. (Photo: Author)

Shepherd's Grove
RAF Upper Heyford
RAF Waddington
RAF Wethersfield
RAF Wittering
RAF Wyton
RNAS Yeovilton

❑ APPENDIX J – United States ICBM Bases

All the Atlas and Titan I bases were closed in the 1960s, and the Titan II sites destroyed in the mid-1980s. Of the 1,000 Minuteman sites that were built, 450 remained in use as of the time of publication. The years represent the times when the missile wings were closed.

State	Air Force Base	Rocket	Closed
AZ	Davis-Monthan	Titan II	1984
AR	Little Rock	Titan II	1986
CA	Beale	Titan I	1965
CA	Vandenberg	Miscellaneous	
CO	Lowry	Titan I	1965
ID	Mountain Home	Titan I	1965
KS	Forbes	Atlas E	1965
KS	McConnell	Titan II	1986
KS	Schilling	Atlas F	1965
MO	Whiteman	Minuteman II	1993–95
MT	Malmstrom	Minuteman II, III	
NE	Lincoln	Atlas F	1965
NE	Offutt	Atlas D	1963
NM	Walker	Atlas F	1965
NY	Plattsburgh	Atlas F	1965
ND	Grand Forks	Minuteman II, III	1990s
ND	Minot	Minuteman III	
OK	Altus	Atlas F	1965
SD	Ellsworth	Titan I	1965
		Minuteman II	1990s
TX	Dyess	Atlas F	1965
WA	Fairchild	Atlas E	1965
WA	Larson	Titan I	1965
WY	F.E. Warren	Atlas D, E	1965
		Minuteman III	

❏ APPENDIX K – Nike Missile Launch Sites

Many of these sites were first equipped with the Ajax, then with the longer range Hercules. Most of the Nike batteries were closed in 1969 and 1974 after Congress decided the Soviets did not really have much of a bomber force to worry about; the Soviets had in fact concentrated much of their strategic efforts in ICBMs. By the time of the Nike's final retirement in 1974, only 48 sites remained out of a high of 134. The sites listed show in brackets which city or base they were meant to guard. Hanford refers to the nuclear research and weapons complex in southeastern Washington state.

<u>Alaska</u>
Fort Richardson
Ladd AFB

<u>California</u>
Angel Island (San Francisco)
Berkeley (San Fransisco)
Brea/Puente Hills (Los Angeles)
Castro Valley/Lake Chabot (San Francisco)
Chatsworth/Oat Mtn (Los Angeles)
Coyote Hills/Newark (San Francisco)
Elmira (Travis AFB)
Fairfield (Travis AFB)
Fort Barry (San Francisco)
Fort Cronkhite (San Francisco)
Fort Funston (San Francisco)
Fort MacArthur (Los Angeles)
Garden Grove (Los Angeles)
Hyperion/Playa Del Rey (Los Angeles)
Lambie/Dixon (Travis AFB)
Lang/Magic Mtn (Los Angeles)
Long Beach Airport (Los Angeles)
Los Pinetos (Los Angeles)
Malibu (Los Angeles)
Milagra/Pacifica (Los Angeles)
Mount Disappointment (Los Angeles)
Mount Gleason (Los Angeles)
Palmdale (Los Angeles)
Playa Del Rey/LA Int'l (Los Angeles)
Point Vincente (Los Angeles)
Potrero Hills (Travis AFB)
Presidio of San Francisco (San Francisco)
Redondo Beach/Torrance (Los Angeles)

Rocky Ridge (San Francisco)
San Pablo Ridge (San Francisco)
San Rafael (San Francisco)
Signal Hill/Long Beach (Los Angeles)
So. El Monte (Los Angeles)
Travis AFB
Van Nuys (Los Angeles)

Connecticut
Ansonia (Bridgeport)
Avon/Simsbury (Hartford)
Cromwell (Hartford)
E. Windsor (Hartford)
Fairfield (Bridgeport)
Manchester (Hartford)
Milford (Bridgeport)
Plainville (Hartford)
Portland (Hartford)
Shelton (Bridgeport)
Westhaven (Bridgeport)
Westport (Bridgeport)

Florida
Florida City (Homestead AFB-Miami)
Key Largo (Homestead AFB-Miami)
Opa-Locka (Homestead AFB-Miami)
Southwest Miami (Homestead AFB)

Georgia
Armena/Sasser (Turner AFB)
Byron (Robins AFB)
Jeffersonville (Robins AFB)
Sylvester (Turner AFB)

Hawaii – Oahu
Bellows AFS
Ewa
Kauka/Kahuku
Waimanalo/Dillingham AFS

Illinois
Addison (Chicago)
Alton/Pere Marquette (St Louis)
Arlington Heights (Chicago)

Burnham Park (Chicago)
Fort Sheridan (Chicago)
Hecker (St Louis)
Hegewisch (Chicago)
Homewood (Chicago)
Jackson Park (Chicago)
Lemont (Chicago)
Libertyville (Chicago)
Marine (St Louis)
Montrose (Chicago)
Mundelein (Chicago)
Naperville (Chicago)
Northfield (Chicago)
Orland Park (Chicago)
Palatine (Chicago)
Palos Heights (Chicago)
Porter (Chicago)
Scott AFB

Indiana
Gary (Chicago)
Hobart/Wheeler (Chicago)
Munster (Chicago)
Porter (Chicago)
South Gary (Chicago)

Iowa
Council Bluffs (Offutt AFB)

Kansas
Gardner (Kansas City)
Leavenworth (Kansas City)
Schilling AFB

Louisiana
Bellevue (Barksdale AFB)
Stonewall (Barksdale AFB)

Maine
Caribou (Loring AFB)
Caswell (Loring AFB)
Conner (Loring AFB)
Limestone (Loring AFB)

Maryland
Accokeek (Washington, DC)
Annapolis/Skidmore (Washington, DC)
Brandywine/Naylor (Washington, DC)
Cronhardt (Baltimore)
Croom/Marlboro (Washington, DC)
Davidsonville (Washington, DC)
Edgewood Arsenal (Baltimore)
Fork (Baltimore)
Fort George Meade (Washington, DC)
Gaithersburg (Washington, DC)
Granite (Baltimore)
Jacobsville (Baltimore)
Laytonsville/Derwood (Washington, DC)
Mattawoman (Washington, DC)
Phoenix (Baltimore)
Pomonkey (Washington, DC)
Rockville (Washington, DC)
Tolchester Beach (Baltimore)
Towson (Baltimore)

Massachusetts
Bedford (Boston)
Beverly (Boston)
Blue Hills (Boston)
Burlington (Boston)
Cohasset (Boston)
Danvers (Boston)
Fort Duvall, Hull (Boston)
Nahant (Boston)
Needham (Boston)
Reading (Boston)
Rehoboth (Providence)
South Lincoln (Boston)
Squantum/Quincy (Boston)
Swansea (Providence)

Michigan
Auburn Heights (Detroit)
Carleton (Detroit)
Carleton/Newport (Detroit)
Commerce/Union Lake (Detroit)
Franklin/Bingham (Detroit)
Fort Wayne (Detroit)

Grosse Ile NAS (Detroit)
Kercheval (Detroit)
Marine City (Detroit)
River Rouge Park (Detroit)
Riverview/Wyandotte (Detroit)
Romulus/Dearborn (Detroit)
Selfridge AFB (Detroit)
Utica (Detroit)

Minnesota
Bethel/Ishanti (Minneapolis)
Farmington (Minneapolis)
Roberts (Minneapolis)
St Bonifacius (Minneapolis)

Missouri
Lawson (Kansas City)
Pacific (St Louis)
Pleasant Hill (Kansas City)

Nebraska
Cedar Creek (Offutt AFB)
Ceresco (Lincoln AFB)
Crete (Lincoln AFB)

New Jersey
Fort Hancock (NYC)
Franklin Lakes (NYC)
Highlands AFS (NYC)
Holmdel/Hazlet (NYC)
Leonardo (NYC)
Livingston (NYC)
Northvale (NYC)
Ramsay/Darlington (NYC)
Sicklerville
South Amboy (NYC)
South Plainfield (NYC)
Summit/Watchung (NYC)
Wayne (NYC)

New Mexico
Hagerman (Walker AFB)
Roswell (Walker AFB)

New York
Amityville/Farmingdale (NYC)
Fort Slocum (NYC)
Fort Tilden (NYC)
Grand Island (Niagara Falls)
Hamburg (Buffalo)
Hicksville (NYC)
Lancaster (Buffalo)
Lido Beach (NYC)
Lloyd Harbor/Huntington (NYC)
Lockport AFS, Sanborn (Niagara Falls)
Model City (Niagara Falls)
Orangeburg/Mt Nebo (NYC)
Orchard Park (Buffalo)
Ransom Creek (Buffalo)
Rocky Point (NYC)
Roslyn AFS, Hempstead (NYC)
Spring Valley/Ramapo (NYC)
White Plains (NYC)

Ohio
Bratenahl (Cleveland)
Dillsboro (Cincinnati-Dayton)
Felicity (Cincinnati-Dayton)
Garfield Heights (Cleveland)
Lakefront Airport (Cleveland)
Lordstown (Cleveland)
Oxford (Cincinnati-Dayton)
Painesville (Cleveland)
Parma (Cleveland)
Warrensville (Cleveland)
Willowick (Cleveland)
Wilmington (Cincinnati-Dayton)

Pennsylvania
Berlin (Philadelphia)
Chester/Media (Philadelphia)
Coraopolis/Beacon (Pittsburgh)
Cowansburg/Herminie (Pittsburgh)
Dorseyville (Pittsburgh)
Edgemont (Philadelphia)
Elizabeth (Pittsburgh)
Elrama (Pittsburgh)
Finleyville (Pittsburgh)

Hickman/Bridgeville (Pittsburgh)
Irwin (Pittsburgh)
Lumberton (Philadelphia)
Marlton (Philadelphia)
Murrysville/Monroe (Pittsburgh)
Newportville/Croydon (Philadelphia)
North Park (Pittsburgh)
Oakdale AFS (Pittsburgh)
Paoli (Philadelphia)
Pedricktown (Philadelphia)
Pittman (Philadelphia)
Richboro (Philadelphia)
Rural Ridge (Pittsburgh)
Swedesboro (Philadelphia)
Warrington/Eureka (Philadelphia)
Westview (Pittsburgh)
Worchester (Philadelphia)

Rhode Island
Bristol (Providence)
Coventry (Providence)
Foster Center (Providence)
N. Kingston/Davisville (Providence)
N. Smithfield (Providence)

South Dakota
Ellsworth AFB

Texas
Alvarado (Dallas)
Austin (Bergstrom AFB)
Camp Barkeley (Dyess AFB)
Denton (Dallas)
Duncanville AFS (Dallas)
Elroy (Bergstrom AFB)
Ft Phantom Hill (Dyess AFB)
Mineral Wells (Dallas)
Terrell (Dallas)

Virginia
Deep Creek (Norfolk)
Denbigh (Norfolk)
Fairfax (Washington, DC)
Fort Story (Norfolk)

Fox Hill (Norfolk)
Hampton Roads (Norfolk)
Herndon/Dranesville (Washington, DC)
Kempsville (Norfolk)
Lorton (Washington, DC)
Nansemond/Suffolk (Norfolk)
Ocean View (Norfolk)
Smithfield (Norfolk)

Washington
Cheney (Fairchild AFB)
Cougar Mtn (Seattle)
Deep Creek (Fairchild AFB)
Fort Lawton (Seattle)
Kenmore (Seattle)
Kent/Midway (Seattle)
Kingston (Seattle)
Lake Youngs (Seattle)
Medical Lake (Fairchild)
Ollala (Seattle)
Othello (Hanford)
Poulsbo (Seattle)
Priest Rapids (Hanford)
Rattlesnake Mountain (Hanford)
Redmond (Seattle)
Saddle Mountain (Fairchild)
Spokane (Fairchild)
Vashon Island (Seattle)
Winslow (Seattle)

Wisconsin
Cudahy (Milwaukee)
Hales Corners/Paynesville (Milwaukee)
Lannon (Milwaukee)
Milwaukee
Muskegon/Prospect (Milwaukee)
Waukesha (Milwaukee)

❑ APPENDIX L – Examples of Cover Organizations throughout the World

- The British wartime signals intelligence station at Delhi, India, was known as the Wireless Experimental Centre;
- The current British intercept station at Blakehill, United Kingdom, is described as an experimental radio station;
- Another signals intelligence station at Menwith Hill in England once had the cover of a communications relay station;
- The Special Operations Executive, the United Kingdom's main commando outfit during the Second World War, was also known as the Inter Services Research Bureau;
- Some of the nuclear bunkers built in the United Kingdom in the 1960s had the cover of Home Office Training Establishments;
- When the US Navy first opened its radio listening site at Sugar Grove, West Virginia, the public was told the large dishes were for radio astronomy research;
- The US Naval Facility at Argentia, Newfoundland, was long said to perform oceanographic research but only in 1991 did the US Navy admit it tracked Soviet submarines;
- The CIA's training school at Camp Peary near Williamsburg, Virginia, has the cover of an Armed Forces Experimental Training Activity;
- The CIA's other training ground at Harvey Point, North Carolina, operates as a Defense Testing Activity;
- At the American Embassy in London, the CIA's cover at one time was the Joint Reports and Research Unit;
- During the Vietnam war, the CIA's cover was that of a Department of Defense organization, the Studies and Observations Group;
- CIA and USAF U-2 spy units used the misnomer Weather Reconnaissance Squadrons (Provisional);
- The CIA's satellite intelligence station at Pine Gap in central Australia works under the guise of a Joint Defence Space Research Facility;
- The US Navy's intelligence collection organization once operated under the name of Naval Field Support Operations Group;
- When the Pentagon decided to build a massive new air base on Diego Garcia, it told Congress it was building a communications facility;
- Some of the CIA's cover outfits in West Germany in the postwar era were the US Army's Management and Planning Unit, Field Systems Office and Technical Analysis Unit;
- In Italy, the CIA also used the army as cover, for example its Europe Southern Projects Unit;
- In France, one of the CIA's offices at the Paris Embassy was the Regional Administration Support Office;

- The CIA has often used US Army units to conduct special operations, including the 1st Rotary Test Wing of Fort Eustis, Virginia;
- In New York City, the CIA's local office near the World Trade Center was that of a US Army Logistics Command outfit;
- The USAF has long operated atomic detection stations throughout the world. One of them was the Special Weather Unit at Puerto Montt in Chile;
- The US Army was also in the atomic detection business operating several Signal Research Units throughout the world;
- The USAF outfit that co-operates with the National Reconnaissance Office is the Office of Special Projects;
- The United States and Canadian governments have always avoided calling nuclear weapons as such. They always referred to them as 'special weapons';
- The CIA's main ground station for satellite imagery operates under the guise of the Defense Communications Electronics Evaluation and Testing Activity at Fort Belvoir, Virginia;
- When the United States government sent planes to overfly French nuclear tests in the South Pacific, the aircraft were painted 'Office of Naval Research';
- When the Australian government set out to build a new emergency communications centre on Wormald Street in Canberra in 2009, it called it a scientific research centre;
- RAF electronics intelligence units in southeast Asia during the Second World War used the cover of 'Noise Investigation Bureau';
- Israel's nuclear complex at Dimona was once known as a textile factory, then a metallurgical laboratory;
- An Israeli organisation that collects technical intelligence is the Bureau for Scientific Relations;
- South Africa's former underground atomic test site in the Kalahari was built under the cover of an ammunition depot;
- France's secret service was once known as the Direction Générale des Etudes et Recherche (General Directorate of Studies and Research);
- The KGB's headquarters at Yasenevo in southwestern Moscow was known for years as the Scientific Centre for Strategic Studies;
- The KGB's school, the Andropov Red Banner Intelligence Institute, sometimes used the cover 'Computing Centre for All-Union Scientific Research on Industrial Information';
- Russian spy trawlers are said to belong to the Russian Academy of Sciences;
- When East Germany existed as a state, the Institute for Policy and Economics was a front for the secret service, the STASI;
- For a long time, the Japanese intelligence service was known as the

Cabinet Research Office. It is now the Cabinet Intelligence and Research Office;

- The German government's signals intelligence station at Hoefen near the Belgium border is said to belong to the Office of Telecommunications Statistics;
- During the Nicaraguan war in the 1980s, the Sandinistas' radio listening post on the Cosiguina Peninsula had the cover of an agricultural station;
- The Soviet MoD's nuclear weapons test site at Semipalatinsk in north-eastern Kazakhstan initially operated as the First Mining Seismic Station, then as an MoD training ground, then as the State Central Scientific Research Test Area No. 2. (The Americans were never fooled);
- The Norwegian government established a signals intelligence station in northern Norway and claimed it was an ionospheric research station; and
- The communist-era Romanian intelligence service's school at Branesti outside Bucharest was officially known as a civilian radio centre.

❑ APPENDIX M – Soviet Strategic Rocket Forces Missile Bases in Belarus

The missiles were either stored in earth-covered shelters or in silos. By 1997 all the rockets were returned to Russia and by then all the bases had been closed.

Unit	Year	Location	Rocket Type
31st Guards Missile Division	1980	Pruzhany	SS-4 (R-12)
44th Guards Missile Regiment		Malorita	
56th Guards Missile Regiment		Zasimovichi	
85th Guards Missile Regiment		Pinsk	
403rd Guards Missile Regiment		Ruzhany	
32nd Missile Division	1985	Postavy	SS-20 (RSD-10)
249th Missile Regiment		Polotsk	
346th Guards Missile Regiment		Postany	
402nd Guards Missile Regiment		Vetrino	
428th Guards Missile Regiment		Smorgon	
835th Guards Missile Regiment		Smorgon	
33rd Guards Missile Division	1985	Mozyr	SS-25 (RT-2PM)
306th Guards Missile Regiment		Slutsk	
369th Guards Missile Regiment		Zhitovichi	
396th Missile Regiment		Petrikov	
398th Missile Regiment		Kozenki	
404th Missile Regiment		Rechitsa	
49th Missile Division	1991	Lida	SS-25 (RT-2PM)
56th Guards Missile Regiment		Zasimovichi	
170th Missile Regiment		Minoity	
346th Guards Missile Regiment		Postavy	

| 376th Missile Regiment | Gezgaly |
| 403rd Guards Missile Regiment | Ruzhany |

❏ APPENDIX N – East German Ministry of State Security Emergency Operations Bunkers

There were to be 2 facilities for each of the country's 15 districts, although it seems only 19 were built. These were erected between 1968 and 1986.

Location	Location
Bad Berka	Bornim
Bornmühle	Briesen
Brodersdorf	Crivitz
Dittersdorfer Höhe	Frauenwald
Gallinchen	Haarberg
Körbelitz	Machern
Ostrau	Schönfeld
Schwosdorf	Tautenhain
Treplin	Vesser
Wörmlitz	

❏ APPENDIX O – German Ammunition Depots with Earth-covered Bunkers

These bunkers were operated by either German, American, British, Canadian, East German or Russian forces and could house conventional, chemical or nuclear weapons. American forces began storing nuclear artillery shells in Germany in 1953. By the late 1980s, they had fifty-nine ammunition depots ranging from 6 to 2,269 acres. The depots were invariably located in wooded areas. Many of these places are now closed. The following list may not be complete.

Location	Nearest City	Comments
Bad Kissingen		East of town
Bentheim	Bad Bentheim	
Beverbruch	Cloppenburg	
Bohlenbergerfeld	Zetel	
Borkener Tannen	Meppen	
Buchholz	Landstuhl	
Burow	Golchern	
Clausen	Pirmasens	Stored United States nerve agents The shells were removed in June–September 1990 under Operation Steel Box

Location	Nearest City	Comments
Dichtelbach		
Differte		
Dreifelden		
Engstingen	Stuttgart	
Fischbach bei Dahn	Pirmasens	
Gießen		NATO Site 4 Stored nuclear weapons Near the town of Rödgen
Grebenhain		
Grunow	Beeskow	
Hellendorf-Eft	Perl	
Hemer		Used by the British and Canadian Armies Stored nuclear weapons Actual location may be north of Apricke
Hochspeyer	Kaiserslautern	
Hünxer Wald	Dorsten	
Kitzingen		
Klosterfelde	Wandlitz	
Kriegsfeld		Stored United States nuclear weapons Operated by the US Army's 92nd Ordnance Company, and for a while by the 619th Ordnance Company

A guard tower and administration building at the Clausen chemical munitions depot. (Photo: Author)

One of the munitions bunkers at Clausen. The bunker entrance was protected by a strong metal mesh cover. Similar covers existed at the nuclear weapons depot at Fischbach. (Photo: Author)

Location	Nearest City	Comments
Marpingen	Saarbrücken	
Miesau		
Morbach	Trier	
Mörsingen		
Müllenbach	Ulmen	In the forest east of town
Nörvenich air base	Düren	On the north side of the airfield
Osterne	Gransee	
Ost-Benthullen	Oldenburg	
Riedheim	Leipheim	Stored nuclear weapons Operated by the US Army's 510th Ordnance Company
Schwarzengraben	Ruppertsecken	
Siegelsbach		Stored nuclear weapons Operated by the US Army's 92nd Ordnance Company, and for some time by the 525th Ordnance Company
Sölten	Dorsten	
Tünsdorf	Mettlach	
Twisteden	Kevelaer	
Waldau	Rheinbach	
Wallhausen	Bad Kreuznach	
Wehrheim	Bad Homburg	

Location	Nearest City	Comments
Weier	Offenburg	
Weilerbach	Ramstein	
Westerburg		
Winsen		Off the highway to Walle

❑ Notes

Afghanistan

1. This is from Sun Tzun's famous book *The Art of War*.
2. The fact the Tora Bora and Zhawar Kili complexes were built near the Pakistani border was not accidental. It is now well known that al-Qaeda forces often sought refuge in the neighbouring country.
3. The existence of Tora Bora had long been known by American intelligence since it was they who helped Afghanis build it during the Soviet occupation.

Belgium

1. In the 1990s, NATO's main communications satellite was called 4A, and its previous one, called 3C, was the back-up.
2. The mobile command centre is known as Fast Break.

Canada

1. Churchill was so good at his job he was personally chosen to design the international fair Expo 67 in Montreal later on. His use of Critical Path Networking there also resulted in him completing the project on time.
2. The latter were more often used to confine the inebriated by the Military Police.
3. By 1993, annual maintenance costs had risen to $1.5 million.
4. An Aleksandr Pavlov was listed as a Soviet agent in John Barron's book on the KGB. See references.
5. In 1971, the squadron was disbanded and all the staff were assigned to the station proper.
6. Canadian Provincial Premiers are the equivalent to American state Governors.
7. See Appendix A for a complete list of the bunkers.
8. In Ontario, these exercises were called Iliad Trillium, and in Alberta, Iliad West. Other exercises were held under different names.
9. Some Filter Centres were also placed underground.
10. In Kingston, buildings such as the Ontario Mental Hospital, Queen's University and Loyalist Collegiate Vocational Institute were considered as public shelters, as were the police station and the offices for the local newspaper, the *Whig-Standard*.
11. Orders-in-Council are the Canadian equivalent to American Executive Orders.
12. As well, in 1964, all the Target Area Headquarters, except for Toronto's and Montreal's, were made dormant.
13. One military historical document indicated that in 1985, Bell Canada was no longer interested in cooperating with Army communications staff at the Ontario REGHQ in testing the remaining Toronto sirens.
14. The Canadian Forces Warning and Reporting System was dismantled in 1993. Most of the air-raid sirens were taken down during that and the following year.
15. Camp Debert was renamed Canadian Forces Station Debert in 1985. Despite this, it was still called a Camp after the redesignation.
16. The sirens were paid for and installed by the Department of National Defence. This was legislated in Order-in-Council PC 1965-1041. According to Canadian Forces Administrative Order 99-8, no less than seven organizations within DND were involved in the siren programme: the Director of Operations, Training and Coordination had overall coordinating responsibility, the Director for Communications and Electronics Plans and Requirements looked after control communications requirements, the Director for Communications Engineering Maintenance was responsible for system design, the Canadian Forces Fire Marshal

conducted noise surveys, the Director of Property Records and Legal Services maintained property records, the Director of Information Services handled public inquiries and the Commander of the Canadian Forces Communications Command managed the siren network (as part of the Canadian Forces Warning and Reporting System). The author vaguely remembers that the siren in Brockville, Ontario, on North Augusta Road had a sign that read 'DND Property 4758'.

17. A few sirens were kept in use, for example, at Sarnia, Ontario, for the chemical plants, and at a nuclear power station in New Brunswick.

18. OCIPEP has since been renamed the Emergency Measures and National Security Branch of Public Safety Canada.

19. Its cost of construction was apparently a paltry $400.

20. The federal government would end up building a new NDHQ in downtown Ottawa fifteen years later. Except for a test shaft, no building construction ever took place at the Corkstown Road site. Highway 417 now passes through the mine's property.

21. On 1 February 1968, the Canadian Army, the Royal Canadian Air Force and the Royal Canadian Navy ceased to be separate organizations and were combined to form the Canadian Armed Forces. Most Canadian Army Camps, RCAF Stations and shore naval bases became Canadian Forces Bases around the same time. Smaller installations became Canadian Forces Stations. In the 1990s, the Canadian Armed Forces were renamed the Canadian Forces.

22. An artesian well is an underground river.

23. Unofficially, the operations centre was known as the Blue Room.

24. The FYQ-93 consisted of two Hughes H5118MEs.

25. Air Movement Data includes flight number, aircraft type, flight type or 'mode' (e.g. normal, VIP etc.), altitude, speed and IFF transponder code.

26. Sergeant Pitcher died when the USAF E-3 AWACS aircraft he was assigned to crashed in Alaska in 1995.

27. In fact, when the City of Toronto asked for funds from the federal government in the 1960s to help convert its underground rail system into a network of public shelters, Ottawa ignored the request.

28. The committee was made up of three persons: the Prime Minister's national security advisor and the deputy minister of public works. The third person was not identified. He was most likely a member of the federal government's emergency measures branch since they are the only persons at the federal level who possess any experience in emergency government management.

China

1. Government buildings in Beijing on Chang An Street near the Forbidden City are also said to have bunkers underneath.

2. The author noticed the phrase 'imperialist running dogs' cast in a metal plaque that hangs in the Korean War museum in Dandong, Liaoning. The Chinese have not yet learned the benefits of political correctness.

3. The troops left two years after the end of the Korean War, in 1955.

4. Had Qian been allowed to stay in the United States, his experience and knowledge could have benefited the American space and missile industry. But there would always be those in counter-intelligence circles who would doubt his political loyalty. In the end, the United States' loss was clearly China's gain.

5. Some scholars claim that another reason China has not developed a large missile inventory is because of its high cost.

6. The estimate came from General Habiger, chief of US Strategic Command, speaking to the Senate Committee on Foreign Relations in 1999. The number of silos may have increased since.

7. The fuel and oxidizer for these missiles is stored separately, possibly in caves. The fact that the missiles are not always loaded with propellant reduces their reaction time, which strongly suggests they are not designed for quick retaliation.
8. The Central Military Commission is the Chinese high command.
9. In *The Iowa Scuba Affair* episode, a new USAF missile was deployed in Iowa under wheat fields.
10. The Chinese press does not seem to use the word 'Corps' when talking about the SAC. They just call it the 'Second Artillery.'
11. See Appendix C.
12. Hongling translates into 'Red Ridge'.
13. It should be pointed out that the 2006 White Paper specifically states that China should never 'use or threaten to use nuclear weapons against non-nuclear weapon states'. According to Schneider, some Chinese officers, such as Lieutenant-General Xion Guangkai and Colonel Zhu Chenghu, have used such threats against Taiwan anyway.

Czech Republic
1. The monument was destroyed in 1962, but the shelter underneath remained. For a number of years, it was used as a potato warehouse.

Denmark
1. Books often refer to its location at Finderup. It is really closer to Viborg.
2. This quotes a NATO fact sheet on the facility.
3. The feasibility of using an ice-sawdust mixture had also been looked at by the Canadian government during the Second World War.
4. Camp Century would not be the only underground research facility on Greenland. The US Army's Camp Tuto closer to Thule also has a research tunnel. This 1,100ft facility was used to test underground fuel and food storage.

France
1. Ironically, one of the detection posts was put at Place du Colonel Fabien, headquarters of the French Communist Party.
2. A Faraday cage is nothing but metal sheeting lining a structure's wall. It prevents internal electromagnetic emissions from escaping, nullifying attempts at radio eavesdropping.
3. The Houilles bunker also had the navy's main backup control centre. The centre was moved to Mont Verdun in around 2002.
4. QRA aircraft are kept on seven-minute alerts during daytime and fifteen-minute alerts at night. The French Air Force also has sharpshooter-staffed helicopters on alert for slow-moving aerial threats.
5. ELEBORE stands for 'écoute, localisation et brouillage des ondes électromagnétiques ennemies' or 'interception, direction-finding and jamming of enemy electromagnetic radiowaves'.
6. French scientists and military officers were not the only ones present that day. Israel had sent some individuals there as witnesses since it had recently taken the decision to build its own atomic bombs.
7. Guillaumat might have been influenced by the events in the Middle East in 1956, when Britain and France agreed to attack Egypt because it nationalized the Suez Canal. Their attack was called off because of American pressures and because the Soviets had threatened them with nuclear weapons. France did not want to be put in a position where it would ever be bullied again.

8. Later tests took place in French Polynesia, but after worldwide protests took place in 1991 over new testing, France used the facilities at Lop Nur, China.
9. The sand was removed by pulling a chain on an overhead hatch and letting gravity do its work. The same system existed at American missile silos and at Canadian bunkers.
10. It has never been revealed if the Minister of Defence or the Chief of the Strategic Air Forces would have the authority to launch nuclear weapons if the President or the Prime Minister were unavailable.
11. One key subsystem found in French LCCs that was perhaps not seen in American or Russian launch centres was their 'Dead Man's' feature. During peacetime, the launch officers were required to send a signal every hour to higher commands to let them know their status. During times of tension, the signal would have been sent every fifteen minutes. If the signals were not sent when expected, Air Commandos would have moved in to investigate.
12. While France left NATO in 1966, it returned to the fold in 1996 as a member of the all-important Military Committee. Conversely, it jealously guards its independence by refusing to allow the inclusion of its nuclear arsenal in NATO plans.

Germany

1. The formal German title of East Germany, the Deutsche Demokratische Republik, has to be one of the biggest jokes of the Cold War since the state was never democratic. Not only did its secret service, the STASI, hold surveillance files on practically everyone, the government itself could not move any pieces on the chessboard of the Cold War without Moscow's approval.
2. Marienthal refers to the name of the nearest town. Unofficially, the bunker was also known as the Regierungsbunker (Government Bunker). The German government used the codename 'Rose Garden' when referring to it.
3. The cost is an estimate since the German government had no official budget for it. It was spread among various ministries.
4. At one time, some of those plans included the relocation of the German government to the United States at Orlando, Florida, during a hot war.
5. Germany then had ten states, which were called Land (in plural, Landen).
6. In 1989, West Germany had 1,560 Geiger radiation measurement points. The network still exists but is now controlled by the Ministry of the Environment.
7. The Warndienst was to have the same identity crisis as in Canada and the United States in that it was renamed a number of times. During the Second World War, it was called the Reichsluftschutzbund (Reich Air Defence Organization), but in 1946 it became the Luftschutzverein (Air Defence Organization), then the Bundesluftschutzverband (Federal Air Defence Association), and later on the Bundesverband für den Selbstchutz (Federal Association for Self-Defence). It became the Warndienst in the mid-1950s, but is now known as the Federal Office for Civil Protection and Disaster Assistance.
8. The bunker is open for tours only occasionally.
9. The bunker for the Central Bank of North Rhine-Westphalia was at Satzvey.
10. Chlorotrifluoride was also studied as a rocket propellant oxidizer. These days, it is used to reprocess uranium from nuclear power plants by converting it into uranium hexafluoride.
11. Many details of the Falkenhagen bunker come from former East German army personnel who were stationed there. One could never obtain such details from the Russian army.
12. The 16th Air Army/PVO bunker was known by two codenames, 'Okean' for the 16th, and 'Nikel' for the PVO.

13. Two other bunkers exist at Zossen. One was a small communications exercise bunker near the PVO facility, and another closer to Zeppelin that was never finished and that was thought to become a new command centre. Also, the camp had an earth-covered vehicle shelter.
14. The radar station on the Erbeskopf is still operational. It includes a bunker.
15. The bunker is now owned by the Rennsteighöhe Hotel, which operates the old resort.
16. The BND has since moved to Berlin.
17. BARS stands for Bronirovani Autonom Radiovani Sistema or Hardened Autonomous Radio System.
18. All the Warsaw Pact countries had these BARS sites, except for Romania. One source claimed this was because Romania did not have the funds for it, although it is now known that that country was never an eager participant in the Pact.
19. The melting point of lead is 621 °F, while the melting point of aluminium is 1220 °F. During a nuclear explosion, when a lot of heat is generated, aluminium-lined blast doors would tend to melt less in place.

Gibraltar
1. The Royal Canadian Engineers built such structures as the Ottawa Tunnel and worked on Gort's Hospital. The Canadian sappers also built a pillbox at Devil's Bellows called Fort Canada. At one point in 1941, the men would use explosives to catch fish, but as this interfered with the navy's submarine detection equipment, they were ordered to cease and desist the practice.
2. The fact the British and American armies were tunnelling in Gibraltar was probably well known to the Germans. Every now and then, a plane flew overhead under what was likely a reconnaissance mission. The pilot was referred to by Canadian soldiers as 'Persistent Percival'.
3. In fact, the British government is allowed by treaty to remain at Gibraltar as long as monkeys live there.

Iraq
1. Some say Saddam was also influenced by the bunkers he had visited in Yugoslavia in the 1970s.

Israel
1. Apparently, the real reason Vanunu was let go was because of his association with certain Arabs.
2. A basement underneath another building contains a waste treatment plant.
3. Rodger Claire reveals in his book *Raid on the Sun* that two days after the 1981 Israeli Air Force attack on the Osirak reactor in Iraq, Israeli Prime Minister Menachem Begin praised the IAF's destruction of the reactor and of a complex 40m below it. The revelation was a slip of the tongue since there was no complex below Osirak; Begin was rather thinking about the set-up at Dimona when he made the announcement.
4. Vanunu was released from prison in 2004.
5. This is a few miles southeast of the Tel Nof air base.

Japan
1. Shun Akiba, *Imperial City Tokyo: Secret of a Hidden Underground Network*, Tokyo, Yosensha, 2002. The book was written in Japanese only.
2. This is a term used in the Basic Law on Emergency Preparedness of 15 November 1961.

3. The Diet is the Japanese Parliament.
4. The hangars, which were east of the Itazuke Air Base, are no longer used for military purposes. A stadium now stands nearby.
5. Japan ceased to use the Nike in the 1990s.
6. The operations centre was put in old military tunnels that dated from at least the Second World War. In the postwar period, the US Navy took over the base, refurbished the tunnels, and brought in radio intercept operators who used SP-600 receivers to listen in on Soviet and Chinese communications. Other personnel translated the recorded messages and sent whatever was useful to the National Security Agency. A fire in the bunker in 1965 killed several men.

Kazakhstan
1. This was in defiance of the 1972 treaty banning biological weapons signed by the Soviet Union.
2. In most books and magazines, writers refer to anthrax as the bug, whereas it is actually the disease.
3. Soviet Premier Josef Stalin, ever so suspicious of everyone, entrusted atomic weapons research to the head of his secret police, Lavrenti Beria. After both died in 1953, such research was performed by the Ministry of Medium Machine Building.

Latvia
1. The base at Zeltini is clearly marked by brown tourist signs.
2. During Soviet times, foreign tourists were quick to buy pins or badges that had the face of Lenin with the word 'Ogre' written beneath him.
3. When the bunker was an active facility, the staff had only fifteen minutes to eat because of space limitation. If one came in late, one was not allowed to eat.
4. One of the engines was used during the fierce 2005 ice storm to power the present rehabilitation centre above and the town of Litgane.
5. At the end of the tour, visitors are treated to what was a typical Soviet meal of macaroni and beef. When they have finished their meals, they are congratulated for having survived the ordeal.

North Korea
1. Yongbyon would later house another more powerful reactor. Also, the original Soviet model would later be upgraded.
2. The South Korean National Intelligence Service had stated in 2005 that it did not believe the North was planning the test, but CIA analysts who had studied satellite photos of the site knew otherwise. Here, the agency was right.
3. It has not been revealed with absolute certainty in the media whether the Taepodongs will live in caves, silos or earth-covered shelters.
4. Adult males who have completed their full-time service must remain in the reserves until age 60.
5. The Korean War Museum in Dandong, China, has a model of an underground North Korean air defence operations centre, but it does not state the location.
6. All the tunnels have been sealed off. Two have become tourist attractions.
7. The 9 October 2006 test was held here. It produced less than desired results as the 12 kiloton warhead only yielded 500 tons of explosive force.

Norway
1. Until recently, the Department included a special forces unit known as HV-016. The unit's exact purpose is not known by the author.

2. According to Wikipedia, its entrances have been digitally removed from Internet satellite search engines.

Poland
1. This is located between the villages of Chocianow and Trzebien.
2. The bunker went from housing one Party to hosting many parties.
3. A similar depot existed at Sulecin.

Russia
1. The stations are outfitted with heavy blast doors that blend with the decor. One hint of their location is the quarter-circle steel beam embedded in the floor upon which the door's roller would travel on.
2. Some civil defence equipment is stored in grey horizontal canisters at every station. This equipment may consist of flashlights and perhaps walkie-talkies.
3. A Russian television news item showed visitors going through the water-logged tunnels under Moscow State University clearly indicating they are no longer maintained.
4. One source states this bunker is really at Zarya.
5. Apparently, the 15th Main Directorate operated out of a bunker near the Yugo-Zapadnaya underground rail station.
6. Other Soviet underground rail systems were also designed for civil defence. Baku, the capital of the then-Soviet Socialist Republic of Azerbaijan, apparently has a underground rail system that was never completed. A declassified 1958 CIA report on Soviet civil defence stated it was built in the mid-1950s with sheltering in mind.
7. Industrial shelters have been reported at Magadan, one as a basement shelter and one as a detached underground structure. These were built in the mid-1950s. The second one could hold 1,600 persons. Another bunker lies next to an administration building at a tank factory in Khabarovsk.
8. While such training was mandatory, the CIA reported in the 1970s that many citizens did not take the training seriously.
9. Logically, the two command posts should be underground, but the author has not found any evidence of this.
10. Given that the Soviets and the East Germans built bunkers under government buildings in East Germany, it is entirely reasonable to think that the Soviets did the same in and around Moscow.
11. Bunkers are also said to exist under the Rossiya Hotel, under the White House and under Christ the Saviour Cathedral.
12. This was discovered by a remote viewer working for the CIA.
13. 'R' for *Raketa*.
14. The Strategic Rocket Forces are known in Russia by the initials PBCH. This translates into English as RVSN (Raketnyye Voyska Strategicheskovo Naznacheniya).
15. In the beginning of the RVSN's history, some missile units were called Engineering Brigades and were included within Missile Corps. The Corps were converted into Armies in 1970.
16. As an example, Unit 21649 is one of the road-mobile ICBM units. Its regiment number is not known by the author. Also, the PBS documentary *Russia's Nuclear Warriors* showed Launch Control Centre 97690 of the Tatishchevo missile base, but this may instead refer to a Regiment.
17. For instance, the 60th Missile Division at Tatishchevo is also known as the Taman Missile Division.
18. During the failed putsch of August 1991, when Premier Gorbachev was held under

house arrest at his dacha, the military aide who carried his Cheget and who was staying in a nearby lodge was ordered back to Moscow, with the suitcase and without the Premier. This begs the question: who does the aide report to? The Premier or his military superiors?

19. This is different than 'launch under attack', which states that missiles should only be fired when there are clear indications that the nation is actually under attack. This can be confirmed by visual sighting or by nuclear detonation detection methods. The disadvantage of LUA is that it gives forces very little time to act. Launch on warning gives a greater window of reaction time.

20. Together, all the communications systems and links, including the 'footballs', make up the Kazbek system.

21. There are indications that after the coup in August 1991, the NGS lost his 'voting rights' and that such rights were transferred to the Commander-in-Chief of the RVSN. This situation may have since been reversed.

22. The preliminary command is also sent by the General Staff to mobile missile regiments and to long-range aviation units and to submarines. Once the order is received, the truck-mounted missiles will move to their launch points, bombers will take off and submarines will proceed to their launch co-ordinates.

23. Under some circumstances, the preliminary and direct commands can be sent at the same time.

24. Some Russian officers claim that normally there is no delay in the launch of a missile. If a full-scale attack is expected, there is not much point in holding some of the missiles back.

25. The Doomsday Machine may not have been entirely a Russian idea, since RVSN officers may have borrowed the concept from the USAF's Emergency Rocket Communications System.

26. One retired intelligence analyst from the Defense Intelligence Agency doubted the 'Dead Hand' system even existed, or that if it did, it was never made operational. Former missileer Bruce Blair and former RVSN officer Valery Yarynich would prove him wrong by revealing details. Yarynich even worked on the system in the 1980s.

27. At one time, Soviet leaders considered creating a fully automated system that would launch missiles by itself if all the detection systems were destroyed. The idea was eventually dropped. The concept was referred to in the 1964 film *Dr Strangelove*.

28. Since then, Russia has installed more satellites that would be in a position to confirm launches.

29. The eighteen-bomb estimate comes from Stephen Meyer's essay *Soviet Theatre Nuclear Forces*.

30. The advantage of a cold launch is that the silo is not severely damaged after the missile has exited. It can thus be re-used, although some say it can take a few days to make it ready again. If Moscow counted on a quick victory, the silos would be useless.

31. See Lithuania for an example.

32. Russian launch facilities are known as Shakhtnaya Puskovaya Ustanovka.

33. At one time, the shifts were eight hours, then twelve.

34. The world of the RVSN is very much male-dominated. None of the launch control officers are female. Women serve only in support roles, such as communications technicians or clerks.

35. When one of the Barnaul division's missile bases could not pay its electricity bill in 2000, the power company turned off the power. After a group of armed soldiers stormed the generating station, the electricity was restored.

36. Some of the Russian spies arrested in the United States in 2010 were said to be looking for information on American 'bunker-buster' bombs.

37. Despite the high security around nuclear weapons, it is still possible for defective

individuals to pass through the screening process. In March 1994, one soldier shot his commanding officer and others with a submachine gun at the Barnaul mobile ICBM base. It was not clear, however, if he was a guard or a missileer.

38. Writing in his essay 'The Nuclear Forces and Doctrine of the Russian Federation', Mark Schneider claims that the Russian government actually considered launching a nuclear strike against the United States because of NATO's attack on former Yugoslavia in the 1990s. Cooler heads must have prevailed.

Saudi Arabia

1. Two locations, at al-Sulaiyil and al-Joffer, are firing bases and another location at Rawdah is suspected of being a storage base. One Internet satellite imaging site shows many entrances to underground facilities at the latter.

South Korea

1. The same media reports claimed the Korean government has its own bunker in Seoul called 'B-1'.
2. It is not known by the author if this alternate command centre is underground.

Sweden

1. Public shelters in Sweden all display the standard orange and blue civil defence sign with the word Skyddsrum.
2. The air-raid sirens still exist today and would be used more to warn the public of natural disasters. They are tested every three months.
3. The sale of Muskö was a reflection of the greater trend in the reduction of the Swedish armed forces. For several years, the Royal Swedish Navy kept mines moored to the sea floor ready to be set off under passing ships during wartime. These were removed in 2010. Also, effective that same year, military service, which had been mandatory since the 1700s, ended.
4. Both the Royal Swedish Navy and the Royal Swedish Air Force would eventually lose their 'Royal' titles.
5. There were also hints the sub was examining or tampering with underwater mines maintained by the Royal Swedish Navy.
6. Wennerstrom died at age 99 in 2006.
7. The Swedish Bloodhounds were considered one of the most secret weapons in the country. Some of the missiles were stored in secret underground shelters that were usually several kilometres from the launching base. The staff even had to wear civilian clothes and drive in ordinary cars or trucks to get to the base.
8. The dummy guns were provided with an internal heat source and were rotated on occasion to fool spy satellites into thinking they were active.
9. More recently, the facility exhibited the Terracotta Warriors of China.

Switzerland

1. This fact was revealed by former KGB archivist Vasili Mitrokhin in his book with Christopher Andrew, *The Sword and the Shield*. In 1998, the Swiss federal police retrieved a booby-trapped suitcase that contained an agent radio near the town of Belfaux. When troops sprayed the case with a water cannon, it exploded.
2. The Swiss government even considered adopting nuclear weapons for defensive purposes in the 1950s.
3. Internet satellite photos also show what looks like a square helicopter landing pad nearby.
4. There were also apparently plans to relocate a number of Swiss federal politicans to

Liss Ard House in Skibbereen, Ireland, during a nuclear conflict. Some say this hotel would have also been used by the Swiss army's secret P26 stay-behind network.

5. A canton is similar to an American state or a British county.
6. Soldiers would appear in civilian dress and change once below. At the end of the day, they would reverse the routine.
7. Jura canton was the only state not to build its own bunker. Instead, it placed its emergency operations centre in an agricultural school at Courtemelon.
8. As of 2010, there were only about 9,500 forts left in operation in Switzerland.
9. The Swiss Air Force's designation for the Bloodhound was BL-64, with the number indicating the year it was accepted by the Swiss Parliament.
10. The Bloodhound-2's continuous wave radar was considered an improvement over the first model since its pulse radar was susceptible to jamming.
11. There may be no signs advertising the fact a nearby airfield is military, but motorists are nevertheless warned to keep on the lookout for taxiing aircraft.
12. The Buochs base is located very close to the Pilatus Aircraft plant at Stans. The plant was used as Auric Goldfinger's factory in the James Bond film *Goldfinger*.
13. Payerne does have several earth-covered hangars instead.
14. Another unit found at Meiringen is the Festungwachtkorps' test centre.

Taiwan
1. Even today, most mainland Chinese will insist that Taiwan belongs to the PRC and should not be considered a separate state. Yet, the ROC has its own passport, currency and its own style of government. Most Taiwanese are not interested in living under communist rule.
2. At one time, Taiwan even considered developing its own nuclear weapons.
3. The island was heavily shelled by the Chinese army in 1958. In addition, there are stories that Chinese frogmen have swum to Kinmen, killed guards and cut off their ears as trophies. It is one of the reasons some of the beaches are mined today.
4. At least one of the shelters no longer exists.

United Kingdom
1. The letters in ROTOR do not stand for anything.
2. Some of the AAORs were located in earth-covered buildings.
3. Initially, it was planned to have sixty-five stations, but the GCI sites at Calvo and Charmy Down were deleted from the roster in 1955. The entire network was only officially transferred to Fighter Command in 1956.
4. AN stands for Army-Navy. This is because the American technical nomenclature system was devised by those two services. FPS stands for: Fixed (as in immobile), Radar, Searching. The Army and Navy could not use the letter 'R' as the second letter because it stood for Radio.
5. If, however, one knew a radar station existed near a certain town, one needed only to spot the symbol for an antenna to find the station's exact location.
6. Britain's main deterrent at this time was the V-bomber force comprising Valiants, Victors and Vulcans. At its peak in 1961, it had 164 such aircraft in 17 squadrons that could be dispersed to about 36 airfields. As of 1969, the nation's deterrence would come from RN submarines only.
7. The Government Post Office then ran the nation's telephone system. This has since been privatized and is now British Telecom.
8. In April 2007, Strike Command amalgamated with Personnel and Training Command to form the new Air Command. Headquarters are at High Wycombe.
9. VIII Bomber Command would become the 8th Air Force later on.

10. It was also described as an underground telephone exchange.
11. James Gibson in *The History of the US Nuclear Arsenal* claims the W84 had an 80 kiloton yield.
12. One of the security features of PALs is the limited-try system. After a few unsuccessful attempts at unlocking it, the system will shut down and new attempts will be ignored. Another feature is a 'command-disable' mechanism. If a unit commander suspects his weapons are about to be stolen, he can enter a special code that renders some of the components in the warhead useless.
13. By 1973, there would be 10 regions in England and Wales, 3 in Scotland and 1 in Northern Ireland.
14. There were also rumours that the bunkers stocked a supply of cyanide, but this has not been confirmed by the author.
15. This too has not been confirmed by the author.
16. One of the problems was chaos in communications. Staff did not know who the messages were coming from or where they were supposed to go. Also, staff did not seem to know what to do with the civilian population if radiation levels were to be high.
17. The bunker at Hack Green, for instance, became RGHQ 10.2.
18. To determine the location of a burst, one unlucky individual had to step outside the bunker to retrieve the recording paper from the camera.
19. By the 1980s, however, only 873 were in operation. Redundancy forced the closure of many.
20. Drakelow was soon dropped as a central government relocation site.
21. Nations represented here were the United States, France, Ireland, Canada, Australia, New Zealand and probably NATO countries such as West Germany, Norway and Belgium.
22. The bunker would also be known later on as 'Burlington' and 'Turnstile'.
23. It was also known briefly as 'Linstock'.

United States

1. One source stated the bunker was 600,000sq ft.
2. The *Federal Register* is an official document that lists all the decisions made by the President.
3. The government also maintains a Strategic Petroleum Reserve. Some of this oil is stored in Texas.
4. Its codename may have been 'Low Point' at one time.
5. There are indications that presidential COG plans still exist today. The White House Military Office presently includes an entity that looks after presidential continuity.
6. On the other hand, many people in town knew there was something there.
7. In fact, one former employee claimed it was the 'bunker that wasn't really there'.
8. Emergency Action Messages can be any urgent message sent to bomber, missile or submarine crews. The most important type of EAM is the Emergency War Order. EWOs would order crews to launch missiles or drop bombs. EAMs are unofficially known as 'Red Rockets' and, for a while, were also known as 'White Dots'.
9. The Navy-Air Force interservice resentment over nuclear arms was nothing new. Certain admirals had revolted in 1949 when the USAF was given generous funding for its bombers and nuclear bombs. SAC in turn had always resented the Navy's development of nuclear weapons, and when its Commander, Air Force General Thomas Power, recommended in 1958 that he control Polaris SLBMs, the Navy went, in a manner of speaking, ballistic. A compromise was reached where the JSTPS, which would be run by the SAC Commander, would have a naval deputy. The Air Force still came out a winner of sorts since the JSTPS would be based on Air Force

territory at Offutt AFB. (Today, the JSTPS is known simply as J-5.)

10. The DIA's Directorate of Analysis includes a section dedicated to researching bunkers throughout the world. It is the Underground Facilities Analysis Center.

11. These quotes come from the Natural Resources Defense Council's *A Time for Change*.

12. China was dropped from the SIOP in 1982 at President Reagan's insistence. Reagan wanted to use China as a partner to contain the Soviet Union. One way the partnership was cemented was by having the CIA help the Chinese government set up two signals intelligence stations in northwestern China at Qitai and Korla to eavesdrop on Soviet missile tests and other military communications. The two sites were code-named 'Chestnut' and were run by China with the 'take' shared with the CIA. But as the Chinese nuclear arsenal grew and as Beijing began its sabre-rattling over Taiwan in the mid-1990s, it was re-inserted into the SIOP in 1998.

13. In 1985, the SIOP had 16,000 aimpoints, which was about one-third of the National Strategic Target Database.

14. In 2010, the White House confirmed that it had 5,113 nuclear warheads in service.

15. The other two SAC operations centres were in surface buildings. The one at March AFB was in Building 2605 on Riverside Drive. It is no longer used.

16. The Defense Supply Agency was renamed the Defense Logistics Agency in 1977.

17. In the early 1960s, the Soviets detonated a 58 megaton device. Had one of these high-yield weapons been used against Cheyenne Mountain, the vibrations caused by the blast wave would have destroyed the operations centre.

18. The Missile Correlation Center was previously known as the Missile Warning Center.

19. The mine was later acquired by Iron Mountain.

20. Consolidated Vultee later became General Dynamics' Convair Division.

21. SM stands for Strategic Missile.

22. Some sources say the silos were rated at 300psi.

23. One of the air intake pipes doubled as an emergency exit.

24. The TPS-39 operated on frequencies between 1710MHz and 1780MHz with a power output of 1W. Its range varied from 10ft to 130ft.

25. The Minuteman would later be known as the LGM-30.

26. The public would later learn that the much-publicized missile gap really did exist, but in the United States' favour. In the early 1960s, the Soviets had a very small number of ICBMs.

27. The adoption of REACT consoles was only one part of the costly Minuteman modernization programme. At the same time, the Guidance Replacement Program saw the acceptance of new TRW NS-50 guidance packages to replace the current NS-20, the Propulsion Replacement Program called for the replacement of missile motors and the Propulsion System Rocket Engine Life Extension Program planned for the refurbishment of the post-boost stage.

28. The problem was dubbed the 'purple plague'.

29. An underground Launch Control Center can be destroyed either by a direct hit or by the vibrations caused by a nuclear blast. If the USAF relied on the latter, perfect accuracy may not be necessary.

30. As of 2001, the Russians had 369 launch control centres.

31. Given this, the W88 warhead carried by the Trident sea-launched ballistic missile would be the front runner for attacks on silos.

32. One source claimed this eight-digit number also armed the warhead, but another source stated that the warhead could only be armed (by itself) after going through a period of acceleration in flight, then deceleration.

33. This Hardened Intersite Cable System was deactivated as part of START.

Confirmations are now probably sent by radio.

34. Missile Wings compete for the Blanchard Trophy at Vandenberg AFB every year. As well, launch crews are tested monthly on launch simulations called Olympic Play. The test results are used in SIOP planning.

35. Bruce Blair revealed that until 1977, the launch enable number was set to 0000 0000. SAC had never issued proper codes because, apparently, it did not want to slow down the launch process.

36. Officers aboard ALCS aircraft would use the shotgun approach to transmit an EAM to an LCC, that is by sending the signal over several different frequencies or over different types of systems. Some of these aircraft belong to the 4th Airborne Command and Control Squadron at Ellsworth AFB, South Dakota.

37. It is not known by the author if this strict policy is still in place, although one source has stated to the author that even when the Alert Response Teams were fired upon by crazies or by disgruntled farmers, they were forbidden from firing back.

38. EMP tests were done on a Malmstrom AFB silo in 1968–72. Some say these tests led to the onset of cancer in workers and ranchers in the area. An attempt to sue the USAF was quashed when the Air Force refused to turn over test data.

39. As of the time of writing, launch crews consisted of three individuals where two would stay in the capsule and a third would remain topside in the MAF. An exchange would occur every twenty-four hours.

40. The Air Force has disclosed that between 1975 and 1990, approximately 5 per cent of applicants failed to pass this screening. Missileers who have serious marital problems can also be rejected.

41. Only in 1993 would a woman command a missile squadron.

42. Blair served as a missile officer at Malmstrom AFB from 1972–74.

43. Some of those other bases included Blytheville AFB, Arkansas, Fairchild AFB, Washington, and Wurtsmith AFB, Michigan.

44. Ironically, the first MX train was to enter service in December 1991, the same month the Soviet Union ceased to exist.

45. Some sources say the Nike's ceiling was in excess of 150,000ft, which, whatever the figure, was much more than the Ajax's 60,000ft.

46. The PAL device was tamper proof. If anyone tried to force it, an explosive charge would go off. The PALs were called 'Kennedy Devices' since they were installed only after President Kennedy insisted upon better protection for nuclear warheads. They were placed mostly on tactical weapons.

47. Another accident took place on 30 September 1955 at the White Sands Proving Grounds while a missile was being tested. The explosion killed one crewman. In yet another accident, at Porter, Indiana, one crewman working below in a magazine died after a Hercules descended upon him.

48. A commemorative stone has since been installed at Guardian Park in Sandy Hook, New Jersey.

49. A decade later, Sharon died at the hands of Charles Manson.

50. Some sites in Alaska and Florida remained open as a defence against the Soviet Union and Cuba, respectively. They were closed in the late 1970s.

51. A long-range missile's mid-course phase takes place outside the earth's atmosphere; thus the term 'exo-atmospheric'.

Appendix E

1. May no longer exist.

❏ References

After The Battle. No. 87, 'The High Wycombe Air HQ'

Air Forces Monthly. Various issues

Alberta. *Public Safety Services Act*, Chap. P-30.5, Revised Statutes of Alberta

Albright, David and Kevin O'Neill. *Solving the North Korean Nuclear Puzzle.* Washington, DC: Institute for Science and International Security, 2000

Alexander, Brian and Alistair Miller (eds). *Tactical Nuclear Weapons.* Washington, DC: Brassey's, 2003

Alibek, Ken. *Biohazard.* New York: Random House, 1999

Amherst. Summer 1994

Amherst College monograph. *Amherst College Underground Storage Facility.* n.d.

Andrew, Christopher and Vasili Mitrokhin. *The Sword and the Shield.* New York: Basic Books, 1999

Aradcom Argus, US Army Air Defense Command magazine. Various issues

Army Logistician. The Official Magazine of United States Army Logistics, July–August 1974

Arkin, William M. *Code Names.* Hanover, NH: Steerforth Press, 2005

Arkin, William M. and R.W. Fieldhouse. *Nuclear Battlefields.* Cambridge, MA: Ballinger Publishing Company, 1985

Arkin, William M. and Robert S. Norris. *Nuclear Alerts after the Cold War.* Washington, DC: Natural Resources Defense Council, 1993

Association of Air Force Missileers Newsletter. Various issues

Aviation Week and Space Technology, 12 May 1997, 25 January 1999, 23 August 1999, 8 May 2000 and 23 June 2002

Baar, James and William E. Howard. *Combat Missileman.* New York: Harcourt Brace & World, 1961

Bahmanyar, Mir. *Afghanistan Cave Complexes, 1979–2004.* Oxford, UK: Osprey Publishing, 2004

Ball, Deborah Yarsike. 'How Safe is Russia's Nuclear Arsenal', *Jane's Intelligence Review*, December 1999

Ball, Desmond. *Can Nuclear War be Controlled?*, Adelphi Papers, No. 169. London: The International Institute for Strategic Studies, 1981

Bamford, James. *The Puzzle Palace.* New York: Penguin Books, 1983

—. *Body of Secrets.* New York: Doubleday, 2001

—. *A Pretext for War.* New York: Anchor Books, 2005

Barnaby, Frank (ed.). *Tactical Nuclear Weapons: European Perspectives.* London: Taylor & Francis Limited, 1978

Barron, John. *The KGB. The Secret Work of Soviet Secret Agents.* New York: Bantam Books, 1974

Beach, B. Personal communication. Hornings Mills, Ont.: 1997

Bergner, Paul. *Befehl 'Filigran'. Die Bunker der DDR-Führung für den Ernstfall.* Basdorf: FB-Verlag, 2001.

Berhow, Mark A. *US Strategic and Defensive Missile Systems, 1950–2004.* New York: Osprey Publishing, 2005

Berman, Robert P. and John C. Baker. *Soviet Strategic Forces. Requirements and Responses.* Washington, DC: The Brookings Institution, 1982

Bermudez, Joseph S. Jr. 'The Rise and Rise of North Korea's ICBMs', *Jane's International Defense Review*, July 1999

Best, Stefan. *Geheime Bunkeranlagen der DDR.* Stuttgart, Germany: Motor Buch Verlag, 2009

Bhatia, Shyam and Daniel McGrory. *Saddam's Bomb.* London: Time Warner Paperbacks, 2002

Blair, Bruce G. *Strategic Command and Control. Redefining the Nuclear Threat.* Washington, DC: The Brookings Institution, 1985

—. *The Logic of Accidental Nuclear War.* Washington, DC: The Brookings Institution, 1993

—. *Global Zero Alert for Nuclear Forces.* Washington, DC: The Brookings Institution, 1995

Bluth, Christopher. 'Russia's Nuclear Forces: A Clear and Present Danger?', *Jane's Intelligence Review*, December 1997

Bobrick, Benson. *Parsons Brinckerhoff. The First 100 Years.* New York: Van Nostrand Reinhold Company, 1985

Bolt, P.J. and A.S. Willner. *China's Nuclear Future*. London: Lynne Rienner Publishers, 2006

Boyne, Sean. 'In the mouth of the tiger: Taiwanese forces on Kinmen', *Jane's Intelligence Review*, May 1997

Bracken, Paul. *The Command and Control of Nuclear Forces*. New Haven, CT: Yale University Press, 1983

Bright, Christopher John. 'Nike Defends Washington. Antiaircraft Missiles in Fairfax County, Virginia, during the Cold War, 1954–1974', *Virginia Magazine of History and Biography*, Vol. 105, No. 3 (Summer 1997)

Brown, D. Clayton. *Rivers, Rockets and Readiness: Army Engineers in the Sunbelt*. n.p.: 1979

Brownell, W. 'In Defense of Peace', *Survive*, October 1983

Brun, Jean-François. 'Le réseau interarmées d'alerte', *Revue Historique des Armées*, No. 262, 2011

Bugas, Paul 'Fritz'. 'Under the Greenbrier Hotel – The Bunker that Protected Our Congress', *Association of Air Force Missileers News*, December 1997

Burrows, William E. *Deep Black. The Startling Truth Behind America's Top Secret Spy Satellites*. New York: Berkley Books, 1986

Calder, Nigel. *Nuclear Nightmares, an investigation into possible wars*. London: BBC, 1979

Calgary Herald, 13 April 1995 and 6 January 2003

Campbell, Christy. *Nuclear Facts*. Agincourt, ON: Methuen Publications, 1984

Campbell, Duncan. *War Plan UK*. London: Burnett Books in association with the Hutchinson Publishing Group, 1982

—. 'War Games', *New Statesman and Society*, 26 May 1989

Canada. Canadian Forces Base North Bay Public Affairs, letter to author, 8 April 1998, file W1000-1

—. Canadian Forces School of Communications and Electronics Archives, 'A History of Canadian Forces Station Carp: Richardson Detachment'

—. Department of National Defence, Directorate of History and Heritage file 112.016 (D12) Canadian National Survival Attack Warning System, Operating Instructions and Procedures, April 1963

—. Department of National Defence, DHH file 81/259, Canadian Army Operational Research Establishment Report No. 106, The Post Attack Situation in Canada, 1960–1970, Casualties and Resources, 1960

—. Department of National Defence, DHH file 72/163, Emergency Measures Organization, Continuity of Government Planning Guide

—. Department of National Defence, DHH file 112.042 (D1), Civil Defence Survival Operations

—. Department of National Defence, DHH file 327.009 (D422), Buildings and Grounds, Nuclear Detonation and Fallout Reporting Posts, Filter Centres & NUDET Posts, Progress Reports, Volume 3

—. Department of National Defence, DHH file 327.009 (D423), HQ Western Command Buildings and Grounds. Fallout Reporting Posts, Filter Centres and Nudet Reporting Posts, ca. 1962

—. Department of National Defence, DHH file 325.052 (D3), National Survival, Organization and Establishment of Nuclear Detonation and Fallout Reporting System

—. Department of National Defence, DHH file 73/1223, Civil Defence

—. Department of National Defence, DHH file 325.009 (D826), Organization and Administration, NSAWS, TAHQ Almonte

—. Department of National Defence, DHH file 112.3S2 (D57), Organization and Administration, Survival, Fallout Reporting System

—. Department of National Defence, DHH file R P Penhold

—. Department of National Defence, DHH file 80/487, Civil Emergency Operations, Nuclear War Plan

—. Department of National Defence, DHH file 1326-1827, Annual Historical Report, 743 Communications Squadron

—. Department of National Defence, DHH file 1326-1828, Annual Historical Report, 731 Communications Squadron

—. Department of National Defence, DHH file 1326-1831, Annual Historical Report, 706 Communications Squadron

—. Department of National Defence, DHH file 1326-2716, Annual Historical Report, RMED Calgary

—. Department of National Defence, National Defence Headquarters, letter to author, 4 October 1995, file 1463-(A)95/0323

—. Report of the Department of Public Works for the fiscal year ended 31 March 1962

—. Reports of the Department of National Health and Welfare for the fiscal years ended 31 March 1963 and 31 March 1964

—. Emergency Measures Organization, *EMO National Digest*, August 1961, February 1962, June 1962, August 1962, October 1962, December 1962, June 1964, April–May 1968, December 1973–January 1974, February–March 1974

—. Emergency Preparedness Canada, *Annual Review*, 1982, 1985 and 1987

—. Emergency Preparedness Canada, *Emergency Planning Digest*, 1974–1998

—. Emergency Preparedness Canada, *Emergency Government Headquarters Operational Procedures Planning Guide*. EPC Publication 7/78

—. Emergency Preparedness Canada, *Emergency Planning Canada Readiness Plan (War)*. EPC Publication 4/78. Revised 1980

—. *Info Source. Sources of Federal Government Information 1997–1998*

—. Minister Responsible for Emergency Preparedness, *Emergency Preparedness Canada Report to Parliament on the operation of the Emergency Planning Act. April 1, 1989–March 31, 1990*

—. House of Commons Debates, 27 May 1960 and 31 May 1960

—. *Wartime Public Protection in the 1980s*, final report of the Task Force on War Planning and Concepts of Operations, 1985

—. Library and Archives Canada, National Defence files, Record Group 24, Accession 1983-84/215, Box 219, File S-2001-91/B33, Vol. 1, 1 Radiation Detection Unit, Exercise Buffalo

—. Library and Archives Canada, National Defence files, RG 24, Accession 1983-84/215, Box 218, File 2001-91/B37, Vols 1–8, Canadian emergency measures

—. Library and Archives Canada, National Defence files, RG 24, Accession 1983-84/215, Box 321, File S-2001-1993/O Vol. 1, Organization and Administration, Emergency Government Zones and Zone HQs

—. Library and Archives Canada, National Defence files, RG 24, Vol. 19161, File S-2090-34/336, Vol. 2, Organization, Civil Defence, United Kingdom

—. Library and Archives Canada, National Defence files, RG 24, Vol. 19161, File S-2090-1, vols 6 and 10, Canadian civil defence

—. Library and Archives Canada, National Defence files, RG 24M, Accession 956002, Layout of emergency government transmitter and receiver sites

—. Library and Archives Canada, National Defence files, RG 24, Accession 1983-84/049, Box 107, File 096-103-6, Vols 1 and 2, Planning-Emergency Measures, Federal Government. Contains Department of Transport emergency legislation, Prime Minister's relocation plan, wartime roles of federal departments, federal relocation sites, Geneva Convention of 1949

—. Library and Archives Canada, National Defence files, RG 24, Vol. 4212, File 69-181-267-3, Comparison of US SAMs

—. Library and Archives Canada, National Defence files, RG 24, Vol. 21394, File CSC-1834-1, Underground Construction

—. Library and Archives Canada, National Defence files, RG 24, Vol. 20736, File 5-11-1, Vol. 1, 'Civil Defence'

—. Library and Archives Canada, National Defence files, RG 24, Vol. 20736, File 5-11-1, Vol. 4, 'Civil Defence'

—. Library and Archives Canada, Department of Foreign Affairs file, RG 25, Volume 10160, File 27-24-3-1, Defence, Civil Defence and Emergency Planning, Organization and Conferences, International Civil Defence Organization

—. Library and Archives Canada, National Health and Welfare files, RG 29, Vol. 654, File 102-2-10, Reports and Returns, Civil Defence Progress Reports

—. Library and Archives Canada, National Health and Welfare files, RG 29, Vol. 654, File 102-3-2B, Cooperation with government departments, Department of National Defence

—. Library and Archives Canada, National Health and Welfare files, RG 29, Vol. 656, File 102-5-1, Civil defence cooperation with USA

—. Library and Archives Canada, National Health and Welfare files, RG 29, Vol. 672, File 106-2-52, Training Exercises and Operations. Operation Alert 1959 (For notes on US emergency management in the 1950s, incl. agency responsibilities and directives)

—. Library and Archives Canada, National Health and Welfare files, RG 29, Vol. 742, File 118-4-1, Nato: Russia, 'Civil Defence in the USSR', 7 June 1957

—. Library and Archives Canada, Emergency Measures Organization files, RG 57, Accession 1983-84/212, Box 3, File 1285-PR/06, Construction and Maintenance, REGHQ, Ontario

—. Library and Archives Canada, Emergency Measures Organization files, RG 57, Accession 1989-90/212, Box 3, File 1010-FD/52, Part 1, Emergency Orders and Regulations, Federal Departments, Canadian Broadcasting Corporation

—. Library and Archives Canada, Emergency Measures Organization files, RG 57, Accession 1989-90/212, Box 3, File 1010-7, Part 1, Emergency Orders and Regulation, Censorship

—. Library and Archives Canada, Emergency Measures Organization files, RG 57, Accession 1989-90/212, Box 5, File 1250-3, Part 1, Construction and Maintenance, Emergency Government Facilities, Department of Public Works Progress Report, Zone Emergency Government Headquarters and Relocation Units, 1963–67

—. Library and Archives Canada, Emergency Measures Organization files, RG 57, Accession Number 1989-90/216, Box 4, File 1140-2, Communications Planning, Canadian Forces Warning and Reporting System

—. Library and Archives Canada, Emergency Measures Organization files, RG 57, Accession 1989-90/216, Box 5, File 1200-4, Emergency Government Facilities, Peacetime Maintenance and Operations

—. Library and Archives Canada, Emergency Measures Organization files, RG 57, Accession 1989-90/216, Box 6, File 1400-61, External Liaison, Romania, Civil Defence

—. Library and Archives Canada, Emergency Measures Organization files, RG 57, Vol. 55, File S-1216-4, Manning, Central Complex, Operational Information Centre

—. Library and Archives Canada, Emergency Measures Organization files, RG 57, Vol. 55, File C-1221-1. Manning, Federal Government Departments, Relocation Centres and Units, General

—. Library and Archives Canada, Emergency Measures Organization files, RG 57, Vol. 57, File 1237-1, Municipal Emergency Government HQs-General

—. Library and Archives Canada, Emergency Measures Organization files, RG 57, Vol. 57, File 1240-PR/06, Vol. 1, Manning/Planning and Administration, Federal/Provincial Government Departments, Relocation Centres and Units, Ontario

—. Library and Archives Canada, Emergency Measures Organization files, RG 57, Vol. 58, File 1245-PR/06. Planning, Administration and Construction, Zone Emergency HQs, Ontario

—. Library and Archives Canada, Emergency Measures Organization files, RG 57, Vol. 59, File 1270-2(4), Construction and Maintenance, Federal Relocation Centres and Units, Arnprior, Ontario

—. Library and Archives Canada, Public Works and Government Services Canada, Freedom of Information request ATI 960569/RM, 16 January 1997

—. Library and Archives Canada, Federal Civil Defence Coordinator, *Civil Defence Bulletin*, No. 43.

Carmody, John and Raymond Sterling. *Underground Building Design*. New York: Van Nostrand Reinhold Company, 1983

Catudal, Honoré M. *Soviet Nuclear Strategy from Stalin to Gorbachev*. Atlantic Highlands, NJ: Humanities Press International, 1988

CBS Evening News, 1 July 1998

Chinoy, Mike. *Meltdown. The Inside Story of the North Korean Nuclear Crisis*. New York: St Marin's Griffin, 2008

Citizen, Ottawa, Ontario, 18 August 1987, 26 December 1994, 10 October 1995, 27 October 1996 and 14 September 1998

Claire, Rodger W. *Raid on the Sun*. New York: Broadway Books, 2004

Cochran, Thomas B., William M. Arkin, Robert S. Norris and Jeffrey I. Sands. *Nuclear Weapons Databook, Volume IV: Soviet Nuclear Weapons*. Washington, DC: Natural Resources Defense Council, 1989

Cockburn, Andrew and Leslie Cockburn. *One Point Safe*. New York: Doubleday, 1997
Cocroft, Wayne D. and Roger J.C. Thomas. *Cold War. Building for Nuclear Confrontation. 1946–1989*. Swindon: English Heritage, 2004
Cohen, Yoel. *Nuclear Ambiguity. The Vanunu Affair*. London: Sinclair-Stevenson, 1992
Cold War Times. The Internet Newsletter of the Cold War Museum. Various issues
Cole, Merle T. 'W-25: The Davidsonville Site and Maryland Air Defense, 1950–1974', *Maryland Historical Magazine*, Vol. 80, No. 3, Fall 1985
Comité de rédaction de la Base aérienne 200. *Les Sentinelles de la Paix*. Paris: Editions du Zéphyr, 1999
Coughlin, T.G. Flt Lt. 'City in a Mountain', *Roundel*, Vol. 13, No. 5, 1963
Current Digest of the Post-Soviet Press, Vol. 50, No. 19, Vol. 55, No. 19, Vol. 55, No. 40 and Vol. 57, No. 25/74
Daily Commercial News (Canada), 31 July 1989
Daily Hampshire Gazette, 9 April 1997
Daugherty, Charles M. *City Under the Ice. The Story of Camp Century*. New York: The MacMillan Company, 1963
Day, Samuel H. Jr (ed.). *Nuclear Heartland. A guide to the 1,000 Missile Silos of the United States*. Madison, WI: The Progressive Foundation, 1988
De Andreis, Marco and Francesco Calogero. 'The Soviet Nuclear Weapon Legacy', SIPRI Research Report No. 10. Oxford, UK: Oxford University Press, 1995
Del Tredici, Robert. *At Work in the Fields of the Bomb*. New York: Harper and Row, 1987
Dewar, M. *Defence of the Nation*. London: Arms and Armour Press, 1989
Dokumentationsstätte Regierungsbunker. *A walk through the Documentation Center for the former West German government's Emergency Headquarter at Bad Neuenahr-Ahrweiler*. Bad Neuenahr-Ahrweiler, Germany: Heitmatverein, 2010
Dube, Simon and the Stockholm International Peace Research Institute. *United States Military Forces and Installations in Europe*. Oxford, UK: Oxford University Press, 1989
Ellis, Stephen. 'The Historical Significance of South Africa's Third Force', *Journal of Southern African Studies*, June 1998, Vol. 24, No. 2
Emerson, Steven. 'America's Doomsday Project', US News and World Report, 7 August 1989
Erkhammar, Bertil and Bengt Ohrelius. *The Royal Swedish Navy*. Stockholm: Raben and Sjogren, 1965
Evinger, William R. (ed.). *Directory of United States Military Bases Worldwide*. Phoenix, AZ: Oryx Press, 1995
Fagen, M.D. (ed.). *A History of Engineering and Science in the Bell System. National Service in War and Peace (1925–1975)*. Murray Hill, NY: Bell Telephone Laboratories Incorporated, 1978
Feiveson, Harold A. and Bruce G. Blair. 'How to Lengthen the Nuclear Fuse', *IEEE Spectrum*, March 2000
Fiszer, Michael. 'Moscow's Air Defense Network. Part 1: Foundations in Fear', *The Journal of Electronic Defense*, December 2004
—. 'Moscow's Air Defense System. Part 2: A Parade of Missiles', *The Journal of Electronic Defense*, January 2005
—. 'Good Fences. The Polish Air Force Tends to NATO's Eastern Frontier', *The Journal of Electronic Defense*, November 2005
—. 'Moscow's Air Defense Network. Part 3: Closing the Ring', *The Journal of Electronic Defense*, April 2006
Flynn, Nigel (ed.). *The Nuclear Duel*. New York: Arco Publishing, 1985
Ford, Daniel. *The Button. The Pentagon's Strategic Command and Control System*. New York: Simon and Schuster, 1985
Forden, Geoffrey, Pavel Podvig and Theodore A. Postol. 'False Alarm, Nuclear Danger', *IEEE Spectrum*, March 2000
Foreign Reports, No. 2483, 12 February 1998
Fortune, December 1958
Fox, Steve. 'Top Secret Acid. The Story of the Central Government War Headquarters', *Subterranea*, April 2010, Issue 22

Freitag, Jürgen and Hannes Hensel. *Honeckers Geheimer Bunker 5001*. Stuttgart, Germany: Motor Buch Verlag, 2010

Friedman, George. *America's Secret War*. New York: Broadway Books, 2004

Galeotti, Mark. 'Emergency Presence', *Jane's Intelligence Review*, January 2002

Ganser, Daniele. *NATO's Secret Armies*. New York: Frank Cass, 2005

Geraghty, Tony. *Brixmis*. London: HarperCollins Publishers, 1996

Gertz, Bill. *The China Threat*. Washington, DC: Regnery Publishing, 2002

Gibson, James Norris. *The History of the US Nuclear Arsenal*. London: Bison Books, 1989

Globe and Mail, 30 April 1988, 2 March 1991, 29 June 1993, 2 April 1997, 14 August 2002, 28 November 2002 and 29 September 2005

Good, Timothy. *Above Top Secret. The Worldwide UFO Cover-Up*. Toronto: Macmillan of Canada, 1988

Gough, Jack. *Watching the Skies. A History of Ground Radar for the Air Defence of the United Kingdom by the Royal Air Force from 1946 to 1975*. London: HMSO, 1993

Gouré, Leon. *Civil Defense in the Soviet Union*. Berkeley and Los Angeles: University of California Press, 1962

—. *Soviet Civil Defense. 1969–1970*. Center for Advanced International Studies, Monographs in International Affairs, University of Miami, Coral Gables, Florida, June 1971

—. 'Soviet Civil Defense in the Seventies', *Emergency Planning Digest*, May–June 1976

Graham, Bradley. *Hit to Kill*. New York: PublicAffairs, 2001

Grier, Peter. 'Keeping the Missiles Up', *Air Force Magazine*, August 1993

Gunston, Bill. *Rockets and Missiles*. United Kingdom: Leisure Books, 1979

Gup, Ted. 'The Doomsday Blueprints', *Time*, 10 August 1992

Habiger, Eugene E. 'Security of the Russian Nukes', *Air Force Magazine*, February 1998

Halifax Chronicle-Herald, 7 June 1994

Halifax Daily-News, 6 March 1994

Haller, Stephen A. and John A. Martini. *The Last Missile Site*. Bodega Bay, CA: Hole in the Head Press, 2010

Harding, Peter. 'UKAIR: The Fourth Region In Ace. *Nato's Sixteen Nations*, September 1988

Harris, Robert and Jeremy Paxman. *A Higher Form of Killing. The Secret Story of Chemical and Biological Warfare*. New York: Noonday Press, 1982

Harrison and Bates Incorporated. Culpeper High Security Office and Storage Facility sales brochure

Hoffman, David E. *The Dead Hand*. New York: Anchor Books, 2009

Högberg, Leif. *Muskö. En örlogsbasi i berget*. Skurup, Sweden: Fort & Bunker, 2006

Holmes, K.J. Lt-Col., retired. *The History of the Canadian Military Engineers*. Vol. III to 1971. Toronto: Military Engineering Institute of Canada, 1997

Hotte, R. 'North Bay FSS celebrates history', *NAV CANADA News*, Vol. 2, No. 1, February 1998

Hough, Harold. 'Could Israel's Nuclear Assets Survive a First Strike?', *Jane's Intelligence Review*, September 1997

Hough, Henry W. *NORAD Command Post: The City Inside of Cheyenne Mountain*. Denver, CO: Green Mountain Press, 1970

Ilnitsky, Andrei. 'Mysteries under Moscow', *The Bulletin of the Atomic Scientist*, Vol. 53, May/June 1997

Institute for Defense Analyses. *The Evolution of US Strategic Command and Control and Warning, 1945–1972*. Alexandria, VA: Institute for Defense Analyses, 1975

International Air Power Review, issues 9, 17 and 19

International Defence Review, June 1978

International Institute for Strategic Studies. *The Military Balance 1978–1979*. London: International Institute for Strategic Studies, 1978

Jane's Defence 96: The World In Conflict

Jane's Defence Weekly, 22 April 1989 and 5 February 1997

Jane's Intelligence Review, September 1994

Jasani, Bhupendra. 'Ukraine's ICBM Arsenal', *Jane's Intelligence Review*, March 1994

Ji, You. *The Armed Forces of China*. London: I.B. Tauris, 1999

—. 'Nuclear Power in the Post-Cold War Era: The Development of China's Nuclear Strategy', *Comparative Strategy*, Vol. 18, No. 3

Johnson, A. Ross, Robert W. Dean and Alexander Alexiev. *East European Military Establishments. The Warsaw Pact Northern Tier*. New York: Crane, Russak and Company, 1982

Kampe, Hans George. *The Underground Military Command Bunkers of Zossen, Germany*. Atglen, PA: Schiffer Publishing, 1996

Kandebo, Steven. 'NMD System Integrates New and Updated Components', *Aviation Week and Space Technology*, 3 March 1997

Kaplan, Fred. *The Wizards of Armageddon*. New York: Simon & Schuster, 1983

Karpin, Michael. *The Bomb in the Basement*. New York: Simon & Schuster, 2006

Keeney, L. Douglas. *The Doomsday Scenario*. St Paul, MN: MBI Publishing, 2002

Kessler, Ronald. *Inside the White House*. New York: Pocket Books, 1996

Kolkowicz, Roman and Ellen Propper Mickiewicz (eds). *The Soviet Calculus of Nuclear War*. Lexington, MA: Lexington Books, 1986

L'Ecuyer, Ren. Personal communication. Victoria: 1998

Libin, Kevin. 'Up and Atom. Or How I Learned to Stop Worrying and Love My Bomb Shelter', *Canadian Business*, 29 April 2002

McCamley, Nick. *Cold War Secret Nuclear Bunkers*. Barnsley: Pen and Sword Books, 2007

McEnaney, Laura. *Civil Defense Begins at Home*. Princeton, NJ: Princeton University Press, 2000

McKinzie, Matthew G., Thomas B. Cochran, Robert S. Norris and William M. Arkin. *The US Nuclear War Plan. A Time for Change*. Washington, DC: Natural Resources Defense Council, 2001

Maloney, Sean. 'Dr. Strangelove Visits Canada: Projects Rustic, Ease and Bridge, 1958–1963', *Canadian Military History*, Vol. 6, No. 1, Spring 1997

Mangold, Tom and John Penycate. *The Tunnels of Cu Chi*. London: Pan Books, 1986

Martel, William C. and Paul L. Savage. *Strategic Nuclear War*. New York: Greenwood Press, 1986

Martin, Thomas L. and Donald C. Latham. *Strategy for Survival*. Tucson, AZ: The University of Arizona Press, 1963

Massachusetts. Emergency Management Agency, letter to author, 8 October 1997

Mastny, Vojtech and Malcolm Byrne (eds). *A Cardboard Castle? An Inside History of the Warsaw Pact 1955–1991*. Budapest: Central European University Press, 2005

Meehan, Dallace Major (USAF). 'Civil Defense in the Soviet Union', *Military Review*, November 1977

Meyer, Stephen M. *Soviet Theatre Nuclear Forces. Part II: Capabilities and Intentions*, Adelphi Papers No. 188. London: International Institute for Strategic Studies, 1984

Moltz, James Clay and Alexandre Y. Mansourov (eds). *The North Korean Nuclear Program*. New York: Routledge, 2000

Moore, Jean-Paul, MSgt (retd). *The Malpais Missiles*. n.p., 1998

Moore, Richard, Capt. 'Carp. Station Underground', *Sentinel. Magazine of the Canadian Forces*, 1983/3

Morgan, Mark L. and Mark A. Berhow. *The Rings of Supersonic Steel. Air Defenses of the United States Army 1950–1979*. San Pedro, CA: Fort MacArthur Military Press, 1996

Morrocco, John D. 'Soviet Strategic Force Upgrade Paces US Modernization Effort', *Aviation Week and Space Technology*, 9 March 1987

Moscow News, 20–26 September 2000 and 3–9 September 2003

National Post, 26 November 1999, 12 January 2000 and 24 March 2001

NATO Review, Spring 1998

NATO's Sixteen Nations, September 1985

Neufeld, Jacob. *The Development of Ballistic Missiles in the United States Air Force. 1945–1960*. Washington, DC: Office of Air Force History, USAF, 1990

Newman, B. and M. Dando (eds). *Nuclear Deterrence. Implications and Policy Options for the 1980s*. Tunbridge Wells: Castle House Publications, 1982

New York State. 'NY State Emergency Operating Center', Division of Military and Naval Affairs, Office of Disaster Preparedness, Report RDAM 2-2E

New York Times, 18 May 1955, 16 June 1955, 10 November 1963, 3 December 1976, 11

November 1979, 20–23 September 1980, 20 March 1981, 14 February 1983, 31 May 1992, 8 October 1993, 1 February 1994, 18 April 1994 and 21 January 1996

Nicks, D., J. Bradley and C. Charland. *A History of the Air Defence of Canada, 1948–1997*. North Bay, Ontario: Commander, Fighter Group, 1997

North Bay Nugget, 4 July 1962 and 10 July 1962

NOVA. *Russia's Nuclear Warriors*. Public Broadcasting System, 2001

Oliveri, Frank. 'Twilight of the Missileers', *Air Force Magazine*, August 1994

Openshaw, Stan, Philip Steadman and Owen Greene. *Doomsday: Britain after a nuclear attack*. Oxford, UK: Basil Blackwell, 1983

Ottawa Citizen, Ottawa, Canada, 31 May 1994, 16 October 2000, 15 July 2001 and 2 May 2008

Ottawa Sun, Ottawa, Canada, 24 January 2000

Õun, Mati. *Salapärane Suurupi*. Tallinn: Sentinel, 2008

Ozorak, Paul. *Abandoned Military Installations of Canada. Volume 1: Ontario*. Ottawa: n.p., 1994

—. *Abandoned Military Installations of Canada. Volume 2: Quebec*. Ottawa: n.p., 1998

—. *Abandoned Military Installations of Canada. Volume 3: Atlantic*. Ottawa: n.p., 2001

Peebles, Curtis. *Dark Eagles*. Novato, CA: Presidio Press, 1995

People's Weekly, 4 July 1988 and 4 June 1990

Podvig, Pavel (ed.). *Russian Strategic Nuclear Forces*. Cambridge, MA: The MIT Press, 2001

Polmar, N. (ed.). *Strategic Air Command*. Annapolis, MD: Nautical and Aviation Publishing Company, 1979

Post-Intelligencer, Seattle, WA, 8 January 1998

Pringle, Peter and William Arkin. *SIOP. The Secret US Plan for Nuclear War*. New York: W.W. Norton & Company, 1983

Project 2049 Institute. *China's Nuclear Warhead Storage and Handling System*. n.p., n.d.

Pry, Peter Vincent. *War Scare*. Westport, CT: Praeger Publishers, 1999

Public Opinion, Chambersburg, PA, 14 July 1985

Pugh, Craig Sgt. 'Mighty Missile Down', *Airman*, April 1980

Quester, George (ed.). *The Nuclear Challenge in Russia and the New States of Eurasia*. Armonk, NY: ME Sharpe, 1991

Raids, Hors-Série No. 4, 'Le 44e régiment de transmissions'

Red Deer Advocate, Red Deer, Alberta, 24 November 1994

Reed, Thomas C. and Danny B. Stillman. *The Nuclear Express*. Minneapolis, MN: Zenith Press, 2009

Richelson, Jeffrey T. *Spying on the Bomb*. New York: W.W. Norton & Company, 2007

—. *The US Intelligence Community*. Boulder, CO: Westview Press, 2008

Riste, Olav. *The Norwegian Intelligence Service. 1945–1970*. London: Frank Cass, 1999

Roberts, K.G. Sqn Ldr. 'Air Defence Goes Underground', *Roundel*, September 1963

Royal Air Force Yearbook. Various issues, IAT Publishing

Royal United Services Institute for Defence Studies. *Nuclear Attack: Civil Defence*. Oxford, UK: Brassey's Publishing, 1982

Ruggiero, F.X. Maj. *Missileers' Heritage*. Student Research Report 2065-81, Air Command and Staff College, Air University, Maxwell AFB, Alabama

Sagan, Scott D. *The Limits of Safety. Organizations, Accidents, and Nuclear Weapons*. Princeton, NJ: Princeton University Press, 1993

Sauder, R. *Underground Bases and Tunnels. What is the government trying to hide*. Kempton, IL: Adventures Unlimited Press, 1995

Schecter, Jerrold L. and Peter S. Deriabin. *The Spy Who Saved The World*. New York: Charles Scribner's Sons, 1992

Schnabel, J. *Remote Viewers*. New York: Dell Publishing, 1997

Schneider, Mark. 'The Nuclear Forces and Doctrine of the Russian Federation', *Comparative Strategy*, No. 27, 2008

Schwartz, Stephen I. (ed.). *Atomic Audit. The Costs and Consequences of US Nuclear Weapons since 1940*. Washington, DC: The Brookings Institution, 1998

Scotcrown Ltd. '*Scotland's Secret Bunker*', press release, 1994

—. *Scotland's Secret Bunker*, official souvenir guide

Scott, Harriet Fast and William F. Scott. *The Soviet Control Structure: Capabilities for Wartime*

Survival. New York: National Strategy Information Center Inc. and Crane Russell and Company, 1983

Shambaugh, David. *Modernizing China's Military. Progress, Problems and Prospects*. Berkeley, CA: University of California Press, 2002

Slattery, Thomas J. 'The Atchison Storage Facility', *Army Logistician*, May–June 1999

Smith, Stephen. 'Blast from the Past', *Saturday Night*, February 1993

Sokut, Sergei. 'Minister Plants a "Poplar". 21st Century Missile Placed on Alert', *Nezavisimaya Gazeta*, 25 December 1997, as reprinted in *Current Digest of the Post-Soviet Press*, Vol. XLIX, No. 52, 28 January 1998

Sontag, Sherry and Christopher Drew. *Blind Man's Bluff. The Untold Story of American Submarine Espionage*. New York: PublicAffairs, 1998

Spotlight, 'FEMA vs Your Constitutional Rights', Special Supplement, May 1992

Stanton, Shelby L. *Vietnam Order of Battle*, Millwood, NY: Kraus Reprints and Periodicals, 1986

Stares, Paul B. *Command Peformance. The Neglected Dimension of European Security*. Washington, DC: Brookings Institution, 1991

Stine, G. Harry. *ICBM*. New York: Orion Books, 1991

Stockholm International Peace Research Institute. *SIPRI Yearbook*, various years. New York: Oxford University Press

Stokes, Paul. *Drakelow Unearthed*. UK: Black Country Society/Paul Stokes, 1996

Stover, Dawn. 'Home, Sweet Silo', *Popular Science*, November 1996

Stukalin, Aleksandr and Mikhail Lukin. 'Bcya rossiskaya armiya', *Kommersant Vlast*, 14 May 2002

Stumpf, David. *Titan II. A History of a Cold War Missile Program*. Fayetteville, AR: The University of Arkansas Press, 2000

Sunday Times, 5 October 1986 and 16 September 2007

Sutyagin, Igor. 'Security of Russian Launch Sites', *Jane's Intelligence Review*, August 1994

Suvorov, Victor. *Inside the Soviet Army*. London: Panther Books, 1984

—. *Inside the Aquarium. The Making of a Top Soviet Spy*. New York: Berkley Books, 1986

Syracuse Post-Standard, 18 March 2000

Talbott, Strobe (ed.). *Khrushchev Remembers. The Last Testament*. Boston, MA: Little, Brown and Company, 1974

Tarnopolsky, Walter S. 'Emergency Powers and Civil Liberties', *Canadian Public Administration*, Vol. 15, 1972

Taylor, R.K.S. *Against the Bomb*. Oxford, UK: Clarendon Press, 1988

Thompson, Redvers T.N. Wg Cmdr. 'Post-Cold War Development of UK Joint Air Command and Control Capability', *Air & Space Power Journal*, Winter 2004

Times-Colonist, Victoria, British Columbia, Canada, 16 November 2003

The Times, 16 February 1984, 19 February 1994, 24 June 1994, 1 January 1995, 17 April 1996 and 3 June 1996

Törnell, Bernt. *Berghangarer. En bok om Flygvapnets berghangarer, bergtunnlar, betonghangarer och bergverkstäder*. Nyköping, Sweden: LAH Bunkertours, 2008

Toronto Star, 29 August 1999

Tracy, Phil. 'The Albany Bunker', *Village Voice*, 15 February 1973

Tunnels and Tunnelling, November 1978, June 1979, June 1980, November 1980, September 1982, November 1983,   October 1984, June 1986, April 1987, October 1988, October 1990 and September 1993

Twigge, Stephen and Len Scott. *Planning Armageddon. Britain, the United States and the Command of Western Nuclear Forces, 1945–1964*. Amsterdam: Harwood Academic Publishers, 2000

Union of Concerned Scientists. *Countermeasures. A Technical Evaluation of the Operational Effectiveness of the Planned US National Missile Defense System*, April 2000

United Kingdom. Ministry of Defence, *Nuclear, Biological and Chemical Defence Training Pamphlet No. 3*, October 1978.

United States. Central Intelligence Agency, *Intelligence Community Experiment in Competitive Analysis. Soviet Strategic Objectives: An Alternative View. Report of Team B*, December 1976

—. Central Intelligence Agency, *Soviet Civil Defense*. NI78-1003, July 1978

—. Central Intelligence Agency, *Soviet Forces and Capabilities for Strategic Nuclear Conflict Through the Late 1990s.* NIE 11-3/8-88, 1 December 1988

—. Defense Civil Preparedness Agency, *Foresight. Annual Report, FY73*

—. Defense Information Systems Agency, *National Communications System. Thirty Years of Progress.* Arlington,VA: 1993

—. Defense Information Systems Agency, letter to author, June 1998

—. DoD Legacy Resource Management Program, *Legacy of Peace: Mountain With a Mission. NORAD's Cheyenne Mountain Combat Operations Center: The Cold War Years,* August 1996

—. Department of Defense, Secretary of Defense, Memorandum for the President, Subject: National Deep Underground Command Center as a Key FY 1965 Budget Consideration, Final Draft, 7 November 1963

—. Department of Defense, *Soviet Military Power,* Superintendent of Documents, Government Printing Office, 1986, 1987, 1988

—. Department of Defense, Marine Corps Intelligence Activity, *North Korea Country Handbook,* Publication MCIA-2630-NK-016-97, 1997

—. Department of the Army, *Air Defense Artillery, Engagement Simulation Guided Missile System Radar – Signal Simulation Station. AN/MPQ-T1* (Nike Hercules), December 1965

—. Department of the Interior, National Park Service, *The Missile Plains: Frontline of America's Cold War,* Historic Resource Study, 2003

—. Federal Civil Defense Administration, *Annual Report for Fiscal Year 1956.* US Government Printing Office, Washington, DC, 1957

—. Executive Office of the President, Memorandum for the National Security Council from the Executive Office of the President, Subject: US Policy on Continental Defense, 14 July 1960.

—. FEMA Office of Emergency Information and Public Affairs, letter to author October 1997.

—. *This is FEMA,* FEMA Office of Emergency Information and Public Affairs, March 199

—. FEMA, Mount Weather Emergency Assistance Center brochure

—. House of Representatives, Select Committee on US National Security and Military/Commercial Concerns with the People's Republic of China, *The Cox Report.* Washington, DC: Regnery Publishing, 1999

—. Library of Congress Public Affairs Office, *Fact Sheet on Culpeper, Va., Facility,* 15 December 1997

—. National Research Council, *Use of Underground Facilities to Protect Critical Infrastructures.* Washington, DC: National Academy Press, 1998

—. US Strategic Command factsheet

—. USSTRATCOM monograph, n.d.

Upmalis, Ilgonis, Eriks Tilgass, Janis Dinevics and Anatolijs Gorbunovs. *Latvija-PSRS Karabadze,* Riga: Zelta gauds, 2006

US News and World Report, 30 November 1964, 22 August 1966, 7 August 1989

Vancouver Province, 26 October 1995

Vogel, Steve. *The Pentagon. A History.* New York: Random House, 2007

Wall Street Journal, 17 June 1981 and 23 July 1996

Waller, J. Michael. *Secret Empire. The KGB in Russia Today.* Boulder, CO: Westview Press, 1994

Washington Post, 14 August 1983 and 31 May 1992

Watson, Robert J. *History of the Office of the Secretary of Defence. Volume IV. Into the Missile Age. 1956–1960.* Washington, DC: Office of the Secretary of Defense, 1997

Weiser, Benjamin. *A Secret Life.* New York: PublicAffairs, 2004

West, Nigel. *GCHQ. The Secret Wireless War. 1900–86.* London: Weidenfeld & Nicolson, 1986

Western Report, 24 October 1994, 12 December 1994, 18 November 1996, 1 September 1997 and 23 February 1998

Williamson, John, (ed.). *Jane's Military Communications,* 15th edn, 1994–95. Coulsdon: Jane's Information Group, 1994

Winnipeg Free Press, 27 March 2010

Wise, David. The Politics of Lying. New York: Random House, 1973

Womack, John. *Titan Tales.* Franklin, NC: Soliloquy Press, 1997

Woolf, Amy F. and Kara Wilson. 'Russia's Nuclear Forces: Doctrine and Force Structure Issues',

Congressional Research Service Publication 97-586F. Washington, DC: Library of Congress, 1997

Worthington, F.F. Maj-Gen. 'Pattern for Survival', *Canadian Army Journal*, Summer 1960

Wrinch, A.E. Maj-Gen. 'Re-entry after a Nuclear Attack', *Canadian Army Journal*, January 1960

Yarynich, Valery E. *Nuclear Command, Control, Cooperation*. Washington, DC: Center for Defense Information, 2003

Yegorov, P.T., I.A. Shlyakhov and N.I. Alabin. *Civil Defense. A Soviet View*. Honolulu, HI: University Press of the Pacific, 2002

Young, Ken. 'A Most Special Relationship. The Origins of Anglo–American Nuclear Strike Planning', *Journal of Cold War Studies*, Vol. 9, No. 2, Spring 2007

Zaloga, Stephen J. 'Russians decide to stay with "Stiletto"', *Jane's Intelligence Review*, September 1997

—. 'The Topol (SS-25) Intercontinental Ballistic Missile', *Jane's Intelligence Review*, Vol. 7, No. 5

—. *The Kremlin's Nuclear Sword*. Washington, DC: Smithsonian Institution Press, 2002

Zuckerman, E. *The Day after World War III*. New York: Viking Press, 1984

❑ Websites Consulted

cns.miis.edu/pubs/opapers/op1/op1.htm
ed-thelen.org
russianforces.org
www.afmissileers.org
www.airforcetimes.com
www.atlasicbm.com
www.atomictourist.com
www.bazezeltinos.lv
www.bundesbunker.de
www.bunker-302.de
www.bunker-alzey.de
www.bunkermuseum.at
www.bunkertours.co.uk
www.bunkertours.se
www.cdi.org
www.cdiss.org
www.channelnewsasia.com
www.chosun.com
www.civildefensemuseum.com
www.coldwar-c4i.net
www.compromat.ru
www.ddr-bunker.de
www.diefenbunker.ca
www.dtic.mil/soldiers/aug95/p40.html
www.ellsworth.af.mil
www.fas.org
www.flygbas.se
www.foia.cia.gov
www.freerepublic.com
www.glcm.us
www.globalsecurity.org
www.icdo.org
www.janes.com

www.joongangdaily.joins.com
www.kjbaudry.com/bunker/
www.kmnp.gov.tw
www.kommandobunker.de
www.lostplaces.de
www.mass.gov
www.mil.se
www.minot.af.mil
www.napanews.com
www.nikemissile.org
www.norad.mil
www.nytimes.com/1999/12/28/
www.oxelosund.net
www.pbs.org
www.russianforces.org
www.rvsn-bvo.narod.ru
www.sciam.com/1197issue/1197vonhippel.h
    tml
www.siloworld.com
www.stasibunker.de
www.stratcom.af.mil
www.subbrit.org.uk
www.subsurfacebuildings.com
www.telegraph.co.uk
www.thebulletin.org
www.tibet.com
www.timesonline.co.uk
www.usarmygermany.com
www.whitehouse.gov
www.whiteman.af.mil
www.wikipedia.org
www.zone-interdite.net

❑ Index